WHAT'S NEXT?

The Process of Starting a New Career

9th Edition

John H. Ruehlin

Ruehlin Associates
- Rhino Publishing -

For information, write, call, or e-mail:
Ruehlin Associates
917 B Avenue, Suite 211, Coronado, CA 92118
(619) 435 - 2220
careers@ruehlinassociates.com

Visit our Website at:
www.ruehlinassociates.com

ISBN
0-9748393-0-2

WELCOME

Most people, including career military and civil service personnel, devote little thought to the process of changing careers, until the moment is upon them. After all, career transition is hardly rocket science. However, there are smart and "not so smart" ways of pursuing a new career. Given the significance of this crossroad and the challenges brought about by the recent economic and social environment, it makes sense to critically examine and understand the finer points of launching a new career . . . and, learn about what works and what doesn't work from people who have "been there and done that." Believe me, it will make the entire effort a lot less painful, and, in some ways, enjoyable!

WHO SHOULD READ THIS BOOK?

This book is written for the military and civil service careerist. However, anyone, private sector people included, leaving one career and moving to a different one will find the book's content useful. The book will not be enjoyed by someone who intends to sit on a stump and vegetate for the rest of their years. It is for someone who would like to pursue another career in any field, be it your own business, a major corporation, a nonprofit organization, or a local place where you just want to lend a hand. The techniques described will benefit all of those efforts.

WHAT MAKES THIS BOOK DIFFERENT?

There are countless books available on the subject of career transition. So what makes this one different? It is different because it is written by a senior officer who *suffered* through the ordeal of career transition, networked into a great job in the private sector, lost the great job due to a financial industry crisis, was recruited to manage another great job with a Human Resource/career consulting company, and now heads a 27-year-old private business specializing in senior military-to-civilian career transition. Of equal importance is that the book shares the experiences of tens of thousands of successful job hunters, and combines that knowledge with a process which has been proven over and over to be right on target.

WHEN SHOULD YOU READ THIS BOOK?

There is little doubt the majority of us wait too long to begin considering our next career. There is always something else to do. Hundreds of officers and senior enlisted personnel tell me they should have read this book and taken our seminar years before leaving active duty. A four-star admiral commented he should have taken the seminar five years before retirement. I recommend this book be read about every five years during a career. This is not to encourage anyone to think about leaving active duty before the appropriate time, but to keep you thinking about what you will do when the time comes. Remember, there are only two ways for a careerist to leave the service . . . retire or in a pine box. This means, of course, you cannot stay forever! Sooner or later you will have to leave, and most of us do so sometime between 20 and 30 years . . . or at around 40 to 55 years of age. Just think, you will have another 20-30 more years to work, and that's enough time to build a whole new career. What an incredible opportunity!

A major reason for considering your "career after service" early on is so that you can give consideration to preparation. That could mean additional education, or the kind of job you ask for while on active duty, or the affiliations you might belong to while on active duty, or earning relevant certifications (e.g., program management). Keeping the second career active in your subconscious will also keep you alert to contacts that might be able to help you when the time comes. I can't tell you the number of times a private sector business person gave me their email address/business cards and said , "Call or text me when you get ready to retire from the service," and the same number of times I pitched those cards in the circular file. Not good planning!

WHAT YOU WILL GET OUT OF THIS BOOK!

What to do; why you should do it; how to do it!

- A *feeling* for the emotions involved when transitioning from a military career to the private sector and some ideas of how to cope with the negative ones. How to cope with what every job seeker will face sooner or later . . . **REJECTION**!

- An approach to deciding what career objective to pursue. The vast majority of career military personnel have not decided upon a career objective when retirement time comes.

- An understanding of the purpose of a resume and how to use it in preparation for a job interview as well as networking meetings.

- An understanding of the importance of Social Media (LinkedIn) and why you must use it.

- An understanding of what networking is all about and why it accounts for more than 90 percent of all jobs that senior career military and civil service land. (75 percent for those in the private sector)

- Insight into the various ways to market yourself and how to make a reasonable and calculated response to the infamous question, "Tell me about yourself."

- How to get yourself organized to conduct a successful job search and how to research areas of interest to you.

- Proven ways to negotiate a base salary and insight into the ways that companies think about salary and perks. In addition, the many ways to determine what various jobs pay.

- How to interview and be interviewed. Understanding the various techniques used in interviewing by professional screening interviewers.

WHAT THIS BOOK WILL NOT DO FOR YOU!

- It won't tell you where the specific job you are looking for is . . . they are everywhere.

- It will not conduct an interview meeting for you or negotiate your compensation package.

- It will not show you a painless method of getting a job. Looking for a job may be the hardest thing you have ever done . . . especially the first time. Wrong, I take that back . . . every time!

- Finally, it will not research for you, write your resume, conduct face-to-face networking meetings, or make social media contacts on Websites like LinkedIn for you. In other words, it will not **DO** the legwork for you . . . **YOU** have to **DO** it . . . but it will tell you how to go about it in an organized and proven way.

This book is dedicated to all Americans who have served their country with honor.

Foreword

As I update this book, our country is still at war against terrorism and a pandemic, and we have troops deployed worldwide. Iran is threatening. Unemployment, as I write this, is rampant. There are all kinds of predictions with regard to where employment and the economy is heading . . . most are lukewarm, at best. Not a rosy picture for someone about to embark on the search for a new career.

On the bright side of all this gloom is recognizing the contribution you have made to our country's defense and freedom and that we are making good headway in the fight to rid the world of terrorism. The other good news is that not all sectors of the economy are flailing. Despite some recent uncertainty, the defense sector, for example, still offers opportunities for highly qualified people. Old and new hi-tech companies and institutions that design and develop hardware and software systems that can detect potential threats are scrambling to fill a market niche . . . homeland security.

Another thing to remember is that this is not the first time our country and job markets have been challenged by an "uncertain economy." Even during these uncertain times, the impact on *re-employment* was not a disaster. In most cases, the consequence is that it simply takes more time to land the next career – taking six months or more vs. four months, on average, to find a job. The reality: talented, experienced people who want to work are **always** in demand.

Finally, there is always a place for the entrepreneur. One of the great strengths of our country and its economy are small businesses. They have been one of the principal reasons for our economic growth, and when all else seems to be going to the dogs, the small business hangs in there and keeps things humming. Managing a small business is not for everyone, but it might be worthwhile to investigate the possibilities . . . be it consulting for a defense contractor, opening your own restaurant, or buying a Starbucks franchise. Keep the faith!

By reading this book, you will take a major step toward preparing yourself to leave a Department of Defense/government career. You have had a rewarding career and are now ready for the next step . . . a private sector career! You are not the first person to leave government service and seek civilian employment. The information contained in this book has been given, in seminar form, to more than 68,000 senior military and civil service members who have found wonderful private sector opportunities and successfully transitioned to satisfying second careers. That is not to say that career transition is an easy process . . . indeed, it may well create more anxiety in your life than any other situation you have previously encountered. But it can be done!

The mindset required to succeed in a career search is similar to that required in any worthwhile endeavor. It will depend on the amount of effort you put forth and how much you want to succeed. In government service you designed programs, led personnel, made and gave presentations, developed budgets, managed programs, improved quality, increased productivity, and just about everything else that a senior manager does in private sector life. There were good times and there were some rough times and you managed your way through all of them . . . successfully!

The transition process described in this book is designed to take you through every aspect of career transition with the focus on *re-employment.* Even if your intention is to develop your own business, be a consultant, or work as a charity volunteer, this program will be of great value to you. Understanding and evaluating what is important to you and developing a system to achieve your goals is critical for personal success. Just taking three or four uninterrupted days to concentrate on yourself, goals, and objective make the entire process worthwhile.

My goal is to provide you with a *road map* or, as some have termed, a *blueprint* for success. Whichever term you choose, the idea is to define a process that enables a person to visualize, plan, and move forward. This program does just that . . . and the process works. My associates and I have received thousands of letter, email and telephone testimonials acknowledging the program's value and the effectiveness of our process.

This book is divided into 23 chapters. Each chapter presents a different aspect of career transition and career planning. As you proceed with the process you will quickly see that no chapter can stand alone. That is because career transition is a process – a system – and not just a series of events. To write a resume, you must know what you want to do . . . your objective. To conduct an information/networking meeting properly, you must prepare yourself . . . through research. To interview and negotiate compensation, you must understand the strengths you bring to the job . . . how you can contribute to the needs of the company. And finally, you must know how your strengths fit the expectations of a potential employer.

Recurring themes. Throughout this book you will notice five recurring themes: ***focus***, ***preparation***, ***networking/referrals***, ***relevance, and the enduring value of key words***. The repetition is intentional. These five themes are critical if you want to be successful in your new career transition.

During the course of your career transition you will meet hundreds of new people. Most of these new acquaintances will be extremely helpful, but others will be of no assistance whatsoever. You will also find that you will receive valuable assistance from people that you have never met before and may never see again. You will also make some good friends. Chances are that the job you land will be introduced to you from one of these "perfect strangers." Opportunities are everywhere . . . some by careful, thoughtful planning, and others by just plain, dumb luck! It is only a matter of determination and persistence to seek them out. Go for it!

What Color is Your Parachute?

"While the internet has shaken up the job hunting business, central wisdom has remained the same since the 1970s. Job interviews are still just two people circling each other, trying to figure out if they like each other enough to actually spend time together in a productive relationship. Human nature has not changed."

Richard Bolles
Author

CONTENTS

CHAPTER 1

OVERVIEW

Rather than jumping into how to write a resume or negotiate compensation, I strongly recommend you read Chapter One and take a few minutes to get your bearings and understand the task ahead. Since this is a process, it is best to learn the process one step at a time, from beginning to end. For example, if you try to have networking meetings or job interviews without taking time to research the industry and/or the company, you stand a chance of making a poor impression . . . or failing altogether. Bottom line: go in sequence, one step at a time.

CHAPTER 2

CHANGE

You are going to confront a change in your life. For some people it will be a major hurdle, while just a "bump in the road" for others. Many look forward to the change and others fear it like the plague. Take comfort in knowing that many people have the same uncomfortable feelings. In our seminars, we begin the first day by asking if anyone has any concerns for the future, and almost always, no hands go up. But when we go around the room and ask each person what their personal thoughts are about transition, nearly everyone has a concern. When the exercise is over, the flip-chart is covered with concerns – some small and some large. You will not be alone.

CHAPTER 3

THE SPOUSE'S PERSPECTIVE

In career transition, the primary focus is on the person behind the wheel, and no one seems to pay much attention to the passenger – the other half of the team. It is important to understand that the stress caused by career transition can be a two-way street . . . in many cases the spouse, and for that matter, the entire family, is under more strain than the job candidate. Also, the spouse can be a major asset during career transition. Spouses can help research and play the "devil's advocate" when critiquing resumes and letters before they are mailed! Another big assist the spouse offers is their own connections that can be used for networking - many spouses have their own professional careers and perhaps have even gone through their own career transition in the private sector. While this chapter is short, it is one you don't want to overlook.

CHAPTER 4

PERSONAL PREFERENCES

We have all had jobs we liked and, perhaps, a few we didn't like. Putting aside personality conflicts, the jobs we did like were probably jobs we found to be personally interesting, we were skilled at doing, and we were respected by our fellow employees. This chapter takes a brief look at personal preferences and how you might consider your strengths and tastes when deciding on your next career. Most of us will be happier doing something that we prefer to do rather than something that we dislike or have to do. It has nothing to do with intelligence and everything to do with preferences. You should also know that many corporations administer personal assessments such as the Meyers-Briggs to determine if you are personality wise the right choice for a position, and if you will "fit" in. It is only an indicator, but you shouldn't be surprised if you are asked to take one of these so-called "tests."

CHAPTER 5

OBJECTIVES

The "Big-three" in job search are: focus, networking, and preparation through research. By "focus," we mean career objective – what are you setting out to do? There are many opinions to the question of having a specific objective, but smart money will side with those who choose the specific objective approach. There are countless reasons for having an objective, and this chapter will try to convince you that having a specific objective is better than a general statement that amounts to "I'm looking for a job and please call if you hear of anything you think that I might want to do." In the end, it will be your choice. All I ask is that you read the chapter very closely and understand the pros and cons of having an objective . . . or not!

CHAPTER 6

RESUME

Except for deciding upon an objective, writing the resume seems to be the most difficult task for most of us leaving government service or anyone changing careers. The development of the resume will be the basis for all conversations and other communications while in a job search role. It is something that must be done, even if your best friend tells you to forget the resume and asks you to come in and interview for a job that is a "shoe-in." This career transition business is all about taking nothing for granted and being prepared; writing a resume is the first step in getting prepared. ***Writing the resume, and the agony you will go through while doing it, is an invaluable learning and meetings preparation experience***

CHAPTER 7

THE JOB MARKET

Understanding the job market will help you determine where to put the majority of your time and effort. There is a danger in asking friends what they think is the best job hunting approach, because they will probably recommend that you follow their lead and do what they did. I don't care how you find your next career, but there are some easy ways and some very difficult ways to find a job. I recommend you try them all, but put more effort on the methods that are statistically proven to be the most productive.

CHAPTER 8

NETWORKING

This book, and our transition seminars, place a lot of emphasis on the subject of networking. The emphasis is warranted based on numerous job market studies and the thousands of job landing feedback forms I have received from job hunters who attended our transition seminars and/or have read this book. Some people will swear by using job hunting websites, and others stake their reputation on newspaper ads. All I can tell you is ***the vast majority of all job seekers' land their jobs through networking*** . . . 75 percent of all people in the country, and over 90 percent of senior military and civil service personnel . . . the more senior, the higher the percentage. It's your choice . . . just consider the odds and place your bets! We will also discuss the difference between "social media" networking, like LinkedIn, and "face-to-face" networking. You need to understand the difference. ***Networking is not job interviewing***.

CHAPTER 9

MARKETING

You will market yourself in person, by telephone, by letter, by e-mail, by video chat and any other means of communication you can conjure up. Marketing yourself in person will, by far, be the most effective, but chances are you will use every method at some time or another. This chapter discusses the various means of communicating with a prospective employer and networking contacts.

CHAPTER 10

ATTIRE

Like it or not, first impressions set the tone; personal grooming, behavior and the clothes you wear tell a lot about you. Remember the old saying, "You never get a second chance to make a good first impression." It is not hard to look and dress appropriately, and it will not cost an arm and a leg. Sharp dress won't guarantee you get the job, but there is a strong chance you won't ever see the inside of the president's office if you dress inappropriately. The rules are simple and similar for men and women . . . but not exactly the same. You want to dress so that you are taken seriously.

CHAPTER 11

THE INFORMATION MEETING

The heart of face-to-face networking is the: information meeting or also known as the networking meeting. This chapter discusses on how to set up and conduct those meetings. It explains the agenda that you will use during a networking meeting and how you manage the meeting. You should have an objective established and a resume written before you implement the suggestions and methods prescribed in this chapter and the next chapter – "Sound Bites."

CHAPTER 12

SOUND BITES

Sound bites are the short, prepared replies you will use in response to a myriad of questions at face-to-face networking meetings, receptions, job interviews and daily interactions with your friends and acquaintances. "Tell me about yourself" and "How can I help you?", for example. These short and to the point sound-bite responses will trigger questions and suggestions that will propel your networking and career search to a higher level. Trying to develop these sound bites without up-front preparation (like writing your resume) can lead to failure and frustration. Complete your objective and resume "homework" first before you attempt to give a sound-bite!

CHAPTER 13

THE JOB INTERVIEW

The job interview is why we came to the party. It is the culmination of all the research, resume writing and networking you have done. People who are successful interviewers understand that preparation is essential. Interviewing will be enjoyable IF you are prepared, and this chapter will help. Interviewing as well as networking, is a miserable event if you are not prepared. Trust me . . . been there, done that!

CHAPTER 14

REFERENCES

References are used in several ways. First, to give a favorable recommendation regarding your strengths and character, and second, as part of your core network and referral system. But your references need to know what you are all about and what parts of your background you want them to emphasize if they are called upon.

CHAPTER 15

COMPENSATION

In government service, your salary and perks were managed by Congress and your service heads. Now you must go forth into the great unknown and fend for yourself. Although salary negotiation may be distasteful to most of us, it is not difficult. But there are some basic and proven rules to follow that will make it easier for you to negotiate, and will most likely result in more money and better perks – just in case you are interested in getting fair compensation for your efforts.

CHAPTER 16

RESEARCH

Together with having a focus and networking, research is the third most critical aspect in job hunting. More people fail at interviews because of not being prepared than for any other reason. It is a pity, because research is so easy . . . just try Google. We provide you with some basic rules – all you have to do is to follow them!

CHAPTER 17

ORGANIZATION

Make a choice: (1) Get your act together, get organized and stay in control of your job search and start your next career in a short period of time, or (2) Let happenstance manage your appointment schedule and your "To Do" list and take forever to start your next career. It's an easy choice to make for anyone who wants to succeed.

CHAPTER 18

RETIREMENT PLANNING

There are many books on the library shelves about retirement – the "when to" and "how to" series. This chapter discusses everything from the financial aspects of retirement to the "what do I do to occupy my time" dilemma. You will soon learn that "my take" on the subject is never retire! Instead, ratchet down and work less, but always work at something . . . be it for pay or a higher calling.

CHAPTER 19

FINANCIAL PLANNING

How much money do you need to retire happily? What should you be doing to get your house in order and plan for retirement? Good food for thought!

CHAPTER 20

READY TO GO

This chapter summarizes many of the critical subjects discussed earlier in the book. It is a good review and, among other things, tells you where the jobs are . . . they are everywhere!

CHAPTER 21

REALITY

What is really going to happen when you step out into the cruel private sector world where the dollars are colored green? What are some of the perceptions civilians have of US military/government types? How can we overcome the negative perceptions?

CHAPTER 22

ON THE JOB

Having survived the career transition process, the next item is getting into the job and doing your best to succeed. You will want to become familiar with your surroundings and get to know the lay of the land before making too many decisions that will impact the profitability of the company . . . or the success of a nonprofit organization. This chapter discusses how to go about working your way into the good graces of the organization.

CHAPTER 23

SUMMARY

A wrap-up chapter that reviews some of the most important aspects of the book - some thoughts on happiness, what we really know for certain about the career transition process, how long it will take to get a job, and Emerson's take on success.

APPENDIXES

INDEX

CHAPTER 1

OVERVIEW

"The trouble with the rat race is that even if you win, you're still a rat."
— Lily Tomlin

About the Book

This book is targeted specifically at senior military personnel, officer and enlisted, and senior civil service personnel. However, the process described is applicable for anyone in the job searching mode. It is written in an informal, personal style, as job seeking is a very personal experience. Because everyone is different in terms of experience, ability and motivation, it is impossible to write one book to cover all situations. But we come close! Please note that all of the advice found in this book also applies to those people in the private sector who are undergoing career transition, not just government-to-private sector, so you can use these same techniques when you are transitioning for your second, third, or fourth time!

Career Change: A never-ending adventure!

The Process

The career transition process explained in this book will, with some effort, result in not only a new career, but also a sense of job security for the future. In fact, job security ranks highest on the hierarchy of career needs. Job security is the knowledge that you have the background and ability to find a new job whenever you want . . . not just this first time after leaving government service. Why do I spend time discussing job search in the future? Because the chances are very high that you will be looking for another job in a year or two after you land your first job out of government service. That is not always the case, but it is the case nearly 50 percent of the time. And, it is not only the case just with ex-government managers . . . private

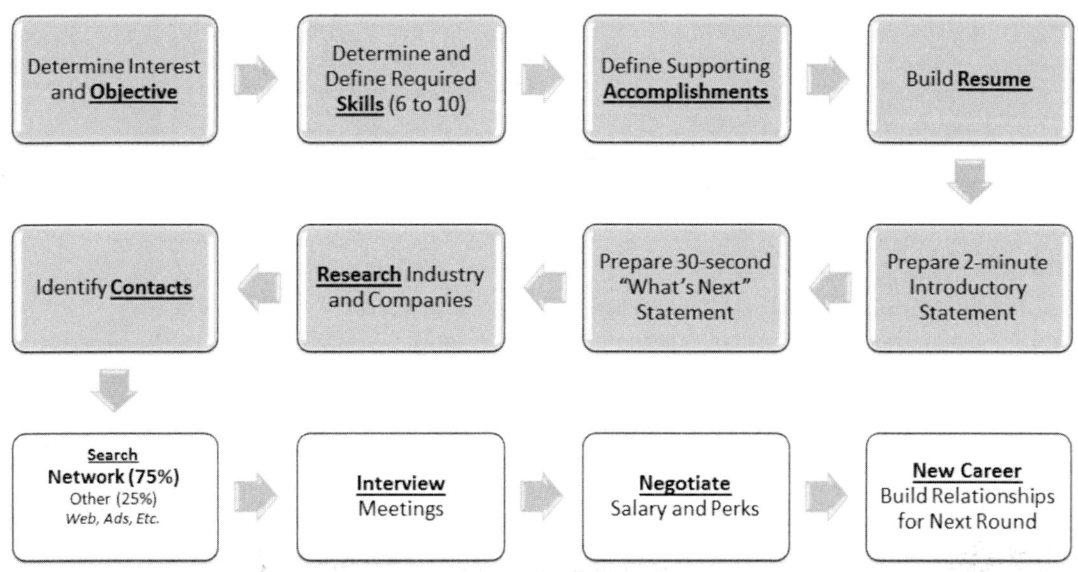

sector managers change jobs on the average of every three to five years. So, the words to the wise are . . . be prepared and keep yourself linked to your network! Use every tool at your disposal; social media sites like LinkedIn and Facebook can help you find and keep contacts, which may lead to referrals. The process of career transition – and it is a process – is like introducing a new item to the retail marketplace . . . to the supermarket shelves. The difference, of course, is that this new item on the shelf is the job hunter. In this case, it is you.

The "take-away" from the flow chart on the preceding page is that ***eight of the twelve major actions involved in a successful career transition are associated with preparation*** . . . getting ready. The better the preparation, the more successful you will be.

Introducing a New Item to the Market Requires:

The Product – What are your strengths and interests? That is, what are the properties or characteristics that make the product useful and attractive? Why should anyone buy it . . . buy you?

Career transition is all about communicating your value to a prospective employer, as well as communicating how well you fit into their organization.

Target Market Needs – Where are your strengths/skills, service attained or otherwise, most likely to be needed or saleable? What kind of work or second career best suits you, your interests and satisfactions? What is relevant?

Target Companies – In which companies or organizations or industries will you feel most comfortable and useful?

Building a Marketing Plan . . . plus a personal commercial! – How can you best find and approach your target market and optimize your chances of success? How will you advertise yourself? **You are the "Director of Marketing!"**

Selling Yourself – How can you best present yourself . . . verbally or in writing . . . so you get attention and favorably impress prospective employers with the idea that your background and strengths are relevant to their business?

Salary and Benefits – How do you negotiate the best overall compensation (base salary and perks) even when the economy is slow and unemployment is high?

Understand the Process

Understanding how the transition process works will give you a major advantage over the typical and unenlightened job hunter. Also, realize that the majority of people do not understand the process of looking for a job – and that includes most who write and publish books on the subject! Additionally:

- When you analyze your strengths/skills, you will realize your military/civil service experience is applicable to most areas in the private sector (unless the career field you are interested in requires specific technical training and/or education . . . such as medicine or law).

- You will have the unique opportunity to choose your own future, as opposed to being assigned where someone else, like a government service detailer, thinks that you are needed most.
- Once you have gone through this career transition learning process you will never have to learn it again . . . although you will probably go through career transition several times, during your remaining work years.

> **Career Transition Basics**
> Decide:
> what you want to do, or
> what you are able to do, or
> what you can be trained to do
> Market yourself by:
> networking personal contacts
> networking social media/websites
> effective communications
> *Floundering should not be an option*

Career Transition Basics

There are many actions involved in transitioning from one career to another and the process gets more complicated when you are transitioning from a different industry or functional area to another. In the end, the graphic on the left outlines the basics. You might think this is over simplifying the problem, but in truth it all boils down to determining an objective and learning how to market yourself – sell yourself, if you like – to a prospective employer.

A Frustrating Experience

Career transition - looking for a job - is at best, a frustrating experience. Frustrating, because after experiencing a successful government service career, with authority and responsibility, you suddenly find yourself in the midst of a new way of life and one where your credentials and reputation don't seem to matter as much. The truth of the matter is that you will find a job that is suitable for you and one to enjoy for years to come. Throughout your job search campaign the process suggested here will become comfortable to you. Look for the underlying meanings and concepts and adjust them to suit your individual style.

Following the process explained in this book will result in finding a job:

■ **With The Best Fit** ■ **In The Shortest Time** ■ **With Minimum Stress**

This requires both self-assessment and knowledge of the organization to assure a proper "Fit." It depends on strategies that include thorough planning, organization and sometimes painful follow-through.

Leave Government Service or Stay a While Longer? The Big Decision!

A factor that sometimes contributes to great personal frustration is making the decision to stay or leave service followed by the after-decision-second-guessing that frequently occurs. Leaving active duty/government service is a major personal decision, and when you make the decision, you are taking a life-changing career and economic step . . . shudder!!! If you are "asked" to leave or you just run out of time (statutory limitation), it is almost better than making the decision to leave on your own accord. Why? Because when someone else makes the decision for you, you don't have to blame yourself for walking away from a nice paying job and all of the security it offers.

The big question: When to leave government service?

So, if the decision to stay or leave is ***not*** made for you by some higher authority – like your service or your spouse – how do you decide? I recommend that you have a frank and honest discussion with your spouse or a very close friend and review the bidding in the most objective way possible. My take on that review decision goes something like this:

IF:

Don't just flip a coin. Make an objective choice!

- ✓ You enjoy what you are doing, and
- ✓ It fits with your life's goals, and
- ✓ There is still a challenge, and
- ✓ There is potential to advance, and
- ✓ You are still making a contribution, and
- ✓ It fits with your family needs and desires, and
- ✓ You have examined the future closely and have ***time*** to do whatever you are thinking about doing for a second career . . . **Then stay** ... if not ... **Go**

Stay until these conditions change or they throw you out! If any of the answers to the above seven decision factors are "no," then you should seriously consider leaving service sometime soon. Remember, it is this year or next year or the next year, but not *forever*! And, the longer you stay, the less time you will have to do whatever you are planning to do (the last bullet above) in your "next life." Time is of the essence!

The Next Big Questions:

What to Do With the Rest of My/Our Lives . . . and Why Do I/We Want to Do It?

Time – the most precious commodity!

Once I made a computer graphic that said, "What Do I Want to Do With the Rest of My Life?" and ***taped*** it on my bedroom mirror. I wanted to remind myself that *time* is precious and I must ensure that I am making the most of the time I have left. A good idea, but turns out that the mirror was the one above my spouse's vanity and she didn't think that having her mirror covered up with a sign was such a great idea. As I was bemoaning the episode and taking the graphic down, I suddenly realized that the message on the graphic was incorrect. It should have read, "What Do **WE** Want to Do With the Rest of **OUR** Lives?" If you have a spouse or significant other, the decisions you make that impact on the rest of your lives should reflect both persons' dreams and desires. So, I made a new graphic accordingly and showed it to my spouse. My spouse agreed with the wording change, but still wouldn't let me put it on her vanity mirror! What does your spouse or significant other want to do? Do you know?

If you have a spouse, talk about where you are headed.

A Full-time Job . . . job hunting is a full-time job

When you are not working, job hunting is a full-time job . . . eight hours a day or more, five days a week or more. You must make a serious commitment of time. We will help you set clear objectives, develop knowledge of your options and prepare you for a successful interview. Facing these opportunities with a positive attitude, because you are **prepared**, will reduce the stress of transition and put you far ahead of your competitors.

The Author's Goal

As we begin to develop a thorough marketing plan, please remember that the author, and the many Associates who contributed to the book, are not therapists. We are seasoned business professionals with a personal understanding of your situation and who have received extensive training in career transition counseling. All have successfully transitioned from a government career to a private sector career. Our objective is not psychological counseling. It is to provide a professional marketing support system. Read and learn from our real-life, real time experiences and more than 27 years of working with military, civil service and private sector professionals undergoing career transition.

Capitalism . . . profit orientation . . . why hire you?

As you read this book, remember that you will be hired for one of two reasons . . . to make the company money or to save the company money. This basic rule applies not only to Fortune 500 companies and small businesses, but to associations and charitable organizations as well. It is called capitalism. No one can afford to put you on the payroll unless you can produce profit or support those who produce profit . . . or, as in the case of the nonprofit, raise funds for their cause and support their needs. This commentary is somewhat foreign to a public servant's ears because they are accustomed to working for a cause . . . national defense. The private sector has other goals in mind . . . the profit motive. By the way, the same reasoning applies if you start your own business – it won't be around very long if it is not profitable!

You will be hired to make money or to save money!

Private Sector (Business) Terminology

The terminology used throughout this workbook is business oriented. Those seeking positions in the corporate world should make a concentrated effort to learn private sector business terms. You should also be able to read a balance sheet and financial statement. There are numerous books on the subject at the library and on-line explanations. One is highlighted in the reference section of this book. Another good source of general information is any college text – graduate or undergraduate level – on the subject of marketing. A good marketing text will cover the majority of the functions of business . . . manufacturing, logistics, finance, productivity, personnel (Human Resources) and the like. Or, go to Google or a business Website and type in 'business terminology definitions' and click on one of the many business dictionaries listed.

What You "Gotta" Do

The challenge in this whole adventure is getting off on the right foot. It all boils down to:

- **Self knowledge** . . . conducting an evaluation of what, you want to do. Easy to say, but many people have great difficulty deciding what they want to do in their next career.
- **Know the product** . . . making sure that you have the strengths, the energy and the desire to move ahead, once you have decided what that career will be.
- **Get organized** . . . design and develop a system for keeping track of all actions and contacts. Keep records of calls and meetings with a computer, as well as manually.
- **Package the product** . . . this is just like introducing a new product to the retail marketplace. Packaging is an important part of the "sell."

- **Have a media plan** . . . as in packaging, you must develop a media plan that will introduce the product in the best way possible. Learn the KEY WORDS associated with your career objective.
- **Develop an introductory statement** . . . a response to "How can I help you?" . . . or the infamous "Tell me about yourself" question.
- **Develop a personal commercial** . . . sometimes referred to as the elevator sound bite . . . a one-liner *sound-bite* that grabs peoples' attention and lets them know exactly what you are selling. **Note**: It is referred to as the "elevator" story because you are supposed to be able to tell a stranger what you want to do – your objective – between the first and second floors of the elevator ride. It's the response to: "What do you plan to do when you leave government service?" It is also known as the "30 Second Commercial."

As you get more and more into your career search campaign, you will find that you build up momentum. Past experience has shown that those individuals who spend eight hours a day or more in their preparation and search, and keep meticulous records, will be successful faster. As with any significant achievement, reward comes through a disciplined, systematic series of actions.

I urge you to avoid networking or job interviews and any conversations about your future plans until you know what you want to do, have developed your resume, and are thoroughly prepared to respond to questions about your future. To wit:

- Don't mention or discuss your service pay or future salary requirements to anyone. Repeat, **do not mention or discuss your present pay or salary requirements to anyone**, even though government salaries are a matter of record.
- Don't burn any bridges with anyone – it may feel good at the time but it serves no real purpose!
- Don't mail out resumes, or start calling and emailing everyone you know.
- Don't contact your primary targets/contacts (I call them silver bullets), until you have become focused, have researched your industry of interest and are well organized. A gem-cutter would not *practice* on a multi-million dollar diamond! He would cut rocks first. Practice, practice, practice!

Instead, first, prepare yourself by: Reading this book from cover to cover twice, selecting an objective, writing your resume, practicing networking, developing a list of contacts, reading LinkedIn for Dummies and researching the industry and companies that you want to target. In other words, get your act together before you begin to actively look for a second career! And remember, you can't go back! You have crossed your Rubicon.

> **Crossing the Rubicon**
>
> *there is no turning back*
>
> *The Rubicon is a small river in northern Italy. In 49 BC Caesar's army stood poised to cross the Rubicon and march on Rome. Caesar knew that if his army crossed the river, there was no turning back – the crossing would be considered by Rome as an act of war!*
>
> The Rubicon
>
> ***When you leave active duty, you cross your Rubicon!***

A Few Other Pointers

Be patient. Success should not be expected overnight. It takes time to land any job and more time to land the right job. Note that, in a faltering economy, it might take a while longer than when things are booming. Typically, it takes four to six months once the effort begins in earnest. You will soon discover that this experience provides a rare opportunity to assess yourself and your future needs, and can broaden your thinking and vision.

Do not think of yourself as entering a vacation or leave period. Your "new" career search assignment is to "package and market" yourself. You should approach this assignment with the same drive and effort that you would use in approaching a new government assignment. Some people actually enjoy it.

Career Transition - The Process

Career transition is a process. The pieces that make it up do not stand alone. To effectively conduct a job interview you must understand "what you bring to the table" and must be able to verbalize your accomplishments.

There is a direct relationship among:

- Your interests
- Your accomplishments
- Your income expectations
- Your resume
- Your strengths
- Your research
- Your objective
- Networking

. . . AND HOW WELL YOU DO IN A JOB INTERVIEW SITUATION! They all come into play in getting offered the job, and in salary negotiations. Think of it as one large *Venn* diagram as shown below. There is nothing mutually exclusive about these facets of a successful job search.

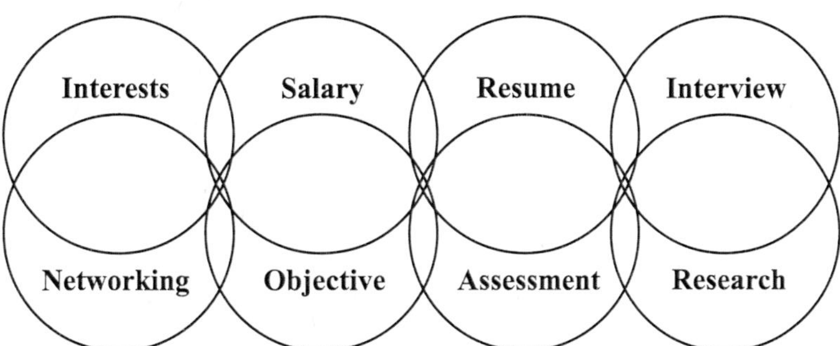

Focus
Preparation
Networking
Referrals
Relevance
Key Words

You begin with deciding what you want to do – your interests – and then assess and determine if you have the strengths and experience to do whatever it is that interests you. Once that is done, research your interests and develop a specific objective. Once the objective is settled upon, write your resume and start networking. If you have prepared yourself along the lines we discuss in this book, this "up-front" preparation will make interviewing and salary negotiation much easier. It all ties together . . . the up-front preparation and writing the resume gets you ready to go do "battle."

Key Words and Career Transition

"In the context of job search, key words are words that evoke a special meaning, memory, enterprise or person when heard, seen or scanned. They are carefully chosen words that will ignite an individual's thought process and/or trip the hot button/s of a computer screening a resume. The word could be a person's name, an industry a functional area, etc. Key words are an essential ingredient of the search process."

Recurring Topics *(as stated in the Foreword)*

As you read the book, you will soon observe that there are five topics that appear frequently. Simply stated they are: ***Focus***, ***Preparation***, ***Networking***, ***Relevance, and Key Words***. The redundancy is intentional and by the time you finish reading the last page of this book, you will fully understand their significance.

Key words remind us of events or people or some kind of situation. Words like: honeymoon, Starbucks, Rose Bowl, retire, Tiger

Woods, Wall Street, *single-malt scotch* and so forth. Each word triggers a thought or memory.

> *"Make sure you incorporate a lot of key words for the kind of job you're looking for. As a recruiter, I run searches through LinkedIn and I look for the key requirements of [each available] job. I look for very specific skills, so have these in your profile."*
>
> Cyndi Klein, Technical Recruiter

Stop and Read the Following:

Appendix A is a *Personal Assessment.* You should complete the assessment <u>before</u> you read the following chapters. Many people have told me that they consider the Personal Assessment to be one of the most valuable parts of the career transition process. Remember this is a process and understanding yourself is part of the process. It will only take an hour or so and will make the rest of the book more meaningful. There is also an assessment for your spouse. Have your spouse/significant other complete their assessment and compare it with yours.

The Career Transition Process Time Line – *examples*

Stage	Time →			
Preparation >assessment >interests >goals >strengths >objective >limitations	 -------- -------- -------- -------- ---------- ------			
Research >options >companies >homework >list contacts >network resources		 ------- ----------------- ------------- ---------------- ----------------		
Determine >market needs >my contribution >is objective valid >research plan			 ----------------- ---------------- ----------- -----------	
Action >preparation >join LinkedIn >networking >interviewing >job offer >compensation >perks >evaluation >acceptance			 -------------------- --------- ------- ---- --- - -	
The new career >on the job >breaking in >contributing >networking >future plans				 ----------------------- ----------------- ----------- ---------- -------

Note: In too many cases, a new job seeker doesn't take the time to do the up-front work and research and as a result, more often that not, attacks the marketplace unprepared for what's ahead. Smart money takes a little longer to get prepared and, as they say, get your act together. The opportunities that may be missed by NOT attacking the marketplace BEFORE you are prepared will be few and far between. On the other hand, I have seen countless frustrated job hunters end up discouraged because they approached the marketplace without knowing what they wanted to do and not being prepared to verbalize their strengths and accomplishments relevant to the opportunity.

Three Vital Lessons

"I'm not getting older, I'm getting better."
— Jerry Baumann

1. RETIRE ... *No!*

Strike the word "retire" from your vocabulary.

You are leaving government service after a successful career. You should strike the word "**RETIRE**" from your vocabulary **permanently**. Not only does it convey the wrong idea to a prospective employer, but it sends a signal to your subconscious that you are on the way out. Just imagine what flashes through a manager's head when they hear you say that you are retired! They think, "This person's just looking for something to do." After all, what's the next step after retirement***? Like stepping into God's vestibule!*** Rather, consider yourself as having just completed the first stage of your work life and that you are now beginning stage two . . . realizing that there are probably several more stages down the road. You are transitioning into a new career, not retiring from an old one! You are simply at "half-time" in the game of work!

2. REJECTION ... *expect it ... but try not to take it personally!*

Look up rejection in the dictionary. You have had a successful career and people were responsive to your telephone calls and needs. When you called someone, they always called you back, or sent a message with the information that you wanted. It may not have been the answer that you were looking for, but at least you received a response. When you are job hunting, getting the job is ***your*** highest priority! But the people that you want to meet have other priorities on their plates and, although you are a nice and talented person, there are other things that come before meeting with you or returning your call . . . things like running their business. Plan on confronting the "feeling of rejection" several times during your career transition. ***Everyone*** experiences it when job hunting or selling. Do not take rejection personally. If you do, it will bring you down to your knees. Rejection plays no favorites . . . everyone, regardless of rank or status, will encounter it! Believe me. It is going to happen!

It hurts, but don't take it personally.

3. PLAN AHEAD ... *the first 72 hours.*

You have been accustomed to being on a fixed schedule for the past 20 to 30 years. Make some concrete plans for the first three days after leaving the service. Paint the house, take a short trip but plan to do something. You have been accustomed to being in control and suddenly you don't have anything to manage . . . except yourself. And, while managing yourself will become a chore all by itself, it is better to ease into this new role. REMEMBER, THAT'S 72 HOURS, NOT 72 WEEKS!

Career Transition - Some Observations

- ✍ **Senior government career transition is unique** . . . but all re-employment, government and private sector, is frustrating . . . you are not alone.
- ✍ **"I can do anything."** You may think that you can do anything, and probably could if you take enough time to prepare and work at it, but telling a prospective employer that you can do anything will discredit you and make you appear to be pompous.
- ✍ **"I will do anything.**" The worst thing that you can say to a prospective employer is that you will do anything . . . that echoes despair and hopelessness. No one wants a loser!
- ✍ **Most companies want specialists** . . . the only generalist is the Chairman of the Board.
- ✍ **Most companies have small staffs** . . . if any. This can be hard on senior government personnel who are used to having staffs assisting their efforts.
- ✍ **Companies want to know what you can do for them** . . . not what they can do for you.
- ✍ **Have something to sell**. Going door to door asking people what they want to buy, is a non-starter.
- ✍ **Maintain accurate and real time records**. Or, you will lose control!
- ✍ **Be NICE to everyone** . . . especially the secretaries . . . but also the receptionists and assistants.
- ✍ **Preparation is everything** . . . know at least ten facts about the company you are talking to . . . know ten other facts about the industry - for each and every visit! Have ten good questions ready to ask.
- ✍ **The resume** . . . understand its value to you as well as to future employers. The Key Words.
- ✍ **Everyone is a potential employer** . . . at minimum, a networking contact or referral!
- ✍ **Enthusiasm pays off** . . . saying "*I'm just looking for something to do*," is counterproductive.
- ✍ **Send thank you notes** . . . you will be more likely to be remembered. Do it!
- ✍ **Follow up every lead** . . . you just never know what will become of it!
- ✍ **You will probably be hired for one of two reasons** . . . to make money or to save money.

Profile of the Ideal Job . . . THE BIG FOUR:

✓ LOCATION ✓ THE JOB ✓ COMPENSATION ✓ ENERGY

Location

While deciding on a location may seem like a simple thing, this is an area that brings more grief to married couples than anything else. Many times one spouse wants to live in one city and the other wants to live in another. If location *is* all important, then make that your first priority. Remember, however, that the next career and compensation you want, may not be available in the location you choose. Everything is a compromise. Also, remember that locating where your children are living may not be such a great idea – they might be forced to move away for employment opportunities elsewhere, just about the time that you are getting settled in and making the first, new house mortgage payment! Note: To determine the cost of living at one place compared to another, check out Sperling's Best-Places (www.bestplaces.net), a company that analyzes and rates data about people and places.

"Hey hon, where will we live?"

> *Tip:* **Do not include location**, let alone salary, when discussing what you want to do – your objective. Doing so might eliminate you from a job opportunity that might otherwise be significant enough to persuade you to rethink your location desires ... at least temporarily.

The Job

For many, the job . . . the new career . . . is the most important element . . . given that almost no one wants to live at the North Pole, regardless of the pay. For the most part, high paying jobs and the power jobs are in the major metropolitan areas. And, if you lock yourself into a specific functional area or industry, that alone may drive you to a given area. Again, it may well be a compromise, for a few years at least.

Compensation

Although the majority of those leaving government service are in search of equal to or higher compensation than their service pay, we recommend that it be secondary in your search for a new career. We have found through thousands of feedback letters that given the right job, compensation usually takes care of itself. If, however, you have ten children attending college at the same time, you may find that compensation must be foremost in your mind.

Energy

We all slow down or, heaven forbid, burn out at different times in our lives. You should assess where you are on the energy curve and plan your objective accordingly. Someone once said, "I don't mind dying. I just object to growing old."

> While some people focus primarily on the financial aspects of career transition, conventional wisdom suggests: occupation, location and compensation, in that order.

Other Career Considerations of the ideal job.

- Corporate Environment . . . the ***corporate culture***
- People . . . *do I like working with the people I am interviewing and working with?*
- Ethics . . . *does the company share your values?*
- Product . . . *selling used cars may not be your cup of tea!*
- Potential . . . *can you move up to more responsible positions?*
- Stress . . . *is it manageable?*
- Learning Curve . . . *how long to be effective?*
- Familiar Surroundings ... *know the territory*
- Ego Satisfying . . . *will you feel good about yourself?*
- Community Involvement . . . *will the job permit it?*
- Family Considerations . . . *amount of travel?*
- Independence and meaningful work
- Responsibility . . . *probably won't be as much as you have now!*
- Staff Reporting to you . . . *will there be anyone? Do you want anyone?*
- Level/Position in The Company, benefits, job security,

PROFILE OF THE IDEAL JOB

Location	Familiar surroundings
Pay	Ego satisfying
Job	Community involvement
Corporate	Family considerations
environment	Degree of independence
culture	Responsibility
People	Level in company
Product	Benefit package
Potential	Job Security
Stress	*ETHICS* and *VALUES*
Learning curve	*Meaningful work*

More than the "job" itself...

What Are My Options?

. . . nearly anything, but not everything . . . those who have successfully transitioned from government service are doing all the following and more!

- Consulting
- Teaching
- Executive Directorship
- Volunteering
- Defense Contractor
- The Trades
- Enter a Monastery?
- Government Service-Municipal/Federal
- Non-Profit
- Trade Associations
- Own Business
- Additional Education
- Private sector retail
- Retire . . . but not a very good option!

The idea is to choose what <u>you</u> will enjoy doing . . . for profit or otherwise.

Remember what Bob Hope, the comedian said, *"At 20, we worry about what others think of us; at 40, we don't care what others think of us; and at 60+ we discover that they haven't been thinking about us at all."* What really matters is what we think about ourselves!

Government and Private Sector Employment Similarities

Military and civil service personnel undergoing career transition often make the statement that their experience does not lend itself to work in the private sector. From experience we can assure you that there are thousands of positions in the private sector that are very similar if not identical to the positions that military and civil service personnel have held. This is especially true in the defense industry. The vocabulary may be different and the acronyms unfamiliar, but the duties are comparable. The following list represents some of the functions/operations in the government that easily correlate to the private sector.

- Finance, budgeting, controlling
- Training
- Customer service
- Planning
- Personnel/Human Resources
- Program/Project Management
- Safety – in office spaces, in warehouses
- Operations
- Contracting
- Communications – information management
- Public Relations

When Should You Begin Your Career Transition?

Our basic answer is that you should begin to think about a new/private sector career five years out from transition, and begin serious planning at least one year before you plan to leave government service. We also believe that your *full-time* job hunting should begin within 30 days after leaving the service. (Attend our three-day career transition seminar if at all possible.) The obvious follow-on question is: "How soon is too soon?" There is an old saying that says "A person with a job is able to find a job faster than a person who is out of work." I have never seen any statistical data on that subject, but it may well be true. The curve at the right depicts that saying. When you have a job you seem to be "hot." When you don't have a job, and are not doing much about getting one, you cool off in a hurry, and people forget about you fairly quickly. As long as you are *out there in hot pursuit*, you tend to stay "hot." It is, no doubt, a function of visibility and people thinking about what you want to do. Think about it before you decide to buy a 40 foot sailboat and cruise around the world for a few years before you settle down and look for your next career! Chances are everyone will forget you by the time you return. Some people take long pleasure cruises . . . that's okay, but why not get your job and then *enjoy* the long cruise? It's your call. By the way, a great percentage – nearly half – of military and civil service people have jobs lined up, or are very close, before they leave government service! Finally, a USA Today study revealed that 56 percent of 356 hiring officials canvassed said that taking a year off for travel or personal pleasure ***negatively*** affects a person's resume, ergo, transition success. See the milestone chart example at the end of the Organization chapter. ***Once again, there have been countless articles written about why it is, or seems easier to get a new job when you already have one than when you don't have one. Not to mention the negative feelings you might have about yourself when all of your friends have jobs and you don't!***

The Job Hunt Temperature Curve

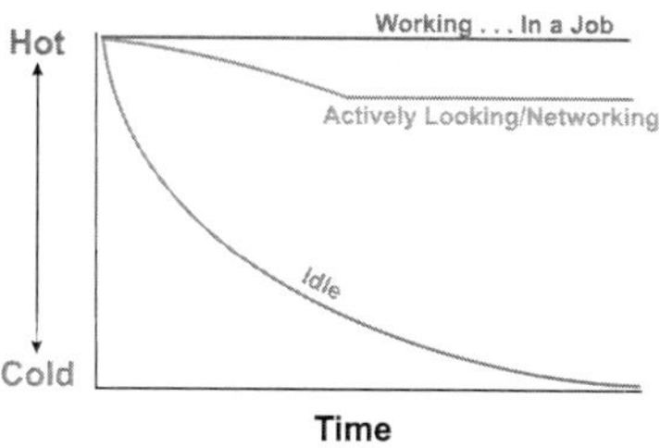

How This Book and Our Seminars are Kept Current . . . up-to-date

Many career transition books and guides are current the day they are written, but over time go stale and become out of date. This book and our seminars are kept current as the result of many actions:

- **Landing reports** – After our seminars we send a letter to each attendee with a landing report form as an enclosure. That form (see Appendix E) asks things such as how the job was found and the salary negotiated. This information goes into a data base and becomes incorporated into the course material and publications such as this. When you land your job, we kindly ask that you fill out the Landing Report form located at the end of this book and mail/email it to *Ruehlin Associates*, 917 'B' Avenue, Suite 201, Coronado, CA, 92118. The information is held confidential, and once the landing data is logged in, the landing report is destroyed.

- **Letters, emails and telephone calls** – All of the *Ruehlin Associates* consultants receive telephone calls or emails from people who have attended our seminars. The results of these calls, which often entail resume critique and salary/compensation questions and advice, interview questions and the like, also go into the data base that supports this book and the formal seminar presentation.
- **Recruiters** – Because of the nature of our business we receive many calls from recruiters, fondly known as headhunters. They are looking for people to fill a job requirement. In return, recruiters share information about the job market and current salaries.
- **Private sector *Outplacement* industry** – several of our career consultants also consult for private sector companies. These contacts help to ensure that our course is on track with or ahead of the private sector. Several other of our career consultants are part time salaried employees for major corporations.

In addition, our administrative staff scans several national business newspapers as well as local newspapers daily and magazines such as Business Week, Fortune, Wall Street Journal and Forbes for career transition related articles. And, they read nearly all of the new books written on the subject of transition and retirement. The material is then reviewed and that which is applicable is incorporated into the book and seminar.

Myths

There are numerous myths associated with government-to-civilian career transition. Some of the most notable are:

- *"I don't need an objective, someone will recognize my talents and hire me." Ho, Ho, Ho!*
- *"Even though this present job market has many opportunities, I will probably never land a job since I was a government employee – so what's the use in trying."*
- *"My friends will find me a job!"*
- *"I can do anything!"*
- *"My spouse fully understands this career search thing."*
- *"If I talk to enough people, I will get hired."*
- *"Sending out massive mailings is a sure way of landing a great job."*
- *"The only thing that will change in retirement is that I will have a different job."*
- *"My ego is not involved in this process."*
- *"Everything will go according to plan, in spite of what this guy Murphy says."*
- *"Being rejected will not bother me."*
- *"I am too old to get a good job."*
- *"A company that is laying off employees is not hiring anyone new."*
- *"An aptitude test will tell me exactly what my career objective should be."*

Hey, look at me!

Obviously, the above comments are indeed myths. If you find yourself believing any of them, conduct a personal reality check.

Parts to the Puzzle . . . A Baker's Dozen

People in transition go through many different phases. Some are quick to move ahead and get involved in the process and others seem to get bogged down in one area or another. We have observed the following "Parts to the Puzzle":

1. **Getting Over The Shock** . . . the shock of not having a job and the concern for the future. Government service is probably the only responsible career you have ever had and suddenly, although you knew it was coming, you are out of a job and out of responsibility = shock!

2. **Deciding What To Do** . . . this is one of the biggest problems that career military and civil service managers encounter. Sounds easy until you try it and then it becomes a major hurdle for most people. And, proceeding without a focus will lead to a less than 100 percent effective career transition plan.

The hardest part of the puzzle is deciding what you want to do!

3. **Adjusting To A New Life Style** . . . it won't be the same. It won't be like you are moving to a foreign country, but you will *feel* the change. This is especially true if you move to a new community where you don't know anyone. If you retire and stay in Washington, D.C. and work for a defense contractor in your area of expertise, then the change won't be as dramatic, but it will be different.

4. **Just *Getting* Going** . . . just getting started . . . where to begin . . . how to begin. For some people, the problem is just getting started. If you feel that way you are not alone. I can think of at least 100 things I would rather do than start looking for a job . . . especially when I like the one I have, and I like the people whom I associate with on a daily basis. Don't procrastinate – start now!

5. **Making Contacts** . . . the target company and people list. To conduct an effective career search, you must develop a list of people you would like to contact and then you must contact them. I know, this is a no-brainer, but you wouldn't believe the number of people who find this a hard thing to accomplish . . . back to getting started.

6. **The Resume** . . . it is a difficult task but it must be accomplished . . . and by you . . . and in the way that it is discussed in the Resume Chapter.

7. **The Information Meeting And Preparation** . . . the fundamentals of networking.

8. **The Job Interview and Preparation** . . . where the rubber meets the road.

9. **Getting Organized** . . . keeping track of your actions and contacts.

10. **Deciding Which Job To Accept** . . . a happy dilemma . . . make it *your* choice!

11. **Compensation** . . . salary and benefits . . . takes practice and preparation.

12. **Moving In** . . . getting along in the new job.

13. **When to Stop Working** . . . sooner or later this becomes a major concern . . . follow the when-to-retire rules, as in the game of marbles.

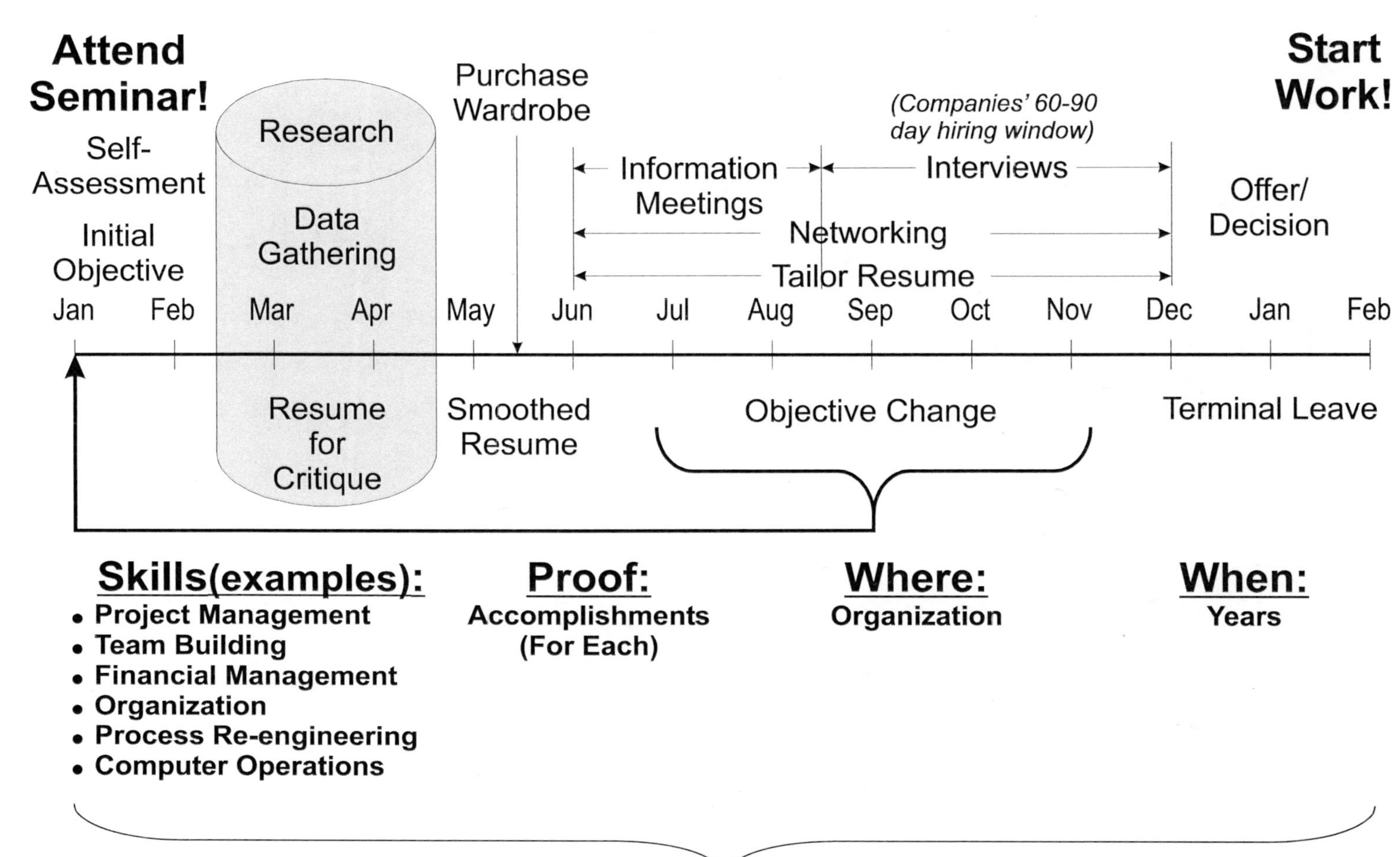

This type of outline will be used as you assess your qualifications skills, accomplishments, work history, education, etc.. It will also provide the "building blocks" for developing your resume.

CHAPTER 2

CHANGE

Dealing with Change

Who Moved My Cheese?

Throughout your new career transition process, a positive frame of mind, oriented toward success, is essential. The same inner reserves of energy, creativity and courage that made you successful in the past are even more important now. One thing we know for certain: change is constant. ***Consider the Pandemic!***

Times Change

> "In times of change learners inherit the earth; while the learned find themselves beautifully equipped to deal with a world that no longer exists."
>
> Eric Hoffer

A person's career decision is influenced by many factors. Times change and people change. Not so many years ago, there were no notebook computers that were truly portable, there were no Apple smart phones, and Google was something that a baby did. In 1992, unemployment was hovering around 7.5 percent. The unemployment rate was only around 5 percent just three years prior, and people feared not having a job. As the economy regained its strength throughout the rest of the decade, jobs were plentiful. The unemployment rate dropped to just under 4 percent, and the head hunters were in hot pursuit. Today, however, things are not as certain, especially with the Pandemic cloud. Layoffs, whether it be caused by the economy or by mergers, acquisitions, climate change and other natural disasters, occur in all sectors. To top it all off, we are still engaged in a war against terrorism and the organizations responsible for attacking civilians in U.S. cities, and cities across the world . . . times change.

Dealing/Coping with Emotions and Reactions

The likelihood that the interruption of your normal routine will be upsetting to you is natural. You have probably taken your lifestyle for granted. Prior to your leaving government service, what you had included:

- Camaraderie and mutual goals
- Economic security
- A sense of belonging
- Esteem, self-respect and respect for others
- Opportunity for growth
- Recognition, structure, social network

Coping With Career Change

Perfectly normal emotions . . .can't escape them

The interruption of this structured support system is usually replaced by some form of frustration, which may include one or more of the following feelings:

Denial - Anger - Fear - Depression - Anxiety - Insecurity

Understanding Your Feelings

> You will not understand the psychological distress of not having a job, (being unemployed) until it happens to you.

In her classic book on death and dying, Elizabeth Kubler Ross describes five emotional stages one passes through while experiencing the death of a loved one. Psychologists tell us that ***along with the loss of a loved one, losing one's job is one of the most traumatic experiences we will ever face.*** This is especially true if the change is unexpectedly forced upon us, like being suddenly laid off from a job because of a merger, acquisition, downsizing or government shutdown! The stages that she describes in her book are, however, common to nearly all change and the important point to remember is that we all pass through them . . . some more quickly than others. So, if you find yourself greatly disturbed, anxious and confused as a result of some traumatic change in your life – like leaving government service after a long career – it is perfectly normal to have the emotions that accompany those feelings. The goal is to get through the stages as quickly as possible, so that you can accept what has happened and get on with your life! To be aware of your emotions is a good thing as long as you understand what is driving them. However, to let these feelings control you for an extended period of time and to indulge yourself in them will be counterproductive. The stress associated with change is best overcome by accepting your circumstances. Realize the reality of the circumstances as they exist today.

> **Responding to Change**
> *the five stages*
>
> 1. Denial . . . denies the message
> 2. Anger . . . at everyone
> 3. Bargaining . . . maintain the status quo
> 4. Depression . . . anger turns toward self
> 5. Acceptance . . . renewed sense of hope and purpose

Control

Many years ago a gent named David Hultgram developed a model about control, or "Spheres of Influence," that addressed the very idea of accepting reality and getting on with life. It says that there are things that you *can* control and influence and there are things that you *cannot* control or influence. Therefore, if you cannot control (change or influence) an event, then put it to bed and get on with other things in your life. Only focus on things that you can control – change or influence. You cannot change or control the fact you cannot remain on active duty/government service forever, just as you cannot influence the time the sun will rise tomorrow . . . so don't try!

Spheres of Influence
David Hultgram

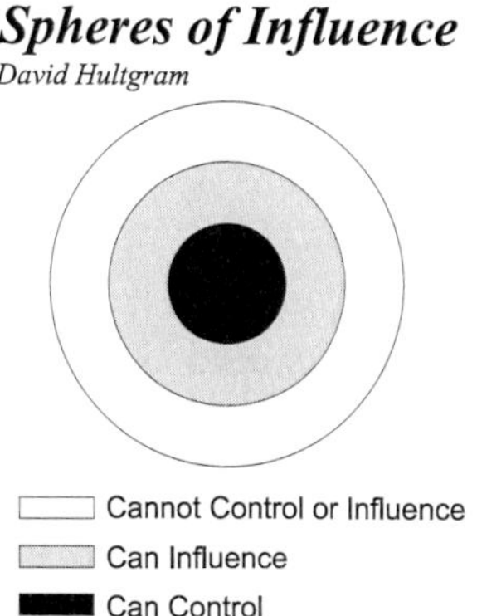

Be Aware of Your Feelings

The process of acceptance starts with an awareness of your changed status. For most people, the problem doesn't begin until the day after you retire. Like the two-by-four that is moving toward your head . . . you know it will hurt but you don't realize how much until it actually strikes you. You will really know you have retired when you turn on your computer to check today's events and find that there is nothing on the screen . . . no meetings scheduled, no trips planned . . . nada! The "cold shower" of reality ... unemployment! Personal experience has shown that while some people can move through all the emotional stages to the final acceptance stage in a blink-of-an-eye, others get stuck in ***Denial***, ***Anger***, or ***Depression*** for prolonged periods of time. It is difficult to conduct a career search and interview for a job with that kind of "baggage" weighing you down. Let it go and begin to look through the windshield instead of the rear view mirror. Chances are that you will cycle through the phases several times. *Denial, by the way, is not a river in Egypt!*

A New Assignment

Career transition is similar to going to a new duty station. You will want to tell your immediate family what is going on. They will want to know what this new "assignment" means to you and them. After all, what is a family for if not to assist you when you've got a need? Talk to them! Include them in your plans. Be positive!

As for your government and civilian friends, we recommend that you *do not talk about specific plans with them* until you have a clear career direction in mind. While it is true that the greater percentage of positions are found through personal contacts and networking, it is vital that these leads be informed at the *appropriate time* and in the *appropriate manner*. Now is <u>not</u> the time to use your silver bullets. The chapter on The Job Market fully explores how business opportunities can be generated from your personal acquaintances.

How you behave around your family, your friends and service acquaintances will determine, in part, how they will behave toward you. Explain to them that you are not going to the poor house and this is just another assignment you are exploring . . . also suggest that they do not tell their own friends what is going on. Adjusting to being "retired," or searching for the next career opportunity as the case may be, may be the most difficult chore of your life. Then again, you may find job searching extremely exhilarating. It is taxing while you are going through it and rewarding after the transition is finished and you have started your new career. Some people actually enjoy the process of career transition.

Job loss can be just as stressful on the family as the job seeker.

You may feel down or out-of-step with those around you, but that's when you need to rely on family and others for support. In some cases, you will have to help them adjust. It will be a new experience for them also. If your approach is rational, confident and well-directed, they will follow suit. Relax, finding the right job for you will be time consuming, but it's not the end of the world. By the way, if you feel a little bit like a second class citizen because you don't have a job while others around you do, you are not alone with that feeling. One day you are in charge of hundreds, or in some cases thousands, of people and the next day you are in charge of nothing. ***Then, you might think that others are pointing at you behind your back and saying, "Poor guy, can't find a job . . . must not be as good as he thought he was!" Not to worry, many have the same feelings when going through this ordeal.***

<u>Who Moved My Cheese</u>? By Spencer Johnson

This short read is a parody about how to deal with the inevitability of change. The story of two little mice named "Sniff" and "Scurry," and two others named "Hem" and "Haw." It describes their frustration while searching for their cheese that had somehow been moved. The story compares "*The waiting for someone to do it for me approach*" with, "*Taking action yourself to make it happen.*" One quote: "The quicker you let go of the old cheese, the sooner you can enjoy the new cheese." Easy, quick to read, and full of real world truths. Are you a Hem/Haw or Sniff/Scurry?

I'm Haw

I'm Hem

Relieving Stress

There are some actions that you can take that will help to eliminate or relieve the stress associated with a job search.

First . . . you must *acknowledge the situation* (what is going on in your life) and recognize that you are going through what everyone else has gone through during the process.

Second . . . *don't procrastinate* . . . get on with the career transition process.

Third . . . *have a support group* . . . family members, good friends . . . people that you can trust with your thoughts.

Fourth . . . *have a plan* . . . lay out the daily, week's or month's plan of action . . . you did it while in government service, it works here as well.

Fifth . . . *Accomplish something daily* . . . that is related to career transition – research, network meeting.

Sixth . . . *set realistic goals* . . . striving for too much will lead to frustration.

Seventh . . . one of your goals should be to *exercise and diet* . . . you will feel better and look better at your interviews. And, you might even live longer. Exercise is a big stress reliever.

Eighth . . . vent frustration . . . get a punching bag! If you don't know what else to do for exercise, ride a stationary bike or just get out and walk for an hour or so each day. It will do wonders for your frame of mind . . . and your waistline!

When you reach a point of acceptance you will begin to feel, sense and realize:

- I had a successful service career.
- I am okay – let's get on with it.
- There **are** plenty of other opportunities.
- What do I want to do?
- How do I go about it?

Vent frustration!

Acceptance and relief, however, may temporarily give way to another hurdle: fear of the unknown and loss of control.

This is evidenced by such questions as:

- What do I do now? (your objective)
- How do I do it?
- How do I determine what I want?

Typical Concerns and questions

Again, you are not alone with your feelings. The following is a partial list of concerns that have been expressed by military and civil service, and private sector personnel undergoing career transition. It is nice that you know you are not alone with your concerns, and it is also healthy to know that it is perfectly normal to have them!

- Just what does happen when I retire?
- Will my ego be able to cope with job hunting?
- The financial impact with kids in college . . . and, "Will I have enough money?"
- Will I have to start at the bottom?
- Where do I begin?
- Will I make enough money?
- Are my service strengths transferable to the private sector?
- How do I find the "right" job?
- How will my lifestyle change?
- How do I choose between two offers?
- How do I cope with loss of structure?
- Where should we live?
- What to do about our aging parents?
- What to do . . . what will be my career objective?
- How do I cope with rejection?
- How to start an interview
- What if I find the job isn't right for me?
- How will I manage my time?
- What about medical care and all that?
- What are private sector values?
- Will my spouse be okay?

"Where Do I Go From Here?"

Is the question that we are asked more often than any other. Meaning that: "I'm not sure that I want to continue in my previous government occupation (functional area) and might want to try something different in the private sector." . . . a very common feeling for people ending one career and looking to begin another.

Our objective is to help you address these concerns, and reduce the fear of the unknown by replacing it with the confidence of knowing a proven way to find:

- The **BEST** possible **JOB**
- In the **SHORTEST** amount of **TIME**
- With the **LEAST** possible **STRESS**

"Rejection" is an Ugly Word!

Stress will come from many directions. The most obvious will be the concern of finding a job and all of the aspects associated with work, income and self esteem. That stress gets compounded when you begin the career transition process and nothing seems to be working. Or, you get the feeling that no one seems to care. A ***THEM AGAINST YOU*** feeling. A feeling of ***REJECTION***! This is a common feeling and one that you will simply have to acknowledge. ***Acknowledging that rejection is inevitable will make it easier to manage.*** It's not that people don't care about you, it's just that they don't know you are out there and what you might have to offer. Everything I have learned about career transition says that it just takes time.

Coping with Rejection

However, it is the waiting period that creates fear and, therefore, stressful despair for most of us. Recognizing up front that this is a **no, no, no** and then **yes** business will help ease the pain. But no matter what I tell you, the stress emotion will be with you until you land your job. The best advice I can give you is, do not take rejection personally. By the way, this is one of the reasons that people in a job search mode join support groups such as 40+, and why big private sector outplacement firms conduct group meetings on a weekly basis and invite their successful job finders to come back and tell their story. It's so people can share ideas and recognize that everyone is undergoing the same emotions. If you keep in mind that most salespeople have to make over 100 calls to get just a few orders, you'll get the idea of what you must do. Think about the rejection tele-marketers get when they try to sell you something over the phone just as you are sitting down for a very special dinner.

A Proven Process

This book has been used by more than 68,000 military, civil service, and private sector personnel of all ranks and levels transitioning to a new career. It is a proven process, and if you follow it faithfully, your career search will be successful. Knowing you are following a proven process will keep you in a positive state of mind and moving forward!

The job hunting process described in this book really works!

Career Search ***... an emotional challenge!***

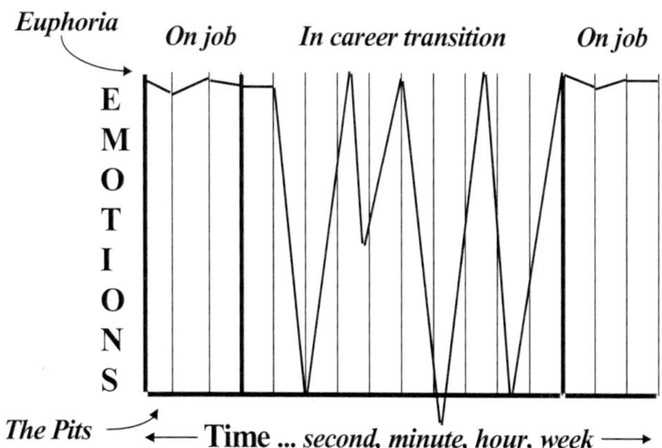

A stressful situation ...

The chart to the left is telling us that, while undergoing a new career search, emotions can swing widely from one extreme to another. While on active duty or actively employed, positive feelings normally run high – in the euphoria area. During the career transition phase, emotions vary based on how successful or unsuccessful the search is going. Dramatic emotional swings can take place over a week's time or an hour. One moment you receive the perfect offer. An hour later you get a call and are advised that the offer has been withdrawn because the company failed to get the "big" contract. Or, you leave an interview after having been told that you were the best person interviewed and that the company will call you in a few days to discuss a great salary and close the deal. Two weeks later you call the company to determine what's going on and learn that they selected someone else. By the way, it is typical for companies in the private sector to "forget" to advise you of a non-selection for a job you interviewed for . . . just the way it is.

Understand that rejection is just part of the process and it is more than likely that you will suffer some setbacks. Don't let the ordeal get you down . . . acknowledge that this is going to happen and when it does happen write it off as part of the drill! Some people liken the job hunting process to riding a roller-coaster . . . it has its ups and downs, can be exciting, a little fearful and happy when it is over!

After you have landed your job, you will again be riding high on the emotion curve. You will stay on that high until you start looking for another job and then you get to go through the whole ordeal again! Ain't it a blast?

Note: For those of you reading this book or attending our seminar who come from a military career, you will probably never have an assignment/job that is as exciting or demanding, or that comes with the same level of responsibility as the ones you had while on active duty. Less stress and more money perhaps, but not the same level and scope of responsibility. So, for most . . .

The **Major Difference**

will be . . .

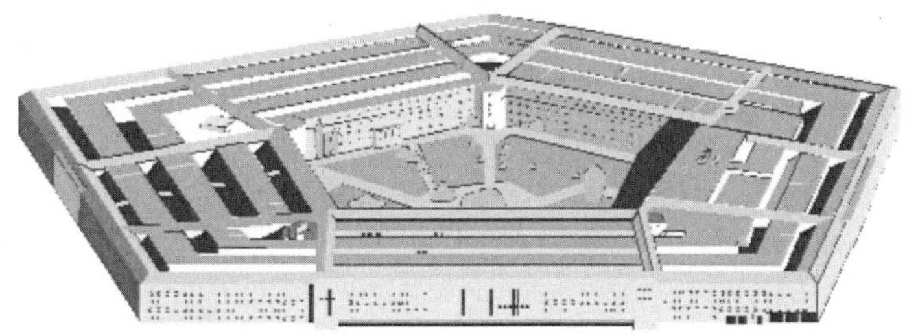

The Change In The <u>Level</u> And

The <u>Scope</u> Of Responsibility

CHAPTER **3**

THE SPOUSE'S PERSPECTIVE

Male or Female

An area of career transition that is often overlooked by many is the impact of the job loss and transition on the spouse and the family. The tendency is to focus most, if not all, of the attention on the trials and tribulations experienced by the job hunter. However, we must be mindful of the impact career transition can have on the job hunter's spouse and family.

Career transition can mean a major change in the living environment when the family is forced to move to a different locale for employment. The financial picture also changes . . . from one of complete security to one of uncertainty. This is true to some extent even though you know that finding a new job is just a matter of time.

The Private Sector Working Spouse

Finances affect lifestyles and changes in lifestyle are usually unwelcome by everyone in the household. Dual income families are not uncommon, which may complicate career transition decisions. For example, this means that there might have to be some hard decisions made as to whose career is the most productive or has the greatest potential, or whatever criteria you want to use. The obvious outcome of all of this can be stress on both sides of the fence.

STRESS . . . It's a Two-way Street

Space lesson: Two objects cannot occupy the same space at the same time.

Another situation that might have to be dealt with during the transition is the change in daily routine. In a two-spouse working family, the routine may not change all that much. But, when one spouse's role is the homemaker, having another person suddenly "invade" the household space can create some difficult times and stress. I have a male friend who discovered this when, during some free moments from job hunting, he offered his spouse some suggestions on how to manage the household chores more effectively. *They are no longer together.* I have another friend whose wife asks me, "Can't you just get him out of the house?" every time she sees me. On a personal note, I tried to rearrange a few decorative objects on my piano one day, and my spouse told me to keep my decorating ideas in the garage. Keep the faith, once a new job is found, things return to a normal state.

The Impact of the Spouse in a Hire

Years ago, the spouse might have played a significant role in the job hire, especially if the job was at an executive level. In today's business/corporate marketplace, the spouse usually plays little or no role in the hire. If you are after a political career, however, then the spouse plays a major role. But, for all intents and purposes, the days of the spouse making or breaking an offer to hire are all but gone.

Wooing the Spouse

Where the spouse might well get involved in the hiring decision is when there is a great job offer but the spouse does not want to move to the job's location. In that case it is common for companies to try and *woo* the spouse by offering to transport the spouse and often their children to the new location and show them how nice it might be. You might think this is a technique used only at the CEO level, but you are wrong. If the person is the right choice for the job, a company would do the same for anyone at any level. It's an inexpensive way to recruit. Another way of wooing a spouse is in the case where he or she has a good job and fears leaving it when moving to another location. Many companies will offer outplacement (career transition assistance) for the spouse to help them get settled and, in some cases, will enlist the assistance of the company's retained recruiter. This is another perk you might consider asking for during salary negotiations, if it applies to your situation.

Understand the Process

One of the most important things a spouse can do for the job hunter is to understand the process of career transition. By reading books like this one and other books on the subject the spouse will understand some of the stresses involved in this process and will also be able to assist in many ways. Just understanding what is going on and being supportive go a long way.

Helping Out

Other ways that a spouse can assist the job hunter are proofing all outgoing letters and resumes, helping with research on the industry and companies being visited, and perhaps most important, being a spokesperson for the job hunter. In the SOUND BITES chapter we will point out several ways for the spouse to help market the job hunter. Getting involved and assisting with the transition will have a positive impact on everyone. A good idea is to reread the CHANGE chapter and how it impacts everyone, especially from an emotional standpoint. Also, the spouse should compile a list of everyone they know and who their friends might know. Spouses often have equal to or better contacts than the job hunter.

> *An efficiency expert concluded a lecture with a note of caution. "You don't want to try these techniques at home." "Why not?" asked a member of the audience.*
>
> *"I watched my spouse's routine at breakfast for years," the expert explained. "My spouse made lots of trips between the frig, stove, table and cabinets, often carrying a single item at a time. One day I told my spouse, "Hon, why don't you try carrying several things at once?"*
>
> *"Did it save time?" the guy in the audience asked.*
>
> *"Actually, yes," replied the expert. "It used to take my spouse 20 minutes to make my breakfast. Now I do it in seven."*

WARNING REPEAT WARNING REPEAT WARNING REPEAT WARNING

Some people, especially those from the male side, will have a tendency to want to give directions in the area of how to manage the household more effectively. While it might seem like a good idea at the time that kind of unsolicited assistance, usually driven by boredom, will most likely not be received with open arms. Stick to your knitting . . . spend your energy working on your career transition and finding a new career!

Remember . . .
all's well that ends well!

CHAPTER 4

PERSONAL PREFERENCES

Personal Preference Type Indicator Assessment Tools

These personality assessment tools are primarily concerned with the differences in people that result from where they like to focus their attention, the way they like to take in information, the way they like to decide, and the kind of lifestyle they adopt. People with preferences opposite to yours tend to be opposite to you in many ways. They are likely to be weak where you are strong, and strong where you are weak. Each type has its own set of inherent strengths. During your job search you may be asked to complete a "personality assessment" such as the ones developed by Meyers-Briggs or Keirsey/Bates, the authors of the well-known Please Understand Me book. Both are common assessment tools in the market today. You will most likely score the same that you did if you took it previously, since the vast majority of people do not change type over a period of time . . . they usually develop stronger preferences as they mature. Remember. There are no right or wrong answers. If the results of the Keirsey Sorter or Meyers-Briggs assessment tools are not *you*, then use a "self select" procedure by reading the various descriptions in a book like, Please Understand Me (available on our Website). This will result in a more accurate analysis of your preferences. You can take the Meyers-Briggs assessments online at: http://www.humanmetrics.com/cgi-win/jtypes2.asp, or http://similarminds.com/personality_tests.html.

Personal Preferences

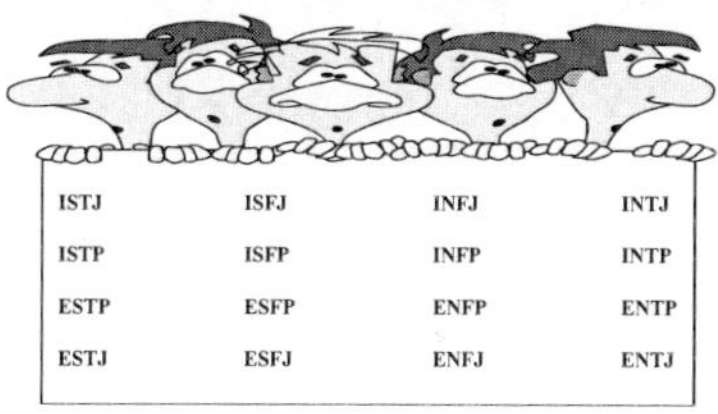

What are your preferences?

To understand why this happens

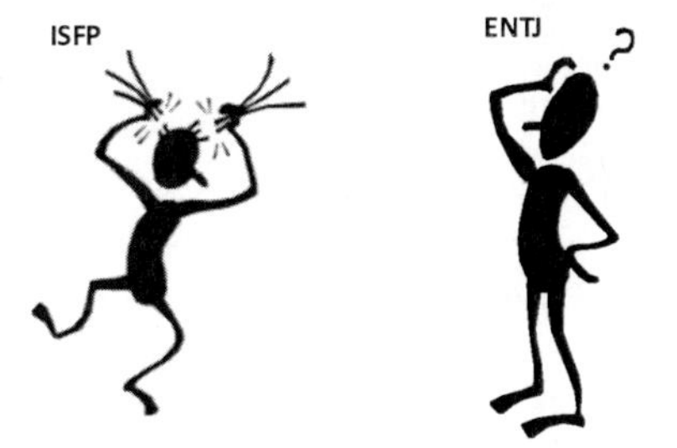

Read the two-page "portrait" of your type and your spouse's type found in Please Understand Me.

The goal of these assessment tools is not to make a value judgement about your strengths or personality but to help you to better understand yourself. The idea being, that if you understand yourself and your preferences, you will be better able to focus on personal development. While some of it borders on the *touchy-feely,* (my opinion), it does have real value when it comes to self improvement; I have received innumerable feedback letters attesting to the value of this assessment tool.

There are hundreds of examples but an easy one to understand goes like this: if your type is "ISTJ," for example, and you are at the extreme borders, you might want to investigate the strengths and shortcomings of that preference. If you are a strong "T" – an objective oriented person, then perhaps you would want to look at how you relate with people. To make this work, you must be candid with yourself.

It is not a test. There are no right or wrong answers to these questions, so don't worry about someone grading your answers. Another aspect to consider is that they do not measure personal strengths or weaknesses . . . only that you have a preference for this direction or for that direction. The MBTI assessment tool is 75% accurate . . . quite high for this kind of device, but not 100%. (See the note at the bottom of the Preferences Chart)

A good demonstration of preferences – Write your name on a sheet of paper in script. Easy. Now write your name in script with your other hand. Not quite so easy. Why? You have a preference for one hand or the other. And, that's all that the MBTI measures . . . it's all about preferences!

What Do the Letters Mean? *. . . some layman definitions of letter preferences*

E Extroversion . . . tends to be more outgoing

I Introversion . . . tends to be more pensive

S Sensing . . . likes detail, factual

N I**N** tuition . . . more global in thinking . . . intuitive

T Thinking . . . objective oriented, logical

F Feeling . . . more people oriented, supports personal goals

J Judgement . . . comes to closure quickly

P Perception . . . likes to consider all of the possibilities

For more detail on how the preference letters relate, read one of the many books published on the subject.

Some statistics: the vast majority of businesspeople in the USA are TJs (objective and come to closure quickly). Around 60 percent of females who have taken the MBTI are "F" (Feeling). Most senior military and civil service personnel we have scored are "S," "T," and "J" . . . with "E" and "I" getting equal representation.

Why Is this Relevant to you in your Career Choice?

- a strong "N" may not enjoy/have a preference for detail work
- a strong "I" may not prefer working with large groups
- a strong "P" may not enjoy a marketing or salesperson job requiring deal closing
- an "N" might get bored listening to details
- an "S" will want to see, hear, touch, lick, smell and feel the details of a plan
- an "F" will tend to want to know how decisions impact on the people involved

Take a Job That Requires Your Preferences

We all have each of the preferences within us. And, we are able to "turn on" being more detailed oriented and/or think more globally based on the need. Knowing that we all have preferences, however, helps to understand what motivates ourselves and others. It, therefore, makes sense to take a job where your preferences are most satisfied. You will be happier. Find a job you enjoy, and you will never have to work a day in your life. Write your letters and what they mean to you here:

____ ______________________________

____ ______________________________

____ ______________________________

____ ______________________________

Frequent Choices Made by Each Type

ISTJ	ISFJ	INFJ	INTJ
accounting medicine financial management teaching administration community service	service occupations teaching medicine social work ministry healthcare	public relations counseling psychology art, music creative writing medicine	scientific consulting financial consulting systems design systems development research forecast
ISTP	**ISFP**	**INFP**	**INTP**
performing arts crafts construction surgery athletics securities statistics	rural/agrarian pursuits construction painting arts/crafts work music	teaching ministry architecture therapy languages creative writing psychology	teaching architecture science, mathematics scholarship/writing research writing complex engineering-problem analysis
ESTP	**ESFP**	**ENFP**	**ENTP**
entrepreneur executive promotion development architecture performing arts	public relations politics selling teaching consulting	sales/advertising drama/acting politics fund raising counseling ministry	business, government organizational leadership innovation entrepreneur journalism consulting
ESTJ	**ESFJ**	**ENFJ**	**ENTJ**
management administration sales medicine/surgery production construction	sales teaching service occupations administration medicine helping professions	sales/marketing teaching/ministry executive psychology psychiatry counseling	business government military leadership public speaking entrepreneur project management

NOTE: The above choices are the averages and may not indicate what your preferences really are. If you complete the indicator or an MBTI assessment form, and the outcome is not you, then in all probability you are one of the 25 percent who make up the invalid part of the statistic. If that is the case, conduct a self-score by reading one of the many, many books on the subject of personal preferences. A book like Please Understand Me has descriptions of the various letter combinations. You can read them and determine if the description fits you or not . . . if not, keep on reading until you find a description that does fit you. This is a worthwhile drill for anyone who desires to have a better understanding of themselves. Please Understand Me is also a great gift for young adults . . . especially young married couples. Another wonderful book on the subject is Gifts Differing, by Isabel Briggs Meyers.

A free, self-directed mini-version of the full blown Meyers-Briggs can be found at www.humanmetrics.com. It is based on the Jung-Meyers-Briggs topology and describes your personality formula, the description of your type, list of occupations and the option to access other descriptive instruments.

You Are Filing a Flight Plan!

Sometimes, you must go with the flow.

A good friend of mine was having a discussion with his wife about taking a trip from Norfolk, Virginia to Seattle, Washington. Once they decided on a departure date, my friend began to lay out a plan. He got out the maps of each state they would be crossing, brought up Marriott Hotels on his Website, and bought a program that would tell him the miles from point to point, the sights to see along the way, where to eat and special events being conducted during the trip. As he was carefully laying out the miles to drive each day and calling Marriott making reservations, his wife looked at him and said, "My goodness, you're not planning a trip, you are filing a flight plan! There must be ten thousand motels, restaurants and hotels between here and Seattle and signs pointing to all of the best sights. Lets just get in the car and GO!" My friend is an ISTJ . . . his spouse is an ENFP.

We all have both!

Just because you are an ENTJ doesn't mean that you will always behave using those preferences. There will be times when your preferences will seem to be ISFP or some other combination . . . and you will perform well in that "mode" . . . it's just that your preferable way of behavior is ENTJ. Much will depend on the environment you are experiencing.

The Difference Between An Introvert and An Extrovert

I was at a Meyers Briggs training review workshop a few years ago and one of the instructors described the difference between an introverted engineer and an extroverted engineer. The difference is that the extroverted engineer looks at the introverted engineer's shoes!

"You Are Just Like Us"

A good friend of mine (George) made some good private sector friends while serving on a charity committee when still on active duty. His friends were in the financial consulting business and they had kidded around for some time about George coming to work for them when he retired from the service. When George retired, he looked them up and went out for an "official" interview. After a friendly welcome the company president introduced George to the company's psychologist who asked George to complete a Meyers-Briggs Personal Preference evaluation. After filling out the evaluation, George returned it to the psychologist who then disappeared into the president's office. After twenty minutes or so, the president and the CEO came out of the office waving the evaluation in the air and declaring, "We knew it, you are just like us." Seems that in their business, the most successful executives, and especially the marketing group, were all ENTJ and that was what they were looking to hire. My friend got the offer and they all lived happily thereafter.

Take it Personally

When interviewing for a job, weigh your compatibility not only with your boss but with potential colleagues too. *"In large part, you fit in with the job if you fit in with the people,"* says Pennsylvania State University psychologist David Day. *"Having a personality different from coworkers leads to job dissatisfaction and poor performance. It is the fact of being different, not one's particular personality, that can hinder job performance and prospects of success."*

The Take-Away. . . "Think of your natural preferences, what you like to do, not necessarily what you have become adept at doing!" (From What's Your Type of Career? by Donna Dunning.) **Hint**: If you are having trouble deciding what you want to do, match your four letters with those in the Frequent Choices Made by Each Type chart and see what others are doing with your preference type.

CHAPTER 5

OBJECTIVES

"If you don't know where you're going, you will end up somewhere else."
— Yogi Berra

"If you hear of something, please let me know."
— Anonymous

In your pursuit of a private sector career, your goal should be to find a career that is **right for *you*** . . . not just another job or just something to do. When you land the right job, you will have the opportunity to utilize your strengths and you will be motivated to strive for greater levels. You will also be a happier person.

Note: Some people try hard to find their dream job, their passion, and I believe that is a worthy endeavor. But, the simple truth is that the vast majority of people never do find their one great passion – the dream job. And for those who do, the passion often fades and they turn to other career areas . . . or "dream jobs." Just the way it is.

Imagine . . .

- What is the name of your company?
- What industry category is your company?
- What is the title on your office door?
- What will you be doing every day?
- Why will that benefit your company?

My Company, Inc
My Title

Assuming the above is true, why not choose a new career that suits you . . . a career where you can make a meaningful contribution and provides a level of satisfaction . . . and get on with life. All the while you can secretly chase your one great passion – but in the meantime you will be able to put food on the table. As a matter of fact, there is a school of thought that says a person should just find a *decent* job that will earn them an honest salary, work five days a week and enjoy the weekends.

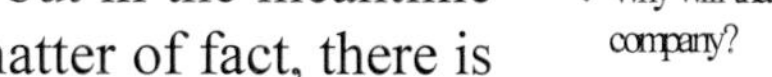

Objective Considerations

1. *You cannot do everything*
2. *You are better at doing 'some' things than other things*
3. *Not enough time to do everything*
4. *Easier to sell what you know than something new*
5. *Focus on your interests*

I have three friends who have gone in different directions. One earns around $250K a year plus perks, works 60 plus hours a week (including some Saturdays) and commutes 30 minutes each way through heavy traffic. Another earns about $170K a year with few perks and works out of the home 50 hours a week as a business developer. The third person works 40 hours a week making around $130K a year with typical perks, drives ten minutes to work, has great job security, and lives in the location that pleases the spouse. Go figure.

I think that Bob Hope nailed it when he said, ***"At 20, we worry about what others think of us; at 40, we don't care what they think of us; at 60+ we realize that they have not been thinking of us at all."*** What matters is what we think of us!

> The hardest thing for most of us is deciding what it is we want and are able to do!

One of the hardest things for most career government personnel, military or civil service, to decide upon is a specific career objective. This is because many have held numerous positions throughout their careers and have experience in several fields. Also, by the time they have 20 or 30 years of active duty most have become general managers . . . leaving much of the detailed work for the younger generation. Nevertheless, it is essential to have a focus, a target, if for no other reason than sounding intelligent, when some prominent business professional asks, "*What do you intend to do when you leave the service*?" More specific is better! A helpful **Research Exercise** can be found at the end of Research, Chapter 16. It makes you *plough* through the process of researching a company you might want to work for. Google does most of the work for you and if you have not done this before, it will be a good experience. It is also a good way to validate a potential objective.

Why an Objective

Keep in mind that the objective serves two purposes. First, it provides a necessary focus that is ***especially important for anyone making a major career change***. If you were already in the private sector and changing jobs within your career path (functional area and industry), this hard personal focus would not be nearly as difficult. For most senior government personnel, however, not working toward a specific objective will result in a tendency to be all over the place . . . like an unguided missile and a very frustrating situation. In the final analysis, if you choose not to put an objective on your resume . . . beginning with a summary statement instead . . . that is your business. But at least you will have an objective *in your mind* and that will serve as a basis for your research and the 30-second drill (see Sound Bites Chapter). I don't know anyone who can write an intelligent resume without knowing what he or she wants to do! You can write a personal profile that will describe your career interests and strengths, but it will not tell you or others what you want to do next. You simply must know what you want to do (objective) if you are to determine the specific skills and strengths required and conduct the necessary research. Second, the objective is what you tell someone who asks you what you plan to do when you leave active service. Not mentioning a focused objective (at the very least, an industry) and relevant key/trigger words, you might fail to gain a valuable referral.

Without an objective you will be like an unguided missile!

Without a Focus, (an objective) You Can't Research

A very practical reason to have a specific objective comes to light when you begin to research an industry. Without a good focus, you will be trying to research every industry in the country or your research will be so shallow that it will be of little help in an information meeting or a job interview. And finally, no one wants to read two pages of type to figure out what this person wants to do. When we discuss the resume in the next chapter you will see that if the resume is properly constructed, the reader will be able to determine your objective. So why not begin with a headline that tells the reader what you want to do?

While some people stumble into the 'perfect' job, your chances will be much improved if you focus on your interests, your strengths and those aspects that will make you valuable to an employer. **Remember. The employer will hire you to fulfill *their needs*,** not yours. It is important that you take time up front to understand what you really want to do. In the end you may have to accept an alternative, but initially you should be striving for the career that interests you the most and, through research, prepare yourself accordingly.

The Universe of Work

There are several up-front decisions that should be made *before* you proceed too far into the career transition process. If possible, try to decide what basic area you would like to work in. The chart at the right indicates some of your basic options . . . and each option will be different in terms of whom you network with and the personal and financial benefits to be derived. There is a mighty difference between a For-Profit choice and a Not-For-Profit choice, let alone civil service.

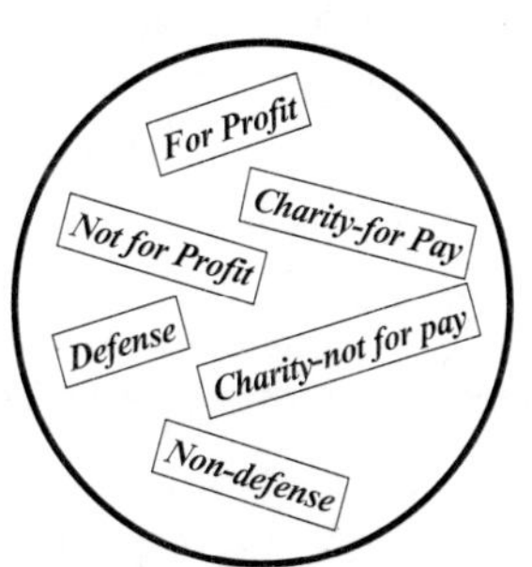

The difference between a For-Profit career (e.g., IBM) and a Not-For-Profit career (e.g., Red Cross) lies mainly in the goals of the organizations. By and large you would use many of the same management strengths in each, but to achieve a different end. In the case of For-Profit companies . . . Defense For-Profit (e.g., SAIC) and Non-Defense For-Profit (e.g., Starbucks) you would use many of the same management strengths and the goals would be the same . . . profit. . . but the *feelings* you have would be different. That is, as a former civil service employee or military careerist, you would probably be much more comfortable in the defense industry, especially if you were involved in work that you were familiar. Not everyone, but most.

Defense or Non-Defense?

There are some fundamental differences between these industries. The pros of aiming for a defense industry second career in terms of effort and ease, far outweigh those of the non-defense industry:

The case for a defense industry

- Easier and faster to enter
- Better long term possibilities
- Shorter learning curve
- Familiar surroundings
- Contacts unlimited
- No or few age barriers
- Fair compensation

The case for non-defense

- Satisfy a passion
- Make a change
- Desire to learn an entirely new profession

Note:

In the context of a career/resume objective, the term "Defense Industry" alone is not an objective. It encompasses too broad an area. The "Defense Industry" is a term that covers all industries that provide material or services to the DoD. If you want to say the "defense industry" is your objective, then you must combine it with an "operational" industry;" "defense aerospace," "defense shipbuilding," "defense communications," or "defense consulting in the IT area," for example. This becomes very important when writing the resume or researching or networking or just telling someone what you want to do. **And remember** . . . Defense industry companies like Lockheed Martin and SAIC are as much the "private sector" as are Starbucks and Sears! Many "defense industry" companies are also involved in "non-defense" business.

Changing Career Paths . . . please read this twice!

If you stay in your current career path, in terms of industry and functional area, your career transition will be much easier. If you seek out an area that is unfamiliar to you . . . that is, no experience in the industry or functional area . . . the effort will be more difficult and more frustrating. Conventional wisdom says that you are much better off sticking to your primary field of expertise than going in an entirely different direction, unless you just can't stand the nature of the work anymore. And even then, you must understand that it usually takes a long time to "catch up" financially in a new area compared to an area where you have experience, contacts and a reputation. Further, a career in the defense industry will facilitate future employment at an older age, because while both defense and non-defense industries are looking for talented people with good management strengths, non-defense industries have a greater proclivity for age bias against *older* workers even though it is illegal to do so. To wit, it would be easier for a 60-year-old to job-hop between defense companies than between non-defense at the same salary and management levels, especially in the same functional area. However, if your objective is to be a Walmart Greeter, then it really doesn't matter ... *not that there is anything wrong with being a Walmart Greeter!*

Just like there is a hierarchy of personal needs, there is a hierarchy of career needs. Decide what is most important to you. A meaningful career or a fancy office with sorf, cushy carpets.

Hierarchy of Career Needs

Title

Influence

Opportunity

Location

Prestige

Recognition

Worthwhile

Satisfaction

Fair Pay

Job Security

Your Goal:
A Sense of Well Being

Definitions ... Career Transition Decision Model

For purposes of our career model the following definitions apply.

- **Interest** - is something that you like/enjoy to do.
- **Ability or skill** - is something you do very well - you have many abilities in many different areas.
- **Strength - an ability or skill that is relevant to your area of interest** - you may have the ability or skill to fly a fighter aircraft, but that ability does not help you become a professional gardener.
- **Marketplace** - where you are going to enjoy and use your interests and strengths.
- **Objective** - reflects your interest, strengths and marketplace needs.

The Ruehlin Associates Focus Filter

Some people have difficulty separating their many skills and abilities from those specific ones that are relevant to the requirements of the objective . . . the strengths. It might help if you thought of all of your skills/abilities having to pass through, what I refer to as ***The Focus Filter***, designed to *permit* only those skills/abilities that are relevant to your job objective, pass. This same thought process applies when trying to decide which of your many accomplishments to use in developing your resume. When you begin to decide which accomplishments to use in your resume or during a job interview you will want to "filter out" those that are not applicable or relevant to the discussion at hand which is hopefully, your fit for the job at hand.

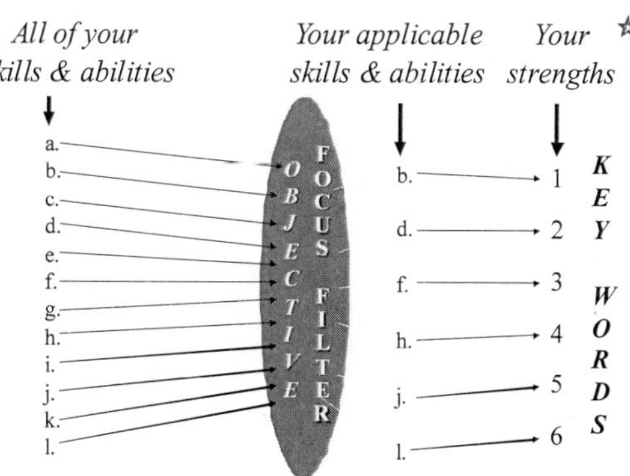

Not all skills/abilities are strengths and relevant to the objective.

The Career Transition Decision Model - how to choose an objective

The model used by nearly all professional career transition consultants consists of three variables: your interests, your strengths, and marketplace opportunities. Where they all come together becomes your objective. If you like horses and are good at making buggy whips, then you have a good match with interests and skills. However, since there is not a great demand for buggy whips you may not be able to earn a living pursuing that line of work. Likewise, if you would like to be a brain surgeon, but have shaky hands, the match falls apart even though there is a very profitable market for brain surgeons . . . you simply do not have the right skills. Happiness, therefore, is having the skills that support your interests and a market that will pay for that combination. Be advised that there are countless opportunities. Also be advised that there are many people in the world that have not found happiness in their careers because of a mismatch between the interests, skills and marketplace needs.

Happiness is doing what you enjoy, having the skills to do so, and being rewarded accordingly.

The ***interests*** in the model refer to the things that make and keep you happy. The ***strengths*** refer to your abilities, experience and knowledge that are relevant to the interest. And the ***marketplace*** refers to the rewards that we seek . . . money, challenge, recognition, charitable giving, and so forth.

Let's examine and expound on the career transition model from some practical viewpoints.

The Interest Approach

Entering the model (*see graphic*) from the "what interests me" aspect, you would determine what occupations you think or know that you would enjoy doing . . . where your interests lie. People who have a *true passion* to do "this or that" are lucky. People interested in medicine or accounting or military service for example. For them, it becomes a matter of acquiring the education and, assuming compensation is sufficient, pressing on toward their interest/their goal. If along the way they find they do not have the required strengths or the compensation is not sufficient, then they have to begin all over again. A personal assessment tool like the Meyers Briggs might be of some valuable assistance in this case in helping to determine interests. Two questions of equal importance to ask yourself: 1) "What do I want to do?" 2) "Why do I want to do it?"

> Upon deciding what you want to do, ask yourself why you want to do it!

The Strengths (skills, abilities) approach

The next approach is to admit that you do not have any career passion . . . strong interest . . . and, therefore, it is not too important what you choose to do. Many people graduating from high school and college fall into this category . . . got the degree but really don't have any great desires one way or the other. For example, I know many very senior military personnel who graduated, entered the service, and stayed because it was the path of least resistance . . . or stayed, as some have said, "by default." In my own case, it wasn't until I had been in the service for five or six years before I realized that I was truly enjoying what I was doing and decided to make it a career. So, if you have no strong feelings about a particular career, you might examine what strengths come easy for you and then determine what occupations or industries or functional areas use those strengths (skills/abilities).

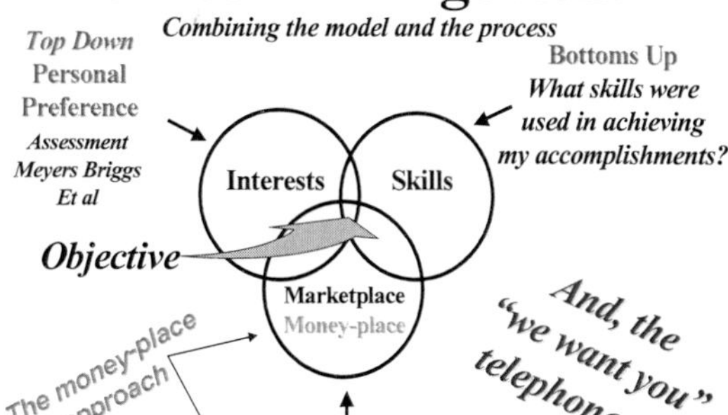

The Marketplace approach

This approach calls for an examination of the marketplace to determine its current needs. For example, a few years ago, telecommunications was the hot spot in the business world. There is presently a high demand for medical professionals. With the current world situation there is a strong demand for security personnel – both internal and external. Therefore, in the "marketplace" case, you would determine the "hot" occupations and make one of them your focus . . . your objective. Again, you must first determine if you have the strengths required.

The Money-Place approach

Along with the marketplace approach is the *money-place* approach. This is similar to the marketplace except that you determine who is offering the best overall compensation package and make that occupation/industry your focus . . . again you must have the required strengths. Note that with the exception of the first approach, where you have an interest – a passion, it really doesn't make much difference what area/industry you choose. You are either looking for an industry that can use your strengths, or one that pays a lot of money.

The "We Want You" happening

This has nothing to do with the model but is closely associated with the previous two paragraphs. What happens here is that you are sitting at home one night scanning Websites for job postings, wringing your hands because no one is answering your calls and letters and applications, and suddenly the telephone rings and an old friend is calling. He begins telling you that he has the perfect place for you in his company and that the pay is good. Such a deal . . . and it might be. It also might be something to get you going, and it might be a good thing for the company, but you might wake up six months later and realize that you are wasting your life away doing things that are not important to you, but you are making a nice salary and living in a nice area. Read on.

All Jobs Are Not Created Equal

I had a good friend who offered me a job with his company because I was frustrated; I couldn't decide what I wanted to do! It was a generous offer, and in a desirable location, but as fast as he made the offer, he said he wouldn't recommend I accept it, because he knew that I would be unhappy in the job. It was nice of him to offer the job, but it was nicer for him to advise me against taking it. I would have been an unhappy camper. Unfortunately, this situation happens to many senior personnel leaving a government service job or any other job for that matter. Think twice before you jump into a situation like this. It ought to be ***what you want to do*** *not what you are able to do or someone wants you to do!* ***Unless, of course, you are starving!***

Some people might offer you a job, but then recommend that you don't take it.

Objective Statement Formula

Your objective statement should contain three basic ideas and an optional add-on value statement:

- **Level of position**
- **The functional area**
- **The industry**
- *Value statement-optional*

Note: As we will discuss further in the Resume chapter, at your level the resume is more for you than for anyone else. That being the case, the two most important of the four basics are the functional area and the industry.

Example: ***Senior financial management position in the aerospace industry where experience, accomplishments and strengths will contribute to increased profitability***. There may even be cases when it would be appropriate ***to state the specific job title*** (when answering an ad or posting for example) . . . Chief Financial Officer or Marketing Director . . . of such and such industry. In this example the operative/critical words are *financial* and *aerospace*.

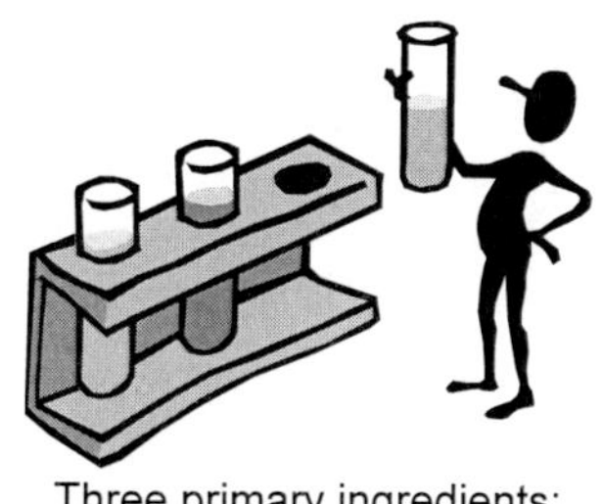

Three primary ingredients: level – function – industry

Select A Functional Area

When you were assigned to a ship or battalion or a shore command, you worked in a specific functional area. Aboard ship for example, some functional areas are operations, navigation, supply/logistics, communications etc. And within a functional area there were probably more specific functional areas. Take logistics for example. While the major functional area is logistics, there are *subordinate* functional areas such as disbursing, food service, material, storeroom management, etc. A functional area should be included in your objective statement. You might have to research specific companies to determine what they call a given functional area.

Functional Area Examples	
• Training	• Logistics
• Public Relations	• Marketing
• Financial	• Legal
• Human Resources	• Medicine
• Program Management	• Administration

Select A For-Profit Industry

The chart at the right depicts examples of some industries. In the research chapter of this book there is Business Week magazine's list of 11 industry categories. An industry should be included in your objective statement. If you are uncertain what industry category a company believes it belongs in, get a copy of their annual report or check out their Website. Several years ago a company's industry would have been obvious, but these days, with the rampant growth in technology, one can't be certain.

Industry Examples	
• Retail	• Shipbuilding
• Aerospace	• Government
• Transportation	• Utilities
• Telecom	• Education

Select a Not-For-Profit Industry

If you intend to pursue a not-for-profit career, remember that there are all kinds of not-for-profit agencies. The figure at the right only shows a few of the many not-for-profit agencies out there. Identifying what kind of not-for-profit agency you are interested in, will make a difference how you research that industry and eventually, how well you do at the interview!

Not-For-Profit Examples	
• Homeless	• Charities
• Education	• Clergy
• Cultural	• Foundations
• Trade Associations	• Government

The rationale for having an objective is readily apparent when you consider that the basic process of the job search involves:

- Personal assessment
- Developing a resume
- Research
- Developing a marketing plan
- Interviewing
- Salary negotiation

With that in mind you can understand that without an objective, stated either on a resume or in your own mind, conducting a successful job search would be extremely difficult. This idea will become clearer as we discuss the information meeting, the job interview, research and salary negotiations. Does that mean if you see an advertisement or hear of an opportunity that interests you, but differs from your present objective, you *shouldn't* go for it? . . . NO! You should, but only if you have the qualifications and can support your case. You would just have to build a new resume . . . possibly from scratch, and conduct additional research.

Determining an Objective

The basic plan for a resume includes your experience, your accomplishments, your interests and values, and your education and training. When we discuss resume development, you will see that these items all support the objective.

Sample Objectives . . . short and sweet

★ Director of Supply Chain Logistics for a major retail company.
★ Senior program management position in the aerospace industry.
★ Director of operations for a nuclear power plant.
★ Chief Financial Officer for a major accounting company.
★ Teaching position in an elementary school.
★ Software programmer in the IT industry.
★ Senior maintenance manager for a major educational institution.
★ Superintendent of a major municipal school system.
★ Mid-level intelligence analyst in the Homeland Security industry.

Note: How you *dress-up* the objective is your choice, but the objective should contain the level, functional area, and industry.

Spin-off Objectives

Sometimes there are areas where you have an intense interest but not the strengths . . . like the brain surgeon objective example given earlier in the chapter. There is also a story of the man who wanted to be a concert pianist, but did not have the piano playing strengths needed to be successful. So, the career consultant recommended that he consider areas related to the piano-music-industry. When the man examined that career field, he found countless areas where he could apply the many strengths he did have and work within the music/piano industry. Don't be stymied in your pursuit of an objective just because the match isn't perfect. Explore all of the possibilities.

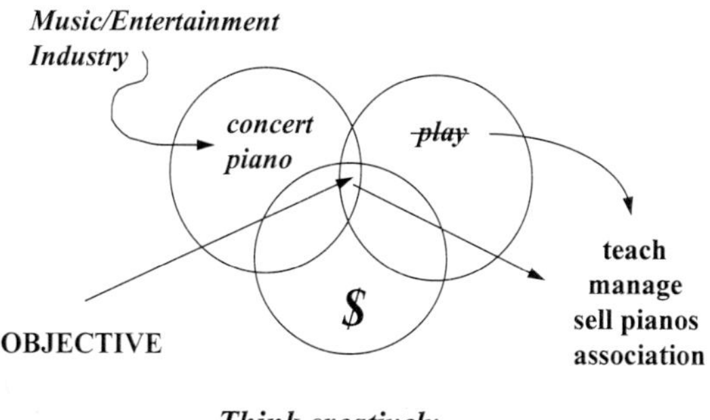

Think creatively ...

Get out of Your Box

Government personnel often get trapped inside themselves. They think that, because they have specialized in one or two different areas, they are limited to doing those same things in the private sector. What you must realize is that you have an abundance of talents. I don't know one senior military/civil service senior manager who doesn't have strong basic management and administrative strengths. There are countless former government personnel in the private sector who are performing well in areas where they never worked before. Don't get boxed in thinking that an unfamiliar area is off-limits to you. And, don't be afraid to ***reinvent*** yourself!

Save the Ads

I read somewhere that a person clipped ads from several newspapers for a year, stuck them in a cigar box, and then dumped them all out on a table and put them into piles by category . . . by industry or functional area. The idea here is that the height of the pile represents interest. The person then selected the tallest pile and focused on that as the area of greatest interest and, therefore, the preferred objective. If you try this *simple,* but somewhat inane technique, please let me know if it works for you, or if you just end up with some paper to start a nice fire. A good drill.

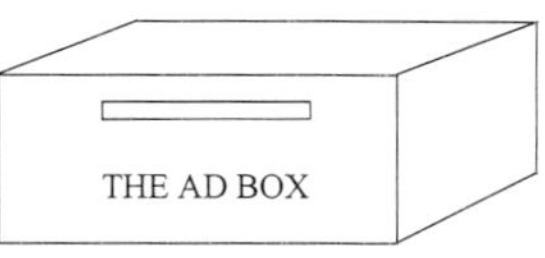

What Do You Do If You Don't Know What You Want to Do? . . . You Force It!

"What to do, what to do, what to do!"

"I don't know" is the statement professional career consultants most often hear from people undergoing career transition. For personnel departing government service the person with the clearest objective is the young technician who has spent the past 10 years working in a technical field and desires to continue in that same field. That person's goal is clear and their background fully supports the objective. However, the more senior the individual and the more responsible his or her duties, the more difficult it is to settle on one or, for that matter, even several objectives. Further, many senior service members focus upon an objective that is unsupportable . . . one in which they have no experience or track record. Heading for a field in which you have no previous experience is fine, as long as you remember that you may have to start at a more junior level. In any case, the goal should be to do what interests you and what you enjoy, and receive commensurate compensation while doing it. As an aside, the vast majority of senior people I have met with have not thought out what they want to do for a second career . . . be they members of the military, civil service or private sector. It's tough to come to grips with career choice.

Forcing an Objective!

There are lots of ways to arrive at an objective. That is, to make yourself select an objective and pursue it. One obvious way, which I do not recommend, is to throw a dart at the want-ad section of the local newspaper and chase whatever job the dart lands on. But, surely there must be a more scientific method. After counseling thousands of senior members, who were undecided as to an objective we devised a system that we call . . . ***Forcing It.***

It's better than wringing your hands!

You can force an objective two different ways:

1. **Top down . . .**
   - ✓ Decide upon five or six different careers/jobs that would be of interest to you, then
   - ✓ Determine the five or six strengths that are required in each position . . . you accomplish this by talking to people who work in those areas or researching Websites such as Google, then
   - ✓ Review your background for accomplishments that relate to the job strengths, then
   - ✓ Prioritize the jobs based on interest or the number of accomplishments, then
   - ✓ Pick one, write a resume for that position/field, and go forward conducting information meetings.
2. **Bottom up . . .**
   - ✓ Brainstorm with yourself and come up with a list of 50 or more accomplishments, then
   - ✓ Categorize the accomplishments into functional areas, then
   - ✓ Choose the area that is most appealing or saleable or marketable, then
   - ✓ Develop a summary statement based on the accomplishments, then
   - ✓ Write an objective based on your summary statement, and conduct information meetings.

Note: More on this subject later in the chapter.

Exploring the Options

Sometimes it makes sense to explore other possibilities in an industry or functional area. Let's say, for example, that your interests lie in the educational field . . . think of it as the "Education industry." When I say education, most people think of the functional area of teaching, when in reality, there are many functional areas that fall under the education industry. There are many facets of teaching. Once again, don't get trapped in the box. The graphic at the right is telling us that the field of education is comprised of functional areas such as administration, training, associations as well as the area of teaching. It is also telling us that you might teach not only in schools, but in private industry and non-profit organizations as well.

Training
Administration
Education
Teaching
. . .
Equipment

Education is not just about teaching – consider what other functional areas are found in the teaching industry or in non-related industries, as well.

Functional Areas/industries

Another example of exploring the options is to put an industry in a center circle and then try to think of all the functional areas that are employed in that industry or all of the industries that use the Functional area that you are exploring.

For example, if you select the Aerospace Industry, you would find that there are innumerable functional areas required by that Industry. The functional areas in the

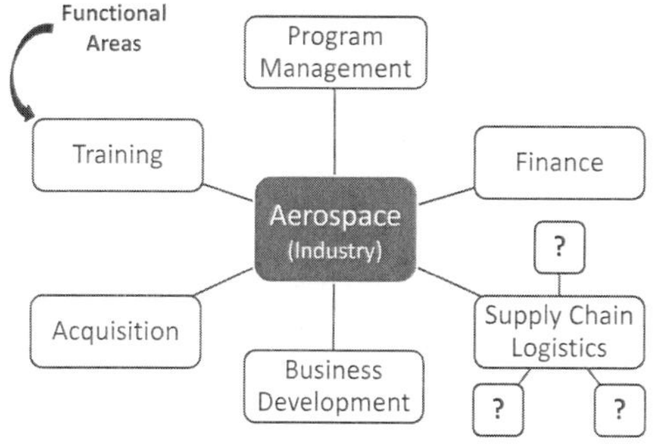

Banking Industry, or in a broader vein, the Financial Services Industry, would most likely be considerably different than those in Aerospace or Outdoor Recreation for example. Play with the idea . . . it is amazing what people come up with.

Objective Summary

By now you realize that the thrust of this chapter is to encourage you to focus on a specific objective. There are many reasons for narrowing down your objective . . . some of the best reasons are obvious when you think seriously about them. Having a specific objective:

- Provides a personal focus for you.
- Helps others to help you . . . they know what you want to do.
- Makes research easier . . . **no, it makes research possible** – how can you research if you don't know what you are looking for? Google can't help without specific terminology!
- Makes referrals easier . . . **no, it makes referrals possible** – how can I recommend you talk to someone in a given area if I don't know what you want to do?
- Enables you to determine the strengths/skills needed for the position.
- Knowing the strengths required, allows you to identify relevant accomplishments which are used in describing your successes.
- Saves the reader time . . . the reader knows up front what you want to do.
- And once again, it makes you *sound intelligent* when someone asks, "what are you going to do when you leave government service?"

The Objective Dilemma

.... Somewhere in between ...

A major concern that most people have when deciding on an objective is that if it is too specific, they might miss an opportunity. And, on the other hand, if it is too general, people will not be able to provide assistance because they won't know which direction to point you. There is no easy answer for this problem, but experience pretty much tells us that the specific approach is more successful by a wide margin. You just need something to focus on. If you still disagree, reread the preceding paragraph. In addition, it is important for you to understand how people absorb and deal with information.

The Brain and Networking Connections

> Key words are an indispensable component of a resume, as well as how you describe yourself and your career objective at networking and job interview meetings. Computers will filter out applicants who don't fit.

Most people do not understand how the brain functions while in a conversation mode. You must first understand that the brain only contains and retains specific information and, therefore, focuses only on the specifics of a conversation. There are countless connections in the brain and when the brain registers a specific bit of information, ***like a key word or phrase***, it automatically links that information with other specific information stored. That's why when someone tells you they are looking for a job in the aerospace industry, you automatically think of all of the people you know in that industry . . . you (your brain) make a connection. That connection usually leads to a comment like, "Oh, have you talked to Steve Bristow who works at Sona Aerospace Inc.?" And that leads to a referral. If you just tell me "You are looking for a job," I either have to ask, "Doing what" or simply say, "Lots of luck." Brain connections lead to referrals . . . referrals lead to networking opportunities . . . networking opportunities lead to job interviews and interviews to jobs and off you go! Once again, you should try to determine what it is you want to do . . . so others can help you! It's a no-brainer!

How Brains Operate

The listener's brain:

- *only records specifics*
- *disregards generalities*
- *"connects" information by association*
- *has countless connections*
- *connections = referrals*
- *referrals = Networking*
- *Networking = interviews*
- *interviews = jobs*

Referrals
Input
Networking Contacts

Without something to connect or associate with, e.g., a key word or phrase, there is no referral!

How Many Objectives Can I Have?

Answer . . . as many as you want! However, for each objective you will need a corresponding resume. For each objective you will have to research accordingly. For each objective you will have to inform your references accordingly. For each objective you will have to memorize a different set of data. For each objective, you will have to change your LinkedIn profile. Too many objectives will dilute your efforts and what do you say when a high roller asks, "What do you plan to do when you leave government service?" And, by the way, what do you really want to do?

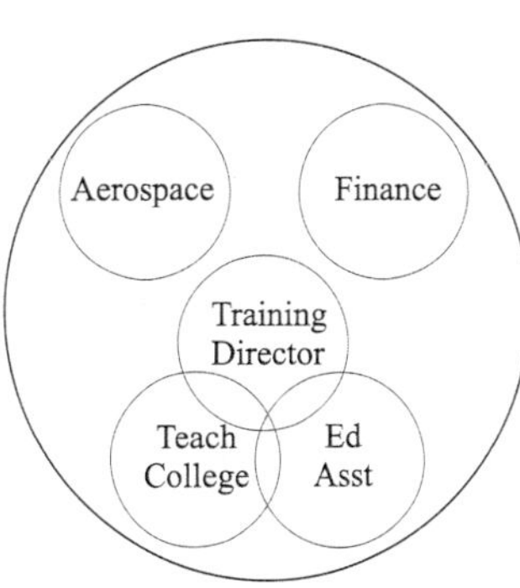

Looking at the illustration on the left you can see that various objectives in the educational area work together very well. However, when you start adding *foreign* objectives such as aerospace and perhaps finance, unless it is finance within the educational area, you begin to dilute your efforts. Therefore, happiness is having an objective in a specific functional area and a specific industry area.

After saying all that, it has been our experience that about half of those who attend our seminars end up doing something different from what they set out to do. And that's okay. How does that happen? Say you have decided to make your objective "Project manager in the aerospace industry." Next you find yourself conducting a networking

The Moment of Truth

Bill Gates says:
"And what do you plan to do when you leave active duty?"

And you say?: "____________
____
____________________."

What can he do for you?

meeting or even in a job interview and at the end of the session the other person says, "We are full up with project managers, but after talking to you for the last half an hour it seems to me that you could fill the position as the senior operations supervisor at our new plant. Would you be interested in exploring that opportunity?" You think about it for a moment and realize that you might enjoy such a position, and three weeks later you find yourself happy in a career much different than what you had originally intended. This kind of scenario happens more often than you could possibly imagine.

If All Else Fails . . . Take the Path of Least Resistance

If, after you have beaten your head against the wall eight hours a day for 30 straight days, and still have not determined an objective, then say to blazes with it and take the *path of least resistance*. Free fall. Look back on your career and determine:

The path of least resistance. It's better than sitting on your hands!

- The ***most obvious*** job/objective you could accomplish based on your background . . . like it or not.
- The ***career direction*** you have had most of your career.
- Where you have the best or ***most contacts*** that could provide the best network.
- ***Most credible***
- Where you might have the ***highest comfort level***.

So now you must be saying, "Why would I do that after just being told I should self-assess and decide to do something I really want to do?" Because, if you can't figure it out, you are better off doing something other than staying home wringing your hands. Do something and if you can *force* yourself into an area that is at least familiar to you, you will be confident in going forward in that area. When you get there, chances are that you will recognize other things that may be more appealing, or that what you have chosen is in fact the best choice, on an interim basis, at least. After all, it's not forever! **And, if what you want to do is what you have been doing, you have a slam dunk!**

A Position or a Job?

One last consideration to make, and one that applies mostly to the more senior personnel involves the job or position decision. Years ago when the defense industry was booming, large corporations often had service representatives on their staffs to serve as a liaison between the company and the services. While this practice has diminished significantly, it is still practiced by some. More often you will find these people in corporate positions in strictly a staff role . . . some people call them door openers . . . business development. Among other things, a door opener is a person who, through whatever means, gets an entre to the decision maker, for other people. The door opener is a highly respected person but probably doesn't understand all of the technical aspects of the business . . . just there to enable others to get into the room to make the sale. There is nothing wrong with any of these positions if that is what you want to do. Just be sure of your long term objective.

Which Is Which?

Everyone has his or her own way of describing what is a job and what is a position. Some would say that a position is staff and a job is line, but there are many staff assignments that can have a significant impact on the company's profits and, therefore, I would have a difficult time calling them positions. The easiest way to distinguish between them is to remember that, in this discussion, a *position* has little to do with the day to day operations of the

POSITIONS AND JOBS

Positions:	Jobs:
Door openers	CEOs
Representatives	COOs
Some staffs	CIOs
Boards	CAOs

company and the person with the *job* is the day to day and long-term decision maker. There are no *positions* in a Special Warfare forward deployed SEAL team . . . there are a slew of them among the many bureaucrats in DC.

(Note that the term *position* has two meanings in the context of career transition. The above meaning refers to a senior staff person who most often has no direct impact on the success or failure of the business . . . a "door opener." The other use of *position* is when describing an objective . . . "a position as the Chief Operating Officer of a retail manufacturing company involved in worldwide operations.")

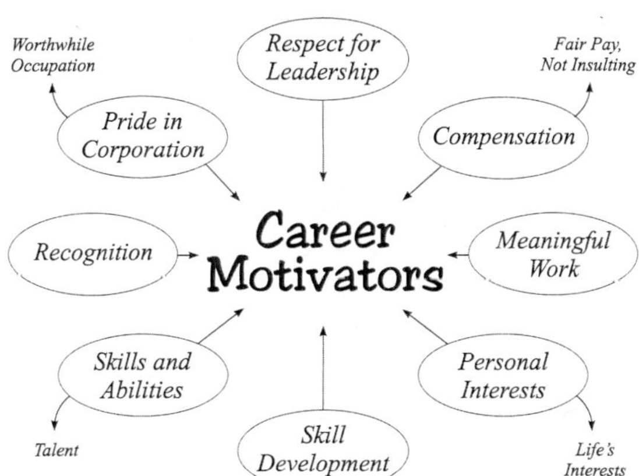

This all raises the point about doing what turns you on and what you will most enjoy doing in your next career. A study called "100,000 Executive Survey," examined the things that motivate employees the most. They found that in addition to the three basic areas we mentioned previously, (interests, strengths and the reward) that ***pride in corporation*** **and** ***respect for the leadership*** were very significant. You might want to take those points into consideration when thinking about your next career. Also note, fair pay . . . not insulting!

Finally, what would be your dream job? The job you would take if you won the Reader's Digest contest and received a check for $20 million.

Exercises

On the following pages are some exercise worksheets and/or *systems* that will help you to determine what a good objective might be for you. Fill them out before reading the rest of the book. You might need to use some additional paper. Here are the directions for each . . .

"WHO AM I" Worksheet

Go to your computer, and, on one page, describe yourself in the terms indicated. Don't spend a lot of time pondering the subject – just get something down. The idea here is that if you write down what first comes to mind, your objective might become very clear by the time you get to the last subject. If that happens, then go back and refine your descriptions. You might even have your spouse or a good friend fill the page out in your behalf and then compare their comments with yours.

"FORCE AN OBJECTIVE - TOP DOWN" Worksheet

Line A: Write four functional areas that would be of interest to you. The areas could range from financial management to marketing to program manager to bridge builder – any functional area. Hopefully they will be somewhat realistic.

Line B: Write six strengths you believe or discover are needed to be successful in that functional area. Obviously, it would be helpful if you had an idea which industry you would apply the functional area . . . aerospace, telecommunications, education or whatever.

Line C: Write an accomplishment or two for each of the strengths listed on line B. Don't worry about length at this time, but do try to explain what you did using the skill and the tangible results. Just saying you "Did good" doesn't hack it. Tangible means dollars saved or x percent improvement in a process, for example.

Line D: Label each item from line A in priority sequence . . . number one being what you think would be the best focus for you.

Line E: Write down some names of people whom you could talk to about what you have decided to focus on in line D. And, then go do it!

"FORCE AN OBJECTIVE - BOTTOM UP" Worksheet

Line A: List as many accomplishments – up to 100 – that you can think of, or others can think of.

Line B - Categorize: Separate the 100+ accomplishments into categories. It doesn't matter how many categories you have as long as you have fewer than the total number of accomplishments. Select four of the categories that most appeal to you and make four columns. The categories might fall out to be functional areas such as . . . aerospace, telecommunications, education or whatever.

Line C - Determine Strengths: Under each category, write the six strengths you believe are necessary to be successful in the applicable category.

Line D: Choose the most appealing/supportable category – tie an industry to it if possible . . . for example, you might end up with something like "Program management in the shipbuilding industry."

Line E - Develop a Summary: Using the example in line D above, your summary would be a short paragraph describing yourself in terms of a program manager in the shipbuilding industry with comments and attributes which support that category.

Line F - Objective: An easy follow-on to the summary statement or "A senior program management in the shipbuilding industry . . . yada, yada, yada."

To formalize what you have just completed, go to the **"Objective Exercise"** page and fill it out with the information you determined to be appropriate in one of the previous exercises. And now you have the beginning, and the hardest part by the way, of your resume. Now it is a matter of listing the relevant accomplishments and providing a brief review of your last three or four assignments.

Objective Modifiers

Before you get too far along with your objective, you should ask yourself and your spouse if there are any very ***personal considerations*** that you should take into account. The obvious considerations that come to mind are: personal or family ***health***; your ***age*** and your spouse's age; any special ***financial*** needs . . . like having ten children in college at the same time; ***parents/parents*** in-law's health; ***family business*** needs and so on. At age 45-50 and beyond most of us will have some special needs to consider. They may not have an immediate impact on what career and/or location you choose but sooner or later they will come into play. In nearly every live seminar we conduct, the concern over parent's health is already a concern for about half of the attendees. If you are between 45 and 55 years old you are in the *sandwich generation* . . . meaning, halfway between your children's and your parent's age.

Personal Objective Exercise

This exercise (later in this chapter) is one of the best and most enjoyable exercises in the book. I strongly suggest you and your spouse, or good friend, sit down and complete this exercise. You may have to repeat the exercise several times to get it right, but sooner or later it will all make sense and lead you to a useable objective, if you cannot determine one in a more formal manner. And, even if you determine an objective without using this exercise, you should give it a try a few times if only to validate your objective. The exercise will require a few bottles of good red wine!

"Follow Your Shadow" . . . from Forbes Magazine

How do you start a "shadow career?" Here's some advice from New York career counselor Dee A. Soder, founder of the CEO Perspective Group. Note: A shadow career. "Individuals who are in shadow careers are not fulfilling their own desires, but instead are standing in someone else's shadow. Many people I have known are living a shadow life — it's not that they are doing anything wrong or bad; it simply means that they are spending a lifetime doing something similar to their true calling, but without the real work, or risk or ***reward*** of the calling they know they should be following." Deb Sofield

Plan ahead. Too many people wait until their 50s or 60s to start thinking about work alternatives. That doesn't give you time to get the credentials to develop the contacts you need for a second career.

Don't overlook your weaknesses. You may have thought you were a great manager back when you were executive vice president of Megacorp, or the Commanding Officer of a ship. But without the fancy title . . . and without the clout that comes with it . . . you may be a lot less persuasive.

Be prudent. You could lose your savings in a franchise, demanding startup capital. Another way to go bankrupt: taking a board seat on a company that doesn't have an adequate Directors and Officers (D&O) liability insurance policy.

Do your homework. What's the demand for the strengths you are offering? "Most people spend more time buying a house or a car than they do researching a post-retirement career," says Soder.

Do a "tryout." You may think someone with your vast experience should make a great teacher, but you don't know if you are suited until you stand in front of a classroom.

Prepare yourself. If you spent a business career surrounded by subordinates, being a solo consultant will be a shock to your system. So, consider leasing space in an office building or joining up with another firm. "Otherwise," says Soder, "It's just you, your spouse and the postman."

Choose wisely. Don't assume friends make good business partners.

Beware of the dream job. And don't open a country inn!

Business Development (BD) as a Career Objective or Occupation.

We often receive questions regarding the pluses and minuses of a business development career. Business development entails *selling* a product or a service to willing buyers. Someone must be the principal business developer for a company or, simply put, there will be no business . . . and no business means no income . . . and no income means no job(s) for the company employees, let alone the business developer. In truth, ***everyone is in the business of selling company, or their organization's products and services***, but the person whose *sole* job is to bring in new business and customers (the rainmaker), and keep existing customers and their business, is the person standing on the red carpet, about to receive their pink slip, if no business is produced.

"Thank you for your business, we guarantee satisfaction."

Many people do not like the idea of calling on friends, or anyone else for that matter, and "selling" products. And many people do not like nor want the stress of having to make their "mark" (a sales quota) each month. They would rather work in a line or staff position not directly responsible for bringing in new or additional business. When a person leaves government service and gets a job offer in Defense Industry Business Development, it is usually because the person has many personal connections in defense industry companies and can provide introductions (referrals) to the prospective decision makers–a ***strategic hire*** (see page 175). Normally the company will take time to indoctrinate newcomers so they fully understand the company's products/services and can "sell" on their own. Selling quality products which will produce a better "mousetrap" is good for everybody and in the case of the defense industry, is necessary if we are to continue to improve our nation's security.

> Some people do not like the idea of selling but it is an important part of our economic engine, and like it or not, we all do it.

While there are many pluses to a business development (BD) career, a downside often occurs when their personal contacts leave active duty. Suddenly, after about three years, the BD finds themselves with a new and unknown audience. Their best active duty contacts have retired and moved on to the private sector. That doesn't mean it has to happen, but unless the business developer stays current with the product and cultivates relationships with the next wave of active duty managers, they might find themselves training their successor and looking for a new job. Another downside might be the requirement to travel extensively . . . depending where you live and where your contacts/business are located, you could find yourself on the road four or five days a week. A major plus in the BD business, of course, is the opportunity to produce business and see the results of your efforts. I suspect that an *outgoing* person might be more successful than someone who prefers to work alone (please see the Personal Preferences chapter). In any event, make sure you know what you are getting into before accepting a business development job. Anyone involved in BD should be prepared for many turn downs . . . rejection. It is not an occupation for the shy or faint of heart!

"We understand that you have given everything you've got to this company - that's why we are letting you go. You've got nothing more to give."

> **Caveat Emptor**
>
> Business Development is high payoff, but . . .
> - high risk . . . no new business = no job
> - selling contacts
> - constant pressure
> - limited shelf life . . . usually
>
> Check it out first . . . not for everyone

Strengths, skills, core competencies - Examples

For every functional area in a given industry, there are a certain number of critical strengths that are relevant to the job. Depending upon the nature of the job and the industry involved, the skill set will change. Below are a few *examples* of different functional areas and some relevant strengths . . . this is not meant to be a comprehensive list, only to demonstrate the point. In truth, there are probably dozens of highly regarded strengths for any given job.

TEACHING
Behavior management
Curriculum development
Counseling
Leadership
Lesson planning
Course/material knowledge
Communication
Instruction

PROGRAM MANAGEMENT
Marketing
Contracting
Administration
Customer relations
Communications
Team building
Analysis
Scheduling

CONTRACTING
Supplier negotiations
Market research
Buying
Specifications
Requirements
Value analysis
Administration
Supplier quality

LOGISTICS
Facilities management
Packaging
Customer service
Automated systems
Contracting
Transportation
Hazardous material
Inventory management

The same holds true when considering an ASSOCIATION or a CHARITY management position. Some strengths might look like this:

Fund raising
Leadership
Lobbying
Strategic planning
Customer relations

Marketing
Financial management
Administration
Team building
Communications

Additionally, in nearly every management or supervisory oriented position, four factors will be of significance. They are:

- **FINANCIAL** or a financial related skill like cost control or budgeting.
- **PEOPLE SKILLS** . . . being able to deal effectively with personnel . . . coordinate, team building
- **COMMUNICATIONS** . . . verbal, written and presentation.
- **PROBLEM SOLVING** . . . how to make it better, or how to determine what's broken and fix it

After all, isn't that what most managers spend the majority of their time doing?

Who Am I? – *Worksheet (One page, single space, typed)*

- **EDUCATION** . . . principal

- **VALUES** . . . what's important to me

- **INTERESTS** . . . what I like to do

- **STRENGTHS** . . . as I see them

- **GREATEST ACCOMPLISHMENTS** . . . most proud (three)

- **WHAT I LIKED ABOUT MY CAREER** . . . and didn't

- **STRENGTHS** . . . as others see them

- **THINGS I MIGHT WANT TO DO** . . . three

Force an Objective . . . Top down – *Worksheet*

	①	②	③	④
A. **Things I Like to Do**	________	________	________	________
B. **Strengths Needed**	________	________	________	________
	________	________	________	________
	________	________	________	________
	________	________	________	________
	________	________	________	________
	________	________	________	________
C. **My Relevant Accomplishments**	________	________	________	________
	________	________	________	________
	________	________	________	________
	________	________	________	________
	________	________	________	________
	________	________	________	________

D. **Prioritize**

E. **Process** Take each in turn . . . conduct level-one interviewing . . . and choose!

Force Objective . . . Bottom up – *Worksheet*

A. **List Accomplishments**

______	______
______	______
______	______
______	______
______	______
______	______
______	______
______	______
______	______
______	______
______	______
______	______
______	______

B. **Categorize**

C. **Determine strengths**

Area	Area	Area	Area
______	______	______	______
______	______	______	______
______	______	______	______
______	______	______	______
______	______	______	______
______	______	______	______

D. **Choose most appealing/supportable.**

E. **Develop summary based on strengths contained in accomplishments.**

F. **Develop objective supported by strengths contained in summary statement.**

Objective Exercise

This is a simple exercise to demonstrate one way of getting to an objective and then continuing on with the other critical elements in a combination resume.

Step 1. *Over a nice glass of expensive red wine, (or single malt) think about what you have been doing in your service career . . . finance, aerospace, shipbuilding, logistics, medicine, civil engineering, etc., over the past ten to twenty years. Now fill in the below blanks the best you can.*

Objective: A senior ____________________ management position in the _________________ industry.
*functional area** industry**

A reader would think . . . "Well that's interesting."

Step 2. *Over another glass of expensive red wine (white is okay, as is a good single malt) write a summary statement consisting of about five lines of prose describing what you have been doing relevant to that industry for the past ten to twenty years. This will explain why you think you could do well in your objective.*

Summary: Experience in every facet of the ________________________________ industry. Twenty years experience dealing with areas involving ____
____
____
____

If this is done properly the reader would think . . . "Well that's makes sense . . . it figures."

Step 3. After a cup of black coffee, write six of your abilities/skills that made you successful in your objective area – that support your summary statement.

______________________________________ ______________________________________
______________________________________ ______________________________________
______________________________________ ______________________________________

If done properly, the reader should think . . . "Those sound like/are the experience/abilities a person should have to be successful in the ______________ industry."

Step 4. Now (without stretching the point) write an accomplishment that demonstrates success using one of the above abilities listed in step three. **Briefly describe what you did and the results of that action. Quantify the results if at all possible.**

____
____
____
____

*If you don't know the functional area, use "program" for a functional area.
You **must indicate a specific industry (aerospace, medical, shipbuilding, Logistics, etc.) . . . *defense industry* is too broad. Please note that the quality and quantity of the wine is an important ingredient in this process.

IVE

Summary

Relevant Strengths Include:

-
-
-
-
-
-

The Dream Job

Everyone has, or probably should have, a "dream" job or career. What is yours? Many of us have this idea – a dream career – but for one reason or another, don't believe it is achievable . . . too many hurdles.

"What I really want to do is direct traffic."

Dr. Carol Hyatt, in her book Changing Gears, has found that we build our own hurdles a vast majority of the time. I have found the same to be true. There have been many military and civil service personnel who said they would like to pursue something "special" but didn't think they could make it happen . . . only later to find that the very thing they believed to be impossible, worked out for them. They pursued and landed their dream jobs.

The first step in obtaining your dream job is to identify the hurdles . . . write them on the hurdle lines. Then, take them one by one and determine how to get over them. Write down the solution on the line opposite the hurdle. Sound simple? . . . it is. In the majority of cases, if there is the will, there is a way! You will only know if you try. Give it a shot!

To bring some realism in testing your objective decision, once you have decided ***what*** new career you want to pursue, ask yourself "***Why*** do I want to do it!" You may learn something new about yourself.

Your First Private Sector Job Probably Won't Be Your Last

Finally . . . remember that the first choice you make and/or the first job you accept will probably not be the only or last job you will have before you finish your working days. And, if after some period of time you decide that what you have chosen is not what you wanted or thought it was going to be, then there is no shame in leaving it (but carefully) and pursuing something else.

That also goes for those who are undecided. If you are stymied to the point of total frustration, go ahead and take the first reasonable offer that presents itself. It will not be the end of the world. Remember the story of Alice in Wonderland . . . Alice came to a fork in the road and did not know which road to take. So she asked the Cheshire cat, "Which road should I take?" And the cat replied, "Where do you want to go?" And Alice said, "I don't know!" And the cat replied, "Then it doesn't make any difference which road you take!"

Alice In Wonderland

When you come to a fork in the road, take it!

As touched on elsewhere in this book, ***the easiest and fastest route to a life-after-service career is via an industry or a functional area that you are technically familiar with and/or where you have an abundance of contacts.*** For many, that course could be considered as the first job out of service. Once you are out there and familiar with the private sector world, you could begin looking outside of your familiar territory. Managers who lose their jobs in the private sector get the same advice from career (outplacement) counselors . . . that all else being equal, it will be faster, easier and the compensation better if they stay in a familiar area . . . either functionally or industry.

Be assured that I am not trying to dissuade you to give up a dream job or burning desire to do something completely different – but just to make you aware of the facts.

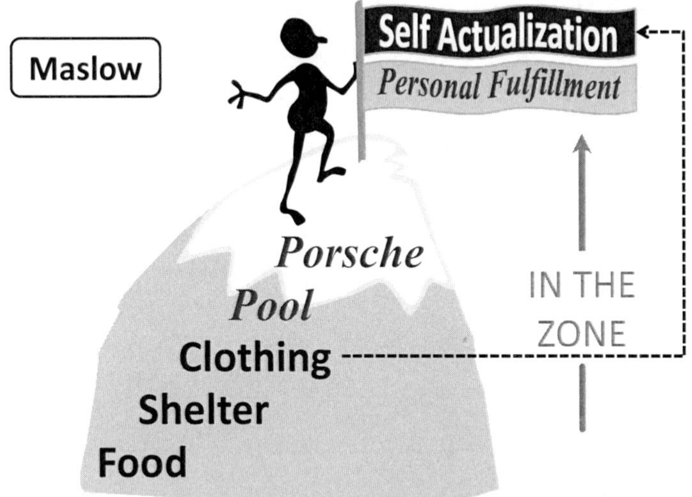

Note: the Porsche and the pool are nice-to-have personal needs!

CHAPTE

RESUME

"I yam what I yam, and that's all that I yam."
— Popeye

The resume is one of the most important tools of your job search campaign. While the resume has many purposes, perhaps *the most important purpose is going through the process of writing it . . .some people would call it the pain!* Writing it can be exhausting! But it forces you to think about your "greatest hits!" We will discuss the many uses of the resume later in the chapter, but it is absolutely critical that you understand its principal use is . . . for you . . . especially at senior levels! Keep in mind that the resume is a forward looking document, not a history lesson.

In a nutshell, the resume:

- **Objective -** Tells the reader (and you) what you want to do
- **Provides** - a brief, pertinent background statement
- **Describes** - your relevant strengths/skills
- **Lists** - accomplishments that substantiate those strengths
- **Describes** - your previous work and responsibilities
- **Notes** - your formal education and relevant affiliations

About this Chapter

This resume chapter has been written in great detail, and with intentional repetition, so that you will understand all of the nuances of writing a meaningful resume for transition from one career to another. We suggest that you ***read it several times before you begin to write your resume****. Understanding the purpose of each section of the resume before you begin to put pen to paper*, will save you a lot of time later on.

Resume writing can be exhausting! In most cases its primary customer is **you**!

After working with thousands of senior managers and professional outplacement specialists, I am convinced that ***the resume is the most misunderstood document in the career transition field and business world***. Most people have been led to believe that the resume is the document that will get them a job; that if you mail hundreds of resumes out to unsuspecting managers, most will respond favorably and offer you a job. And, if you have a really good resume it will just be a simple matter of signing a contract. Nothing could be further from the truth. It certainly has some practical uses, like responding to a job posting. But, ***the resume's basic purpose, for an experienced manager, is to help you focus on what you want to do and to serve as a preparation paper for future networking and interview meetings***. This is especially true in the case of senior military and civil service personnel. With the advent of *social media* sites such as

LinkedIn and Facebook, there have been several articles written predicting the demise of the "traditional' resume because of the opportunities that social media "networking" provide. An important distinction to recognize, however, is that **"social media networking" is *staying connected* or *getting reconnected with friends or acquaintances*, which can lead to *referrals* who can open doors to *networking meetings*** (face-to-face), which is the kind of networking that leads to landing a job. Sites like LinkedIn are also screened by recruiters looking for candidates who have the skill base to fill a position they are seeking to satisfy.

The vast majority of all senior jobs landed in the USA are the result of personal face-to-face networking – through known contacts or those referred to you by a friend or an acquaintance. When you are networking, the objective is to have a face-to-face meeting with someone in the industry of your interest and, among other things, to get exposure, obtain information about the industry and relate relevant information about yourself to the industry. An important purpose of the resume in career transition is to make you focus on what it is you want to do, and to develop the supporting structure for that objective. Certainly, when you are answering an ad you will have to submit a resume in order to be considered. Even in this case, however, the resume is critical in helping you focus and prepare. If I had to put a number on it, I would say that the resume's true value is 70 percent for you and 30 percent for those who might be looking at it. As a matter of fact, ***there is a high percentage of people who are hired as a result of networking, without ever being asked for a resume!***

Note: As much as anything else, the resume is . . . a personal organization, validation of objective, preparation for meetings & discussions tool. An objective way of thinking about a new career!

A high percentage of people are hired as a result of networking, without ever being asked for a resume!

The Purpose of a Resume . . . in brief it serves lots of purposes:

- It tells you what you want to do . . . your objective
- It tells you about you . . . provides a personal focus
- It describes your work history . . . the most recent places you have worked
- It's a snapshot of your work life . . . not your life's memoirs
- It's a guideline for meetings . . . might help someone think about things to ask you
- It's a leave-behind after the meeting document . . . so they can remember you
- It's a preparatory "exercise" to get you ready to talk about yourself when having a networking meeting or during a job interview

The resume is not a historical document or regurgitation of the past. It is forward looking . . . a sales document . . . a focus document!

Special Hurdles for Military and Civil Service Personnel

Government personnel have a unique hurdle when it comes to writing a resume or talking about themselves during a networking meeting or job interview. There is a tendency for them to both write the resume and talk in government or Defense Department jargon . . . referring to a tour in the Pentagon in Code OC495768 working for an Assistant Secretary. (Note: Telling someone that you once worked for an assistant secretary doesn't go very far in the private sector) You must always keep the reader in mind. Sanitize your resume by having several "civilians" read it before you begin handing it out. Show your resume to a good friend and ask him or her to tell you what it says that you want to do, and the rationale that you can do it.

The Audience . . . *who are we addressing?*

The best answer to that question is . . . everyone! Once you hand your resume out or publically post it to a Website, like Linkedin, it becomes public property. That means that it may be reviewed by people such as human resource directors, consultants, recruiters, referrals, future bosses, peers, neighbors, relatives and anyone else who has nothing better to do. In addition, electronic submission or posting of resumes has made it easier for recruiters and managers to "screen" for likely candidates by filtering on specific skills and experience required for open positions. Therefore, you should concentrate on writing it in English. There is nothing worse than trying to read your way through a resume filled with jargon that

> The average manager only spends about six to eight seconds screening an unsolicited resume.
> — WSJ

you do not understand. As a matter of fact, most managers will simply toss a resume away if they cannot immediately understand what the writer is trying to tell them. No one has time to go to the local jargon dictionary . . . even if there was one. (One statistic I recently read was that the average manager spends only six to eight seconds screening an unsolicited resume.) For military and civil service personnel, talking in English is particularly difficult since our worlds are so full of acronyms and jargon. That is not to say that the private sector doesn't have its share of jargon . . . just remember that you are changing careers, and the average man on the street usually speaks and writes in plain English. One more time . . . before you give out your resume or for that matter, any written correspondence, you have another pair of eyes give it the "English only" review. And that someone should not be another military or civil service person. Find a *real* person.

Resume Development – getting started

In most cases, a good working resume is developed in two stages. In the first stage, you gather as much information as you can, from whatever resources are available, and get something down on paper . . . and, hopefully, something that looks like a resume. You then take that first stage resume and conduct some low level networking meetings with close associates that you are comfortable with to get more information about your area of interest. In the second stage, you incorporate what you have learned from your networking meetings and produce a more polished resume. I can promise you that each time you have a networking meeting you will want to tweak your resume. Each time you have a job interview, you will tweak your resume. At each meeting you will learn something new . . . something that you will want to study or research. Remember, the resume is a living, forward-looking document!

> **Note:** Before you begin the resume writing process, you <u>must</u> determine your objective, as described in Chapter 4. If the resume is in response to an newspaper ad or job posting, the resume should be *targeted* accordingly, i.e., your objective should nearly parrot the objective in the ad, and the rest of the resume must address the requirements specified in the ad wherever possible.

Popular Resume Formats - *a comparison*

There are three popular resume formats and many derivatives of each. The different formats are used in different situations as will be obvious from the following discussion.

> **Resume Formats**
>
> Even if your career has been in the same line of work, e.g., civil engineering or medical, and you plan to remain in that line of work in the private sector, it is still wise to first write your resume in the Combination Format. The Combination Format is a superior preparation tool.

The Chronological format emphasizes the functional position held, the activity's name and the associated responsibilities in reverse chronological order. ***<u>May</u> be appropriate if staying in the same functional area.*** *(See box below)*

The Functional format on the other hand, places the emphasis on the relevant strengths learned during your work life and with no mention of the jobs you have held.

The Combination format (Chronological combined with the Functional) incorporates the best of each, with a heavy focus on the strengths relevant to the position you are seeking and a lesser focus on the jobs held and where you worked. Although the combination format is normally the best for someone changing career paths, like military and civil service personnel, I will discuss each of the three formats since, sooner or later, you may want to use one of the others. ***For military personnel, or for that matter, nearly anyone transitioning from one career to another and different career, the combination resume format does the best job of portraying your strengths and we recommend it as the best option. The functional format is definitely not recommended***!

> The combination resume format does the best job of portraying the strengths of military personnel transitioning to the private sector and it is recommended as the best option. The same applies to people that have spent a long time in a particular line of work (e.g., engineering, medical) and plan to remain in that same line of work.

Detailed Descriptions

The Chronological Resume Format

(a misnomer – it should be called reverse chronological) The chronological resume is best suited for a person changing jobs but staying in the same career field . . . and especially, the same functional area . . . finance, marketing, safety, etc. For example, it is ideally suited for a banker, who has had a series of ever increasing responsibilities over the past five or ten years in the banking industry and is building a case that he/she can handle the next higher job on the career ladder . . . in the banking industry. It is also ideal for a civil servant or military person who wants to move to a higher position in the military or public service. But for those (most of you) who are changing career functional areas and/or industry, the chronological resume format can act as a severe detriment, because it focuses on aspects such as the organizations you worked for, which are *usually not* ***relevant*** to the new objective. There are no aircraft carriers for sale at Walmart, and Sears doesn't care how many missions you flew over Afghanistan. Further, it gives the person reading it the immediate perception that this person is a government employee, and could not possibly have anything to offer the private sector.

> **Chronological Format**
>
> **Question**: In what situation, upon leaving government service, use a Chronological Format instead of a Combination Format?
>
> **Answer**: When applying for a job in the defense industry, and you are asked to provide a Chronological Format resume.
>
> . . . the "Relevant Rule" still applies!

The advantages of the chronological resume . . . it's really a *reverse-chronological* resume, are:

- It's easy to follow . . . HR people like it
- It emphasizes continuity and career growth
- It shows strengths that directly relate to the job
- It highlights the names of the organizations where you obtained your experience
- If constructed properly, it makes it obvious that the best next career step is your objective
- It might be a fine resume format for your second job after government service.

Some disadvantages come into play:

- If there are gaps in employment . . . since all periods of time must be accounted for
- If there is a **definite change in career direction** . . . government to private sector or banker to grocer
- It is also a hindrance if the previous employers are less than prestigious

Therefore, use the Chronological format when:

- You want to show positive growth in the functional area of your career
- You want to emphasize the organizations that you worked for

DON'T USE THE CHRONOLOGICAL format when:

- **You are changing career paths** . . . industry and/or functional area
- There are large gaps in your work history
- You have had many jobs over a relatively short time period . . . "job-hopper"
- You have taken two years off to go cruising in the South Pacific

On the government-military side, people who have had careers as civil engineers, in the medical area, the ministry or one of the other professional fields, **and who want to remain in that functional area**, could use the Chronological format. Typical civil service jobs that could also use the Chronological format might be Human Resource specialists, accounting specialists and others whose functional speciality transfers directly to the private sector. Unfortunately, while we all have great management strengths and the ability to learn most anything, for a military aviator or an infantryman or airman to try and sell himself as a banker by using a Chronological resume is going to be a non-starter, unless you have the good fortune of meeting the chairman of the board (as I did) and he believes that he can teach you the ins and outs of the business.

The Functional Resume Format

This format became popular in the early 1960s when many managers in the workforce began to change career areas. Up to that time the traditional thing to do was to work for a company for 40-50 years and/or until you received your gold watch. While the Chronological resume was a good format for a person staying in the same career path (industry and functional area), the Functional resume format was seen as ideal for one who wanted to move into a different field . . . be it the functional area or industry . . . regardless of the reason.

It provides a great amount of flexibility because *the focus is on the strengths that you possess, rather than the organizations that you may have worked for* in the past. In fact, the organizations are never mentioned.

The advantages of a Functional resume:

- Stresses strengths that are marketable
- Stresses strengths that are in demand in your field of choice
- Eliminates any focus on areas that are not relevant to your field of choice
- Requires the reader to focus on the needs of the job, rather than where you have been
- Eliminates the problem of employment gaps or jobs that are not related to your objective
- Helps build personal self-confidence . . . you know that you can do it!

Disadvantages of the Functional Resume:

- Provides no link between your strengths and where you obtained them
- Provides no insight into your career growth pattern

- Makes the reader wonder where you received your experience . . . and when. ***And most importantly, the majority of HR directors and hiring officials don't like them!***

Use the Functional Resume when:

- You are changing careers
- You want to emphasize strengths not used in your current or recent job.
- You are returning to the job market after a hiatus . . . back from the two-year world cruise
- Your background is totally unrelated to the new career you intend to pursue

DON'T USE THE FUNCTIONAL RESUME WHEN:

- You want the reader to focus on career growth and responsibility
- You are applying for a position in a traditional field such as teaching

THE BAD NEWS ABOUT THE FUNCTIONAL RESUME FORMAT

The bad news is while human resource directors and business managers *initially* liked the Functional resume format because it provided an excellent presentation of skills, they soon found out that they couldn't tell where the person obtained those strengths. Most businesspeople want to know something about the people they are lining up for an interview.

The Combination Resume Format – *the **preferred** resume format for career change*

As a result of the dislike for the functional resume format, ***outplacement*** (the name for private sector career transition business) professionals turned to the combination format for those who wanted to change career paths/areas. Although most of the business world still prefers the traditional chronological format, the combination format is seen as a good and acceptable substitute. That's good news for military and civil service leaving government service and seeking employment in a private sector functional area different from their former careers. Otherwise, we would be stuck with the chronological format, and forced to start the resume with a focus on our career jobs . . . once again, big companies like Sears don't need people who fly fighter aircraft, catapult and arresting gear specialists, or battalion commanders . . . but they do need their leadership and management strengths. Except in rare occasions, government personnel, and for that matter people changing career fields in the private sector, are best advised to use the combination resume. It is widely accepted, and I have had hundreds of letters from business people and those who have attended our seminars and/or read the book tell me that it is the best format they have seen.

> Sears and Microsoft don't have military jet aircraft to fly or tanks to drive. They are looking for business managers.

Another and equally important reason to embrace the combination format has nothing to do with the business people . . . it has to do with you – the individual using the resume as a preparatory tool in getting ready for networking meetings and job interviews. Remember that the resume is far more important to you than to anyone else who might read it. Finally, the combination format is highly recommended by hiring officials throughout the country.

The advantages of the Combination format:

- It is easy to read
- It highlights your functional strengths
- It will generate questions about your ability to contribute
- It is great preparation for networking meetings and job interviews

Disadvantage:

- It is somewhat more difficult to prepare, but it is well worth it!

The Structure of the Combination Resume . . . appropriate for one changing career paths.

Objective . . . two or three lines that describe what it is that you want to do . . . level, functional area, and industry . . . and perhaps a value statement. Keep it simple and to the point. Like a newspaper headline or theater marquee announcing the show . . . make it an attention grabber!

Summary . . . a brief, five or six line statement that describes why you think that you can do what you want to do . . . it serves as a "bridge," along with the strengths bullets, between the objective and the rest of the resume.

Strengths . . . usually six strengths needed to be successful in your objective. Remember, a strength is a skill/ability that you do well as ***it relates to your interest.*** These are not personality characteristics. They are the things that you need to be able to do to accomplish the objective. A job listing normally lists four to six specific skill requirements for the position. Most people like to "break out" the strengths in a "bullet" format so that they stand out and focus the reader's attention on them, like a theater marquee. **Many of the strengths/bullets will and should be *key words.***

> **The Summary Statement**
> *and accompanying "bullets"*
>
> **The Statement** . . . a ***bridge*** to the rest of the resume . . . a profile . . . your background as it relates to the objective.
> **The "Bullets"** . . . the *hard* strengths required by the objective.

Accomplishments . . . statements that demonstrate and validate the strengths delineated in the "bullet" portion of the resume. One or two accomplishments for each strength shown. The accomplishments should be quantified, whenever possible. The strengths and accomplishments are the real meat of the resume.

Work History . . . a description of the last three or four jobs you held in reverse chronological order, the location and name of the organization and the calendar years, not months, you were there.

Previous Experience . . . this is really a sub-section of the **Work History** section. It is especially important for someone changing career paths because it provides an opportunity to describe previous ***experiences relevant*** to the objective that may not have taken place in the three or four jobs described previously in the Work History section of the resume. ***This paragraph is not intended to describe jobs you had in the past.***

Education . . . level of education, certificates and degrees held. This will normally be near the end of the resume. The exception to this rule is the *Curriculum Vitae*, used when applying for academic positions at an institute of higher education. In that case the education credentials follow the summary statement. Service schools and short period university seminars may not be relevant to your objective and, therefore, it would not be appropriate to show them.

Affiliations . . . normally the last section of the resume. These are professional organizations that you support or belong to that are relevant to the objective. There may be an occasion to include a ***Personal*** section, but in the vast majority of cases the sections described above will handle the pertinent information.

Security Clearances . . . if you are in pursuit of a defense industry or government job requiring clearances.

A Closer Analysis of the Three Basic Format Structures

1. Regardless of which resume format you choose, all resumes for this discussion begin with an **objective**. We already know what the objective is . . . level of position, functional area, industry and perhaps a value statement.

2. Likewise, all resume formats follow the objective with a ***summary statement***, whose chore is to act as a bridge between the objective and the accomplishments area. This statement will probably be about five or six typed lines long, and introduce the strengths necessary to accomplish the objective. In the summary statement, (some refer to it as a brief personal profile) you should describe your background in terms of what you want to do . . . your objective. Also, words and phrases that describe personality traits would be more apt to be found in the summary statement than included in the strengths (bullets) that follow the summary statement.

3. The Rhino Rule. The **six strengths** (the bullets) should be those strengths which are most critical to performing well, relative to the objective. If you were going to go to Africa to photograph Rhinos for example, and needed to hire a guide, you would advertise for a guide who knew the territory, could track rhinos, could speak English, was familiar with cameras, could communicate with you and be a good instructor. I doubt you would care if the guide had a college degree or great financial strengths. *Oh yes, you would want the guide to be able to run slower than you.* In any event you would come up with a set of strengths that were **relevant** to what you wanted this person to do. The strengths should be in priority sequence . . . the first strength being the most important. The strengths should be no more/longer than two words; don't number the strengths.

A strength is a skill that is relevant to your objective.

The objective, summary statement and strengths for each of the three formats are identical. After that, they dramatically depart in format. To wit:

The Chronological Format

After the six bullets, comes the **WORK HISTORY** section. On page two describe your work history in *reverse chronological order*. On the first line you have a choice . . . to state either the job title that you held, or the name of the organization where you worked. That choice is driven by what you want to stress. If job title would be more relevant, then begin with that. If the places that you worked would be more relevant and impressive to the reader, then use the name of the organization. In either case, at the end of that first line, indicate the years that you held that position . . . not months, just the years. You cannot omit any period of time. Do so, and they will think you have been in a Toledo penitentiary. They will not understand.

On the next two or three lines describe what you did in that position with **a heavy stress on those things that are relevant to your objective**. Following that description, give two accomplishments that illuminate on one or two of the strengths listed following the summary statement.

After describing your previous work organizations and responsibilities you cite education, relevant affiliations and any other relevant information, such as security clearances.

The Functional Format – I do not recommend it except in a few very unusual cases!
Following the six bullets comes the **ACCOMPLISHMENTS** section. Since the Functional resume focuses on strengths and not job titles or organizations, the resume is made up of the strengths relevant to your objective and some accomplishments about each. Label the next area accomplishments. The idea here is to demonstrate to the reader that you have the strengths to perform the objective and can demonstrate that you have done so . . . through the accomplishments. What this really says is that one shouldn't care where or when you got the strengths, what is important is that you have them and can substantiate them through quantified accomplishments. After you have discussed your accomplishments, your education and relevant affiliations are listed.

As mentioned earlier, while this resume format served the career changing person very well, the managers reading it wanted something more . . . something that would provide an indication of where and when this relevant knowledge and experience were obtained. Thus, the combination resume was born. Submitting a resume without some indication of where and when you have been working will probably result in having it delivered to the circular file.

The Combination Format

There is little doubt that this format serves the vast majority of military and civil service personnel the best. It is somewhat more difficult to write, but is a far better presentation of your strengths and an excellent preparation item for future networking and job interviews as well. I have never had an executive tell me he/she didn't like it. And, I have had numerous unsolicited letters from managers who have said it was the best resume they had ever seen. It's your choice.

Following the six bullets comes the **ACCOMPLISHMENTS** section. In this section you will put each bullet . . . strength . . . indicated above, in the left-hand margin. Immediately to the right of the bullet, you support the strength with an accomplishment . . . quantified if at all possible. The descriptions should be straight forward, even in a Kiplinger style, and to the point. There will not be room for a lot of flowery language and no one that I know will want to read, what the industry calls, fluff. Two accomplishments per skill will usually suffice. By the time you have stated and supported all six strengths, you will be somewhere at the top of the second page and ready for the next section.

The next heading is **WORK HISTORY**. The work history section of the combination resume format is similar to the *Chronological* resume format in that you describe the organizations you worked for and your responsibilities, but at that point they differ. In the Combination resume format ***you only describe the organization and your job responsibilities*** because the accomplishments have been described on the first page in the accomplishments section.

In the **Work History** section, (usually begins at the top of the second page) describe the last three or four assignments that you held, in reverse-chronological order. See the example at the end of this chapter. Once again, what goes on the first line will be your choice . . . either the title of your job and the years, or the organization you were assigned to and the years. ***Do not include any accomplishments in the Work History section of the Combination resume, they have already been addressed***

> **Carefully Script Work History Job Descriptions**
>
> *"Sometimes I found that when I handed someone my resume, they glanced at the first page with the 'strengths and accomplishments,' and quickly went to the page with 'job descriptions/experience'"*

in the accomplishments section. Likewise, ensure that you do not describe job responsibilities in the accomplishments section . . . a common failing.

An important thing to remember when writing a resume in any kind of chronological or combination format, is to ensure your service job descriptions are as relevant to your objective as possible. The biggest single mistake that military and civil service make, is describing their job responsibilities in Defense Department terms, and failing to describe what they did relevant to the objective on the resume. (The "What do you do for a living?" 45 second Personal Response is an example; see Chapter 12). What this also means is that you may not be able to describe some of the most important aspects of your responsibilities because they will not be relevant to your objective.

The biggest mistake military and civil service people make in the work history section is describing the job responsibilities in DoD terms/lingo, instead of describing what they did relevant to their objective.

Next, write the **"Previous Experience"** paragraph which you may use for any purpose that suits you. I recommend that you utilize this paragraph – five to six lines – to describe previous experience/s relevant to your objective that were not included in the Work History job/assignment descriptions. An easy way to start this paragraph is "Previous experience includes:" There are no bounds in terms of time on this paragraph. You could go back to your early years in service or restrict it to the most recent . . . just keep it relevant. It is a way of getting to information and experience that took place in assignments prior to the three or four assignments that you have identified under Work History. ***Don't simply regurgitate all of your past assignments in this paragraph*** – keep it relevant.

Note: Education and Affiliation information is the same for all formats. Add any certifications such as Program Management, if relevant.

Determining Strengths for a Given Functional Area and Industry

While you might think it is going to be hard to determine the strengths required for a given functional area, in truth it is relatively simple. It will take some doing to determine them, but it will be worth the effort. You will use them to write the accomplishments for the resume, as well as during networking and interview meetings and salary negotiations. You will find them in:

- Newspaper ads and Websites
- Books written on the subject
- People currently in the business
- Personal experience
- Trade association publications
- People who have been in the business

Skills-Abilities-Key Words

where to find them

- Google skill requirements for the position
- Newspaper ads/Web postings
- Trade association literature
- People in the business - now and previously
- Books written on the subject

***Note**: I have personally gone to Google and typed in "Skill requirements for the name of the job" and every time several of the Websites that appeared provided useful insight regarding the job, and, in most cases a list of skill requirements for the job . . . often in order of importance!* Also try: O*Net at www.onetonline.org/skills/ for skill/strength keywords. Examples are provided for a given functional area/industry. Well worth a look!

For example, if your objective is to be a *Senior Program Manager in a hi-tech Industry*, after poking around, you might end up with a list of strengths like this:

- Marketing
- Team building
- Government business
- Technical knowledge
- Contracting
- Customer relations
- Administration
- Scheduling
- User knowledge
- Finance/budgeting
- Analysis
- Communications
- Product control

Selecting Which Strengths to Use

From these 13 possible strengths used by successful program managers for example, you select the six that you deem to be the most important. Or you may have discovered an ad in the newspaper, such as the one shown, that has different strengths required or some that you had not considered. Or, in talking to a referral, you find that *user knowledge* is the most important strength that a company is looking for . . . someone with lots of hands-on experience. In any event, you put your six strengths into your resume . . . in the order of priority ***most important to the company***. Remember, for each skill you choose to use, you will have to write an accomplishment or two, to demonstrate that you have experience in that area. ***It is one thing to know the strengths necessary to accomplish the job. It is another to have had successful experience with each strength. In other words, you must be able to "belly-up" to each strength you choose***. Also, remember that you will use this same information, strengths and accomplishments, during interview and networking meetings!

Example: A newspaper ad for a IT Program Manager:

The successful candidate will be responsible for working with Engineering at all stages of product development to customer delivery. You will create plans that include product design, development, testing, and documentation. Duties to include: interfacing with Engineering, Product Managers, and Operations, Finance, and other departments to determine resource requirements; manage schedules and budgets; implement manufacturing procedures and manage overall product control. You will brief upper management on status.

Accomplishments . . . *validate the strengths.*

Try to develop at least 50 accomplishments. You will find this is easier said than done. Most of us have not maintained a daily diary nor have we maintained any kind of record of our accomplishments. Yearly evaluations and awards can provide a source of accomplishments. Some ideas:

- ***Asking friends*** what they remember about your career accomplishments.
- ***Brainstorming*** your career by thinking through each assignment and recalling the more challenging aspects of them.
- Carefully ***reviewing performance evaluations/fitness reports you received*** during your career. This is best accomplished by reading each evaluation, highlighting action items or functional areas and then repeating the process and expanding on each word or phrase highlighted. The next step is to put the action or accomplishment in the format mentioned earlier . . . state the problem, describe the action you took, and describe the results of that action. Following that, try to quantify the results in terms of dollars saved or increased productivity. For example, in your first pass you may come up with "increased

competition by 75 percent" . . . which would lead to "Spearheaded a program to increase competition in contracting . . . resulted in a savings of $200,000." If contracting is a ***strength*** that is relevant to your objective, you have an accomplishment. On the other hand, if contracting is not relevant, then the accomplishment is a *throw-away* as it relates to this particular objective.

- *Review the **evaluations of others** . . .* evaluations that you wrote. This process will sometimes serve as a mind-jogger and help you recall your own accomplishments.
- ***Ask your spouse*** or another friendly native (trusted friend). Many times the things we consider to be routine operations are impressive to others.
- *Talk with **former supervisors**.* They often recall what you did that impressed them the most. Hopefully they will have something nice to say.
- Consider ***the achievements of others***. Again, you are in a personal brainstorming mode, trying to recall all of the things you have done over your career. Sometimes just considering what someone else is doing or has done will be enough of a mind-jogger to help you recall a similar situation.
- Review the ***resumes of others***.

Accomplishments can be thought of in terms such as:

- improved quality
- reduced costs
- improved productivity
- reduced operations time
- improved retention of employees
- achieved a new technological process
- increased profits
- delivered a product on time and within budget

> **Accomplishments**
> When writing a resume, an accomplishment is what you did on active duty (what you accomplished) not the position you held while on active duty.

Quantify Your Accomplishments

Ensure that your accomplishments are quantified and demonstrate the six strengths in action. ***Being the Commanding Officer of a ship or the CEO of a large corporation are most certainly accomplishments. But, in the context of resume accomplishments, it is what was achieved in those important positions that count.*** In other words, you must extract the things that you did in the position and describe them in terms of the results achieved. To be a civil service Personnel Officer is one thing . . . to be a Personnel Officer who was able to increase retention by 25 percent, or reduce travel expenses by 10 percent, or design a new training program which accomplished the training in one half the normal time, is another thing. To determine this takes some doing, but it is necessary if you want someone to understand what you might be able to contribute to the private sector. They should translate to bottom line profits or savings, or *improved* something. An accomplishment consists of the following three factors:

Quantify your accomplishments!

✓ **The problem** . . . state the problem. Describe what was going on, or what was broken and needed fixing.

✓ **The action taken** . . . describe what action you took to solve the problem.

✓ **The results** . . . state the results of your actions. Quantify the results whenever possible. To say that you implemented a new system to eliminate this or that problem is nice, but what were the results? Accomplishments without results are like crackers without cheese.

Problem, Action Taken, Results

While an accomplishment contains the problem, action taken, and results achieved (quantified), you may have to omit describing the problem on your resume due to space constraints. If you are networking or interviewing with a person (company) who would be familiar with the situation, you may omit defining the problem and they will easily understand.

After you have written all three areas down, rewrite the accomplishment omitting the problem statement (you won't have room on the resume to describe a lengthy problem), and then boil the action taken and results down to about three lines or less. Example:

Show that you are cost conscious

"Designed and implemented an automated stowage system that improved inventory accuracy by 22 percent and reduced labor costs by 10 percent."

Action Words for Resume Accomplishments

When you are writing your resume, use words that depict action taken when describing your accomplishments. Here are some examples of words you can use when brainstorming for accomplishments. And, of course, ensure that you weave in ***key words*** relevant to your objective.

Management

administered	conducted	contracted	controlled
coordinated	directed	enacted	established
exceeded	executed	expanded	implemented
initiated	maintained	managed	obtained
organized	performed	produced	responsible for
retained	revised	supervised	undertook

Methods And Controls

analyzed	arranged	budgeted	catalogued
compared	compiled	completed	computed
expanded	increased	indexed	redesigned
reduced	reorganized	restructured	reviewed
revised	scheduled	synthesized	systematized

Public Relations

advised	counseled	employed	grouped
guided	handled	hired	monitored
motivated	sponsored	trained	***terrified***

Creativity

arranged	conceived	created	designed
developed	devised	enabled	formulated
innovated	invented	originated	refined
reshaped	resolved	solved	structured

Promote

accounted	convinced	created	improved
influenced	marketed	promoted	recommended
persuaded	represented	secured	sold

Communications

approved	counseled	demonstrated	disseminated
edited	facilitated	instructed	interviewed
moderated	participated	presented	presided
served as	wrote		

Resourcefulness

accomplished	awarded	diverted	eliminated
extraordinary	identified	improved	pioneered
rectified	strengthened	surpassed	

Negotiations

assured	determined	evaluated	procured
negotiated	proposed	sorted	

Research And Analysis

automated	classified	determined	developed
differentiated	equated	experimented	investigated
related	searched	synthesized	theorized

ONE MORE TIME *. . . at the risk of sounding repetitive . . .*

The accomplishments should contain ***quantified*** results whenever possible. Quantified results are important because anyone can say that they did something big and worthwhile. ***It is how well you did something big and worthwhile that counts***. Being the Commanding General of a Base or the Master Chief of the Command or a GS-15 responsible for a large organization's financial management plan, or an Air Group Commander, or a Battalion Commander are important accomplishments, but again, it is ***how well you performed in the job that counts***. Think of it this way, you don't get an award or personal citation for just having the job, you get it for doing good things while on the job – some noteworthy accomplishments. You get a personal medal for doing a superior job, not for just being there!

Private sector: a focus on cutting costs.

It is not necessarily *how much* you saved or increased, what is important to the private sector is that you *think* in those terms. ***Remember. There is a perception in the private sector that military and civil service personnel care little about saving money and none about making money.*** That is why you may get blank stares from business people when you tell them you are interested in this or that private career area. More on that subject later in the Information Meeting Chapter - 11.

Education/Certifications

At the end of the resume, there should be room left for your educational credentials. One quick comment on education. Many military and civil service personnel have been fortunate enough to have earned advanced degrees. If you are one of those, that's fine. However, keep in mind that you probably won't be hired because you have an MBA received some 20 to 30 years ago. You will be hired for what you bring to the table . . . contributing to the financial bottom line, or however the organization measures success . . . and that will be mostly based on your experience and accomplishments relevant to the position you are seeking. I know many former military and civil service managers who didn't have an undergraduate degree, let alone a Masters, and have gone on to be very successful in the private sector. It's what's in your head and what you want to do that counts! By the way, the vast majority of small business owners and millionaires in the USA do not have advanced degrees, and many never attended college!

Not to worry . . . It's your experience that counts!

More Education?

I often get asked whether or not an "older" person should pursue an undergraduate college degree and/or undertake a Masters Degree. I answer by saying that if you are so inclined, do so. Smart money says you should work on the degree while still in government service, if at all possible. The services have all kinds of programs that help individuals obtain additional education. All things being equal, the person with the highest education level will almost always win . . . it is a tie breaker, if nothing else. Most career counselors will tell you that the financial break even point for PG school is somewhere between 40 and 45 years old. After that, the payback in terms of income will be marginal at best. Regardless, additional education will never hurt and if it feels good, then do it . . . at any age!

Affiliations

Affiliations that deal in some way with the functional area or industry that you are interested in should appear here. ***Affiliations that have no relationship to the objective should not be listed***. *If you do not belong to an association that represents the area of your interest, it might make good sense to join one now.* If nothing else, it demonstrates you have a genuine interest in the objective area, and it may offer points of contact for networking purposes – like the local chapter head. One exception to the general rule: if you know that the networking contact, or job interviewer, has a personal interest in an organization that you belong to, you might consider listing it, regardless of its relevancy. That will be your call, and it will be made on a case-by-case basis.

Security Clearances

Include, but **only if relevant to the job** . . . the defense industry or government service.

Popular Resume Formats – Side-by-Side

CHRONOLOGICAL	FUNCTIONAL	COMBINATION
Objective	**Objective**	**Objective**
Summary *(Six strengths . . . bullets)*	**Summary** *(Six strengths . . . bullets)*	**Summary** *(Six strengths . . . bullets)*
Work History *Organization or Job Title* *Year(s)* *Job Description* *Accomplishments*	**Accomplishments**	**Accomplishments** *Skill* *Accomplishments* **Work History** *Organization or Job Title* *Year(s)* *Job Description* **Previous Experience Includes**
Education **Affiliations**	**Education** **Affiliations**	**Education** **Affiliations**

Exercise: When you are finished with this chapter, write a resume in each format . . . *just for drill.*

In a Nutshell . . . 8 Steps to a Solid Combination Resume

1. Develop an Objective of two or three lines that states the level of responsibility, the functional area, the industry, and perhaps the value that you bring to the organization.
2. Write a summary statement that broadly covers your experience in terms relevant to your objective. You should be able to accomplish this in four or five typed lines or less.
3. Next, *break out* the six strengths (under the summary statement) in one or two word bullets that you wish to showcase. (See example)
4. Write a series of relevant accomplishments that support the strengths listed under the summary statement. Show the strengths in the left-hand margin. Each should be supported by at least two accomplishments. The accomplishments should be quantified . . . the action that you took and the results that you achieved.
5. Briefly describe your work history. Using the format at the end of this chapter list your last three or four assignments in reverse chronological order. Under each assignment describe the nature of the job . . . keeping in mind that everything in the resume should be relevant to the objective. The assignments must be consecutive and only the years, not months, should be shown.
6. **Write a short paragraph describing your work experience (Not your work assignments!)** prior to the assignments accounted for above. Keep in mind to always stress those elements of the jobs that relate to your objective. This should ***not*** be a regurgitation of all of your career assignments!
7. Education will normally be *the last section* of your resume unless you are applying for a position in an educational environment. In this case your educational credentials should follow the summary statement. (Note: Educators will want to see up-front what your educational credentials are. If your credentials are weak or you don't have the right kind, your resume won't make it past the filing clerk's desk.) **Unless you very recently, *within five years,* completed a degree in a field directly related to your objective it is unnecessary and could be counterproductive to show the dates of graduation.** If in doubt, leave them out. Likewise, while military service schools are important while in uniform, unless they relate directly to the objective, omit them. Degrees should be listed in order, most advanced degree goes first.
8. Identify your affiliations with professional or honorary organizations (only if they support your job objective).

The next few pages show the outline of the combination format, followed by an example of a combination resume . . . remember, most of you should use the combination format. I have declined to show a multitude of sample resumes, even though I probably have a thousand or more in my files. This is because I want you to go through the process of collecting the data and writing your own resume without "cutting and pasting" from one written by someone else. The struggle you will go through by writing your resume from scratch will pay big dividends when you get to the networking meetings, job interviews, and salary negotiations.

If you are desperate, there are countless books in the library with countless resumes written by others. Most of them are marginally satisfactory . . . many are horrible. Look at them if you want, but write your own resume!

> You may download the ***Ruehlin Associates*** combination resume template by going to our Website **www.RuehlinAssociates.com.** Click on *Client Page* on the navigation bar. The username is: **racareers**. The password is: **rares09.** It is so easy a cave man could do it!

Combination Resume Outline

NAME - ADDRESS - TELEPHONE - E-MAIL . . .

OBJECTIVE

✓ Level
✓ Function
✓ Industry

SUMMARY

Bridge

❶ ❷ ❸ Strengths/Skills/Key Words

❹ ❺ ❻ Strengths/Skills/Key Words

ACCOMPLISHMENTS

❶

❷

❸

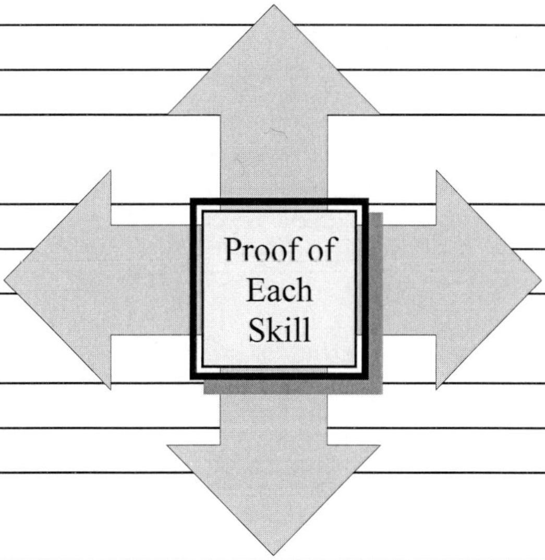

❹

❺

❻

Proof of Each Skill

NAME

WORK HISTORY

Organization or Title

Years Only

Job Description

PREVIOUS RELEVANT EXPERIENCE

Objective Related

EDUCATION and Certifications *if applicable*

Highest Level First - no dates

AFFILIATIONS

Only if Relevant

SECURITY CLEARANCE

If Applicable

Combination Resume – Example *(Courtesy reprint)*

Matthew J. Pittner
(619) 123-4567/mpittner@email.com

Level, functional area, and industry

OBJECTIVE Director of Supply Chain Logistics for a Retail company.

SUMMARY Extensive and hands-on experience in every facet of retail distribution and material management. A proven record of achieving the highest levels of productivity and efficiency. An experienced manager and effective communicator with exceptional organizational, administrative, and people strengths. Distribution experience includes:

Break out the six strengths here

- **Warehouse Processes**
- **Customer Service**
- **Inventory Management**
- **Automated Systems**
- **Transportation Management**
- **Facilities Management**

ACCOMPLISHMENTS

Start each accomplishment with an action verb

Warehouse Processes Processed over 700,000 receipts and issues annually. Improved productivity of warehouse workers 22 percent by streamlining work processes, reducing rework, and implementing employee cross training programs. Increased production rate per employee to 5,196 units.

Customer Service Improved the quality and timeliness of products delivered to the customer by implementing process improvements based on analysis of distribution processes and customer feedback. Reduced distribution errors from 7.2 percent to 6 percent and improved on-time delivery to 99.7 percent.

Inventory Management Increased inventory and location accuracy 11.3 percent by improving material receipt procedures and implementing an active inventory and location audit program. Reduced investment in inventory 20 percent while improving material availability 8.6 percent by establishing Just-in-time delivery contracts from suppliers and eliminating unnecessary excess inventory.

Try to quantify each accomplishment

Automated Systems Implemented new automated material handling systems and improved utilization of the existing automated stowage, tracking, and retrieval system. Downsized work force 11 percent while increasing throughput 8.7 percent. Reduced cost of operations 21 percent while improving productivity and product quality.

Transportation Management Developed innovative methods to expeditiously ship and deliver material at reduced costs. Solicited bids from local shipping and trucking companies to obtain quality service at the lowest possible cost. Established contracts that resulted in a 33 percent improvement in product delivery time and an 8 percent reduction in transportation costs.

Facilities Management Improved the material condition and energy efficiency of all warehouse facilities. Initiated a Facilities Planning Board to identify and prioritize improvement projects. Projects were reviewed, accepted, and completed based on their impact on safety, structural integrity and potential energy savings.

Matthew Pittner **Page 2**

WORK HISTORY **(years only)**

Make descriptions as relevant as possible

Deputy Director of Logistics Management –
Commander, Naval Surface Force, Norfolk, VA

Directed the material distribution and retail sales for over 200 activities worldwide. Managed 97 personnel, 401,890 items of inventory, a $600 million operating budget, and retail stores that accounted for over $30 million in annual sales.

General Manager, Defense Distribution Depot –
Somewhere, FL

Planned and managed the efficient receipt, stowage, inventory, packaging, and distribution of material. Managed 135 personnel in the processing of over 700,000 receipts and issues annually. Developed and controlled an annual operating budget of $14 million.

Material and Requirements Planning Manager –
Large activity, Jacksonville, FL

Managed the material requirements planning for 180,000 items of inventory and a retail store with $2.7 million in annual sales. Directed computer analysis in the development and analysis of automated tools and programs. Supervised 42 personnel in the performance of their duties.

Previous relevant work experience includes: Distribution manager for an 800-person organization with 25,000 items of inventory valued at over $750,000, and a $7.9 million annual operating budget; Distribution and Retail Manager for a 450-person organization with 33,000 items of inventory valued at over $18 million, $200,000 in annual sales, and an operating budget of $1.5 million; Inventory Manager for 19,000 items of inventory with annual sales of over $185 million.

EDUCATION Certifications MBA. Business Management, Michigan State University
B.S. Business Administration, **The** Ohio State University

Only those relevant

AFFILIATIONS National Association of Logistics Managers

SECURITY CLEARANCE Top Secret (date) – ***only if the defense industry***

CERTIFICATIONS (if applicable)

Don't say:
"References available upon request."

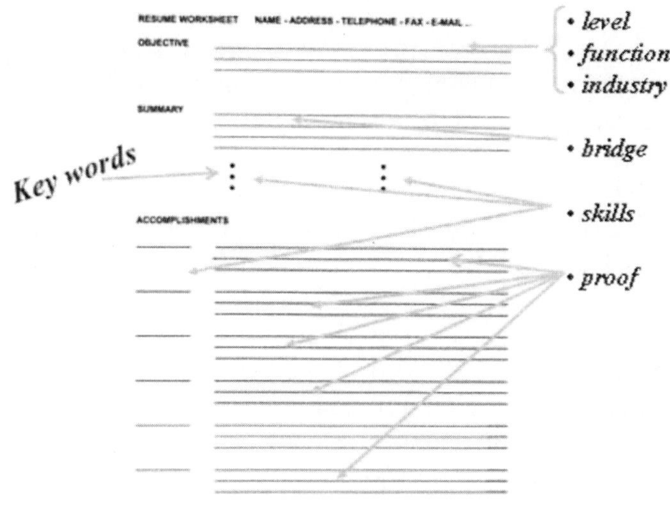
RESUME WORKSHEET
NAME - ADDRESS - TELEPHONE - FAX - E-MAIL
OBJECTIVE
SUMMARY
ACCOMPLISHMENTS
• level
• function
• industry
• bridge
Key words
• skills
• proof

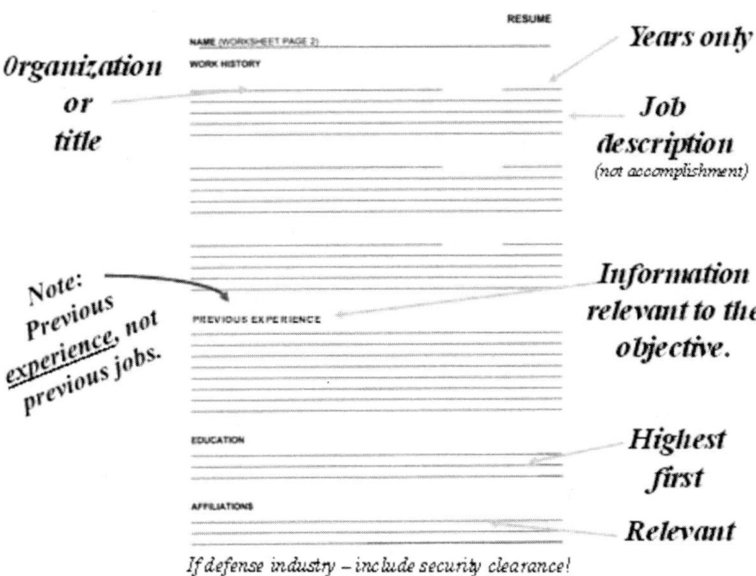
RESUME
NAME (WORKSHEET PAGE 2)
WORK HISTORY
PREVIOUS EXPERIENCE
EDUCATION
AFFILIATIONS
Organization or title
Years only
Job description
(not accomplishment)
Note: Previous experience, not previous jobs.
Information relevant to the objective.
Highest first
Relevant
If defense industry – include security clearance!

Technical Considerations of Resume Writing

Length . . . How Long Should it Be?
You will find that one of the hardest things about writing a resume is to get all the information on two pages. Space becomes critical, therefore, your writing should be short and to the point. This is not the time to describe your life history. Another major frustration that will confront you is the desire to write accomplishments that do not relate to the objective.

There are many schools of thought, but for starters, ***I recommend your resume be no more than two pages long***. There are always exceptions, including the *Curriculum Vitae* used when applying for jobs in the educational teaching field, but most managers resent anything more than two pages. A one page resume is a Human Resource manager's delight, but for most of us, one page will not adequately describe our strengths and, or why, we are suited for the goal we are seeking. People who are well-known national figures can often get away with a one page resume. Bill Gates, of Microsoft fame for example, could get away with a one liner . . . it would probably say, "Bill Gates" and that he was interested in the computer industry. So one page is great but difficult to get enough hard core facts thereon, and three or more pages are just too much. Stick with two pages and remember that the resume is not intended to be the story of your life . . . it is a *snapshot* of your work background which is relevant to your objective. I have a friend who is a long time professional in the outplacement business and he told a USA Today newspaper reporter that he would "knee-cap" anyone who wrote a resume longer than two pages. I thought that the comment was appropriate and humorous . . . the company that he *used to work for*, did not. There is a fine line between an effective resume and one that doesn't do the job. A resume with so much information in it that an organization can make a hire-no-hire or see-not-see decision without ever seeing you, is counterproductive. You always show off better in person.

Two pages max . . . with one exception!

As strong and as committed as I am to the two page resume, however, there will be cases other than the educational situation where a more lengthy one is appropriate. If the person whom you are going to interview with tells you to write everything that you have ever done along the lines of the job in question and don't worry about length, then write to your heart's content . . . but even then, don't go off the deep end. Don't ramble. Or, if you are asked for a resume and a complete description of all the places you worked and what you did, then add that page to your resume as an addendum. In any event keep it relevant to the case on hand. I recently read a comment made by a for-fee "Resume Assistance Company" stating the resume could be as long as you want to make it. I can tell you most executives will simply ignore a resume longer than two pages . . . chances are the people screening the resumes (HR, secretaries) will pitch it first! Concise, relevant, and key words is what counts . . . especially if the resume will be posted on a Website.

Fonts
Use any executive font, but the ones that I prefer are "Times New Roman" and "Arial." Most of this book is written in "**Times New Roman**" (This is "Arial"). It's your choice. Don't use anything like, Bradley Hand or Comic Sans MS.

Print Size (pitch)
Use 12 point. I can read size 11 but any smaller than size 12 I throw the resume away. No one wants to squint to read a resume . . . a resume is supposed to be user friendly. If you find yourself stretched and need to get just <u>one more line</u> on the page, use the"make it fit" feature on your software to make two pages into

one. The change in point size will be imperceptible. Another trick is to decrease the line space slightly, or decrease the one inch margin slightly. In any event, a crowded resume will not be looked upon favorably and probably won't be read. *Try to stay with 12 point pitch* . . . smaller is too hard on the eyes.

Paper
If you use any paper other than bond paper you are selling yourself short, and the preferred weight is 24 pound instead of the daily 20 pound weight that most of us use on our computers. The preferred paper color is white . . . standard 8.5" x 11". Light gray, light cream or ivory are also acceptable but white does the best job. Envelopes should match in color. Some people prefer to use heavier paper, but the major outplacement firms use 24 pound . . . it is more than satisfactory. Print color should always be black.

Margins
One inch on the sides and top and bottom. A tad less won't hurt, but remember the "don't crowd me" advice.

Graphics
Don't get clever. The resume should appear as professional as you can make it. You want to keep in mind that most bolding and different font sizes are not read well if your resume is put on the Web. The Web/computer screening programs likes things as plain as you can make them.

Resume Change Management . . . Making Changes to the Resume
Unlike the old days, when job hunters would have 200-300 resumes printed in advance, you will only print a few at a time and on your own laser printer or one you use at FedEx/Kinkos or Office Depot. Besides, you will be changing the resume to make it fit the occasion. You can easily tweak your resume . . . change the objective to make it more relevant and modify the strengths, skills, key words and supporting accomplishments accordingly. You have never had it so good.

STOP!
Return to GO! Before you make any kind of distribution of your resume, and that is a subject that I will discuss in depth later, you will want to ensure that it is letter-perfect in the truest sense of the word. If you are like most people, you have a tendency to read mostly for content and not for spelling or grammar mistakes. I know that my personal biggest writing failure is lack of attention to detail. Like many others, on the computer I write "from" instead of "form", "you" instead of "your", and often omit words that I know should be there. To make matters worse, since I wrote the incorrect word/s in the first place, my tendency is to overlook the error when I do my own proofreading. That's okay when you are dropping a note to your Uncle Matt, but it is not to your advantage to error in a resume or other correspondence when looking for a job . . . or any other professional endeavor.

Choose words carefully

"The difference between the almost right word and the right word is really a large matter. It's the difference between the lightning bug and the lightning."

Mark Twain

Proof Reading Hints

So, after countless hours of blood, sweat and tears you finish your first resume. After jumping for joy, you go to your printer and begin to run off a bunch so that you can send them out to your friends. Sounds like a good idea, but it has some drawbacks. You should:

1. Use Spell Check and Grammar features on your computer.
2. Read the resume out loud to yourself.
3. Read the resume backwards, word for word.
4. Have another person read it to you out loud.
5. Have another person read it and ask the person to tell you what your goal is.
6. If desperate, find a high school English teacher.

Resume Do's . . . Do,

- open with an objective statement
- use the combination format
- use a direct writing style
- include key words
- write out numerals up to nine
- keep it simple
- use good paper – 24 pound
- proofread until you can't stand it
- emphasize accomplishments
- keep sentences short
- use bullet statements when appropriate
- use plain English
- two pages (normally) use only one side of the paper
- use private sector terminology
- be consistent in format
- finish the sentence on the page it begins . . . no run over
- use a laser printer
- have another person proof the resume before you use it
- put your security clearance on your resume if the company is defense oriented
- get feedback from a non-military, non-government person
- keep the reader in mind . . . you are not the reader!

Resume Don'ts . . . DO NOT!

- use first person . . . "I" . . . "me," "my" or "mine"
- mention present salary or salary requirements
- misrepresent yourself
- use military or government terminology
- indicate your age . . . but don't try to hide it
- mention marital status
- write in jargon
- print on both sides of the paper
- overwhelm the reader with billion dollar numbers
- include a photo (***except when putting your profile on LinkedIn***)
- make it too personal . . . marriage, children, golf, etc.
- mention untruths
- include fluff . . . or stretch the truth
- over emphasize education . . . unless it is relevant and very recent
- be vague
- skip an assignment in the Work History section of the resume
- be long winded
- mention your hometown, your health, your dog's name or favorite sport
- include references or say that they are available upon request
- abbreviate
- write the word "resume" at the top or bottom of your resume
- staple it together
- bold the first word of each sentence
- put the year of graduation from college or graduate school, unless it is **very** recent
- mention that your last three spouses left you for unknown reasons
- start the summary paragraph line with more than "20 years experience" . . . if any!

Typical Questions about Resume Writing

How many resumes can I have?
This question really relates to a previous discussion in the Objective Chapter about how many objectives a person can have and manage satisfactorily. Obviously you will need a resume for every objective you intend to pursue. It gets difficult, because for every objective and resume you have, there is a corresponding amount of research involved. That takes time. It gets more complicated when you are asked the question, "What do you want to do? While I recommend that you think through what you want to do and follow that course, you can handle several objectives and, therefore, several resumes. In truth, what usually works best is to have a basic "core" resume on your computer, and when you need to tweak it (make minor changes to accommodate the situation), tweak it to fit the occasion. ***A tailored resume***. And, there will be times

when you see a job advertised which is different from your present objective but one which you believe you have the ability and experience to handle. In this case you will be starting largely from scratch and will have to proceed accordingly.

Where should I have them printed?
I recommend that you have your resume printed on a laser quality printer. The ink jet printers do a nice job, but the laser does it better. If you don't have a laser printer go to a Office Depot or a Government Transition Assistance Center with your computer thumb drive and do it there.

Should I pass them around?
There are pros and cons to that question and the real answer is - it all depends who is passing your resume around and to whom. If it is the President of Bank of America passing it around to his senior Vice Presidents, then it's a good idea. If it is a casual acquaintance, then it could do more harm than good. If, after a successful networking meeting or job interview, the person asks for a resume so that he/she can share your strengths with some others in the organization, then by all means have at it. I would not pass it around indiscriminately.

Should I publically post my resume on a Website?
You should have your resume or personal profile on LinkedIn. The statistics say that less than 5 percent of jobs are landed as a result of being posted to an Internet site, but that number is growing and you can get some good leads and ideas about whose hiring, and you might get a "hit" by a recruiter's computer screening for potential job candidates. If you are a technical type or perhaps have great tradesman skills and include relevant key words, your chances of success are much better than if you are a general manager type. It can't hurt. Just don't sit back and convince yourself that this will be the answer to all or any of your problems. For senior management positions, the chances of a hit are slight! *More than 95 percent of the jobs landed, and reported by our seminar attendees, were obtained through face-to-face networking as described in this book!* By the way, if you post your resume to a Website, stand by for an avalanche of unsolicited e-mails selling everything from computers, to resume assistance, to home loans to used cars. UGH! I would however, encourage you to read other people's resumes and job ads posted on the web. By all means avoid putting anything like your social security number or other personal data on your resume or social media profile.

Note: Job Search Websites are changing faster than we can get them into print.

Should I use a resume writing service?
It probably won't be necessary. The resume is best written by you . . . using your words, your style and your thoughts. Some of the writing services can be valuable if there is no other person around who can help you with sentence structure and grammar . . . assuming you need that kind of assistance. I have found that military and civil service personnel have enough friends who are good at writing that they do not have to seek "paid for" help. I had a person in a seminar once who was concerned about grammar and structure. Sitting next to him was an Admiral's writer who immediately offered assistance. When she finished his resume, it looked as professional as I have ever seen. Use your resources at hand.

Do it yourself or writing service?

An experienced and mature job seeker will find their job by networking. The great value in writing your own resume is the preparation you will receive and use when conducting a networking or job interview, and during salary negotiations.

If you are desperate and must go for commercial help, make sure you get an up-front understanding of what you are going to get for your money. The last fee I know of was $650.00 and the customer thought it was worth the price. Make sure the service uses your words and expressions. Have them show you how to make changes as well, so you won't have to return and pay for every little change**. Remember. The resume is as much a preparation document for you as anything else.** Check out, *The Resume Place* Website for assistance if you are desperate.

What response should I expect from a resume mass mailing?
One to two percent at best! Hardly worth the cost and effort! And, "response" means response . . . not a job offer.

Should I mail the resume folded?
It is perfectly acceptable too tri-fold your resume when mailing it. ***However, in this day and age most of the time you will email it.*** You should carry a folded resume inside a matching envelop whenever you are out and about. If you know for certain that your resume will be scanned, then mail it unfolded. If you mail a lot of resumes unfolded, in large envelopes, you will soon be calling me for a loan.

Should I, mail or email a resume?
All else being equal you will probably be asked to email the resume. Regular mail, snail mail, can take forever. Email or hand carried is preferred. E-mailing resumes is generally acceptable. **If you do E-mail a resume make it an attachment and send it in PDF format.**

How many times must I write it before I am satisfied with it?
Probably about 10 to 20. A Colonel once told me he rewrote his resume more than 50 times. A good friend of mine who is a professional outplacement consultant answered that question like this, "There is no such thing as a perfect resume, there are only millions of imperfect ones." The reason for that comment is that you will never be totally satisfied with it and you will be forever tweaking it. It's like my biography . . . every time I read it I make some small changes that might, but probably don't, make it very much better.

Should leadership be considered a skill?
This is a tough call. A few years ago if you talked about leadership, you might be considered a little touchy-feely. However, in recent years, leadership is being discussed in the business magazines, the newspapers like the Wall Street Journal, and by the military services more and more. If you are going to mention leadership, do so in the ***Summary*** section and be sure that you can respond to the question, "What do you think leadership is?" or "Give me an example of how your leadership enhanced productivity." The Appendix contains some more thoughts on the leadership subject. Leadership is hard to quantify, so be careful about using it as a skill or ability in the six "bullets" (strengths) section of the resume. Think of it this way . . . There are ***soft skills*** and there are ***hard skills***. Hard skills are those that are "technically" required to do the job or that can be easily taught. Soft skills, like *leadership* are those that are more management oriented. For example, a person working on an automobile production line must have the hard skills to do their job. The President of the same company must have more soft skills, like leadership. The President knows what the laborer does but probably couldn't do it (without training) because he doesn't possess the necessary hard skills.

Should I get fancy?
NO! NO! NO! Keep your resume as straightforward as possible.

Should I attach a list of all of my previous jobs?
No . . . but have one prepared in case you are asked to provide a list of your previous jobs . . . in reverse chronological order. And, when you describe your jobs make sure that you do so with your objective in mind. Keep the jobs descriptions relevant to your objective!

How do I get the "bullets" in the resume?
If you are using a program like MS Word, use the "columns" feature, or create a table. Another method, although a bit laborious, is to write the bullets and strengths in PowerPoint and import them into the resume. The problem with the latter method is that you will be working with a graphic object, so you need to pay attention to alignment and positioning as you create regular text within your document. The easiest way to do this is to use the template from our Website, as previously mentioned. Go to www.RuehlinAssociates.com select *Client Page* on the navigation bar, and open the template using **racareers** (username) and **rares09** (password). You have never had it so good!

Should I attach a list of my references or reference letters?
NO . . . 99 percent of the time it will **not** be the thing to do. If you are answering a job listing and it asks for references, then you might include them. However, since 95 percent plus of the people reading this book will land their jobs via networking, it is a moot point.

How do I answer a newspaper ad with a resume?
You write what's called a "Tailored" Resume ... see below.

Must I change/update my LinkedIn profile when I change objectives? **Most certainly!**

Are there special ways to respond to a civil service job announcement ad?
Yes. You want to use the same thought process as explained in this book and get a copy of **Kathryn Troutman's "Ten Steps To A Federal Job - (current) Edition."** for tips and strategies or responding to a government ad. She has become the expert on the special needs and requirements for writing a civil service resume. And, don't forget to get any unique requirements from the Website of the activity making the job announcement. Go to Troutman's website for more info.

New Topics

Answering Ads With A "Tailored" Resume
All that means is that you tailor your resume to fit the job advertised. The first thing to do is dissect the ad. Break it down into parts . . . job title, job description, strengths required (their bullets), years of experience desired, educational requirements, and salary requirements. Then note any strengths that you don't have and determine how critical they might be. If you have a close fit, continue. Do a side-by-side cover letter as described in "The Job Market" chapter. Assuming that you have met most or all of their requirements, use ***their*** bullets and key words as a guide instead of those you may have determined previously to be appropriate. Your resume objective should be what they are advertising for . . . but don't use their company name. If American Airlines is looking for a Chief Maintenance Officer, your objective would read something like this . . . *Chief Maintenance Officer in the commercial airline industry* or *Senior maintenance management position in the*

> **Responding to an Advertisement**
>
> When submitting your resume in response to an ad, the "objective" and "skills" should be the same or close as what is in posted in the ad . . . relevant. In most cases omit the name of the company or organization.

commercial airline industry. The next page shows an example of a strategy to use when responding to an ad.

Develop a "Core" Resume
Once you have decided on an objective, develop a core resume that contains as many of the related strengths, key words and accomplishments that you can think of... always relevant to the objective. Then, when you have a need to put together a two-page resume with six strengths and relevant accomplishments, you will have a ready resource from which to tailor an appropriate target resume. ***The resume you use for company 'Alpha' may very well be different than the one you use for company 'Bravo' even though they are in the same industry and produce the same kind of product.***

Should I "Google" myself to see what others are saying about me? I would hope so! Take a deep breath first!

The ad below is from the Wall Street Journal. The underlined portions (my underlining and italics) tell you the strengths that the company is looking for in the successful candidate. From this ad, you should be able to write a "tailored" resume . . . providing, of course, that you meet the qualifications.

Business Development Planning

The XXXX **Engineering Company**, is seeking a **Business Development Planning** professional. The successful candidate will be responsible for diverse functions in the area of <u>financial and business planning</u>, including <u>corporate development</u>, <u>business acquisitions</u> and <u>divestitures</u>, <u>operations</u>, <u>strategic planning</u>, <u>performance and financial analysis</u>, and <u>forecasts</u>. Position requires a *highly analytical professional* with 8-10 *years experience* in business development and planning and a *degree* in finance, materials management, or accounting. Must possess excellent <u>verbal and written strengths</u> and detail orientation. Send or fax resume and salary requirements to:

Here is a first cut at developing a resume from the previous ad. Read these two boxes closely and you will see how, by closely examining an ad, you can tailor your resume to fit the bill. Again, you must have the qualifications, or at least most of them.

Objective: Senior Business Development Planning position in the XXX engineering industry.

Summary: Over 15 years of hands-on manufacturing experience ranging from line operations to the senior management level. Possess excellent verbal and written communications strengths. Experience ranges from manufacturing hydraulic pumps to sophisticated hi-tech components. Special strengths include:

- **Business Development**
- **Financial Planning**
- **Forecasting**
- **Strategic Planning**
- **Business Acquisitions**
- **Analysis**

Exercise: For practice, take any ad in the newspaper that interests you and try to dissect it as I have done . . . develop an objective, a summary statement and six bullets. Do this a few times and you will soon get the knack of "dissecting" an ad.

Most Common Mistakes Made When Writing a Resume

One of the services we provide to personnel who attend our Career Transition seminars is the review and feedback on their resumes. Most often, if the resume is sent to us in a reasonable amount of time, all we really have to do is tweak the resume. Other times we send it back with a polite note that says "You are off to a good start," which is code for try again," or, "You must have slept through the resume writing portion of the seminar." In any event, the most glaring errors that we see from the resumes we critique on a daily basis are:

- No functional area mentioned.
- No industry indicated.
- Accomplishments not showing quantified results.
- Work history not described in terms of the objective or stressing relevant strengths.
- Accomplishments in the Work History section of the resume, instead of the accomplishments section.
- Work descriptions in the Accomplishments section.
- In general, including things that are not relevant to the objective.
- *Your* name or street name spelled wrong . . . you take for granted it is correct.
- Failure to identify and use "**Key Words**"

Every once in a while, someone will add a ***Personal*** section at the bottom of the resume and include: gross weight, color of eyes, height, and facts about a happy or unhappy marriage. The worst case was when a person mentioned his dog's name and how much he enjoyed going hunting with him. This kind of information is not needed . . . do not include it!

If you follow the direction in this chapter and use the self-critique review that follows, you will be among the top 1 percent of resume writers in the country.

Resume Review List

This review list is based on a Combination resume. It may however, be used as a guide to review other formats.

OBJECTIVE:
A personal headline that tells the reader what you want to do.

Does the objective:

- Show the level of position?
- Use business language/terminology?
- Indicate the industry?
- Describe the functional area?
- Clearly describe what you want to do?

SUMMARY:
A background statement which supports the objective in terms of the attributes needed to qualify.

Does the summary statement:

- Briefly discuss your background as it relates to the objective?
- Include other pertinent information?
- Use civilian business language?

BULLETS:
Do the six strengths (bullets) following the Summary Statement support the needs of the objective? (contain some key words?)

ACCOMPLISHMENTS:
Support the summary by offering proof.

Do/are the accomplishments: (contain some key words?)

- Relate to the objective?
- Support each of the strengths?
- Direct and to the point?
- Include key words?
- Begin with an action word or phrase?
- Clear and concise?
- Quantified? . . . dollars saved . . . percent improvement!
- Written in civilian terminology?

WORK HISTORY:
To show how work experience relates to the objective

- Is the most important information listed first? Job title, job function, (organization)?
- Are jobs shown in reverse chronological order?
- Include key words
- Are the years shown on the far right of the first line and year to year?
- Are the jobs described so that a non-government type person can understand?
- Does the description include major functions?
- Is specific information included about the reporting level and responsibility and number of personnel managed?

Ask Yourself:
Have I included key words? Words or language that will attract the attention of a computer resume screening program or human resources screening clerk?

PREVIOUS EXPERIENCE:
To convey your past experience relevant to your objective.

EDUCATION\CREDENTIALS
Relates to intellectual capacity.

- Are the government courses relevant to the objective? If not scrub them.
- Are the highest level of academic credentials listed first? Have you shown the degree major when it is relevant to the objective and omitted it when not?

AFFILIATIONS and ORGANIZATIONS:

- Are they ***relevant*** to the Objective? Have you held officer positions?

OVERALL REACTION:

- Is the resume the proper length? . . . *normally two pages!*
- Does the resume catch your eye? Is it forward looking?
- Are there lots of open spaces . . . looks organized?
- Is it easy to read? Have you shown it to a "real" (non-DOD) person?
- Is your eye drawn to the most important information?
- Does it pass the common sense test?
- Does it contain applicable/relevant key words?

Note: In addition to the above you may want to add a statement to the effect that you are leaving active duty . . . with the rank or level that you held. Normally this will be at the end of the resume, since most of the people that you will be talking to will know your status. This is your choice . . . and will normally depend on who the resume is going to. If I had to go one way or the other, I would omit it.

If you really want to impress the reader, you will ensure that your resume's accomplishments are loaded with hard numbers and percentages to quantify your strengths. There is no better way to impress a reader and to sway skeptical private sector managers than to demonstrate quantified accomplishments. Isn't this fun!

I've never had so much fun!

Some Final Thoughts About Resume Writing

Other Resume Formats
During this chapter we introduced you to the three main resume formats, but there are a few outliers. Certain industries have their own unique resume templates; examples include: the US Government, the airlines, school districts, etc. For the government, you will be required to submit a resume using USA Jobs. The resume format within USA jobs can be quite cumbersome, repetitive and long. Most government resumes are 4 to 8 pages long! But, if you want a government job, you will need to comply. Also,

industries like the airlines have specific templates you will need to follow. The airlines are most interested in flying qualifications and certifications of their pilots, not their financial or management skills. They want to compare apples-to-apples, so they have standard templates pilot applicants must follow. One last example - universities and colleges typically ask for CV's, which are a fancy way of documenting academic credentials such as books written, research completed, articles published. Many CV's are 10 pages plus! So, bottom line - you may encounter resume styles and formats that do not conform with the standard Chronological or Combination resumes. Roll with the punches and submit whatever resume template/format the company asks for.

On taking advice from others

While I wholeheartedly recommend that you solicit opinions from others, beware of the individual whose personal interests may play too heavily in his or her opinion. The person who lands a job by answering an ad in the Chronicle of Higher Education with a chronological resume believes that the best way to land a job is by answering an ad in the Chronicle of Higher Education using a chronological resume. Also, keep in mind that you are coming from government service and are probably changing career paths. Much of what is written in the career transition books found in book stores and on the library shelves does not apply to you! In fact none of the books I recommend that you read during your career transition speak to the special needs of the military or civil service person. They assume that you are going from one functional area in a given private sector industry to another one. Banker to banker - hotel management to hotel management, used car salesman to used car salesman, etc.

"I was supposed to be a horse!"

Beware of taking free advice from just anyone.

If you have read this chapter carefully, or have attended a *Ruehlin Associates* seminar, I would tell you that you already know more about resume writing than the vast majority of business people. So, if you get advice that differs from what you read here, you should give it careful consideration . . . and maybe consider it not relevant to your situation! As a matter of fact, we tell people who attend the seminars that if they hear any advice that differs from ours, to consider it suspect! At least think it through. ***You do not want to get so much differing advice that you end up with a camel instead of a horse.*** *Ruehlin Associates* is very confident because the information we provide is derived not only from literally thousands of feedback reports written by successful job hunters, but from 27 years of personal experience working with military, civil service, and private sector people of all levels. Not a day goes by when we don't receive a telephone call from someone who has attended the seminar. And, each time we go to school on their experiences . . . what is working and what is not working . . . and we add their thoughts to this book and our seminar.

More Thoughts on Putting Your Objective on Your Resume

A clear, concise, and verified objective is the key to a well written and well received resume. It is important to keep in mind that the resume serves several purposes. First and foremost it helps you focus, and if you do it right, it ***makes*** you think about the industry and functional area that you want to pursue. The objective is especially important for retired government personnel, because of their tendency to go in many directions. Secondly, it serves as a preparatory paper for networking meetings and job interviews (see Networking). And finally, it is something that, after making it fit the occasion, you can send in response to an ad or in response to a job posting on the Web.

There are many opinions about the role of the objective on a resume. Everyone, it seems, thinks that you need a personal career objective. But some think that putting an objective on a resume is either counterproductive or unnecessary. Others believe that putting the objective on the resume is an absolute must. I can make a case either way. However, when the dust settles, it seems like the prudent thing to do is to put the objective on the resume.

Make It Reader Friendly

If you write a resume that is logical and is going to be easily understood by the reader, then the reader will know exactly what you want to do, even if there is no objective on the resume. If the reader cannot figure out what you want to do, then it is a lousy resume . . . or is so general in content that it does not support anything. If you go along with that logic, then why not go ahead and put the objective on the resume. It will save the reader time and will provide a constant focus for you. Personally, when I screened resumes for my first company as a "favor" to the CEO, if there was not an objective on the resume, I threw it away. A professional outplacement consultant recently wrote, "Why should a person have to read two pages of type to determine what someone wants to do?" I agree wholeheartedly. But, you say, what if I see an ad in the newspaper about a job that I have the strengths for but the objective on my resume is different from what the ad calls for? Easy, change your objective to fit the ad. **And, change anything else in the resume that supports the *new* objective.** Remember, the objective drives everything in the resume . . . the summary statement, the strengths, most certainly the accomplishments, and even some of the affiliations that you may include. Can you submit a resume without an objective to answer an ad . . . or take one to a networking meeting with the idea of leaving it behind? You can if you want to. But if you are in one of those circumstances, why not put the objective on the resume . . . it will be more impressive because the person reading it will know that you are truly interested in the line of work that he or she represents.

In the End, It's Your Choice

Finally, some would say that if a person puts an objective on a resume it might restrict the possibilities . . . that there might be other things that he/she would want to do and people reading the resume might think that the originator of the resume only wants to do what the objective states. Nope, it doesn't work that way. There have been countless reports of people who are networking for this or that job, who end up being hired for an entirely different job. In my own situation, I was networking for a position as a senior corporate contracting officer, whatever that is, and was hired by the Chairman of a Bank to be the Director of Institutional Investor Relations . . . the guy who interfaces between the corporation and Wall Street major institutional shareholders. During our networking discussion, he learned that I had some finance in my background, had given many stand-up presentations, and had the other attributes of the position. He also thought that he could teach me the other strengths that were necessary to be successful in the job, and he did. From the countless feedback reports I have received from military and civil service people who have attended my seminars, I know that people in a like situation get hired in the same way. I also know that every time I receive a resume without an objective, it is going to be a lousy resume and does not support anything . . . and I throw it away!

Why Do Resumes Fail?

I have read more than a thousand resumes. Many of the resumes were written by well-educated men and women and many others by self-proclaimed scholars. **However, nine out of ten resume writers fail to apply the basic rules of resume writing content.**

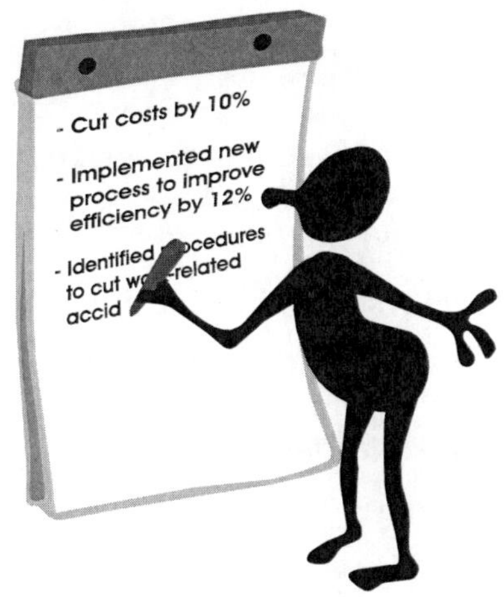

Major reasons why resumes fail

- ***Lack of focused objective and/or the skills/strengths are not relevant to the objective.***
- ***Poorly Organized. Wordy and/or not neat in appearance.***
- ***Lack specificity. The accomplishments are not quantified using concrete examples. Instead, has general comments about past work experiences.***
- ***Accomplishments in the work history section and job duties in the accomplishments section.***

Accomplishments . . . ask:

✓ ***How good?***

✓ ***How much better?***

✓ ***The quantified results were?***

Start quantifying accomplishments now!

Resume Check-off List

Before distributing your resume please ensure:

___ **It is not more than two pages long, except under unusual circumstances**

Unless otherwise requested by the organization or is a CV.

___ **It is in the combination format.**

Unless otherwise requested by the organization or is a CV.

___ **The objective includes the <u>industry</u>, a <u>functional area</u> if possible, and <u>level</u>, if appropriate.**

They want to see if what you want to do is what they need - no more than two lines in most cases

___ **There is a summary statement that addresses your experience, relevant to the objective.**

They want to see if your background and job requirements match

___ **There are six strengths, broken out in bullet fashion and relevant to the objective.**

They want to see if your strengths are what is needed to be successful in the job

___ **There is at least one accomplishment for each skill/ability.**

Do the accomplishments coincide with the requirements of the job

___ **The accomplishments are quantified whenever possible.**

Does the candidate measure the results of actions taken

___ **You have attached a one page cover letter.**

If responding to a request or an ad or job posting on the web

___ **Personal information is accurate and you have not exaggerated any facts.**

Exaggeration will only get you in trouble ... now or later on

___ **It contains relevant key words.**

___ **I have not "stretched" reality**

"Frankly Mr. Grundies, if this were my resume, I would have lied."

CHAPTER 7

THE JOB MARKET

How People Find Jobs

"I am looking for a lot of men who have an infinite capacity to not know what can't be done."

— Henry Ford

How Do People Find Jobs and Start New Careers?

I know there are jobs out there somewhere!

When you picture a job hunter, the vision that comes to mind is a person pouring over and circling the want ad's section of the local newspaper or scouring the thousands of job postings on websites. Some people think that the best way to land a job is to send out hundreds of letters or resumes in hopes that someone out there . . . wherever that is . . . will receive and read the correspondence, call and offer a job. Others think that if they just post their resume on LinkedIn and Facebook the offers will pour in. And, many people believe that if they go door to door handing out resumes and telling managers that they are available for employment, they will be inundated with job offers. ***Wish it were so!***

Before you attack the job marketplace you must understand how most jobs are found. According to many national surveys, including those of the Harvard Business School, there are two kinds of job opportunities . . . opportunities which are *formally advertised*, like in newspapers and Websites, and therefore *visible*, and the *informal* opportunities . . . those which you find in the *Hidden* or *the Invisible* market. The jobs in the *Hidden Market* are job opportunities that have not been advertised, and are most often filled by word of mouth. They are often the jobs that only the 'boss' knows are opening up. Since your objective is to make the best use of your time and land the right job quickly, you need to understand how the marketplace operates.

The Visible (Formal) Market . . . the classic approach to job hunting

- The "Help Wanted" ads
- Search firms (headhunters)
- Placement agencies
- Personnel offices (where they post the jobs on a bulletin board)
- Ads placed in newsletters published by associations
- Private sector websites like LinkedIn, Facebook and Indeed.
- Job listings found on Google and Yahoo and other sites
- Ads in military and government newsletters
- DoD Websites

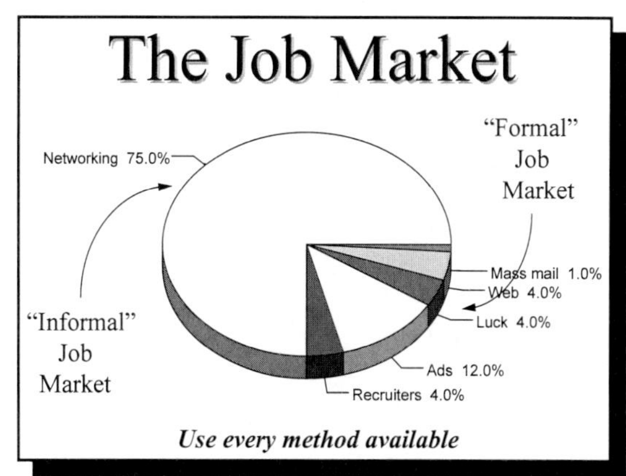

While you would think that the "formal/visible" market would represent most job opportunities available, nationally, it only accounts for about 25 percent of all the opportunities. And, the ***higher*** you go in terms of responsibility and compensation, the smaller that figure becomes. Unfortunately, most people spend the vast majority of their time looking for jobs in the visible/formal marketplace. ***The feedback from senior government personnel who have attended a Ruehlin Associates seminar, indicates that overall, 90 percent of jobs were landed through face-to-face networking . . . the informal marketplace.***

The Hidden (Informal) Market

The hidden, also known as the informal job marketplace, is made up of jobs like those that have often not been identified by anyone but the functional manager, or jobs where someone is retiring but only the boss knows, or a job created when just the right person comes along, etc.. There are many senior managers who will not run a newspaper ad or post an opportunity to a Website because they do not want to suffer the avalanche of applications and go through the time consuming and painful screening interview process. They would rather quietly put the word out that they are looking for a senior manager who can accomplish "whatever," or have their HR department quietly screen sites like LinkedIn/Facebook. That's what the hiring network is all about. And, by the way, networking is how recruiters find most people to fill the senior jobs they are working on to fill.

The good news is there are lots of jobs waiting for you . . . the bad news is you will have to find them.

> **Job Boards**
> While Job Boards do produce some results, applying to the company's or organization's website directly may well produce better results. You might also learn some useful info and terminology.

How People Find Jobs

There are millions of people hired into jobs each year in this country alone. They land them anyway they can, but for the most part they waste a lot of energy and create a lot of frustration shopping in the wrong job mall. When you ask someone the best way to get a job, the answer will usually be the way that person got his or her job. How do people find jobs?

- **Ads** and **Website** postings (like Career Builder)
- Agencies/recruiters (headhunters) screening social media Websites
- **Personal networking . . .** ***referrals/personal contacts***
- Cold calling
- Professional journals and associations
- Job postings like indeed.com
- Putting your resume on LinkedIn, et al.
- Part-time . . . leading to full-time
- Temporary work . . . leading to full time
- Newsletters . . . search bulletins
- Start your own business
- Buy a Franchise
- Social media "networking" . . . **for referrals**
- Friends
- Nepotism
- Dumb Luck Opportunities
- Win the Lotto!
- Job Search newsletters

"Futurestep"

Several years ago, Korn/Ferry International (www.futurestep.com), one of the nation's largest executive recruiting firms, announced a new venture aimed at filling middle-management jobs through the Internet. The program has been named ***Futurestep*** – an online recruiting service. The skeptics say that on line recruiting of management personnel won't work, but Korn/Ferry obviously thinks differently. When someone signs up with ***Futurestep***, they are required to complete a lengthy questionnaire about their background and work style. The program targets middle-and senior management jobs that pay $75,000 to $200,000 (I could live with that). The program opened in 1998 on a limited basis on the West Coast . . . it is now on both coasts and some 100,000+ have registered on the Website. Give it a try?

Regardless how you land your first job after leaving government service, you should try to find something that you want to do. Jobs are not difficult to find. The right job, in the right place, at the right salary will take a little effort.

Answering Advertisements and Job Postings on the Web

People **DO** land jobs as a result of answering a newspaper/internet ad. The problem with this approach to job hunting is that you are competing with hundreds if not thousands of other people. Unless you meet almost every qualification mentioned in the ad, you will be screened out early in the game. If you see an ad that appeals to you and you do meet most of the requirements, then by all means send in your application, but do it smartly.

You will have to sniff them out!

- Answer the ad as soon as you see it, and again after seven days. Why? When the ad hits the street there could well be an avalanche of responses and a good chance that your application could be overlooked. Sending in another response seven days later, will most likely ensure that your submission will be read by the screener at least.

- In your cover letter, ensure that you mention the name of the newspaper, magazine or Website, the date that the ad appeared, and the position advertised. This is important because the company might be running several ads for different positions at the same time. Lay out their requirements for the position and your qualifications alongside. This way they will be able to see that you do in fact have the experience and strengths that they want. **If at least some of the strengths or requirements listed in the add do not appear in your cover letter and resume, chances are you will be screened out by their computer screening program.**

Web Site Postings

"I found my job by a Google search. Just typed in "civil engineering job opportunities in the Seattle, WA area" and there it was. Completed the application and everything fell into place. Three group interviews "on site" over a two day period."

- Nearly every ad will ask for salary history and/or requirements. <u>**Do not**</u> list it. Instead, ask for a meeting to further discuss the job and your strengths. **However**, if the ad says that if you do not provide your salary history, your resume will be discarded and fed to the dogs, then provide a ***range*** based on what you believe the position should pay. See the Compensation chapter regarding salary research. Note that nearly all companies use an Applicant Tracking System.

- If the name of the employer is in the ad, make a follow-up telephone call. Calling, not badgering, will show that you have more than a passing interest.

If you can identify the company and determine the functional manager that initiated the ad, send that person a copy of your response to the ad. If you know someone that works in the company and knows the functional manager, try for an information/referral/networking meeting.

There will be occasions when you will hear of a position opening before there is an ad posted on a website or placed in the newspaper. Even though you do not know the functional manager or are unable to get a referral into the functional manager, consider making a direct approach. Write directly to the functional manager and suggest a meeting to further discuss the position. Later, when the ad appears, respond to it as you would to any ad. One caution, make sure that you don't send the letter to the person whose job you are seeking.

Another approach to answering ads is to try and find someone who knows a senior member of the company and have that person make a call in your behalf . . . a referral. I have a friend who wanted to work in the florist industry (An industry which he knew nothing about, I might add) and bring his knowledge of Total Quality Management to make a company more productive. He saw a 1" x 2" ad in the paper and called a friend to get some information. To make a long story short, after talking to six people he had never met before, he discovered a person who knew the president of the company that had placed the ad, and since he also knew the referral, offered to vouch for him. The next day the president called my friend and suggested that he come in for an interview. The meeting resulted in an offer and he landed a job as the Chief Operating Officer of a major company on the East Coast. A great example of how networking can work for you when answering an ad. Having a personal referral (not necessarily a personal friend) into the company is worth its weight in gold!

Heads-up ... "Nearly two-thirds of top employers in the USA do not notify job seekers that they are not being considered for positions." - WSJ

Note: A WSJ study showed that having a current employee of the company you are interested in recommend you, is the surest way of getting an interview within the company.

Submit resumes to actual people. Nearly 80% of jobs landed are through referrals.

Government Websites

All of the services are using USAJobs.gov to post job openings. That is the easy part. You can ask your personnel officer the exact location of your service's Website and the address of any special places they offer opportunities.

Veterans Preference

- Honorable discharge required.
- Retirees O4 and above not eligible, unless disabled.
- Additional preference for 10+ point disability (without this, you won't make the first cut).

Action: ensure you document any disabilities, regardless of how minor.

The government has recently started to use a resume format when applying for positions. While the format and guidelines are basically the same between agencies, individual services often have some rules of their own. Get a copy of the agency instructions that you are interested in. As mentioned previously, we also recommend that you read a text on the subject. One that is widely recommended is the "Electronic Federal Resume Guidebook" by Kathryn Troutman. It comes with a CD that contains useful information.

One last thought about government resumes . . . remember to use the ideas and thought-process that you learned in our discussion of resumes . . . they apply when writing a federal government resume as well as a resume for a private sector position.

Search Firms, Recruiters and Agencies

Search firms, recruiters and agencies are all organizations that work at filling positions for their clients. The client pays the firm, not you! Therefore, their focus is on the client and not on you! They work at finding the right person for the client, not the right company for the person in need of work. The basic difference between recruiters/search firms and agencies is the level of the job being filled. Agencies usually fill the lower paying jobs. Within the recruiter/search firm arena there are contingency and retainer-based recruiting companies. A retainer company, such as Korn/Ferry, is hired by a company to fill a particular position and is paid up-front. The contingency company is paid when and if they deliver the goods. They are all endearingly referred to as "headhunters." The chances of one of these firms sponsoring you, as a newly retired government person, to fill one of the positions that their client is seeking, are slim. After you have landed your first civilian job, however, they *could* be knocking at your door. It is common practice for a recruiter to offer a position to someone that already has a job. They "steal away" managers who have already proven themselves in their industry. While the search firms may like you personally, they prefer to present a known and *private-sector-proven* candidate to their client. At this point in your career your private sector credentials are probably nil, unless you have some very specific talents and technical strengths. Further, don't be disappointed when you send your resume or a nice letter to them offering your strengths and you don't receive a response. At best, you will receive a post card or form letter, advising you that they had filed your correspondence in the appropriate receptacle. In the event that you are approached by a search firm, make every effort to meet with them face to face and treat them as you would a prospective employer. You want to become a living personality . . . not just a resume to fill a job. Note that the exception to this *rule* is when the recruiter is conducting a search for a defense industry company who has asked specifically for a person with a strong military/government background.

> **Recruiter Sources**
>
> ***Find candidates for a client by:***
>
> ***Referrals from their active data base***
> ***Cold calls to incumbents in like areas***
> ***Screening social media sites***
> ***by computer or manually***
> ***Soliciting previous placed candidates***
>
> ***By networking ... just a little devious***

Korn Ferry receives 1 million unsolicited resumes each year.

Note that these firms do screen social media websites like LinkedIn and Facebook for possible candidates.

The bible for looking up recruiters and learning what areas they specialize in is The Directory of Executive Recruiters, published by Kennedy Publications. It is available in the public library, usually in the business research section and probably chained to a post – because people like to rip them off! It is worth reviewing. It explains the relationship between the client and the recruiter and the job seeker . . . important to understand. It also has some helpful hints for those in the job market. The book recommends that you avoid:

- Floating a resume with photo and a written reference from your aunt.
- Phoning and asking if they received your resume.

- Phoning again in 60 days to ask, "What's up?"
- Cornering a recruiter at a social event and asking him to help you find a job . . . bad taste.
- Saying that so-and-so gave you his/her name and suggested you call (but I would do it anyway).
- Lying about your age, education, work history, etc.
- Missing an interview date.
- Failure to take the recruiter's advice on the appropriate dress.
- Refusing to take the recruiter's call after you get the job.
- Asking: "What did you think of my resume?" Get that kind of advice elsewhere.

Finally, recruiters specialize incertain industries and trades . . . such as: Generalists, General Management, Manufacturing, Human Relations, Marketing, Finance and Accounting, Procurement, R&D, Packaging, Administration, International Operations, and Specialized Services.

Some of the largest executive recruiting firms are: Korn/Ferry, Russell Reynolds, Dunhill, Spencer Stewart, Heidrick and Struggles. Check out their Websites. They all have good job hunting tips.

Headhunter story . . . why they normally don't like to offer up military/civil service personnel without some private sector experience.

A good friend of mine left active duty and proceeded to look for a new career in supply chain management (physical distribution) in the private sector retail world. He was exceptionally well qualified.

He set up networking meetings with companies all over the country but the meetings led to zero opportunities. He called Korn Ferry . . . recruiter . . . and through a personal contact he was able to reach a senior recruiter . . . Mr. Jones. In short, the recruiter would not give him the time of day because he had "No real life qualifications" . . . even though my friend had worked in the same functional area in the military for many years.

He went back to networking and after nearly a year his prayers were answered and he landed a great job in Denver as the director of supply chain management for a major retailer . . . company X. He and his wife bought a nice new home and settled in what he thought would be the perfect situation. Six months later when he was conducting company business in Atlanta, his secretary called him and told him to "Come home" as soon as possible. He asked why and she told him that the movers were unloading his office because company Y had acquired his company and that he no longer had a job . . . the new company's supply chain manager would take over his responsibilities. (How does that grab you?)

Sidebar: A word to the wise. *Regardless of what you may be told, when one company acquires or merges or "swallows" another company, many of the management personnel from the company being taken over, both senior and mid level, eventually go out the door. You will be told that this will be "one big happy family," but in truth, that ain't the way it normally goes.* Watch your back.

We are all one big happy family . . . yea, sure!

My friend returned to his office and while he was packing his personal belongings his secretary knocked on the door and told him that he had a telephone call from Korn /Ferry . . . a Mr. Jones. Mr. Jones told my friend that he was aware of the acquisition and his circumstances and was wondering if my friend would be interested in being the director of supply chain management for a similar company on the east coast. My friend replied in the positive and then asked why he was making this offer now when six months ago he wouldn't give him the time of day. The recruiter replied that my friend ***now*** *had credentials and experience in the real world. My friend was essentially the same person, technically, that he was six months earlier.*

Analysis: In this case the recruiter's concern is obvious . . . he didn't want to risk his reputation by offering up a person with no private sector credentials . . . meaning someone who had never worked for a private sector company, even though my friend had all of the technical qualifications. The company X job in Denver, which he found through networking, became available because the senior person my friend met with listened to his qualifications and believed the **fit** was "right." If the company that retained the recruiter had made "DoD background" part of the qualification requirements, then the story would have been different from the beginning. Just the way it is.

Job Fairs

One excellent resource to find a job is at a job fair. Job fairs come in all kinds, sizes and shapes. Some are held on military bases. Some are at large downtown convention centers. Usually you need to arrive with a resume and you approach tables hosted by various vendors. These vendor tables are typically manned by HR personnel looking to fill positions in their company, but also to showcase the products/services their company provides. My advice to you is to research and prepare as much as possible before showing up at a job fair. Which vendors will be there? Create customized resumes for each of the firms you are interested in. Approach the vendor table fully armed with good questions and enthusiasm for the company(s). Find out prior to the job fair whether there are any openings for someone like you. Smile, relax and be patient; job fairs can be crowded, busy and a bit "desperate." But it's worth giving it a try. Bottom line, you will build your business intelligence and network while attending a job fair. Also, consider a virtual job fair. Everything above applies, but you will be sitting at home a participating via video cam and chat rooms.

Part-Time/ Temp Work

The beauty of taking on part-time or temporary work projects is that these opportunities can lead to full-time work. If you begin some sort of project based work, you get a chance to interact with the employees and leaders of a firm; obviously you will impress them with your intelligence and work ethic. Basically, it's advanced Networking! There are many famous Temp Work agencies; the best known is Kelly Temp Services but others include Adecco Group and Manpower Inc. A second way to get part-time work is to form your own consulting company and bid on work projects being advertised via the web. See the next section on how to start your own business. Once you've done a great job as a consultant, many times you are offered full-time employment with your client.

Starting Your Own Business

Many people give serious consideration to starting their own business. It might be buying and running a franchise, or consulting on your own, or just beginning a business from scratch. The reasons they give are numerous, but most of them simply do not want to work for someone else again.

It is not the purpose of this book to get deeply involved in starting and running your own business of any kind (there are plenty of how-to books in the library on the subject), but I will

Starting Your Own Business!

- **Think it through**
- **Study it**
- **Work for another first**
- **How much $ needed**
- **27 hours a day**
- **9 days a week**
- **Temperament**
- **Personal assessment**

... ***you must have lost your mind!***

share some thoughts from my own experience and from those of others.

There is probably nothing more satisfying than to start your own business and have it succeed. However, there is nothing that takes more energy and personal effort than being a small business owner. Most small businesses do not make a tremendous amount of money . . . at least not at first. There was a statistic published a couple of years ago that said it takes from three to five years for a person who begins his/her own business to catch up with the counterpart who went to work for a private corporation. I think, on the average, that is being very optimistic.

The Staff are YOU!

Self Employment
Someone has to:

- ✓ Design the program
- ✓ Finance the business
- ✓ Write the book
- ✓ Write the proposals
- ✓ Conduct the marketing
- ✓ Pay the bills
- ✓ Invoice the customer
- ✓ Create the presentations
- ✓ Do the research
- ✓ Take the risk

When you work for someone else, ***they*** carry all of the risk . . . ***they*** must meet payroll and hire an accountant, ***they*** float the loan, and ***they*** pay social security taxes, and ***they*** provide a medical plan and so forth. When you do it yourself, ***you*** are ***they***! On the other hand, the gratification that comes with a successful business and making a respectable income is wonderful.

Buying a franchise is one way to get into your own business, but, Caveat Emptor – buyer beware! Know what you are getting into and conduct the due diligence required. Keep in mind that there are companies that specialize in conducting due diligence on franchises.

Starting your own consulting company is also a popular way to go. However, friends tell me that it can be a lonely business - working on your own - and you must work hard at staying abreast of all new developments or your relief will have your customers in three years . . . when you are old news!

The Business Plan

Above all, if you are going to pursue your own thing, then **make certain that you write a business plan** before taking one more step. I often receive calls from people asking that I give them some help/advice in starting their business. My response is always, "Send me a copy of your business plan, and I will give you some feedback." Their response is often, "I don't have one." How does it go? "A fool and his money are soon parted?" There are plenty of software programs available to help a person walk through the steps of writing a business plan, and the results may change your mind against the concept, or validate that it is a profitable idea. The SBA also has seminars on how to start your own business. DO IT! **SBA.gov is a great web resource** and well worth the read. Another great way to validate your plan or idea is to take your Business Plan to a bank and ask if they will loan you the money to start up. If they say yes, you know you have a responsible venture. If they say no, you had better rethink your idea.

You absolutely must write a business plan and have it approved by a commercial lending bank, regardless of the financing source.

If a bank won't approve it, it is a bad plan!

The Business (Calling) Card

The business card is but a 2" x 4 ½" small piece of heavy paper that tells people you meet where and how they can contact you. It is one step better that writing your name and phone number on the inside of a match book cover. Business cards do not have to be, nor should they be, fancy. Plain white paper and black ink are just fine. Again, the idea is to have something with your name on it to hand out when the situation calls for it. Most print shops sell them for about $40 for 500 cards. Some people like to put their photo on the business card. Not a good idea in most cases, since most of us aren't that good looking and ugly doesn't sell! Others like to use the front and back. For your purpose that is not necessary. Nor should you use colors. You may if you want but it isn't necessary. Just a nice executive type print on a stiff paper . . . which means that you will not want to go on the cheap and print them on your home printer . . . the paper isn't stiff enough and flimsy doesn't sell either!

Stores sell expensive holders for business cards. They are fancy and make great presents for people who are about to go job hunting. They make you feel good. They are impractical. The tendency is to cram so many cards in the holder that when the time comes, the cards won't come out. Just put some in your shirt or coat pocket or wallet or purse or whatever you are carrying. If they get beat up, throw them away and take out some more. Carry business cards with you at all times. There is no excuse for not having a card with you, unless you are in a swimming pool and then put one in your shoe. ***Note: I know that you can exchange info by just tapping your smart phones together, but it is just not the same. Get and use the cards.***

The card should have your: name, address, telephone number(s) where you can be reached, your Cell phone number and your E mail address. If you are military, ***do not*** put your rank on the card once you have retired. Professional engineers and doctors should put their professional credentials on the card, if that is the line of work they are pursuing. The relevancy criteria applies here as well as on the resume. If you are going to be a Wall Mart Greeter, then the fact that you are an MD or have a Phd in engineering doesn't matter.

Business Cards

Purpose:
- Info Meetings
- Interviews
- Receptions
- After 30-second Soundbite
- Anytime/Anywhere

No:
- Rank
- Degrees (unless relevant)

You've got to have 'em!

Name

Email Address — LinkedIn Profile
Address (optional) — Phone Number

Hint #1
When you receive a business card, write: who (position), when, where on the back.

Hint #2
Email recipient(s) the next day and tell them you enjoyed the conversation.

While you are still associated with the government, it's Okay to use your government business card. The minute you retire, you must have your own. Give the cards out everywhere . . . networking meetings, social occasions, receptions, on the street corner, to anyone that asks for one. The problem with the government business card is that there is no personal telephone on it. A good case for having your own card . . . maybe give out both! ***Remember to write: who, what, where and when on the back of another's business card so you remember them and send a "nice to have meet you" email . . . networking.***

Cold Calls and Mass Mailings

"Cold call" – a telephone call to a person you do not know and does not know you or anybody that you know – may bring the greatest amount of frustration possible in a career search because the rejection that goes along with them is simply unbearable for most people. The only career search vehicle that offers more rejection than cold calling is a mass mailing. The reason these techniques are so lame is that people have become so wary of the telephone sell . . . telemarketing . . . that they avoid them like the plague. In a true mass mailing . . . *not a liturgical event!* . . . hundreds of letters are sent out to anyone that may be a potential employer and in some cases, just anyone. Those letters are received with about as much enthusiasm as the letter you receive at home that says, "OPEN NOW! THIS INFORMATION IS IMPORTANT TO YOU" and so on and so on and so on. As a matter of fact, most mass mailing letters do not make it past the mail room attendant unless it is directed to a specific individual, and then some file clerk will probably intercept it and place it in the circular file. Unless there is no other way, I would avoid making the cold call – just too hard on the ego, at least when you first leave the service.

Referral Calls

The great value of a referral call as compared to a cold call is that you have a personal entre to the person you are trying to make an appointment with . . . much easier and many times more productive. If done right, it is very hard to turn down a referral from a friend, especially if the person is a veteran or long-term federal government employee. **Having a good referral into a company/ individual is like hitting the mother load!**

The Unsolicited Telephone Call

You are sitting at home one evening, wondering if you will ever work again and the phone rings. Turns out to be an old friend who you worked with on active duty some five years ago. After some pleasantries he mentions that he heard you were about to retire and wondered what you were going to do.

You now have three choices:

1. You can say that you don't have the faintest idea (**not good**)
2. You can say that you are considering several options and when you decide, they will be the first to know.
3. Assuming you know what you want to do, you say . . . "A program manager in the aerospace industry" . . . or, give him your 30 second commercial response (see Sound Bites chapter)!

Regardless of how you respond, his next comment might be . . . "Well my boss was asking if I knew anyone who might be good at managing one of our new aerospace programs, and when I mentioned your name he asked, "What I thought it would take to bring you to the table?" (That is code for how much money do you think they will want?)

Your response should go something like this. ***"While compensation is an important part of any job, my goal is to start a new career that interests me and where I can make a meaningful contribution. I am certain that when the right fit comes along, compensation will fall into place. So, I'd rather defer discussing compensation until I find the right fit and have an offer on the table to consider."***

Rule: *Do not divulge your compensation desires until you have a job offer on the table (refer to the Compensation Chapter).*

The Headhunter Calls

What if you receive an unsolicited telephone call or email from a headhunter who tells you that they receive many calls from companies looking for people with your background and skills, and that they would like a copy of your resume to pass around to potential customers? What do you say and why? Note that we are talking about a recruiter whom you have never heard of, not a major one like Korn/Ferry and the like.

We recommend that you respond with: "Thanks for the interest, I have already talked to some companies and I will call you when I take my search to a higher level. In the meantime, if you receive a firm requirement, call me and we can discuss the position and fit." Then thank them again and hang up. Next, go to the Directory of Executive Recruiters, or Google them on your computer and learn a little about them. If they are for real, call them back in a few days and ask if they have any need specific requirement for a person with your skills . . . meaning do they have a contract to find someone to fill a position . . . not just bottom fishing.

Why answer in this manner? There are many, many small recruiting companies who gather resumes from anyone they can, and then try to present them to HR directors in hopes of making a sale. Some of these companies are very legit but many are not. A major recruiter would never try this approach. They would call you and ask if you are interested in whatever and then suggest a meeting somewhere to discuss the position. Please understand that many of the "unsolicited" callers are legit so you will have to sort them out and determine if it is worth your while to work with them. You just don't want some guy standing on a street corner handing out your *dog-eared* resume in hopes that someone wants to hire you.

The "Walk in and Ask for a Job" story

A few years ago a friend of mine was struggling in his attempt to find a job. He wanted to work in banking but since the banks in San Diego had all failed years before, he decided that he would pursue his second love . . . the hi-tech industry. Now this person did not have a hi-tech background in terms of maintenance or development, but he had been a user and knew the capability of each piece of equipment.

In a moment of desperation he called and set up a networking meeting with the CEO of a successful IT company. After the initial introductions were over the CEO asked my friend what he could do for him. My friend gave an unusual reply, he said, "I would like to work in the IT industry and although I am not a IT person I have been a user and have a great interest in the business. What I would like to propose to you is this . . . bring me on with your company and assign me to your best program manager . . . pay me anything you want to and in six months evaluate my performance. If I do well, and I am sure I will, then we can negotiate a long term salary and if I don't satisfy your needs I will be on my way and you will have lost nothing."

Give me a chance!

The CEO liked what he heard and said "okay!" Six months later the senior program manager went to the CEO and told him that my friend had learned all that he could teach him and that all of the programs he had assigned were in the black and that customer satisfaction was at an all-time high. Long story short . . . my friend was hired and ten years later was made president of a spin-off company.

Analysis: This technique is very risky for a company and most corporate executives would not buy into this kind of an arrangement. (However, they might be willing for a senior military or civil service manager who recently left government service.) They would be concerned that you might be a spy or a *nutcase* or both. This particular CEO was very entrepreneurial and since my friend was a senior officer with great references the CEO decided to give it a try. Obviously, things turned out well for both of them. So then, why do people do these things like cold calling and sending out mass mailing letters if they are not profitable and the rejection rate is so high? Why do some people throw themselves off of a 10-story bridge at the end of a bungee cord, held by someone they have never met before? Why do people bet on the long shot? . . .

because, it is doing something and *sometimes* they win. And, that is the same thing with cold calls and mass mailings. Sometimes you get a hit. It's your choice, but our advice is to dedicate the vast majority of your time to networking (95 percent) and answering ads and surfing the Web for research purposes. A much better use of your time and proven over and over to be more profitable. As this last paragraph is being written, I received a letter from a seminar attendee who just landed his job as the result of a cold call. Give it a try if you feel you must.

The Best Time to Look for a Job

Keep up the job search effort at all times. You never know who will be reading your signals!

Much has been written about the best time to look for a job. The simple answer is, "When you already have one or when you think you are about to lose one." Unfortunately, it doesn't work that way for most of us. (Note: It does work for most military and civil service personnel. We know that we cannot stay in government service forever and in many cases know the year and day that we will have to leave.) So, the next question is, "What time of year is the best time?" My answer to that question is: "Look for a job whenever you don't have one, or know that you are going to lose one, and let someone else worry about the time of the year being right or wrong." Certainly, during the holidays the business sector slows down somewhat, but it doesn't stop. And, while a company may not hire you in December, many companies are developing plans and budgets for the next year and if you have met with them, your name will be fresh in their minds when it comes to making a choice to fill a new position. Some people will tell you that in the summertime everyone goes on vacation so there is no point in searching for a job. Nonsense, some management must stay around to run the business and often, since things do slow down a little, the managers might have more time to meet with you. Also, keep in mind when the company's fiscal year ends. The bottom line to the question is keep the job search in high gear at all times – just remember that the responses may not be as plentiful during the summertime or during holiday seasons.

Hidden/Informal Job Seeking Approaches

For the vast majority of those seeking management positions by far, the most productive approach will be in the hidden/informal job market. The informal or hidden market contains the majority of positions that you will be looking for and you will find that your success rate will be higher there. Working/networking the informal market will allow you to:

- Locate positions that you otherwise would have never heard of.
- Develop your network . . . (more in the Networking chapter).
- Place you in a less competitive arena.
- Meet some of the most influential people in town.
- Make some good friends.

You will be more successful with the informal (personal) approach because:

- Meetings with the decision-makers are easier to obtain if you say you are there looking for information as opposed to asking for a job . . . even though they know the purpose for the meeting. They know, that you know, that they know, and so on.
- The meeting with the decision-maker will be more relaxed. You will be able to ask questions about the industry but probably **not** the company. You may even be offered a job on the spot or a chance to interview for one. It happens more than you think . . . tell them that you are interested in exploring

opportunities but don't accept on the spot! Thank them for the offer and go home and think about it!

- You will receive valuable referrals, and perhaps, learn about openings at other related companies . . . some people will offer referrals but you will probably have to ask for them.
- Since many positions are never advertised in the paper and in some cases not shared with the personnel office, you may learn of inside positions that would otherwise be hidden to you.
- Since it takes time, energy and considerable preparation, fewer people bother to investigate the informal marketplace . . . you will have less competition.

Meetings: Networking, "Look-See," Job Interview

A short but important note about meetings: In this book we will be discussing three different types of meetings. **There are major differences between each.**

The Networking Meeting . . . *face-to-face*

The first is a ***networking meeting***. While the stated purpose of the networking meeting is to get information, the *true purpose* is to get face time and exposure as well as information. You initiate the meeting. You prepare by researching the industry and the company. You always have an objective!

The Look-See Meeting

The second meeting is what I refer to as the ***look-see*** meeting, the stated purpose of which is to have an informal discussion about your future plans – a company gets an opportunity to talk to you in an informal way. In the look-see meeting, *the company initiates the meeting* as compared to the networking meeting when you initiate the meeting. It works this way – *you get a call from a company* (probably someone you know) asking if you could visit with them sometime and discuss your plans for the future. They are not offering a job – more like fishing around to see how you might fit in their organization. However, this is closer to an interview than it is to a networking meeting so be alert. You prepare by researching the industry and the company. You always have an objective! *There is probably a better name for this meeting than Look-See and if you can think of one let me know.*

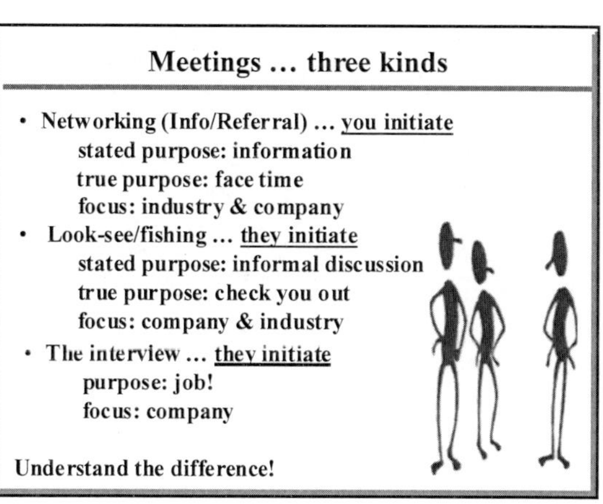

Meetings ... three kinds

- **Networking (Info/Referral) ... you initiate**
  stated purpose: information
  true purpose: face time
  focus: industry & company
- **Look-see/fishing ... they initiate**
  stated purpose: informal discussion
  true purpose: check you out
  focus: company & industry
- **The interview ... they initiate**
  purpose: job!
  focus: company

Understand the difference!

A Look-See Meeting Story

A good friend of mine had been stationed in the same area for several years and became involved with some charitable organizations. In one of the organizations he was a member of the board of directors. As the date approached for him to leave active duty, a fellow board member asked him what he was going to do when he left service - sound familiar? He replied that he wasn't sure and with that, another board member spoke

The "Good Old Buddy" Get-together

Question: *Is it appropriate to meet with an old friend/s and discuss my situation?*

Answer: *Most certainly, but:*
Know your objective
Be prepared
Don't take them for granted
Consider them as a possible reference

up and asked if he might be interested in the aerospace industry since he knew that my friend had been involved in support of Navy and Marine Corps aviation. My friend replied yes and the board member asked if he would like to meet and talk with so and so corporation - a major aerospace company. My friend answered yes but how would he do that? The board member replied that he himself was on the board of the so and so company and could set up a meeting for my friend. Two weeks later the so and so HR director called my friend and invited him to visit the company.

After spending three days with the company picking up all costs including cross country air fare and giving him the company's benefit package to look over, my friend returned home. He sent his expense bill to the company and a thank you note for the nice visit and did nothing more. Several years later he bumped into one of the people from so and so company who had shown him around the plant. The person asked my friend, "We were really impressed with you . . . why didn't you ever call us back and tell us what you thought of the benefit package and let us know you might be interested in working for us? We were ready to make you an offer!" My friend was dumbfounded and replied that he didn't realize he was being interviewed. Ouch!

Lessons Learned. (1) This was obviously a look-see meeting that could have led to an interview. A company just doesn't call you and ask you to come over for a visit unless there is some interest in having you work for them – especially if they are picking up an expensive travel claim. (2) Companies listen carefully to members of their board and if a member suggests that the company take a look at someone, chances are very good that they will. A board member may not be able to get you a job but they can nearly always get you an entree (a referral) into see someone senior in their company. (3) Be alert and follow up. If my friend had read this book before he went for the visit, he would probably be working for the company now.

> If they ask you to stop by for a visit and discuss your plans, it is probably a look-see meeting!

The Job Interview meeting

The third meeting is of course the job ***interview meeting***, the purpose of which is for you to determine if you would like to work for the company and for the company to determine if they want you to work for them. Heavy research on the company and their competitors. (See Chapter 13)

The purposes and the formats of these three meetings are significantly different. The preparation is basically the same.

Traditional Job Search Steps

Answering ads, mass mailings, Websites, making direct approaches to companies, and using search firms represent approaches to the formal marketplace that, *at best*, represent about 25 percent of the entire job market. When you enter the market through one of those avenues, you will probably go through a series of steps:

- Pre-screening . . . a screening of your resume or cover letter to determine if, on paper at least, you meet the requirements.
- Screening interview . . . a brief meeting, usually with someone from the HR Department.
- Selection interview . . . usually conducted by the functional manager and a host of others.
- Approval interview . . . a meeting with the more senior personnel in the department or company.
- Follow-on interviews . . . they want to be certain that you "fit in" the organization.
- Reference checks . . . to find out if you are what you say you are.

- The job offer.
- Salary negotiation.
- Job acceptance.

*THERE **MUST** BE A SMARTER WAY ! . . . AND THERE IS ! . . . IT'S CALLED*:

NETWORKING!

Attendee letter: "I probably sent out 70 resumes to companies advertising on the Web or in the newspaper, etc. The only time I got a call back was when my resume was submitted in coordination with networking."

CHAPTER 8

NETWORKING

The Magic of Association

Every meeting and every conversation is an 'interview.'

You have been networking all of your government service life. Every time you begin a new project and seek advice from a source unfamiliar to you that has been recommended by someone you already know, (a referral) you are networking. The big difference is that when you were on active military duty or with the civil service, you were networking on behalf of your organization to improve defense readiness; when you are job hunting you are networking on behalf of yourself. Some people have trouble with the concept of networking because they have the feeling that they are using their friends and their friends' friends. One person told me that he felt like he was groveling . . . begging for help. Rest assured that if you feel that way you are not unusual . . . however, you must also realize that networking is how the vast majority of the *quality* jobs are filled . . . and nearly all **senior** management and executive level positions. Remember the graphic at the beginning of the last chapter? It shows that, nationwide, about 75 percent of all jobs are found through personal contacts (face-to-face) networking). And, more than 90 percent of military and civil service people find their jobs through networking. Think of it this way: the person that you network with today to land your job will probably be networking with you sometime within the next five years to land his or her next job. However, if you still object to networking you are not alone. By the way, it's not groveling!

> "When it comes to finding a job, many times it's all about who you know. Network, network, and network. When someone recommends someone for a job, their reputation is on the line, so you don't recommend a slouch. I trust peoples' judgement."
>
> — Phil Blair, CEO, Manpower of San Diego

Networking

As used in this book, ***personal networking*** is having ***face-to-face meetings*** or ***telephone calls***. In contrast, ***social media "networking"*** is ***connecting electronically through the internet*** with people who might be able to help you find a referral or meet with an individual you are trying to arrange a networking meeting with. It is *using* the internet to look for jobs or tell people you are looking for a job and/or just making an electronic communication with people . . . LinkedIn, Facebook, Twitter and the like. The most noted and professional-based social networking Website is LinkedIn, and if you do not have an account, you should join. There are several good books on the subject, namely Social Media Networking (SMN) and LinkedIn for Dummies. These books go into great detail regarding every aspect and nuance of SMN and should be read before

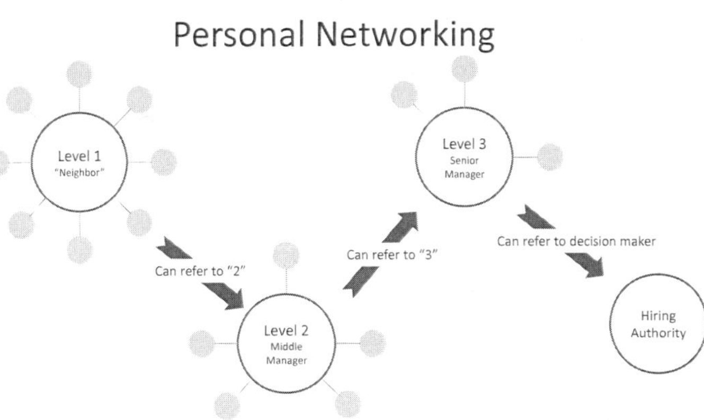

getting started. In this day and age you would be wise to use both traditional *face-to-face* and *social media* networking, although the more senior you are in grade, the higher the probability will be that you will land your job by *face-to-face* networking.

Note: Regardless of what you might think or hear, in the end, you will have to undergo a face-to-face interview meeting(s) with one or more people. Except under very unusual circumstances, no position of any consequence is filled sight unseen based on a resume or recommendation from whomever. And, all else being equal, if you obtain the interview through face-to-face networking or a strong personal referral, you will have a leg up on someone who obtained the interview by answering a newspaper or social media advertisement. There is nothing more powerful than the HR Director receiving a note from the CEO suggesting that they interview "so-n'-so" for the "whatever" position.

Why People Object to Networking - They think:

It doesn't work . . . saying or thinking that networking doesn't work is just denying a fact of life. All you have to do is talk to any professional career transition consultant or recruiter or corporate manager and ask how people land jobs and/or how they found out about the jobs that they landed.

People will think I'm imposing . . . our experience has proven that this belief is incorrect. Most people enjoy being asked for their advice and giving out information as long as it is asked in the right spirit. We have found that not only do people enjoy giving out advice (it's a bit of an ego trip), but many become personally interested in your career and will mentor you until you land a job. Bear in mind, good managers are <u>always</u> on the lookout for promising hires with potential. ***Also remember most people are "Good Samaritans."***

It is just too hard . . . true, getting into the networking mode takes some doing, but once you have done it a few times, it becomes easier and easier. Like most of us, you will probably never become totally at ease with the process, but then you don't have to. On the positive side, during your career search you will meet some wonderful people and most likely make some permanent friendships. Also, realize that you have a distinct advantage over your private sector counterparts. As a senior government member, most managers will be eager to provide assistance because they realize that this process is foreign to you. Like everything else, you have to get in the water if you want to learn how to swim.

They Are Not Waiting For You, But!

This is not to say that every busy executive has a shingle hanging outside of their office soliciting job hunters who are networking. They are busy just like you, but if approached in the right way and if you are willing to accommodate their schedule, you will eventually have an opportunity to conduct an information seeking meeting . . . a networking/information/referral meeting.

Note: In this book the terms *networking, information, and referral* meeting are used interchangeably. For all intents and purposes the terms mean the same thing when looking for a job. Some books use one or the other but they are all getting at the same thing . . . an informal meeting with another person for the purpose of getting exposure and information that will eventually lead to a job in their company or someone else's company. The referral term creeps in because, often times, the only way you can set up a meeting is through a referral's recommendation, and or introduction.

Networking Rules

Networking Rules ...*overview*

1. Industry focus only
2. Be prepared
3. Never ask for a job
4. Never discuss money
5. Use the correct level
6. A 20 minute meeting
7. Two minute responses
8. Record the meeting
9. Always a thank you letter
10. Always an objective

And, always network – even when you have a great job!

- **Focus**. Your focus when networking is on the industry. As a matter of fact you should ***never mention the company of the person you are meeting with*** . . . even though you have researched that company along with other like companies in the industry. The one exception to this rule is if the person you are meeting with asks if you have any questions about their company. So, you better have some questions, just in case.

- **Preparation.** If you go to a networking meeting, let alone a job interview, without having spent a minimum of three hours studying the company and the industry you aren't very bright. This is the area where most people fail and, as result, end up losing valuable opportunities. ***Being prepared separates the successful from the failures! Knowing applicable key words and being prepared to use them is critical.***

- **Never Ask For a Job.** You will learn that one of the conditions for setting up a face-to-face networking meeting is that you will not ask for a job. They will know that you are looking for a job but you should never ask or even hint of asking for a job. More on this subject in the Sound Bites Chapter.

- **Don't Discuss Money . . . Even if they ask what kind of salary your are looking for!** It is inappropriate to discuss money at a networking meeting and for that matter you should not discuss money in any form until you have been offered a job. See more on this subject in the Compensation Chapter.

- **Correct Level**. It is okay to have a networking meeting with management people junior in the company's hierarchy. When you become serious however, you should aim for the most senior person you can reach in the company.

- **20 minutes**. When you set up the networking meeting, you will ask for 20 minutes of the person's time. Therefore, you should spend no more than 20 minutes in the meeting. If you are asked to stay longer and you believe they are sincere, (not just being polite) then stay another ten minutes or so. Remember, this person is giving you their time and the last thing you want to do is overstay your welcome.

- **Two minute response.** Simply stated, your response to any question should never exceed two minutes. If the person you are meeting wants to hear more on the subject they will ask for more. We all know how bright you are but please don't tell me everything you know all at once.

- **Record the Meeting**. It's okay to take notes during the meeting, and it is very important to expand on your notes and what you heard as soon as possible after the meeting is over. But be polite; *ask* if it is okay to take notes.

- **Thank you.** A thank you note following the meeting is mandatory. It doesn't have to be elaborate but it must be done . . . the next day at the latest.

- **An Objective.** If you attend a networking meeting without first ensuring your resume is well-written with a solid objective, you have missed an important goal of this book.

Making Networking Contacts Is Fairly Simple *(first know your objective)*
Let's say that you are interested in ***a program management position in the aerospace industry***. If you already know someone in that industry, you ask if you could schedule a meeting with them to discuss the industry and get their thoughts about opportunities in the industry . . . being careful to mention that you are *not going to ask* the person for a job or expect the person to know of any job opportunities. At the end of a short 20 minute meeting, you thank them and ask if there are any other people that they could recommend that you talk with . . . referrals. If you do not know anyone in the aerospace industry, then find someone who does, and ask that person if you could get a *referral* to an industry manager. It sounds too simple to be true. It works!

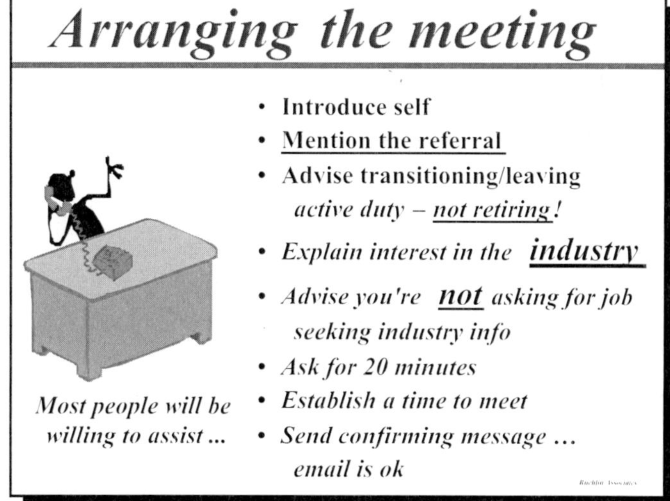

The Referral
A referral is usually someone you know who provides you with an introduction to someone you do not already know. Many companies offer their employees a significant financial reward for referring a potential employee to their company for employment.

When making the initial call and after you have introduced yourself you might say something like this:

"George Smith (your referral) suggested that I call you. I am presently serving on active duty as a Captain in the Navy's aerospace community and am about to embark on a career change. George suggested that you would be a good person to talk to. I am in the initial stages of gathering information and promise you that I will not come in and ask you for a job or ask if you know of any opportunities. I would appreciate it, however, if I could have about 20 minutes of your time when it is convenient for you."

It's Always Easier with a Referral
It is always easier to set up a networking meeting if you have a referral – from outside the company or from within – but you can do it without one! Make the call, mention the referrals name and why you are calling. ***Be careful not to ask for a job. In fact, you will purposefully state that you are not requesting the meeting to ask or ask for a job, you are just seeking/gathering information about the "whatever" industry. A very big difference.*** The reason the referral is so important is because the referral will most likely have a business or social relationship with the person you are trying to meet. In any case it is important that you do not abuse the referral's

> Even though a person is a "retired" CEO or President or Chairman of The Board of a company, they are still well connected and can provide meaningful leads and referrals!

kindness in any way. For example, don't try to sell your referral's friend any Tupperware or Mary Kay products while you are there. And once again, you will tell the referral that your purpose is to gather information . . . not to ask or interview for a job. I know this, "I'm not going to ask you for a job" bit may sound a little corny, and perhaps odd, but read on.

The "Wall of Disbelief"

For many military and civil service types there exists an invisible *"Wall of disbelief"* . . . private sector on one side and you on the other . . . meaning that you don't bring anything to the table in the private sector. Having a referral helps to get you over the *"Wall of disbelief."* When a friend or business associate refers you to another friend or business associate it sends a signal that you might have something to offer. In any event, they would not lend their name as a referral if they did not think you had something to offer. Why? Because if you meet with the referral and had nothing to offer, or demonstrated bad form, it would destroy or weaken the relationship!

Tracking Referrals

You will have to build some kind of system to keep track of your referrals and networking meetings. Without a system, you will forget how you networked to a particular referral. I know it sounds like a simple thing to keep track of, but many people end up having hundreds of names in their network, and find themselves "lost in the woods." Some people I know connect names with circles, some use a matrix and others, the system to the left. *I knew one person who had flip-chart size paper taped all over his dining room walls with the names of people he had spoken to and connecting lines to those who referred him to them. It worked for him, although his spouse was not very impressed.* A Personal Management System, as discussed in the Organization chapter, will be invaluable in assisting you with the tracking problem. An organized way of keeping track of your referrals, linking one to another and having all relevant communications at hand (written and verbal) is mandatory.

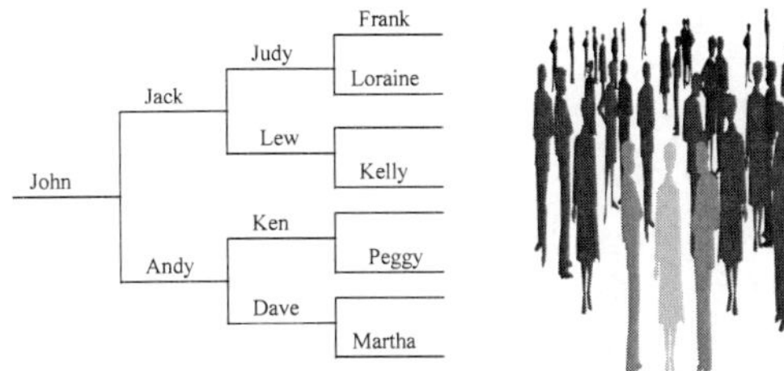

Give it a try ...

The Man On The Beach Under the Tree . . . who are you talking to?

Part One: Shortly after a military friend of mine retired, he and his spouse were invited to attend an end of the year beach picnic at a small resort on the Atlantic ocean along with a few dozen other military and civil service personnel. The party turned out to be somewhat dull and my friend wandered out onto the beach and there saw another guest sitting under a tree with what was left of two six-packs of Bud. My friend walked over and introduced himself to the "beach man," John Smith, who then invited him to have a beer. They chatted for a while, and John Smith asked our member what he did for a living. He replied that he had been in the service but that he had just "retired" and was on his way to San Diego to look for a new career. The beach man said "Wow, my Naval Academy roommate Joe Dokes lives in San Diego and you should look him up. Our member asked what Joe Dokes did for a living and found that he was a lawyer (mentally, our member dismissed a lawyer as a possible contact because he did not want to be a lawyer). The conversation then went to other matters and after the beer was all consumed our member excused himself and

Want a nice cool one?

returned to the party. My friend did not ask what the man on the beach - John Smith - did for a living, he assumed that he was a fellow military officer stationed at the Naval Academy.

Part Two: A month later my friend was in San Diego and frustrated as can be because be was making no headway in his search for a new career (It would have helped if he had a clear objective). Whereas on the east coast he had many contacts, he found that he knew no one in San Diego. (actually he had many possible contacts) In a moment of desperation he remembered the lawyer's name and thought "What the heck, I might as well call this guy and say hello to him for John Smith." So he made the call and after he introduced himself and passed along the good wishes of John Smith the lawyer and asked, "how is John's company doing?" With that, it suddenly dawned on our guy that John Smith was most likely a Company Commander at the USNA or had some other leadership job there and as he was about to say something really dumb the lawyer cut him off and said, "I mean his steel company of course, did they ever merge with US Steel Corp?" Turns out that good old John was president of one of the largest steel companies in the country . . . of course our guy had not bothered to inquire about what the man on the beach did for a living . . . you will of course! *That meeting led to a series of information meetings (see above) , including an information meeting with a bank chairman, which resulted in landing a job.*

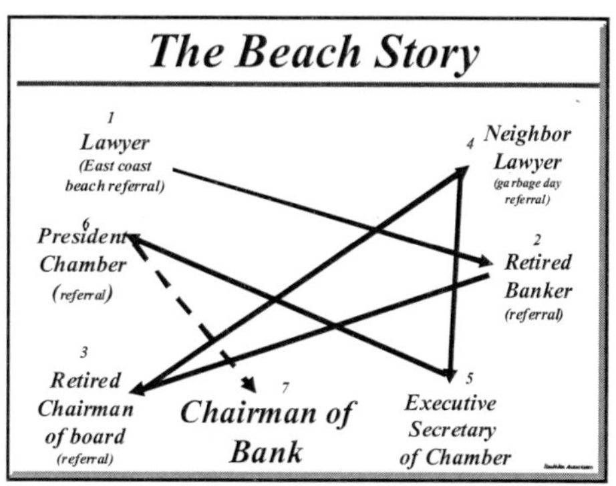

Lessons Learned:

1. You never know who you are talking to or what they do, so just ask.
2. Just because a contact is not associated with the industry you are interested in doesn't mean that they cannot make an introduction to a person in your area of interest. It's all about personal contacts and referrals. While our subject did not want to work for a steel company either, *John Smith* would have been a big time contact and referral (a silver bullet) because of his business knowledge and his nationwide contacts.

As it turned out, the lawyer invited our member to have lunch, and that meeting led to a meeting with the executive that ultimately hired him. All's well that ends well!

The Business Manager's Point of View - *why meet with you?*

Finally, look at it from the business manager's point of view. When a manager grants a meeting with a job seeker who has been referred by a colleague, the manager gains as well as the job seeker. How's that? The meeting provides the manager *an opportunity to talk with another professional, in an informal, unthreatening setting, who may be of value to the manager's company.* There are innumerable cases where the job seeker walks into a meeting expecting to ask for information and walks out with a job offer. It does not happen the vast majority of the time, but it does happen.

If you have done it right, they will want to hire you!

The **information/referral meeting** . . . networking . . . allows you to bypass the formal job screening process, allows the manager to take a look at you without the stress of a formal interview meeting, and enables you to learn more about the manager's company and industry, perhaps even sharing ideas. It is a win-win situation. Also keep in mind that, *"60% of companies look outside their organizations for senior-level candidates,"* according to a study conducted by Thorndike Deland Associates, a New York executive search firm. The reason given for choosing an outsider over "on-hand" employees is the bottom-line pressure to get the best people. There is also the idea of bringing "new blood" and fresh thoughts into the organization.

The Objectives of Networking

To get exposure . . . the world will not know that you are out there unless you get out there and make your presence felt. Networking is advertising your interests!

To get information . . . this is even more important to government personnel since most do not have a foundation in the private sector business world and many are changing their vocations. This is also an opportunity, however, for government personnel to make the business manager understand how many government responsibilities and experiences relate to private sector business.

To give information . . . you will have an opportunity to share information.

To get referrals . . . along with the objectives of exposure and information, you will want to get referrals. The referrals will extend your network and increase your exposure in the marketplace.

To build your data base of contacts . . . for now and for the future. So when the first job does not work out or you grow tired of it, you will have a resource to call upon. And trust me, that will happen.

To validate your objective . . . making certain that your objective is really what you want to do.

And most important, that's where most of the jobs are to be found! 90 percent+ for senior/career government personnel . . . military and civil service.

Networking is NOT asking for a job or going from door to door talking to anyone that will talk to you. You network with a purpose and with the people that can assist in your pursuit of employment. Networking ***without a purpose*** will lead to many conversations and a lot of good lunches, but not to a job. Networking really makes sense when soliciting for a charity, looking for a job or getting more business if you have your own company. You may begin with a small number of contacts but as you have more and more meetings (of the right kind and with the right people), your network will grow. As a result you will have hundreds of people thinking about you and your objective. As these numbers increase so does your coverage of the job market in your chosen industry.

Where to Face-to-Face Network

The short answer is . . . anywhere and everywhere. Following is a list of sources for contacts. ***Jot down some names now, the ones you can think of off-hand*** . . .

Friends . . . neighbors ... your barber
References
Politicians
Classmates . . . and college professors
Professional and business magazines
Social acquaintances
Relatives
Chamber of Commerce
Bosses . . . fellow workers
Bankers, Doctors
Accountants
Small business owners
Members of associations
Clergy
People on airplanes
Bars
Reserve officers and enlisted personnel
Contractors, sub-contractors and contractor reps
Purchasing agents
Contracting officers
Civil Service personnel
Rotary and other clubs
Business executives, company directors or stockholders
Dumb luck opportunities at hotel bars

And, Dumb Luck Opportunities

Dear John,
Thanks for all of your help and and advice. Networking really does work and so do the "dumb luck opportunities" that networking allows. While having a drink at a hotel bar in between networking meetings, I fell into a conversation with a head-hunter who was looking to fill a job. He asked what I was doing there. I explained and before I knew it, I was being interviewed for the job he was trying to fill and I got the job!
Go Figure!!

All the best and thanks ...

Start now with people you know . . . once started, you could have at least 300 names . . . try it!

Levels of Face-to-Face Networking

There are many levels of networking but to simplify matters let's just assume that there are two levels.

Level one . . . is where you begin – with close friends you know very well and perhaps some long-term business acquaintances that you have gotten to know over the course of your career. These are people that you feel comfortable with and can "practice" on, so to speak. However, even though you know these people very well, do not take them for granted. If you are going to ask them for 20 minutes to discuss their industry, or even just to pick their brains, you should be prepared. Study their industry and have well thought out questions for them. They will appreciate your preparation and will be flattered that you took the time and put out the effort to learn something about their business.

Networking Resources

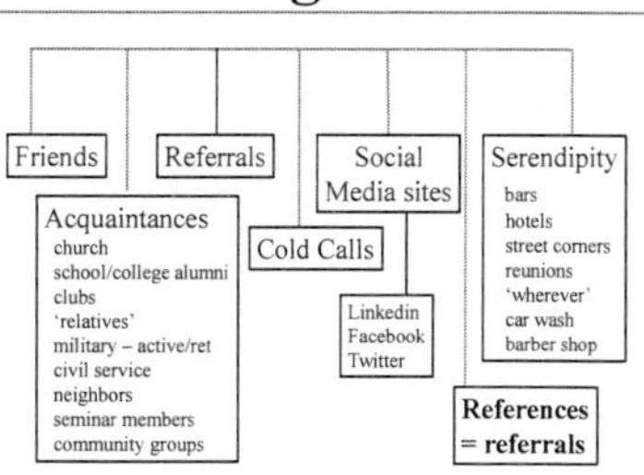

There are several approaches you can use in the **<u>level one</u>** stage.

A. The "good-old-boy" approach . . . without the slightest clue of what you want to do, you visit a good, but not "powerful," friend and discuss what they do and how they enjoy their job. 20 minutes of general conversation – but never asking for a job or what they think you should/would want to do.

B. The "investigative" approach . . . another "low-level" networking meeting with a close friend when you have a few objectives in mind, but are not certain which is the most viable – but never asking what they think you would want to do. **Note**: never use this approach on a "silver bullet" (defined below).

C. The "hardcore" approach . . . you have a solid and "tight" objective (e.g., Director of supply chain management for a manufacturing company in the aerospace industry) and are ready to go for it!

Note: *Regardless of the approach you use, or level you are in, you should always use the "I'm not here to ask you for a job" spiel. (See Sound-Bites Chapter) Further, never use a "silver bullet" for anything other than the "hard core" approach. That is to say, whenever you approach a senior executive – a high roller, a silver bullet, an influential manager – you should have a well-defined objective and be able to verbalize it clearly . . . the Thirty-Second Commercial - Chapter Twelve.*

Level two . . . is networking with people who are big-time door openers you have never met before or people you know are high rollers. I refer to them also as "silver bullets." A silver bullet could be the person across the street or even a close friend. You want to save these second-level contacts until you are comfortable and confident in your personal presentation. By now you are saying to yourself that the author can't be serious – that you have been talking to and working with people for years and don't need the practice. Well perhaps, but you will be better served if you practice on the well-known before you engage with people you have never met and/or who are powerhouses in the business world. It's your call.

Networking Prospects

Use the form on the following page to list people who might be able to assist you in your job search.
Companies. List companies you think you might want to work for . . . who do the kinds of things you are interested in, or where you might have some good contacts.
People. List anyone you know or your spouse knows who is working or has just finished working, and who might bc of assistance as a referral, or be able to provide information.
Influential. List people who you know, or have known who may not be working in your field of interest but could be a "door opener" for you. This might be a Congressman or the civilian Co-Chair of a charity fund you worked on, for example.
Special. Special people might be a favorite college professor or a classmate you have remained in contact with. (*A good reason to send out Christmas cards)*

Networking Prospects

COMPANIES	PEOPLE	INFLUENTIAL	SPECIAL
1.	1.	1.	1.
2.	2.	2.	2.
3.	3.	3.	3.
4.	4.	4.	4.
5.	5.	5.	5.
6.	6.	6.	6.
7.	7.	7.	7.
8.	8.	8.	8.
9.	9.	9.	9.
10.	10.	10.	10.
11.	11.	11.	11.
12.	12.	12.	12.
13.	13.	13.	13.
14.	14.	14.	14.
15.	15.	15.	15.
16.	16.	16.	16.
17.	17.	17.	17.
18.	18.	18.	18.
19.	19.	19.	19.
20.	20.	20.	20.
21.	21.	21.	21.
22.	22.	22.	22.
23.	23.	23.	23.
24.	24.	24.	24.

. . . How about teachers and college professors?

Sophisticate Your Network

You can sophisticate your network by identifying top decision makers. These would be people who are in the industry you are targeting, or other areas . . . such as:

- those with high visibility
- association heads
- recently retired "experts"
- those with an in-depth understanding of the industry
- outside consultants
- investors
- venture capitalists
- accounting firm heads
- law firm partners

Once you have developed such a list, you can prioritize it by determining:

- who has the largest network
- who has the most knowledge of the industry
- who you know best

But Won't They Know I'm Networking?

But, won't they know I'm networking?

Most certainly . . . because that is how they got their jobs and that is how every outplacement company in the country teaches their clients how to get a job. They will know, that you know, that they know, that you know, and so forth, that you are networking. ***But, please don't say the word, networking***. Sometimes a secretary will ask if you are networking. Just reply that so and so (your referral) suggested that you call and that you are trying to get as much information about the *whatever* industry as you can. Secretaries don't like networkers, because secretaries are paid to protect their bosses from time-gobbling people like you. Most bosses however, don't mind networkers because they know that in five years or less they will be knocking on your door, having the same conversation with your secretary! Ain't it wonderful?

Be Prepared

Networking can be a lot of fun and you will have an opportunity to meet interesting people who may well become friends, although not employers. Preparation is mandatory. There have been countless networking meetings destroyed because the job seeker took the opportunity for granted and failed to research the industry and company being visited.

Meeting Preparation

Needs	**Contribution**
What the company is looking for	*What you bring to the organization*
• special skills *• special contacts* *• special knowledge*	*match point by point*

Needs source: ads, PD, contact, research

Breakfast Without Research Doesn't Mix - Story

I personally blew a networking meeting when I had an opportunity to have a breakfast meeting with the CEO of a major corporation. After a great meal and much conversation about the weather in San Diego and how happy I was to return to that fine city and how much I enjoyed sailing in the bay, I asked him if there were any tips he could give me as I pursued my second career. He replied that, "You could spend a little time preparing to meet with the person you are having breakfast with and learning something about his company and industry." . . . OUCH! I never did that again! A great lesson for me and for you!

The Telephone Networking Meeting

A situation where many networkers falter is in setting up their networking meetings. It has become commonplace for the person you wish to network with to say, "I don't have time on my schedule to see you for several months, so why don't we take time now (over the phone), to discuss your situation and answer any questions you may have." If you are not ready to carry on the conversation, you send the wrong signal that says, "I'm just poking around, and if I get a hit, I'll take time to do some research." That is a bad message to send, and your verbal stumbling will be easily recognized by potential employers or information meeting managers as someone who doesn't have their act together.

Be Prepared!

The innocent telephone call could lead to an information telephone meeting. Have good questions ready!

Don't get caught off guard!

How Face-to-Face Networking Leads to a Job

There seems to be a great mystery about how networking leads to a job. In truth, networking doesn't lead to a job . . . it leads to and exposes you to people who are working and might need or know of a need for someone like you . . . which, in turn leads to a *job interview* which can lead to a job.

To understand how networking works, you must first understand that *the business world is just as incestuous as the government.* Everyone either knows everyone else in a particular area, or knows someone who knows someone who knows someone. Second, you must recognize that there are a million jobs in a state of flux/transition at any given time and managers are eager to fill them with qualified people that they like. (Quality people are the single most precious commodity in the marketplace . . . in *any* economy and in *any* business) Third, understand that people - even competitors - in the same industries talk to each other at meetings, seminars, on the golf course and other social meetings . . . just as you and I do. During those conversations, "Who is working where?" and "What is so and so doing?" and "Do you know anyone who would be good at this or that," are discussed and networking conducted.

Networking Meeting Questions

- **New industry developments**
- **Current industry problems**
- **Opportunities in the industry**
- **What do you like most about the industry?**
- **Describe a typical day**

And, you should know ten facts! *Ruehlin Associates*

Therefore, taking the previous comments into consideration and knowing that 75 percent+ of all jobs are landed through networking (as many as 90 percent plus for senior government and especially in the defense sector), and that many of the jobs are unannounced and/or created by the mere presence of a qualified individual, some of the mystery that shrouds the networking process should fade away.

Once you enter the "network," and people in that network know that you are available, want to work, and have useable strengths, you become a marketplace commodity and the process takes over. Obviously, you must enter the "race" before any of this will happen!

You have to enter the race to have a chance to win! And, there must be a finish line to know which direction to run!

How Face-to-Face Networking "Really" Works

I am often asked how networking actually leads to a job interview. No one seems to know! There are many theories on the subject but the real truth lies in the infamous black box.

As you contact more and more people, hopefully in the same industry, and tell them your objective (conduct information meetings as described herein), more and more ***people will begin to think about you, talk about you and associate your subject-objective with your name***. Those thoughts and conversations generate more thoughts and more conversations and are somehow (I am not allowed to tell you how) introduced into our black box. The black box somehow matches up people's objectives and strengths with company needs and produces interviews. The wise man or woman does not ask how it works. ***It may well be a psychic phenomenon but it's probably a computer matching a company's needs with the key words in your LinkedIn resume or one person mentioning to another that they have a need for and new employee and they recall your 30 second commercial and mention you to their friend. (The Faraday** **<u>effect/phenomenon:</u>** **Michael Faraday, English Scientist - 1845)***

The *Faraday* Effect

96,500 coulombs

NETWORKING ⇒ **BLACK BOX** ⇒ INTERVIEWS

Don't worry about it, it just happens!

So, What Do You Get For All of the Effort?

- Perhaps a job offer . . . it happens frequently.
- Some information about the industry or the company you are meeting with.
- A referral to other people in the industry . . . helps to build your network.
- A suggestion as to where there might be employment opportunities.
- A recommendation to an associate.
- A call back for a job.
- Make a new friend.
- Get you out of the house.
- *A free lunch.*
- A "dumb luck" opportunity.

"It's a Bill Marriott again – he wants to know if you are still interested in the Executive Vice President's job. I told him we were watching TV and to call back tomorrow."

A late evening callback!

Why Not Ask for a Job When Networking?

Earlier in this chapter I said, **"When you are networking, never ask or even hint of asking for a job . . . in fact you never discuss or ask questions about the person's company unless the person "opens that door" and asks if you have any questions about his or her company."**

Why <u>Not</u> Ask?

the conditions of the visit

- **Introduce self**
- **Referred by**
- **20 minute audience**
- **Discuss industry**
- **Not to <u>ask</u> for a job**

Ask for a job and you violate the conditions!

Ruehlin Associates

So, once you are there, why not ask for a job? It all has to do with how the meeting was set up. Most business men and women do not have time to meet with every Tom, Dick and Mary that call looking for work – even though they might be calling at the suggestion of a common acquaintance, a referral. So, let's say you reach the person by phone and you tell them you are leaving service and looking for a job or want to ask for a job . . . the odds of there being an opening at that very moment are low, and, therefore, the referral will probably respond with "I'm sorry, we have no openings at this time, but lots of luck." Instead, you advise the person that you are in transition from a government career (military or civil service) and (your referral) suggested that he/she would be a good person to talk to about the industry. Then you mention that you are only asking for about twenty minutes of their time, and by the way, "You are not going to ask for a job and don't even expect the person to know of any opportunities." Having said that, if you ask for a job or a job opportunity with the company during the face to face or telephone meeting, you have broken your pledge and destroyed your credibility and probably the credibility of the person who referred you. Your goal is face time!

They Know That You Are Looking for a Job

There is no doubt the person you are meeting with knows that you are looking for a job and that you would probably hop out of your seat if offered one. But the idea here is to avoid putting the person you are meeting with on the spot. No one likes to say "No," especially to a friend or the friend of a friend/referral. And by the way, remember that you probably would not have gotten the face to face meeting to begin with, if you had told the person on the phone that you wanted to come in and discuss job opportunities with his or her company. If you had said that, the response would most likely have been, "Sorry we only hire from within or we don't have any openings at this time."

Networking Faux Pas

Networking is easy once you get the hang of it but there are easy ways to trip up:

- Just not doing it - not networking
- Asking for a job while networking - ***the ultimate sin!***
- Not being research-prepared for networking .- *not using key words*
- Arriving late and/or staying too long
- Ignoring the administrative staff
- Not keeping in touch with the contacts
- Not thanking people for their help
- Not writing thank-you letters
- Burning bridges with past employers

All this effort is to get you to the interview table. No one gets hired without an interview.

Conclusion

Networking is not asking for a job or job leads. It is getting "face time" with a manager and asking a lot of good industry related questions, getting input from many people on subjects related to your objective (industry and functional area) and then carefully reviewing what you have learned and then determining how to use the information.

One-on-one face time and being prepared are what count.

Of the countless, and I mean countless, letters that my associates and I have received, (see one below) the single most common comment is ***"networking is the only way to go."*** It's up to you to decide how hard you want to work using this technique. I personally feel so strongly about networking, I am confident I could go to any major city in the country and develop a network that would lead to satisfactory employment. It would not happen overnight, but it would happen. The same applies to you. Try it. You will like the results!

Letter: *"It's the people who you know and know your capabilities, work habits and work record that will help you find the right job. It is impossible to overemphasize the importance of networking! Networking was clearly the key to my successful job search!"*

Overseas Networking

"Dear John,

I thought that I would give you an update on my transition status. I have found employment . . . good job and good money.

The process that you taught us is exactly what people need to follow to get good employment - post-military. I can tell you that I had started the process about 4-6 months before your seminar in (overseas). Networking was most useful and offered me several interviews even by telephone. Most of those were networking meetings . . . gave me facts and information . . . good practice for interviews. Everyone that I talked with was happy to help, and when I offered to end the conversation at the agreed time, they wanted to continue to tell me more.
Being overseas does make the process harder, but it is manageable if one decides to stay focused on the process. I worked about 20-30 hours a week after getting home from my work, submitting resumes tailored to the job and networking.

I had a couple of telephone job interviews and several face-to-face interviews for employment. Most people did not know how to interview . . . except one gentleman with a non-governmental humanitarian organization. He was good. The other interviewers primarily told me about the company benefits . . . which were not new to me since I had read (mostly on their Website) about the company ahead of time. This allowed me to bring up questions and make comments about the company very easily.

I also found that if you provide a good resume that matches what the company/website is looking for - you could get by the HR person. I applied for several positions via websites. Most of those applications go to the HR manager, but with a couple of well-timed phone calls and explaining why I was a good fit, the HR manager passed me to the person wanting to fill the position. I received some responses that the company hired someone else, but that is okay and I got interview practice and some information.

Networking is what finally got me the job. However, I have to call it reverse-networking. I had someone that I had worked with, and was not necessarily good friends with contact me unexpectedly and told me about a job I could be working in. He told that he felt that I would be a good fit. I applied; the company and their client were impressed with my resume and immediately started to prompt me to return to the states for an interview. It took a couple of months to get things worked out but at the end of the interview, I was offered a job on the spot.

Since I was already in the States, I arranged for some other interviews . . . mostly from networking sources in the same period. I was offered a position from another company with more money and the benefits a little better. However, I was more comfortable with the first offer so I went back to them . . . was up front . . . said that I did not intend to start a bidding war and that I was very comfortable with them, and asked them to match the salary. They did immediately. I trust that this information has been helpful. By the way - I followed all your rules - find the location early, visit the bathroom to check hair, etc. and all the other things in preparation. Oh, lay out your clothes - early - the day before and check that you have everything."

The Lawyer and the Garbage Can . . . getting referrals

One of the most bizarre ways that I found a referral/made a new contact that led to a job offer happened on a Saturday morning in La Jolla, CA. Story goes like this: A friend of mine told me that a good person to network with was the past President of a major company in San Diego. After many calls I finally made contact with this gent and he said that he would give me thirty minutes on the following Saturday morning at 0700. Seems that he was a very early riser and went jogging at 0600 every day. I showed up promptly at 0700 and he was waiting at the front door in his sweats. We had a great visit and I got some important referrals and good advice about focusing on the job I really wanted.

I left promptly at 0730 and went to my car. As I was opening the door, I noticed the man next door carrying out his garbage can for the Saturday morning garbage pickup . . . he was still in his pajamas. He gave me a funny look and said, "What the hell are you doing here at 7:30 AM on a Saturday morning wearing a suit and tie? When I explained my purpose, he all of a sudden got interested and said, "I can help you too . . . wait a minute and I will get you some telephone numbers of some of my important clients and you can say that I said to call them. One of those names he gave me was the banking executive that I eventually met with and who hired me! It took seven networking meetings to get there.

What in the blazes are you doing here at 7:30 am?

Lesson Learned:
1) You just never know!
2) Determine the garbage pick-up days!

Thank You Letters Pay Off!

Dear Judy,

Just a note to let you know that I have landed a job with (xxxx) corporation in upper New York state. The position is exactly what I wanted. As I indicated in my landing report - attached - the salary and perks are beyond my expectations. You may be interested to know that it was my thank-you letter that got me the job . . . plus my charming personality . . . ha-ha. I was on the short list and the competition was strong. After I was notified that I got the job I asked the CEO why they selected me over the other candidates. Their response was something like this, "All of the candidates were strong and the last few were pretty much a tie. You were the only one to send a thank-you letter and we were impressed with your manners."

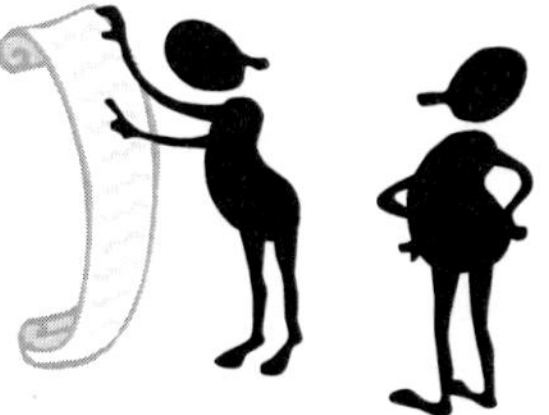

Look at the nice "Thank-You" note we received from Mark Flaherty..

Thanks again. The coaching really did pay off. Especially the emphasis on the thank-you letter, even though I must admit I thought it was a bit corny when I heard you talk about it during the seminar."

Sincerely,

Mark

Working The Crowd – Networking a Group

There are no hard and fast rules about networking a large group. Most people tend to move from person-to-person, or a small group-to-small group, simply because they want to see who is there or talk to some old friends. When you are networking for a job some easy to follow guidelines are:

- Stay away from the food tables unless the person you want to meet with is standing there. You are there to meet and talk to people, to get referrals and set up face-to-face meetings, not to fill your face with goodies!

- ***Stay away from the alcoholic drinks***. Grab a cup of coffee or a glass of punch instead of a double martini. Avoiding alcohol will keep your brain alert and your tongue under control.

- There won't be time to meet with everyone in the room but in an hour's time you should be able to spend some quality time with five or six different people.

- When you are talking with a person, try not to always be looking over their shoulder to pick out your next target. It is very impolite and the other person will notice what you are doing. Engage the person you are talking to directly and sincerely.

- Make certain that you have a supply of business cards to hand out and make sure that you put the cards you receive in a different pocket than where you keep your own cards. Otherwise, you may find yourself handing out another person's card and they will get the call . . . and the job!

- When you receive another's business card, discretely write who, what, where, when and any message on the back of the card so you can remember the person and what was discussed.

- It is bad form to actively network people at a private dinner party or a truly social function! How would you like me to come to a dinner party at your house and start selling magazine subscriptions or Tupperware to your guests? That is not to say you can't tell people that you are leaving service when they ask, and what you want to do, but openly soliciting appointments or asking for referrals will irritate people more than any results it will produce. If someone you are talking to does have an idea that would help you, they will offer it to you – but let them make the offer and then ask if you could call them in a day or so to discuss their idea further. You don't want to be like the insurance salesperson acquaintance I used to know, who always tried to sell insurance to anyone in the room, regardless of the occasion, i.e., social gatherings, funerals, weddings, religious confirmations, etc.

"It's not where you go, it's who you meet along the way." (Alice in Wonderland) or maybe Tiny Tim.

And What Do You Do? Story

A friend of mine had recently left active duty and was in the networking mode. He had read somewhere that airplanes were a good place to network and that you should strike up a conversation whenever possible. On one of his airline trips across country he tried to start up a conversation with the person seated next to him but the try was in vain – his seat mate was not interested in engaging in small talk conversation. After several attempts – asking "Where are you going?" and "What do you do?" – his seat mate told him that he was in the frozen food business, and that he was going to visit his home office in Saint Louis. My friend had recently been in charge of a government division that bought food for the armed forces and said, "Food is an interesting commodity, in my last job I was responsible for contracting for several billions of dollars worth of food a year and in fact your company was one of our suppliers." With that comment the seat mate gave my friend his undivided attention for the next hour and invited him to visit their corporate offices on his return trip. He did of course and he was later offered a job.

Lessons learned:
1) You just never know with whom you might be talking to.
2) A little persistence can pay off in great dividends.

"Luck affects everything. Let your hook always be cast; in the stream where you lest expect it, there will be a fish."

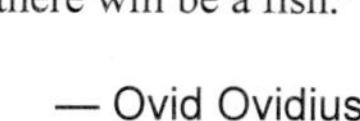

— Ovid Ovidius
43 BC

Networking Works Because:
I know that some people are leery of the value of networking and wonder if it is really as effective as we say it is, so here are some of the reasons that networking works so well.

- Most people are cordial.
- Most people respect their friends and business associates.
- Most business people are busy but willing to give up twenty minutes to a referral.
- Most people do not like to reject others – especially if the other person is a friend of their friend.
- Most people want to be helpful.
- That's how most people got their jobs.

Letter From a Successful Networker
"I followed your rules of networking to the "T" and generally found that everyone I contacted was willing to help in some way, either by referrals to others or mentoring. I developed a few key contacts which I will call "hubs." These hubs were skilled networkers and rapidly expanded my web. One hub was especially valuable (I received his name from six different people!). He spent several hours with me in separate meetings to help me focus and also sort through the offers once they started coming in. He was the stepping stone to the company that eventually hired me. In the end my list of "B" and "C" contacts grew to over 150 names, of whom I contacted over 120 by phone or in person over a four-month period. I expect to continue to use this list in my day to day work here in the Washington, D.C. area. I sent a thank-you note to everyone that helped me and then some."

"Social Media Networking"
Stay In Touch – many social media Websites can help you to *connect* with networking/referral possibilities. A favorite of mine is LinkedIn. It is free (for the most part) to join and will assist you in finding colleagues, job opportunities and even research. We are seeing LinkedIn playing more and more of a major role in the job search effort . . . especially when combined with personal (face-to-face) networking. But before we get too deep into the mechanics of LinkedIn, I want to mention two other excellent "Mentorship" groups: American Corporate Partners and Onward to Opportunity. Using their websites, you will be matched/connected with a volunteer business person who will serve as an additional guide through your military to civilian transition. Please take advantage of as many networking opportunities as possible.

Why Bother with social media sites like LinkedIn?

As previously stated, social media "networking" is not the same as face-to-face networking, and may or may not get you a job. Nor does it take the place of a resume or the hours of preparation needed to get ready for networking and interviewing. Remember, it is just another tool in your bag.

Social Media is used by:
Job hunters - looking for jobs
HR managers - looking for talent
Recruiters - looking for talent
Friends - looking for friends

The value of LinkedIn and similar programs . . . it's a no-brainer

1. *Finding referrals/leads that will result in face-to-face networking meetings,*
2. *Publically announcing your capabilities in hopes that a company screening resumes/profiles will detect your resume and make you a candidate for a job interview, and*
3. *Enable someone, a recruiter or an HR person for example, to "discover" you as a result of your resume description – by screening for the key words relevant to their job requirements.*

How do you get started?

1. Open account . . . get a free **Premium** account at: https://veterans.LinkedIn.com.
2. Read LinkedIn for Dummies.
3. Follow LinkedIn format.
4. Explore the features.
5. Research . . . Google: "LinkedIn Job Search and Career Building."

An invaluable resource

Then . . .

Create a Profile . . . *in a nutshell* (use your resume for basic information)

- Photo: ***Professional*** . . . a Wall Street Journal survey found that "LinkedIn profiles with photos are 11 times more likely to be viewed than those without." Make it a head shot – a pleasant smile is okay. Wear business casual – coat/jacket, with or without a tie or scarf.
- Headline: Load with relevant key words; describe how you want to be known and in what industry (the essence of your resume objective).
- Summary Statement: Describe your relevant background and objective; include key words.
- Strengths: List six skills (key words) applicable to your headline.
- Experience: Jobs (in reverse chronological order) stressing strengths relevant to your objective.
- Education: Schools and colleges attended with the highest first.
- Include: email address.

BEWARE: If you are in or recently have been in a sensitive position, check with your security manager to make sure you are not including sensitive information in your profile.

Then . . .

- Get connected with 50+ persons.
- Share information.
- List references.
- Obtain endorsements.
- Get referrals.
- Explore companies/jobs.
- Search for job leads.
- Post a resume.
- Demonstrate strengths.

Talent Finder

LinkedIn manages a program called "Talent Finder," which is used by companies to screen LinkedIn's database for suitable job candidates . . . using key words, not generalities.

There is no cost to you . . . another good reason to sign up!

The LinkedIn staff says that "Your profile is the front page of your story." Your profile should reflect those attributes/core skills that are most often identified with the position you are seeking. Pretend that ***you*** are writing the computer program that will be the vehicle used to screen thousands of resumes and profiles. Which attributes and job titles would ***you*** choose for the computer program to search? Discard those attributes that are not relevant. This is basically the same advice that you have read in the Resume Chapter. *Use appropriate* ***key words***! When recruiters scan the LinkedIn data base looking for people to fill jobs, they load the search program with key words. If your profile has the same key words, you are likely to get a call asking for additional information or possibly an interview. ***After reading your LinkedIn profile, the reader should be able to determine: your soft and hard skills, and the sector/industry and functional area you are interested in and qualified for***!

Note: There are many resume writing services on the internet . . . many specialize in assisting writing a LinkedIn profile. Check out www.theresumecenter.com. They charge about $104.00 and guarantee satisfaction. Call: 1-914-233-3337 for more information *(not an endorsement, just an example).*

Read: Social Media Networking For Dummies.

Facebook, of course is another well-known social media Website. Whereas LinkedIn is perhaps better known as a "professional" business tool, and, according to the Wall Street Journal, preferred by business men and women, Facebook tends to be more on the *lighter* side. However, I would strongly recommend posting your profile to Facebook as well as LinkedIn. Keep it professional! Unflattering material can come back to haunt you . . . once it's out there, it's out there. Another book you may find useful is, Social Media Marketing For Dummies.

If you are few years out from leaving service, these miracles of the World Wide Web can help you build a contact database, and can help you stay connected/reconnect with friends and associates who might be able to assist you in your job search. So, start building your contact base today! You simply can't have too many personal and professional contacts.

LinkedIn/Facebook ... Why?

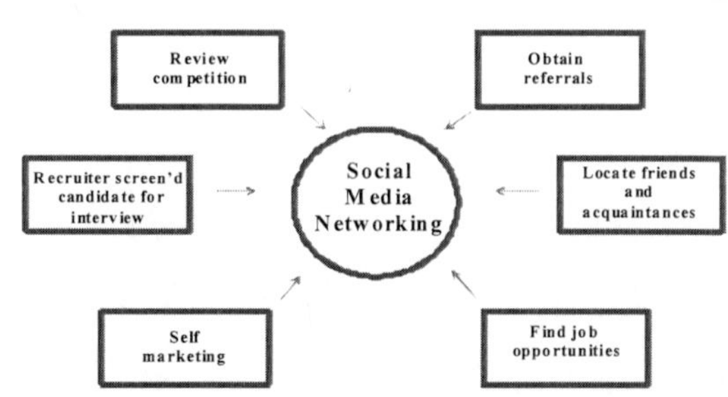

LinkedIn Etiquette
Check out http://topdogsocialmedia.com/linkedin-etiquette-infographic. This is a wonderful Website that, among other things, lists "20 LinkedIn Do's and Don'ts." In summary:

DO

- Personalize connection requests. Tell them your reason for connecting.
- Have a profile picture so people can see who they are dealing with . . . have the photo taken professionally if at all possible and in a square format. Ensure the photo makes you look ***serious*** but "approachable." Dress for the job you want; not for the job you have . . . that rules out the uniform in most cases.

Photograph or not?

on Linkedin resume and profile

Most pros say yes, but make it
professional photo
head shot
square format
business casual
coat and tie but no tuxedos

Conventional wisdom ... better with than without

- Try to Personalize your recommendation requests and offer to reciprocate.
- Turn off notifications when updating your profile.

> *"Make sure you incorporate a lot of key words for the kind of job you're looking for. As a recruiter, I run searches through LinkedIn and I look for the key requirements of [each available] job. I look for very specific skills, so have these in your profile."*
>
> *Cyndi Klein, Technical Recruiter*

- Keep it professional and only share information relevant to business.
- Send a nice welcome message that provides value.
- Regularly nurture relationships. ***Building relationships is not a numbers game***.
- Make your contact list open to your connections.
- Offer to introduce your connections to others in your network.
- Respond promptly to messages . . . 1 or 2 days.
- **Remember it's not about you . . . it's about them!**

> "LinkedIn profiles with professional photos are 11 times more likely to be viewed than those without."
>
> WSJ

DON'T

- Send *spammy* messages.
- Over post – once a day is good enough.
- Ask people you don't know for LinkedIn connections.
- Criticize or comment negatively.
- Post self-serving content in groups that holds no value to members.
- Send messages to multiple people without un-checking the option "Allow recipients to see each other's names and email addresses."
- Ask people to "like" your Face book page.
- Ask new connections or people that you don't know to endorse you.
- Send messages starting with "I see you have viewed my profile." It's creepy.
- Treat LinkedIn like Facebook or Twitter.
- Overuse words/phrases such as "extensive experience," "results oriented," "proven track record," "team player," "fast paced," "problem solver," "entrepreneurial," "innovative," "dynamic," "motivated" . . . you get the picture.

Networking . . . Is it Overrated?

"Unemployment is an emotional ***roller coaster****. Our employer loyalty, pride in our work is suddenly an issue when we've been terminated. Fact is, we've been rejected! Coupled with this rejection is fear. We see it in our spouse's eyes, face it when the house payment is due, and tremble each time we dip into our savings account. And then, somebody tells us the solution to all our problems is to go out in the marketplace, feeling like a beggar, and NETWORK!!! Selling ourselves when we've just faced a huge emotional trauma . . . loss of a job is second only to the loss of a loved one. Most people are not salesmen, and now we are suddenly confronted with trying to sell ourselves! Like it or not, this is the world today!"*

— William R. Thompson

CHAPTER 9

MARKETING

"The hard part will be the marketing."

Now that you have settled on an objective, written a resume and conducted the pertinent research, you are ready to begin the process of marketing yourself. Not before! Marketing yourself is much like marketing any product. In this case, you are the product! You need a plan, you need a Personal Executive Summary of your plan, and you need to know what the product is all about.

Understand that YOU are the Director of Marketing

Personal Executive Summary . . . you're not serious unless it is in writing! Break out your computer and take a few minutes to write a personal executive summary about yourself using the following as a guide. You will probably find that you don't know nearly as much about your objective as you thought you did. This is a great review to help you determine the holes and shortcomings, if any, in your plan.

- A breakdown of your target industry segments.
- A list of potential contacts.
- An assessment of your knowledge of the industry and your relevant strengths.
- Your plan to approach the hidden and visible job markets.
- A proactive strategy for approaching your job search campaign.
- An assessment of your financial resources.
- Your time management plan . . . how will you allocate your time.
- Your organizational management plan . . . staying in control.

And, Before You Begin, You must Know:

- Your objective.
- The company and industry.
- How you relate to the company/industry.
- Your accomplishments that are relevant to the company/ industry.
- How to verbalize your accomplishments and experiences.
- What you "bring to the table."

Gentle Reminder

Since ***everyone*** is a potential contact and referral source, it pays to be considerate of everyone . . . especially contractors.

Meetings, Telephone Calls and Letters

As you market yourself, you will be using several kinds of tools, namely, the telephone, letter writing, personal referrals, social media and face-to-face meetings . . . face-to-face is always best!

Meetings

Information/referral/networking meetings . . . the goal of these meetings is to introduce you to people in the industry, to learn more about what is happening in the industry and to get exposure. These are not job interviews . . . they are information gathering and sharing meetings.

Face to face is nearly always best ...

Screening meetings . . . a meeting usually conducted by someone in the Personnel Department (usually in response to a job posting) to determine if you meet the minimum qualifications.

Recruiter meetings . . . a face-to-face meeting with an agency or recruiter to discuss a job opportunity.

Job interviews . . . where the rubber meets the road. A meeting with one or more people from the functional manager's office. Sometimes it could be the personnel officer but normally it will be conducted by people that you will be working with or for.

Follow-on meetings . . . it is usual for a company to call a candidate back for one, two or more, follow-on interviews. These are just as important as the initial interview.

The Telephone

The telephone will be one of your most effective tools while searching for a job. It can also create a great deal of anxiety. Making a *cold* call (calling someone you do not know or do not have an introduction to through a referral) is one of the most difficult things that a professional salesperson must do. And for the senior government job hunter, it can be a traumatic experience. Just as a salesperson always tries to get a referral introduction to a potential client, you should work hard at getting a referral to the person you are trying to reach. It is always better to make the call saying that a good mutual friend (the referral) recommended that you call, rather than to try and explain why you selected the person's name out of the *telephone directory or LinkedIn* one afternoon when you had nothing better to do! You don't have to write a letter before you make the call, but if you do not have a referral, writing a letter can help. Your letter can introduce you and end with a comment that you will call for an appointment in a day or two. It is almost always better to do that than to make a flat-out cold call.

Telephone Protocol

- Be prepared
- Be pleasant
- Have an outline ready
- Have questions ready

There are some major advantages to using the telephone. For starters, it is faster and once you get the hang of it, more effective than letters. It can save you hours in doing the letter writing paperwork. You get a chance to talk with the person, before he or she has a chance to go over your paper credentials and decide that there is no job for you here. On the phone you come across as a real person rather than a piece of paper that can be tossed aside (that's the same reason that the face-to-face is the best of all forms of communication). On the phone, you can modify your approach as the conversation changes . . . with the letter, you are locked into what you have written. **Suggestion**: Stand up and smile when you talk and your voice will sound better!

Telephone Techniques

There are some good telephone techniques that will help you overcome any fears you may have and, at the same time, make you a more effective presenter:

✓ Be prepared. Know what you are going to say so that you appear businesslike. Write an outline of what you are going to say . . . have it in front of you when you place the call.

✓ Who are you . . . identify yourself . . . smile, you will sound better.

✓ How did you get the person's name?

✓ Ask if this is a good time to talk . . . smile!

✓ State the purpose of the call . . . what do you want and why are you calling.

✓ Make all of your calls at the same time . . . you eliminate start-up anxiety.

✓ Record some practice calls so that you can hear what you sound like.

✓ Practice first with close friends.

"Your call is important to me Mr. Buffet, but not as important as the call I have on call waiting."
Please don't do this!

✓ Your manner will determine how you are received . . . smile.

✓ If military, do not use your rank as part of your name when you introduce yourself. However, do use it when you explain that you are leaving active duty . . . if it seems prudent.

✓ You desire an information meeting, you don't expect a job.

✓ Mention times that you are available for a meeting . . . have a calendar handy.

✓ Thank the caller and confirm any arrangements that you have made.

✓ Keep a record of what, who, when, where, why and how.

✓ Build a relationship with the secretary.

✓ Call early in the morning or late at night to circumvent the temple guards.

✓ Remember, "persistence and determination are omnipotent."

✓ If cold calling is just not for you, **write** a letter or email first.

✓ If they are out, you call back. Don't leave a message asking them to call you back . . . it will save you waiting by the phone all day . . . and perhaps forever.

WebCam and Virtual Marketing/Meetings

Many companies are now hosting meetings, networking and interviewing via WebCams enabled by software systems such as Zoom, MS Teams, and WebEx. The COVID pandemic has pushed our economy towards WFH - Work From Home. So, similar to the discussion above about Telephones, you will need to be prepared to market yourself via video conferencing. Let me give you some tips on being prepared for WebCam meetups:

Tips for Using Video Conferencing

1. TEST TEST TEST – be sure you know how to use their video conferencing system. Check for browser compatibility – practice with your computers at home, with a friend, or with the help desk. Make sure your computer camera and microphone work well. Dig into the program and try all the "buttons" and functions before your meeting. Be ready to present documents via the conference platform, including your resume. Remember, companies are looking for Tech Savvy candidates – show them what you've got.

2. Attire/Background – Dress for Success; nuff said. Don't be in your pajamas and please wear pants!! Be careful about your lighting; make sure they can see your face; this may require some makeup; kidding … but maybe not. Also, check to make sure that your room is tidy and devoid of any items that may be embarrassing.

3. Alert the Family – There are plenty of epic Zoom Fails being posted on the Internet right now. Suffice it to say, make sure everyone in the family knows that you are going to be on an important call. Maybe put a "Busy" sign on your home office door. Don't forget your animals – be sure they are put in a quiet place, away from the camera and the postman.

Letter Writing: Cover, Approach, Thank you

Letter writing will be an important part of your campaign. Letters can set the stage for future meetings and of course are indispensable for long distance job hunting efforts. Since this may be the only impression that the reader will have of you, it is critical that letters are perfect in form and content.

Letters-Five Steps

1. **Plan it**
2. **Write it**
3. **Edit it**
4. **Edit it**
5. **Edit it**

Proof, proof, proof, prooooof !

A typical letter is composed of three paragraphs:

- ✓ An opening statement to get the reader's attention. If you are answering an ad, you should make reference to the newspaper, date and nature of the ad.
- ✓ A second paragraph which highlights your career, discusses your strengths and how your background is relevant to the reader's industry.
- ✓ The third paragraph should close with an action statement . . . that you will call the reader to set up an appointment or a number where you can be reached. It is almost always better to take the lead and say that you will initiate the call.

Note: As with all correspondence, the wise person asks another person to review what has been written.

Use Letters and email-if appropriate to:

- Ask for appointment.
- Respond to advertisements.
- Convey your thanks for a meeting.
- Sell yourself to potential employers.
- Follow-up with a contact.
- Follow-up to a meeting
- As a cover letter for a resume.
- Ask for information about a company.
- Correspond with a recruiter.
- Accept an offer or confirm the details of the offer.
- Present new facts thus providing the basis for another meeting.
- Delay accepting an offer while you consider other opportunities.

Write a thank-you letter after each meeting and nearly every telephone call. You will be unique, and you will be remembered. DO IT!

Your Email Address

Conservative - *recommended*:

Frank.Jones@yahoo.com
Mary.Smith@gmail.com

Wild - *not recommended*:

Red.Baron@tutifrutti.com
Lost.it@gmail.com
Ship.Ahoy@live.com
chopsticks@yahoo.com

It's a business address, make it professional!

Cover Letters

There was a time when you would never send a resume in response to an ad unless there was a cover letter attached, although some people did – obviously without thinking. The cover letter served two purposes . . . as a letter of transmittal and, second, to mention things about your professional background that did not appear in the resume. With the advent of the personal computer, a resume sent in response to an ad should be a "stand alone" document. It's just a matter of tweaking (targeting) the resume to fit the job description.

That said, **you still need a cover letter**, if for no other reason than to make you look professional, and to include some information about the ad and something pertinent about yourself that is in addition to the content of the resume. And, of course you can't just put your resume in an envelope and mail it – you need some kind of transmittal letter. The cover letter is also a way to demonstrate that you are an effective communicator . . . an attribute that all hiring managers are looking for. The cover letter should always contain:

- The date of the ad.
- The title of the job.
- Any identifying number or codes assigned to the ad.
- The name of the paper, website or journal where it appeared . . . (the company could have many ads running at the same time in different newspapers, journals and websites).

The cover letter should contain three sections: an *introduction, content, and closing*. With few exceptions, it should never be longer than one page. When writing the cover letter, use the same logic you use when you write a resume or prepare for an interview: (See example in this chapter)

- use ***key words***, specific to the industry
- use action verbs when describing qualifications
- if you cite an achievement, try to quantify it
- use bullets to highlight major points
- if responding to an ad or Web posting, show interest by asking for a meeting to further discuss your qualifications. Be careful not to duplicate information contained in the resume. Include your telephone number, e-mail address and LinkedIn profile.

Note: ***Key words*** are becoming more important than ever before as companies use computer software to screen resumes . . . for key words applicable to the needs of the position. As I said before, if your resume does not contain certain and relevant key words it won't even make it past the assistant mail-room clerk.

Email Correspondence

Email correspondence should be written as though you are writing a paper for a professor of English.

Avoid:
- jargon
- incomplete sentences

Check for:
- grammar
- misspelled words

Approach Letter for an Information Meeting

Date

Mr. Nelson Hendricks
President
Hanging In There Corporation
156 East Bay Street
Wherever, USA 12345

Dear Mr. Hendricks,

Your name was given to me by our good mutual friend, David Ruble, whom I know through my government/military service. Dave mentioned that he respects your knowledge of the XYZ industry and is impressed how you have built your business to be an industry leader.

Dave suggested that your thoughts and ideas would be helpful to me as I transition from the military service/government service to a civilian career. I am presently looking into several areas of the XYZ industry, one of which is information technology. Please be assured that I do not expect you to have or know of any specific position. My goal is to meet with you and discuss the field, and get some input from you as to what my opportunities might be in the industry.

My experience is in telecommunications and information technology. I am leaving government service as a ______ (optional) and have spent more than 18 years in management positions associated with those fields. One thing that I have done is design and implement a computer driven, cost account tracking system that increased productivity and decreased the cost account error rate by 28 percent.

I am looking forward to meeting with you and will call you next week to arrange a mutually agreeable time.

Sincerely,

Bob Milligan

NOTE: Use 24 pound bond letterhead. Include mailing address (home <u>or</u> business), telephone number (home <u>and</u> cell), and e-mail address (if applicable).

Letter Response to an Advertisement/Cover Letter

Date

Mr. Mark Flaherty
Director, Financial Services
Dowe-Cheatem-And Howe
1457 India Street
San Diego, CA 12345

Dear Mr. Flaherty,

I am responding to your advertisement for a controller which appeared in the Washington Post on January 15, 20__. As the following shows, my experience and background match well with your requirements.

YOUR REQUIREMENTS	MY QUALIFICATIONS
Ten years of financial management experience	17 years in-depth experience in every aspect of financial management. Designed management systems and reduced costs. Administered groups ranging from 17 to 135 personnel.
Knowledge of accounting and financial management	Hands-on experience in all phases of financial management and accounting. This includes generating input and analyzing output. Trained accounting staff. CPA credential.
Strong leadership and communication strengths	Proven stand-up presenter and strong writing strengths. Designed new operational procedures and internal financial management books.

I will call you in a few days for an opportunity to discuss the position for a Controller with you.

Sincerely,

Dave Grundies

Dave Grundies

NOTE: This same format is useful when preparing for an interview. List the requirements for the job in the left column, and an example of a personal accomplishment in the right column. It is a wonderful exercise. Use 24 pound bond letterhead. Include mailing address (home or business), telephone number (home and cell), and e-mail address (if applicable).

Thank You Letter

Date

Mr. Mark Flaherty
General Manager
Paramount INC.
3456 Utah Street
Blissful, Maine 12334

Dear Mr. Flaherty,

Thank you for taking time from your busy schedule to meet with me yesterday. It was a pleasure to talk with you. You assisted me greatly in seeing areas where I might fit in the computer industry.

I was particularly interested in your comments regarding the new technique for networking computer systems via satellite and appreciate having your insight into the benefits associated with the equipment.

Presently, I am in the process of contacting Jack Young and Dave Bunten as you suggested. Thank you for recommending them to me. I will be sure to let you know how my meetings with them turn out.

Thank you again for the assistance that you provided to me. I will keep you apprised of my progress.

Sincerely,

Steve Bristow

Steve Bristow

Some people scoff at thank-you letters . . . they just don't know any better!

NOTE: Use 24 pound bonds with a letterhead. Include mailing addresses (home <u>or</u> business), telephone number (home <u>and</u> business), a cell phone number and e-mail address.

Telephone Planning Log

TELEPHONE NO. ____________________ DATE ______________ TIME ___________

NAME ______________________________ TITLE ______________________________

COMPANY: ____

ADDRESS: ____

____

____

SECRETARY _________________________ OTHER NAMES _________________________

____

REFERENCE MATERIAL NEEDED: ____

____

OBJECTIVE OF THE CALL: ____

____

____

REFERRAL: ____

____

OPENING STATEMENT: ____

____

____

____

QUESTIONS: ____

____

____

CONFIRM/CLARIFY INFORMATION OR NEXT STEPS: ____________________________

____

CLOSE/THANKS: ____

The Dinner Meeting Story . . . or, "Don't blow off your dinner partner"

"When a friend was about six months away from retirement his boss asked him to represent him at a Navy League dinner meeting. He was living in Boston and the meeting was in DC so his spouse opted to stay home . . . where he really wanted to be . . . so he attended the party alone. When he arrived he found that he was seated at one of the sponsor's tables next to a matronly "older" woman and her pouchy husband. That was 10 years ago - today he would describe the woman as mature and attractive.

The speaker was nearly as boring as the table conversation and as he was about to excuse himself and head for home when the lady next to him said, "You must be a Navy boy because you are wearing a dark blue uniform." Then she asked him what he did in the Navy and after a long sigh he explained his job and that he was leaving active duty in a few months and going into the private sector with the idea of running a manufacturing company. He thought that would put an end to the non-productive conversation but instead she pushed her chair back and turned to her husband and said, "Frank, you should talk to this Navy Boy . . . he has an interesting background. "Now you have done it" he said to himself, "Why didn't I just say that I was a party crasher and here for a free meal." At any rate, he repeated to her husband what he had said earlier and to his great surprise the husband said, "We can use people like you in our company." Turns out that her husband was the third senior executive in one of the country's largest IT manufacturing conglomerates and had about thirty companies reporting to him. He gave him his card and three names to call including the Chairman of the Board in downtown LA. That led to several meetings and one offer. He didn't take the offer but he learned a great lesson."

And what do you do? (The classic ice-breaker question.)

Lesson Learned:
You just never know who you are talking to or how they might be able to help you. **Communicate with everyone!**

Lunch or Dinner While Networking or Job Interviewing

Sometimes while looking for a job you will be invited to a lunch or dinner meeting. While this seems like a good idea, my recommendation is that you try to avoid meetings that entail food if at all possible. The problem is that if there is no other way to get together, the meal meeting is the only alternative.

The reasons that meal meetings are not recommended are several. You cannot talk with food in your mouth and more often than not, many people order something which is sloppy to eat and end up with some of it on their tie or jacket or blouse. That situation, however, is controllable – order manageable food!

What is not controllable is the well intended person who comes over to your table, just as you are making an important point, and breaks into the conversation to talk about last weekend's golf outing or some other personal event. If that occurs you will just have to roll with the punches. If the person is your friend, politely ask if you can call him/her later and continue the conversation. If it is your luncheon mate's friend you will just have to sit there while they finish their conversation. Either way it is disruptive. Be as it may, if you must have a luncheon meeting, there are some basic rules that I recommend you follow:

1. **At breakfast or lunch.**
Under no circumstances consume an alcoholic beverage! Make no excuses even if your host is having an alcoholic beverage. Simply say that you will have water or an ice tea or coffee. *Don't say that you have been on the wagon for the past six months and don't want to go back to your old ways*! The only exceptions to this rule is when you are being entertained in the company's cafeteria at an October festival luncheon and the Chairman of the Board offers you a stein of beer, or your host is a wine connoisseur and has ordered a 200 year old bottle of Chateauneuf-du-Pape. Other than that – avoid alcohol.

The Business Lunch
No mess, no booze, no smoke . . . be civil to help

2. **At dinner.**
You are not required to have an alcoholic beverage but if you want one then order <u>one</u> drink **or** have <u>one</u> glass of wine with your meal. Please do not order a drink with a colorful umbrella or a piece of fruit sticking out of the glass or any other exotic concoction designed to be consumed at a beach bar on Waikiki. If the host is not drinking an alcoholic beverage then skip one yourself and order ice tea or some other non-alcoholic beverage. You do not have to apologize for not ordering an alcoholic drink!

Why no booze! First of all it might be a test. Some companies are leery of people who drink during the day or too much in the evening, so the drink offer might just be a character test. But a better reason is that alcohol can loosen your tongue and cause you to say things that would have better gone unsaid. So the conservative approach is to simply avoid alcohol and play it safe.

Be civil to the restaurant employees. Many employers judge job candidates by how they treat the *hired help* . . . the waiters. It can be an indicator of how you might treat employees at their company if you are selected for the job.

<u>Finally, above all do not order the most expensive item on the menu. Regardless what the others might select, you order something priced conservative . . . mid-range.</u>

You Must Know!

- Your objective
- The **<u>company</u>**/industry info
- How you relate
- Your relevant accomplishments
- How to verbalize
- What you bring to the table

It's all in the preparation!

CHAPTER 10

ATTIRE

The old saying, *"**You never get a second chance to make a good first impression**"* couldn't be more applicable than for people who are networking and job interviewing. While dress most certainly isn't the final determining factor in hiring, it plays a big part in answering the "Would this person fit into our organization?" question . . . ***reread; can do, will do and fit explanation***.

Dress the part ...

"You never get second chance to make a good first impression."

In General ... your goal is to be taken seriously.

When it comes to advising people on what to wear when looking for a job, be it a job fair, networking or interviewing, conservatism reigns supreme. Most managers in major corporations dress conservatively and most expect their personnel to do likewise. Obviously, there are many exceptions to that rule . . . hi-tech company computer programmers and research lab technicians being the most obvious, wearing pony tails, tank tops, earrings, Fu-Man-Chu goatees and the like. You might get away with dressing down for an interview if you were Bill Gates, but other than that, most management personnel in the public eye dress conservatively. If you own your own business and work out of your home, you can wear most anything or nothing for that matter. But, when you leave home to market your products most of us must conform to what is accepted in the marketplace . . . like it or not. ***If you dress inappropriately for the occasion, no one will take you serious.***

> **Wall Street Journal**
> *on corporate attire*
> **"Clothes generally won't be the determining factor in whether a person moves up the corporate ladder - but the company does look at it as a sign of emotional intelligence. Conventional career wisdom holds that dressing like the boss helps advance one's career."**

There has been a lot in the news about the Friday casual dress down day, or about some companies that say, casual is okay most anytime. Don't believe it! Before you show up for a job interview in a tank top and flip flops, check the building out and see if anyone else is dressed the same way. And, even if they are, you should show up looking your very best.

There are some obvious don'ts . . . don't wear a clip-on tie . . . if you do, it will knock at least $10,000 off your starting salary; don't wear three earrings in each ear; don't wear any clothing that dates you . . . like the suit and ties or dresses you bought ten years ago but never wore out. Don't wear a sport coat unless the position is a casual one and you don't want to impress anyone; don't cut your hair so short that you look like G.I. Joe undergoing basic training. Remember, the idea is to *blend in.* After you have the job, you can wear anything you want, although if you like working there, you will probably want to dress like the senior company officials . . . *especially if you ever want to be one.*

> **Attire**
> When networking: conservative
> When interviewing: conservative
> When hired: check out the boss

Whether you are a man or a woman, the most impressive dress for interviewing or networking is usually a nice conservative suit. And, the most important aspect of those suits is that they fit you. Cheap suits usually don't fit very well. If you tell me that you don't want to spend the money to outfit yourself with well fitting clothes and this year's style necktie, then you are missing the whole idea. And, in the long run, the money you spend will be the best investment you could make. The bad news is that while it can be expensive for men, it is *very* expensive for women. Once again, the payback is worth the investment! JUST DO IT!

Men's Attire

There are no hard and fixed rules governing what to wear while in a job search posture except to look neat and clean whenever you are meeting with a prospective employer. We believe that it pays to be on the conservative side, meaning suits and ties, unless you know that the office dress is extremely casual and that you would definitely be out of place if you showed up in your believable blue suit and "power" tie. There are organizations where the employees work in cutoffs and wear flip-flop shoes. However, the vast majority of organizations resemble what you see walking down the city streets of America every workday . . . a suit and tie or a conservative sport coat and tie. If in doubt, always wear a suit. Our recommendation is to err on the conservative side and we suggest that you dress accordingly whenever you are in public . . . except of course if you are at the beach or on a golf course. It's your call. Therefore, for men:

Suits

The most important aspect about a suit is that it fits you properly and was not manufactured in the roaring twenties. There are many great looking suits in the marketplace that look good on a mannequin, but hang like a sack when you put them on. I recommend that, when looking for a job, you wear a suit whenever in a public place . . . other than the beach or a family picnic. Styles do change, so be on the lookout for what people are wearing in different parts of the country and in different industries. Cuffs on pants are also the "in" thing. Cuffs tend to make a short person look somewhat shorter, so you will have to consider your physical characteristics as you plan your wardrobe . . . all said, I would still cuff my pants. A small break in the cuff is desirable . . . no one wants to see your *white* socks showing between your pants and shoes! If in doubt, wear cuffs! Besides cuffs could catch any loose change that you might drop! (Just kidding about the white socks!) Seriously, cuffs add a little weight to the bottom of the pant legs and keep them from flopping around so much.

Second to fit is style. Only wear a suit that is in style. That means the correct lapel width for this year, the correct number of buttons and perhaps the width of the shoulders. Two and three-button suits are both in style as I write on this subject but two-button suits have made a strong comeback. If you wear a three-button suit, you should be in great physical condition – tall and **slim** . . . three-buttons and pouchy don't go together. A Brook's Brothers salesman recently told me that he would not recommend a three-button suit to anyone overweight or anyone who had a chubby face. Any good retail store will carry this year's style suit. I also recommend a natural fiber, like wool. Many people are wearing year-around wool materials . . . somewhat lighter in weight than the heavy winter wool and very comfortable. Look around and see what the typical, downtown businessman is wearing. *Leather fight jackets are not recommended unless they are well-worn, covered with bright and colorful squadron patches, and have tattered sleeves.*

Dark colored suits are more acceptable for job hunting than lighter ones. We recommend dark blue or dark grey . . . not charcoal grey, and not black. A blue or grey suit is acceptable everywhere and goes well with white and blue shirts. The idea is to keep it simple. Brown is not recommended for job hunting. A thin pin stripe in the material is fine but not the broad 1/4" white stripes on black suits that was popular in the late 1920's.

Most people do not wear vests or braces/suspenders. You need at least two nice suits to job hunt . . . more after landing your job. **Tip**: dry-clean suit jackets as little as possible . . . brush them instead. Dry-cleaning tends to break down the fabric backing, and eventually the suit will not hold its shape and you will look like one of the Marx Brothers.

How Much?

If you can find a great suit that fits you well for free, go for it. The chances are however, that you will have to pay for a good one. Most decent suits range in cost from four hundred dollars to many thousands. I cannot tell you how much to spend . . . just that the suit must fit you and should be of a quality that will last for more than one wearing. If I had to pick an average dollar range for suits, it would be between four and eight hundred dollars. Many high end retail stores, like Nordstrom and Brooks Brothers, have sales once or twice a year and they are good opportunities to get quality at a more reasonable price. Some Brooks Brothers stores give military personnel a substantial discount; ask for it. I believe Brooks Brothers has the best all-around quality for men's clothing. Don't overlook The Men's Warehouse and Jos A. Bank. They have perfectly acceptable quality suits, and you can usually catch a great sale.

Shirts

We recommend that you wear a light blue (light oxford blue) or a white, button-down or straight collar shirt. Other colors may be okay, but you will always be safe with white and oxford blue colors. And, both go with dark blue and gray color suits. Straight pin-point collars are okay, but you will feel more like a business person if you wear a button-down collar. I prefer a combination cotton and synthetic material because it doesn't wrinkle as much as a 100 percent cotton shirt. It is your call. A fairly recent development in the shirt business is a new near-wrinkle-free, no-iron shirt with something called a TAL treatment. They have been nicknamed Botox-for-Broadcloth and are available at Brooks Brothers, Nordstrom, Dillards, JC Penny and Jos. A. Bank for $50-70. A common mistake when buying a shirt is getting the wrong sleeve length. Get the sleeve length that is correct for you . . . 34" length instead of a 33/34" *mixed* length. If you do buy a *mixed* length, try it on before you take it home! Watch out for the shirts that have a white collar and a colored body. When I see them I always think that the person took two worn-out shirts and made one good one. How much for a shirt? . . . $40 - $65 for a decent shirt at a military PX . . . $80 - $100 at Nordstrom and other expensive department stores. *A note on collar style: If you have a chubby face, go for a wide collar. If you have a very narrow face go for a narrow collar.*

Shoes

There are many styles of shoes on the market but the most acceptable for job hunting are black or cordovan color and wingtip or oxford design. A plain toe civilian shoe is okay but you will feel better with the wingtip or cap-toe. Some people like wearing loafer style shoes, but they are somewhat informal for job hunting. If you insist on loafers, make sure that you take the pennies out of the shoes before the interview. Shoes with laces are preferred. Brown shoes are OK, but I prefer black or cordovan for job hunting . . . especially if it is a formal meeting or ir if the meeting takes place in the evening. If in doubt, wear black shoes with laces. And what can I say about tassels? Promise me that you will not wear your Exchange-bought, high-gloss military shoes. How much for shoes? Buy the most expensive shoes that you can afford. A good pair of shoes will last you the rest of your working life and your feet will love you for it!

Ties

Whatever you do, make sure your tie is made of silk – never polyester – is conservative in design, and the width commensurate with the today's style. We do not recommend bow ties or special effect ties like fish, dogs, golf clubs, red peppers or military aircraft. There are many tie designs that are acceptable including: regimental, club, paisley. A good place to see these styles is in a Brooks Brothers catalog. Jos. A. Bank usually has a good selection at reasonable prices. Another option is to visit the Nordstrom Men's Department. Some of Nordstrom ties are horribly expensive, but at least you can see what's "in." Remember, neckties come in different lengths and widths . . . get the length and width that's right for you and in style. Why do ties come in different designs and widths? Because the retailers want to sell more ties and we are dumb enough to go along! Ties should just cover the belt buckle; no shirt should show between the belt and the end of the tie. Recently, I have seen some people wearing their ties hanging three or four inches below the belt. When I see this, I always wonder if their pant's zipper is stuck. The large part of the tie (the yoke) should be longer than the narrow part . . . (the tail). It's not fair to tuck it in your shirt or in the front of your pants. If it is too long . . . re-tie it! Knots should be on the small side and should complement the width of the shirt collar . . . the wider the collar the larger the knot and vise-versa. Try to put a *dimple* in the knot . . . takes a little time and practice but looks nicer and more professional. You can buy a cheap tie for $5 but, in the long run, you will be happier with a tie that costs $30 to $40 to $50, or more! **Please, please, please no clip-on ties and no tie-tacs** – they are passé, for now. Width - 3" to 3 1/4". Lastly, be careful of "fad" colors. The tie manufacturers introduce new colors and styles and different widths to sell more ties, not to make you look any better . . . e.g., the purple ties being worn some newscasters and politicians who want to appeal to the younger generation. Note that there has been a recent trend to wear very narrow ties . . . about 2 inches wide ... especially among the young, avant guard, GQ Magazine age group. Don't do it! Recently some men's stores have been pushing the "old fashion" double knit, solid color ties . . . about two inches wide. Maybe okay for a sport coat but I'd hold off wearing with a suit . . . for now, at least.

Please . . . no clip-on or bow ties!

These designs are **acceptable**

Paisley

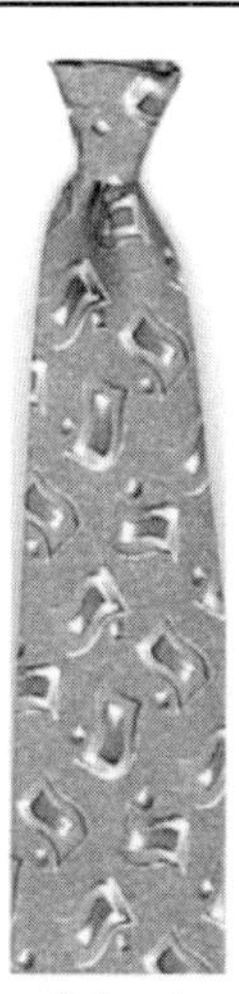
Patterned

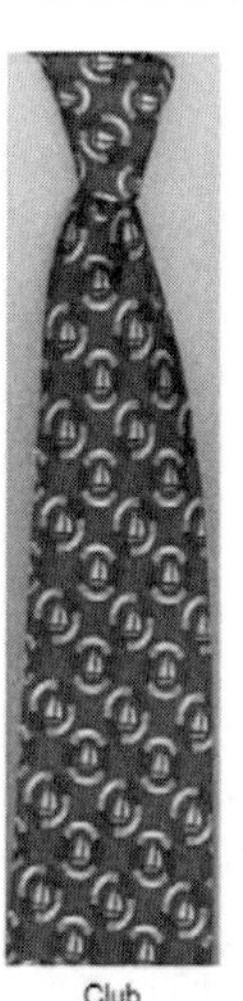
Club

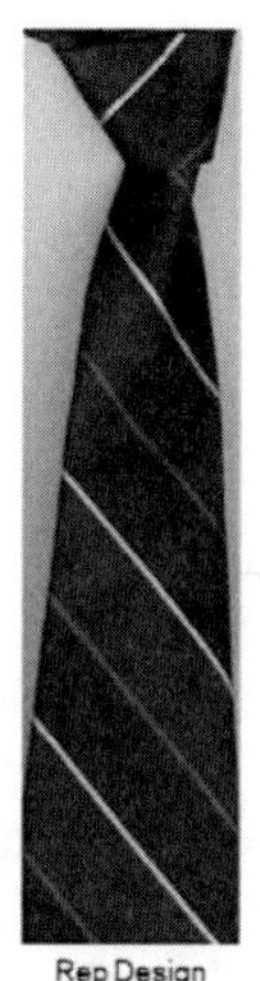
Rep Design

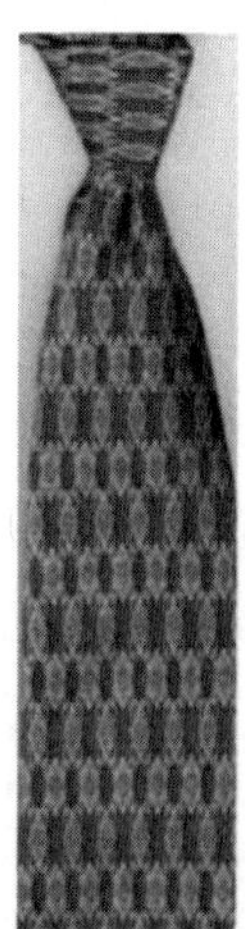
Horizontal

Wear one of these designs if you **never want to work again**!

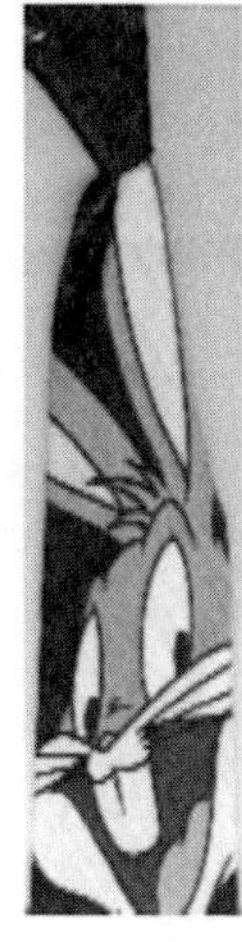

Belts
Your belt color should match the color of your shoes. Buy good quality leather belts and they will look better and last longer. No motorcycle or eighteen wheeler buckles! Coach company makes a leather belt that will last for a lifetime and they are sold at some government exchanges. For future planning purposes, buy a belt an inch or two longer than you presently require . . . you will be glad you did.

Socks
Socks should be darker than your pants and over-the-calf/knee length, unless you shave your legs. No one wants to see a big hairy leg hanging out of your pant leg. If you have a blue and a gray suit, all you will need are dark-blue socks. No school colors or argyles.

Accessories
The short answer is none . . . no tie-tack, no lapel pin, no handkerchief in the pocket. While these things are attractive and interesting to look at, they can be distracting in a meeting. The interviewer is more interested in what you have to say than in a fancy tie-tac. And, if you are military and want to wear medals, wear small medals. *Call me if you think I am serious about this last item!* Finally, please ... no pocket protectors unless you are wearing a slide rule . . . *this is not a baseball term.*

Glasses
We recommend that you wear good civilian business frames, and certainly not the service's "birth control" frames. Avoid wearing sunglasses and the lenses that darken outside and lighten up when inside. Dark lenses make you look suspicious . . . like you just got out of jail!

Braces (suspenders)
Most businessmen don't wear them . . . and never with a belt. If you research the industry or company and learn that they are wearing them, then go ahead if you have the desire. Otherwise we suggest that you stick with a belt.

Lotions . . . None!
This is not the time to improve the way you smell! While many people wear after shave lotions, many others are offended with the smell. Avoid them! Do wear a moisturizer like Lubriderm or another high quality moisturizer.

Watches
Wear a conservative watch. Leather bands are nice but not required. Some people wear large watches that tell you everything except what you are having for dinner. Other people think that these large watches are unprofessional. Some people are also offended by people who wear very expensive watches . . . like a fancy $20,000 gold and diamond Rolex . . . I like them to look at, but some people think they are pretentious. **Some executives think that people *who do not wear a watch* are not professional because it sends a signal that they are not concerned with the value of time and that time is money**. I wear a watch from morning to night but often check the time on my cell phone. Go figure. Wear a conservative watch . . . no Disney characters indicating the hour and minute. If the diameter is more than an inch and a half it is too wide. Note that once you get the job you can wear anything you like.

Raincoats
This is an easy call. The classic dark blue or khaki single-breasted raincoat with the removable liner is perfectly acceptable and the price is right. Some of the "big city" types are wearing the double-breasted coats . . . see Humphrey Bogart in Casablanca . . . but the majority of business people keep it simple. Hopefully you won't be conducting an interview in the rain so the raincoat is not much of a big deal! This is good advice for both men and women.

Hair Length, Beards and Mustaches
Most military members keep their hair short as compared to private sector business people. Civil service hair length is usually okay. ***Most senior people in the corporate private sector are clean shaven . . . no beards and not many mustaches***. Be careful of the fad style of looking like you haven't shaved for a week – and have the "bushy" look. ***That might be OK for a 25 year old but most of those reading this book are further along than that . . . don't be a lemming.*** Give some thought to looking "just like them" at least until you are hired. One thing to consider if you are on the "a little older" side, is to shave the beard/mustache to make you look younger. White hair in beards and mustaches make you look ten years older. If you are a little light on top-balding, you might consider a toupee but we do not recommend it . . . with the exception of the guy below! ***Once you are hired, wear and look as you please, and/or can get away with.***

When in doubt conservative reigns

The "half-shaven" craze that some men are sporting is not recommended when job hunting.

One last comment on appearance. While women usually take great care of themselves, many men, especially as they grow older, have a tendency to let things go to pot – both figuratively and literally. You should take special note of your fingernails, complexion, and, most notably, eyebrow, ear, and nostril hair. Keep it where it belongs – properly trimmed or out of sight! See *Habits I Wish I Didn't Have* at the end of this chapter. A good skin cream like Neutrogena (SPF 30) will help keep your skin looking fresh and healthy.

Women's Attire

The rules for women's attire are similar to men's. **Conservatism is the key.** Most women pay better and more attention to their attire than do most men. If you are uncertain about what people are wearing, a visit to a nice women's clothing store in your locale (like Nordstrom) can be of assistance. Many of the women news commentators dress very well and have a distinct professional look.

More variety and more costly!

Suits

Suits are appropriate for any business meeting. They should be conservative in style and in neutral colors such as navy, gray, and black. Like men's clothing, they should be in the current year's style. The length of the skirt is hard to comment on because it changes too frequently. Just not so high that you look like a high school girl, and not so long that you look frumpy. About knee length seems right. Suits with pants are becoming more and more popular and are fine but you will always be safe with a skirt. ***Perhaps the decision maker would be to wear whatever you look best in . . . be it skirt or pants.***

Blouses

Blouses should be silk or cotton and in flattering but conservative colors.

Shoes

As with suits and blouses conservative is the word here. Leather pumps, a classic style with a medium heel are good for most business occasions. Do not wear the trendy block-high heel that some people refer to as lumberjack footwear. And no extreme pointy toes or heels more than two inches high.

Belts

Should be leather and should match your shoes and handbag.

Handbag

Should match your shoes and belt. Carry a handbag or portfolio but NOT both. I suggest the portfolio or thin briefcase over a purse.

Jewelry

Keep it simple . . . gold, silver, pearls. No dangling earrings. It's faddish these days to wear a ring on each finger. Wear only two max . . . one on each hand.

Perfume

Either none or very light . . . **recommendation: none**.

Hosiery

Neutral color. Carry an extra pair of hose . . . just in case! Bare legs are a bit casual, especially at the more senior level. Note: The basic rule is, wear what makes you look the most professional.

Hair

Styled, shoulder length or shorter or whatever the length in style for your age group.

Makeup

Wear it, but as natural as possible. *As a general rule, less makeup is better than more.*

Lipstick
Keep it very conservative . . . stay away from blood red.

Glasses
No dark rims, no sunglasses.

Earrings
One in each ear. Keep them simple and appropriate for the attire. But wear them.

Finger Nail Polish
No flashy reds, greens, blues or purples . . . no colors! No sparkles or little faces on the nails. Keep it simple. Recommend a clear finish/natural buffed and well manicured, of course.

Hint
There are more and more executive women in the business marketplace these days and you may want to observe their attire. Most good clothing stores will be able to offer suggestions as to what the successful businesswomen are wearing in your area. Nordstrom, for men and women, is always a resource for advice and ideas. If you shop there or at a first rate store like it for clothes, however, select a "mature" salesperson who will understand your purpose. Above all, dress conservatively and in this year's style!

Note . . . for Both Women and Men

The idea is to look successful. To *blend in* with the company you are meeting with. For ideas on how they dress at a particular company, ask someone who works there . . . look at what the Board of Directors are wearing in the Annual Report, or walk in their lobbies and see first hand. Observe what well-dressed executives are wearing on television . . . in Fortune magazine . . . in Business Week and the company's social media site. Again, scout out what people are wearing in the organization. Would you report to a new military assignment in other than your best attire? A good-looking suit is always acceptable in a business setting . . . for any level or position, for men or women. ***For men, a sport coat is for "light weights."*** On the other hand, if you are applying for a construction job, management or otherwise, show up in whatever is appropriate for that occupation. Along that same vein, if you have an imposing personality, consider wearing the classic gray suit with a light blue shirt; and, if you are a bit shy, wear a dark blue suit with a white shirt, and a tie with shades of dark red. The former will tend to soften your bearing and the latter will tend to enhance it. In any event, your dress should demonstrate that you are serious about your career.

The goal is to look successful!

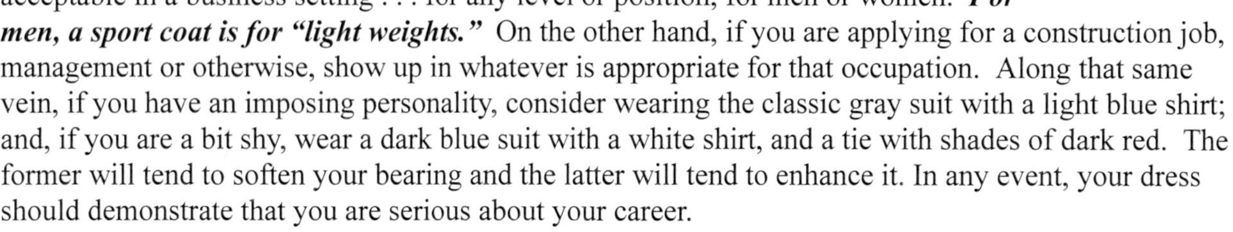

Finally, make it your goal to dress one level higher than the level of the job you are going after, but not better than your boss or the Chairman of the Board.

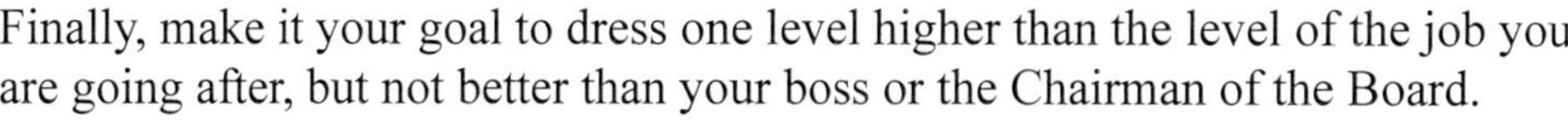

Habits and/or Characteristics I Wish I Didn't Have

We all have some undesirable habits or characteristics and would give anything to be rid of them. And, unfortunately, some of us do not realize we have bad habits, traits, or gestures, so someone must remind us that many of these habits can be annoying, especially during a networking meeting, let alone during a job interview.

Some of the more common bad habits we have observed over the years are as follows:

The eyebrow discovery!
Mostly applies to men who have a nervous habit of playing with their eyebrows while in the midst of a conversation. They just can't keep their fingers out of their eyebrows. I am sure that there is a prize or something special in there somewhere, but for the life of me, I have not been able to find anything worthwhile or at least what I would want to tell you about.

Smoke gets in your eyes!
Grownups are doing better and better with this one. You should never smoke at a networking meeting or job interview. Many companies have unwritten rules about not hiring smokers and nearly all have rules about not smoking in their office buildings and/or with clients. Some of this is driven by the fact that smoking bothers others but also because of the medical implications. Smokers are not as healthy as non-smokers on the average and companies don't want to risk the medical costs that might be associated with the habit. 'Nuff said!

Messing with the hair trick!
Almost always applies to women . . . who play with it. All it really entails is taking some strands of hair and slowly twisting them while pulling them away from the head – and when they have reached their maximum extension, letting go, so the curled hair suddenly springs back to the head. I watched my daughter perform this trick with great fascination when she was younger and even asked her where she learned how to do it. Her answer was that it just came naturally! This is a bad habit because it is distracting, and you will find the other person more engrossed with the hair manipulation than in what you are saying.

Eyebrows gone mad!
This is an event that is usually associated with men as they grow older and has to do with their eyebrows growing long and gnarly. We have all seen what I am talking about – more hair growing out of the eyebrows than out of the head. In case you didn't know, the eyebrows on the right side of the head are supposed to grow to the right and those on the left to the left. Most barbers will trim eyebrows if you ask them to and some trim them without your asking – when they do it without your asking you know you are long overdue.

Talking through your knuckle!
If you have a habit of talking through your hand or knuckle you should realize that it is often hard for the other person to understand what you are saying. In a networking meeting or job interview, you will not *show* very well if you do this. The best guidance in this matter is to keep your hands off of your face – when speaking or listening.

I know what you are going to say!
Most of us who have been married to the same person for many years will sometimes anticipate what the other is going to say and answer their question or finish their sentence before they have completed it. While you might get away with these poor manners with your spouse – once in a while – it will not play well during a networking meeting or interview.

The return of the Wolfman!
I have a friend who has blond hair. While he is very well groomed and a great dresser the hair in his ears grows fast and long, for whatever reason, and *hides* in the folds of his ears. There is nothing wrong

with this happening except if he is standing in front of a bright light and there is any static in the room, the hair springs out from the folds and he looks like the wolfman on his way to a meal. Your barber can assist in this case, as well.

The nose breathing dragon!

This is another male happening as they grow older (Maybe the same for women, but women tend to take better care of themselves throughout their lives). At any rate, as men grow older, one of two events take place: either the nose itself begins to shrink or the nostril hair begins to grow faster and longer (Might be a connection here with the eyebrows). To make matters worse, the nostril hair begins to turn gray as they age so you have the worst of all combinations. For those who do not understand human body mechanics, understand that the nostril hair is there to prevent things from flying up into the nose, not to reach out and catch things as they go flying by. Hopefully you get the picture and again, your barber can be of assistance if you are too timid or shaky to do it yourself.

Other shortcomings!

No doubt you have some other shortcomings and would like to have them identified. That being the case, I recommend that you ask your spouse or a good friend to sit down with you and be as candid as possible in describing any bad habits or characteristics you might have. You will probably have to provide several bottles of good wine to get things going, but it will be worth it. You might also think about setting a time limit. After all, there is a limit as to how much we really want to know about ourselves. Cheers!

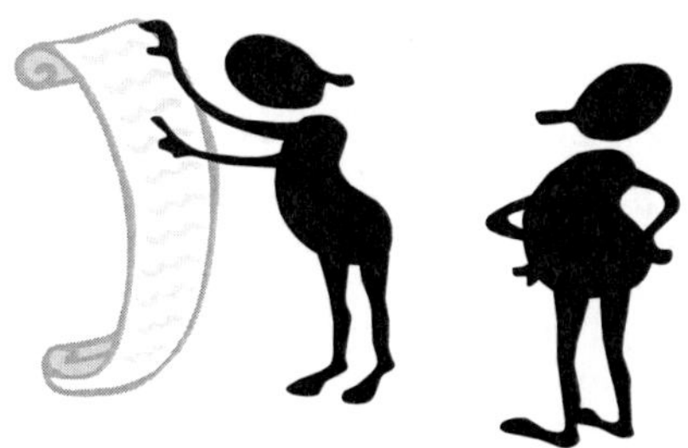

Ask a friend to identify your bad habits . . . but set a time limit!

Bad Habits . . .

✗ ____________________ ✗ ____________________

✗ ____________________ ✗ ____________________

✗ ____________________ ✗ ____________________

✗ ____________________ ✗ ____________________

✗ ____________________ ✗ ____________________

✗ ____________________ ✗ ____________________

✗ ____________________ ✗ ____________________

✗ ____________________ ✗ ____________________

✗ ____________________ ✗ ____________________

✗ ____________________ ✗ ____________________

✗ ____________________ ✗ ____________________

✗ ____________________ ✗ ____________________

✗ ____________________ ✗ ____________________

✗ ____________________ ✗ ____________________

Takeaway

for men and women

- ★ Conservative is the word . . . ***no extremes***!
- ★ Check out business attire . . . ***stay current*** . . . examples:

    - ♦ Professionals in the business district
    - ♦ Department stores . . . *Nordstrom, Brooks Brothers, etc.*
    - ♦ Business magazines
    - ♦ Senior industry leaders on TV

The idea is to blend in . . . but it's a moving target!

CHAPTER 11

THE INFORMATION MEETING

. . . referral - information - networking . . .

How to Use Your Contacts/Network

Once you have determined your objective, written your resume, developed an initial networking/contact list and have selected your target companies, you are ready to begin networking. Rule one, and never to forget is: **Never, Never, Never** ask or hint of asking for a job during a networking meeting (commonly referred to as an information and referral meeting). The idea is to meet with a contact who can share information about the industry that you have targeted. The processfor setting up and conducting an information meeting is as follows:

When you arrive . . .
"Decompress" the meeting

"As I mentioned on the telephone (in my letter), I'm not here to ask you for a job . . . (I don't even expect you to know of any openings) I am here to ask you about the _____ industry."

It will put everyone at ease . . . mention the referral!

First - Write or telephone (I prefer the telephone) your contact and say that you are calling at the suggestion of your mutual friend or referral and that you would like to have 20 minutes of their time to discuss the (*fill in the blank*) industry. At this point, ***the contact's primary concern may be that your intention is to come in and ask for a job***. You can defuse this concern ... this tension by telling them that you are looking for industry information only and to rest assured that your purpose is only that . . . and not to ask for a job. While this may seem a bit corny, the "I'm not going to *ask* you for a job" comment will allow the conversation to go more smoothly. Otherwise, your contact will be waiting for *the other shoe to drop*. You both know you are looking for a job, just not asking! The operative words here are ***not asking.*** Schedule no more than two or three meetings a day and allow sufficient time in between them. You never know when twenty minutes will lead to two hours . . . a green light. Be prepared for a telephone meeting.

Introduction Protocol

All else being equal . . . by first name!

Personal note: *I am forever receiving telephone calls from people whom I have never met asking if they could interview with me for a job as an instructor in my company. Since I don't need any more instructors I politely thank them for their interest but "No thanks." I am no different than the many business people I know who do the same thing. If however, a person calls me and says that a mutual acquaintance suggested that I be contacted to discuss the career transition environment in the San Diego area and, only needs about 20 minutes of my time and, say that they do not intend to ask me for a job, they have a pretty good chance that I will meet with them. This assumes of course that their referral is someone I know and respect.*

Second - Dressed in your finest, show up 10-15 minutes early for the meeting and introduce yourself to the secretary or *administrative/executive assistant*, as many secretaries now days prefer to be called. If the secretary was instrumental in getting you on the calendar, thank him or her accordingly. Be nice to everyone!

Third - The first two minutes of an information meeting (and interview/s) are most important. As they say, "first impressions are hard to change." When you meet the contact, introduce yourself, give a firm handshake (don't pump, but no dead fish shakes either), mention the referral's name, thank him/her for their time, and remind them that, as you mentioned on the telephone, you are not there to ask for a job but to gather information. If you are offered a refreshment, (see story below) our recommendation is that you politely turn it down with a simple "no thank you." The last thing that you want to do is spill your coffee all over the poor fellow's new computer, let alone all over yourself! Ask permission to take notes . . . offer your business card. More than likely you will be offered a business card . . . if not, politely ask for one.

No "fish" handshakes

"Coffee Goes Right Through Me"

When you go for a networking meeting or job interview your host will often ask if you would like a cup of coffee or something else to drink. One of the most unusual responses I had was from a young man who was interested in banking and came to see me to get some "industry"information.

Careful with the drinks!

As we were walking into my office, I offered the young man a cup of coffee. Instead of simply declining it by saying no thank you, he slumped forward, in a crouch, his hands covering his lower stomach, and said, "No thank you, it goes right through me." I tried not to laugh but my secretary, who was there to get the order, nearly fell down with laughter. There is no requirement to give anybody personal body signals in response to a refreshment offer, a simple "no thank you" will suffice.

Once again, I recommend that, until you are very confident in yourself and have had several networking meetings, you decline the offer of refreshments.

Fourth - Now you are in the person's office. Start with some icebreaker conversation but don't spend too much time on that subject. Remember that you only have 20 minutes and your purpose is to get information, give information, get to know the contact, get some referrals, and have the contact get to know you. As in the case of the resume, keep the information relevant to your reason for being there. At this point you will probably be asked, "Tell me about yourself" or "How can I help you?" or "What can I do for you?" These are the most common ice breaker questions asked. You respond with the core Two-Minute Opener statement, tailored to fit the question. See the Two-Minute Opener section the "Sound Bites" chapter.

Fifth - The next period should be spent discussing the industry (and the company <u>if</u> they give you the opportunity). **You want to know what is going on in the industry (before you get there) and how your strengths might fit. You should have at least six or more thoughtful questions prepared to ask.** You will want to make sure that you connect with the contact by referring to your background experiences and how they relate to the industry. Once again, don't forget to ask permission to take notes . . . and do take notes! You will weave key words applicable to the industry in your discussion.

Sixth - At the end of 20 minutes, or an agreed upon period, thank the contact for his or her time and the information you received and prepare to leave. Ask if there are others (you are asking for referrals) in the industry or a related industry that you should meet and talk to. Tell the contact that you will keep them apprised of your progress and how the meetings with the referrals go. Unless the contact insists that you stay, you should be on your way.

What to say if they ask you if you have questions to ask about <u>their</u> company? Lucky you! They have just opened the door for you to ask questions abut their company. Before, you were constrained to asking questions about the <u>industry</u> only. Have 6-8 great, well thought-out questions to ask. Have the questions ready in your notebook.

What to say if asked to stay a little longer? On occasion you might be asked to "stay a little longer" because the person is enjoying the conversation. So, what to do? It is a situational decision – if you think the person is asking you only out of courtesy, then a polite reply "That you have taken enough time already, but thank you," is fitting. However, if the person insists and/or there has been great chemistry between you, then stay on. I can't tell you how to decide – trust your senses.

What do you say if the person says they are having lunch with two other company officers and invites you to join them? You should very graciously accept the invitation and go have lunch – unless your spouse is waiting for you in a parked car on a hot sunny day somewhere! They may just be looking for a fourth for bridge, but, more likely, the person thinks you have your act together and wants to show you to other senior people in the company. This is a green light in terms of interest! You will be glad you did your research!

"How about lunch? Who pays?

What do you say if the person says something like "I have enjoyed our conversation and I think that we have a great opportunity right here at our company so why look further?" You might respond with something like, "Well I didn't come here expecting there would be an opportunity/opening here (assuming that is the case) but I would most certainly like to explore possibilities. When researching the industry I also researched your company and am impressed by many of the things you are doing." In this case the person has turned a networking meeting into a job interview. Be prepared! It will only happen a small percentage of the time, but it will happen.

Seventh. Thank the secretary again, leave a business card and depart. Get into your car and ***sit on your car keys***. If you sit on your keys, you won't start your car and drive off and forget all that was discussed! Write down everything that was said at the meeting. What you promised to do . . . what information you learned about the company and the industry . . . what is your next step. What follow up action should I take?

Note Taking

at all meetings

- 3x5 'calendar' notebook *is a good size*
- Electronic organizer *may* be OK
- Company facts
- Industry facts
- Notes
- Questions
- Company names
- Referral's name/s
- Your name!

Ask permission first . . .

20XX

Eighth. When you arrive home, write a thank-you note that night and mail it by the next morning. If the secretary or anyone else was especially helpful, write them thank-you notes as well. Most people do not write thank-you notes and you will stand out if you do . . . besides, it is the courteous thing to do.

"Keep walking and keep talking."
— Tiny Tim

Note . . . stay in control!

One of the most difficult aspects of networking is maintaining management control of your contacts and referrals. You must develop a system to manage this part of your career search or, after time, you will be unable to recall who made the referral. There are several organization techniques described in Chapter 17 but bear in mind that you must be organized to conduct the search effectively. At minimum, use a contact card that shows the name, address and telephone of the contact and the name of the person that referred you, and their relationship. You cannot overkill this part of the process.

The Information/Networking/Referral Meeting - *Agenda - in a nutshell*

1. **ESTABLISH RAPPORT** . . . *when you first meet*:
   - thank the person for the meeting
   - defuse (decompress) the tension by reminding them that you are ***not here to ask*** for a job . . . I know that telling them you are ***not here to ask* for a job** sounds a little corny but believe me it will take the pressure off both of you and you will honor the words you used to set up the meeting
   - remind the person of **who referred you** . . . what/who is the connection
   - ask permission to take notes . . . as soon as the opportunity presents itself
   - say "no thanks" to refreshments . . . but, that's your call

2. **OPENING COMMENTS** . . . *around two minutes* – see 2-minute-opener format in Sound Bites chapter
   - two minute opener . . . will most often be the response to "tell me about yourself" . . . remember to always close with what you want to do . . . your objective
   - background information . . . keep it relevant to the objective
   - opportunities in the industry . . . you are asking about the industry, not asking for or about a job

3. **DISCUSSION** . . . *around ten minutes*
   - general questions about the industry
   - why you are interested
   - industry problems
   - new developments
   - incorporate key words
   - how/why you relate to the industry

4. **SPECIFIC QUESTIONS** . . . *around five minutes*
   - the person may ask if you have any questions to ask about their company. At this point, since they have opened the "company" door, it is fair game to ask about the company you are visiting . . . have 6 to 10 good *company* oriented questions ready in addition to the ones about the industry. ***Do not**, repeat , **do not**, ask or even hint of asking or mentioning anything about salary! If you are asked about salary, default to the stock answer: "While compensation is important, I am sure that when*

the right opportunity presents itself, compensation will fall in line." . . . or words to that effect.

5. **REFERRALS** . . . *around one minute*
   - ask if there is anyone they can think of who they would suggest you talk to about the industry.
   - you may have to jog the person's memory . . . mention companies or people you may be considering talking to if they don't mention anyone.
   - ask if it is OK to use their name when calling referrals

6. **WRAP UP** . . . *around two minutes*
   - summarize the meeting
   - advise that you will contact the referrals
   - keep the person informed . . . mention that you will advise how the referral meetings work out, and how your search is going
   - thank them for their time, and thank **everyone else** as you leave the office

7. **YOUR NEXT STEP** . . . *after you leave the building*
   - think – what's the next step – what do I do next?
   - sit on your keys!
   - write up the meeting in the greatest detail that you can, **before** you drive away

8. **SEND A THANK YOU NOTE!**

Contacts

Contacts are everywhere. Fill in the columns below with the names of people you know in each area. (*Instant Rapport* is someone you know very well; *Bridging* is someone who can lead you to a decision maker: *Decision Maker* is the one who has the power to hire).

Instant Rapport	Bridging	Decision Maker
____________	____________	____________
____________	____________	____________
____________	____________	____________
____________	____________	____________
____________	____________	____________
____________	____________	____________
____________	____________	____________
____________	____________	____________
____________	____________	____________
____________	____________	____________
____________	____________	____________
____________	____________	____________

Bridging Contacts

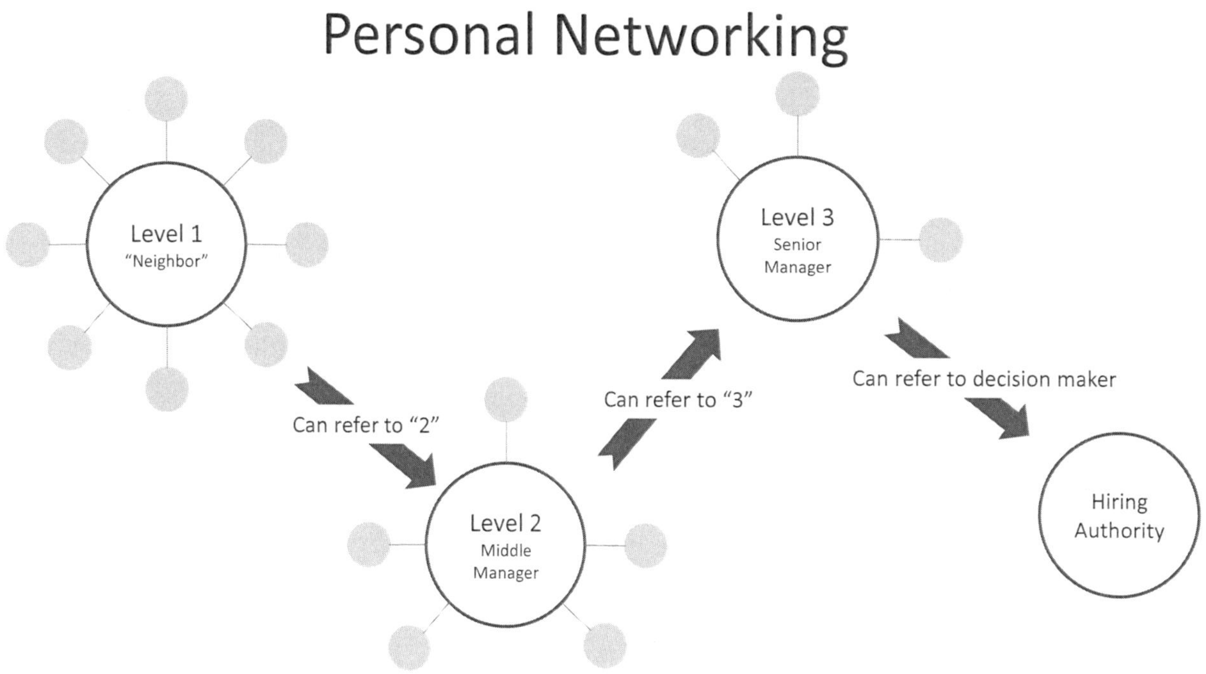

Personal Networking

Level 1
"Neighbor"

Can refer to "2"

Level 2
Middle
Manager

Can refer to "3"

Level 3
Senior
Manager

Can refer to decision maker

Hiring
Authority

CHAPTER 12

SOUND BITES

How can I help you?
Tell me about yourself.
What can I do for you?

Throughout your networking and interviewing experiences you will be asked a multitude of questions. Many of them are simply ice-breakers such as, "**How can I be of help to you?**" to "**What do you think you could bring to the table in this industry?**" This is especially true in the networking stage and when you first begin to explore private sector opportunities. You really have two options when it comes to responding to a query, such as "**Tell me about yourself.**" You can stutter and stammer like most unprepared people do, or you can do a little preparatory work and have an informal, yet structured, thoughtful, and meaningful reply . . . a reply that will stimulate further conversation, make you sound interesting, knowledgeable, and someone with possibilities. The decision is a no-brainer!

The Two-Minute Opening Statement/The Two-Minute Opener

One of the most useful tools that you will use in your job search campaign is the "Two-Minute Opener**.**" It can act as a *bridge* to the civilian marketplace. *(see the worksheets at the end of this chapter)* It is composed of:

- Your education . . . **only in special cases** where an advanced degree is a prerequisite . . . and then very brief ... if searching for a job in education that requires educational credentials, then you would begin with your educational credentials including your dissertation
- Early work experience . . . *briefly unless very relevant*
- Recent experience, quantified accomplishments . . . and using your strengths . . . and how they are relevant to the industry . . . ***incorporate key words***
- Functional responsibilities . . . breadth, experience, depth
- Applicable accomplishments
- Your objective . . . functional area and industry

Note: The Two-Minute Opener commentary answers a multitude of questions including the notorious, "Tell me about yourself."

Consider the basic two minute response as "***core***" information to be used in different situations. You will need to "garnish" (customize) the beginning and ending of the response somewhat to fit the specific question, but the core information will be about the same. The ***"core" is the foundation*** for a response to icebreaker questions such as:

- "Tell me about yourself"
- "How can I help you?"
- "What can I do for you?"
- "What are your plans?"
- "How may I be of service?"
- "What do you bring to the table?"
- "Why should I hire you?"

The 2-Minute Opener

Goal: a short, relevant two-minute response.

Plan to spend no more than 15-20 seconds discussing your early years and education. Your goal during these two minutes is to show that you have experience applicable/relevant to the manager's industry and some accomplishments to prove it. You also want to whet the manager's appetite. See the outline/format at the end of this chapter.

What Is the Contact Person Thinking?

If a <u>non-defense</u> company, the contact will realize that you are a former military or civil service member and may be thinking, "What could you and this industry possibly have in common?" After all, Navy people drive ships; Air Force people fly airplanes, Army people drive tanks, Marines storm hills, Coast Guard tend buoys, Civil Service support the war fighter, etc. In these few minutes it is critical that you discuss your strengths succinctly, without sounding like a braggart. You will find that you will use the Two-Minute Opener throughout your job search campaign . . . in one form or another. A defense oriented company, on the other hand, will realize your potential value and will be looking more for where you might be useful in their company.

What if they <u>don't</u> say "Tell me about yourself?" What if they say, "How can I help you" or "What are your plans?" or "What can I do for you?" etc. Then you must tailor your response to fit the question, using the basic two-minute response. "Perhaps you would best understand if I explained what I have been doing for the past several years" or some other rendition of the basic response. ***The goal is to convey you have experience in their industry and have some relevant strengths***. Always ending with your objective.

Practice - Practice - Practice

I recommend that you write out your two-minute opener and practice this drill in front of a mirror. Practice in front of a video camera. Record it on a cassette player and listen to it in your car. Practice with your spouse and/or your friends. Practice, practice, practice. The Two-Minute Opener is not intended to tell your life history. It is a short statement to relate some background and relevant experience and to spark interest in you as a potential employee. *See the two-minute form at the end of this chapter.*

The Personal Response

. . . ***to, "what do you do now?"****, while still in government service.*

"And, what do you do?"

- **Describe your career in terms of your <u>civilian</u> objective**
- **Use business terminology**
- **Use English ... no lingo**
- **In 45 seconds or less!**
- **And ... "*leaving service!*"**

Keep it relevant ... the perfect fit!

How do you respond when someone asks what you do in the service? Many military people simply say that they work in the Pentagon or are assigned to this ship or that battalion. Most will not take a moment and describe the requirements and/or mission of the job itself in terms that a businessperson can understand, let alone relate to the private sector. Civil service personnel usually say, "I work for the Department of Defense" or whatever their government agency is and let it go at that. You should say something like, "I am presently on active duty in the Navy assigned to the *USS Good Ship managing the information technology programs. I have thoroughly enjoyed my service life but plan to leave active duty this summer and pursue a new career in the private sector."*

The value of the Personal Response is that it allows you to describe your present job in civilian terms, stressing the parts of the job that are most relevant to your next career objective. The idea is for the Personal Response to be a *prologue* to what we call the 30-second commercial. So when someone asks you what you do, your response should contain the information **and key words** most relevant to your next career objective and end with a comment that you have enjoyed government service, but intend to leave it and look for employment in the private sector. **It should last no longer than 45 seconds**! This will probably prompt the question, "What are you going to do when you leave the service?" . . . and you answer with the 30-Second Commercial.

The Thirty-Second Commercial

A related networking tool often used during the process of career search is the 30-second commercial. This is used when you have but a brief moment to answer the often asked question, "What do you plan to do when you leave military/government service?" Most people are not interested in hearing a 10-minute dissertation on your future goals, but it is advisable to leave them with something of substance. What you often hear when that question is asked of someone leaving service or looking for a job is, "I don't know, but if you hear of anything, let me know." Believe me when I tell you that the listener has not the faintest idea what you want to do and will forget your comment the moment you are out of sight. You would be better off if you said that you want to paint manhole covers pink. The 30-second commercial is composed of, **in order**:

Question: "What are you going to do when you retire?" Ans: "I dunno."

- A brief background statement
- A brief accomplishment statement
- Your objective . . . always ending with the objective

Thirty-second Example

The idea is to provide the listener with a short but meaningful comment that states your objective and describes your credentials. Practice the 30-second commercial by writing it out and then summarizing it in three words, (one for each short paragraph) that you can recall instantly. Ensure that you include relevant key words. A short commercial might go something like the following:

Example 1. *For the past six years I have been involved in computer operations of all sizes. I've found that I have a talent for taking user requirements and translating them into programs that will increase productivity. For example, I designed and carried out a computer network program that linked together the key operations in our organization via satellite. The program saved more than $85,000 in inventory costs and has reduced paper and telephone line costs by 23 percent. So I am going to focus my objective as the director of computer operations in aerospace manufacturing.*

He blew it!

Example 2. *For the past 20 years, I've been involved in building and leading teams of all sizes in operational positions, as well as supporting them in IT program management positions. During my career I became certified in both program and acquisition management. I've enjoyed both sides of the business and found that I have a talent for taking user requirements and quickly and efficiently turning them into useful products – often ahead of schedule, under budget and exceeding customer expectations. For example, I recently led the production of eight, multi-million dollar IT defense systems on schedule and developed a highly technical undersea and ground sensor network system during an extremely compressed period, meeting all program goals within budget. My objective is to be a senior, program manager in the hi-tech, ship building industry.*

The order in which you deliver the three short paragraphs is extremely important. When you ***(or your spouse)*** first begin responding to the "What are you going to do?" question, most people will expect an "I don't know" or similar inane response and won't be in a listening mode. Knowing that this is the situation , you begin by giving a short *background* statement that "sets up" the following *accomplishment* and *objective*. Note that you always want the last words out of your mouth to be your *objective* . . . at minimum, the functional area and the industry. Done correctly, the 30-second commercial will almost always generate a beneficial response from the listener and result in a "come see me" or a suggestion of someone or some company that you should visit or think about. It works, and will be one of the most useful tools in your bag!

Two men in an elevator story

Why Critical?

"the old elevator story"

"and what do you do?"

Relationships and referrals

Our person (call him Joe) wanted to work in high tech, clean room manufacturing but was unable to find a position so he accepted a job in environmental clean-up. While attending a conference in Chicago, at lunch time Joe found himself riding down in an elevator with a man (call him Sam) who was attending a conference on the same floor . . . about the 25th floor. With silence and nothing else to do for few minutes Sam turned to Joe and said, "What finds you here?"

Joe replied that he was attending a conference on environmental clean-up. Sam said, "Do you enjoy that kind of work?" Joe replied, "Well I spent a career as a senior officer in the Navy managing high technology manufacturing and wanted to work in that field but couldn't find anything, so, wanting to work, I accepted this current position." (Ergo - his 30 second commercial) Then Joe said, "And what are you doing here?" Sam replied that he was the head of a nine company conglomerate and was holding his semi-annual management meeting here." *(A moment of silence)* then Sam said, "I was just thinking . . . Mike Evans just told me that he was retiring soon so I should be looking for a General Manager replacement" . . . pause . . . "Maybe you would like to put your name in the hat for his job." Joe said "What sort of business is it?" Sam said, "It is a ball bearing manufacturing plant in LA." Joe grimaced and said, "Thank you but I am looking for hi tech clean room opportunities." Sam said, "I understand, but these ball bearings are for shoulder, hip and knee replacements . . . we are the leading developer and manufacturing company in the country making joint bearings as well as other hi tech medical devices. Our work force is composed of orthopedic surgeons, chemists and other professional types."

The rest is history … Joe interviewed, got the job and lived happily ever after … even though it was in LA and not San Diego!

Lessons learned:
(1) You just never know who you are talking to!
(2) If you don't tell them what you want to do (in 30 seconds) there will be no "connection."

Two-Minute Exercise . . . Keep it Relevant!

(Education):

___

Early Work Experience:

___

___

___

___

Recent Work Experience:

___

___

___

___

Functional Responsibilities:

___

___

___

Strengths Gained:

___

___

Accomplishments:

___

___

Career Objective:___

___

The Key Words – strengths that are applicable to this objective are:

1. ___ 2. ___
3. ___ 4. ___
5. ___ 6. ___

Personal Response Exercise . . . in 45 Seconds or Less

Objective: Develop a **Personal Response** to the question: "What do you do?" while still in the government service.

Goal: To respond to the question in **ENGLISH**, and in the ***context*** of what you want to do when you leave government service.

And: To end your response with a statement like: ". . ., however, I am leaving government service/active duty soon and intend to begin a new career in the private sector." *(When asked: "Doing what?", follow with your 30-second Commercial.)*

The Key Words – strengths that are applicable to this objective are:

1. ______ 2. ______

3. ______ 4. ______

5. ______ 6. ______

Personal Response Exercise . . . in 45 Seconds or Less
(Spouse)

Objective: Develop a **Personal Response** to the question: "What does your spouse do?" while still in government service.

Goal: To respond to the question in **ENGLISH**, and in the ***context*** of what your spouse wants to do when he/she leaves government service.

And: To end your response with a statement like: ". . ., however, he/she is leaving government service/active duty soon and will begin a new career in the private sector." *(When asked: "Doing what?", follow with your 30-second Commercial.)*

The Key Words – strengths that are applicable to this objective are:

1. ______________________ 2. ______________________

3. ______________________ 4. ______________________

5. ______________________ 6. ______________________

Thirty-Second Commercial Exercise

Background:

___

___

___

___

___

Accomplishment:

___

___

___

___

___

___

___

Objective:

___

___

___

___

___

. . . Background, Accomplishment, Objective

The Key Words – strengths that are applicable to this objective are:

1. ______ 2. ______

3. ______ 4. ______

5. ______ 6. ______

Thirty-Second Commercial Exercise
(Spouse)

Background:

____

____

____

____

____

Accomplishment:

____

____

____

____

____

____

Objective:

____

____

____

____

. . . Background, Accomplishment, Objective

The Key Words – strengths that are applicable to this objective are:

1. ______________________ 2. ______________________

3. ______________________ 4. ______________________

5. ______________________ 6. ______________________

CHAPTER 13

THE JOB INTERVIEW

Up to this point, all of the effort you have put forth in terms of research, contact development and networking has been in preparation for the Job Interview. Unless you are the brother of the company's owner, you will have to go through the interview process. If you have *networked* yourself into the interview, as opposed to getting the interview through an advertisement or web job posting, then you will probably already know several of the people that will be interviewing you. However, in nearly every case there will be "tire kickers" who will want to take a look at you and pass judgement. The person who will be most interested in the interview is the one whom you will be working for.

You will feel like this . . . unless you are prepared!

Stop . . . and read this!

Before you read further, stop for a moment and consider the differences between a face-to-face *networking meeting* and a *job interview meeting*. Referring to the chart below, you can see that there are major differences, especially in the duration, level of stress, and focus. Preparation, for all intents and purposes, is about the same except you will want to conduct a little more intense study of the company for an interview than you did for the networking meeting. You will want to have some specific pieces of information that you can mention at the appropriate time. If you have been doing your research properly, you will know a lot about the industry, the company's competitors, and basically where the industry is headed. Unfortunately, ***most senior business people are not good interviewers***, and unless they have received some professional training or guidance, you may have to help them along . . . don't worry, it is not hard. Finally, remember that job interviewing is a two-way street. You are looking over the company much in the same way they are looking over you. You want this to be a win-win arrangement. Before you get too far into the interview, ask if the interviewer minds if you take notes . . . and then by all means do so.

Meetings . . . A Comparison

	Info/Referral/Networking	**Job Interview**
Nature	Informal	Formal
Duration	20 minutes	Unlimited
Goal	Information	Job
Info	For you	For them
Close	You initiate	They initiate
Focus	Industry	Company
Stress	Low	High

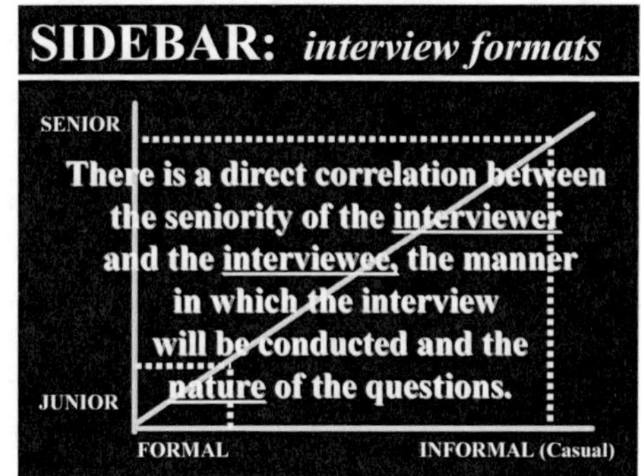

Three Basic Types of Interviews - as a result of \answering an advertisement

1. ***The screening interview*** . . . this is normally conducted by someone in the HR Department and lasts about 10 to 20 minutes. The goal is to determine if you meet the basic qualifications. The screening could also be conducted by a computer program searching for words that indicate you have the required skill set. **Include relevant *key words* in your statements.**

2. ***The job interview itself*** . . . this is an in-depth meeting that can last one or two hours . . . even all day. During this interview they are looking for fit, as well as your personal demeanor, your interest in the company and the job, your enthusiasm, your skills, and of course, what you bring to the table . . . i.e., your ability to contribute to the profitability of the company. Include relevant key words in your statements.

3. ***Follow-on interviews*** . . . return visits to the same or different people that interviewed you previously . . . there may be many. Better a follow-on interview(s), than none at all!

Parts of the Interview
Percentage depends on needs of the job

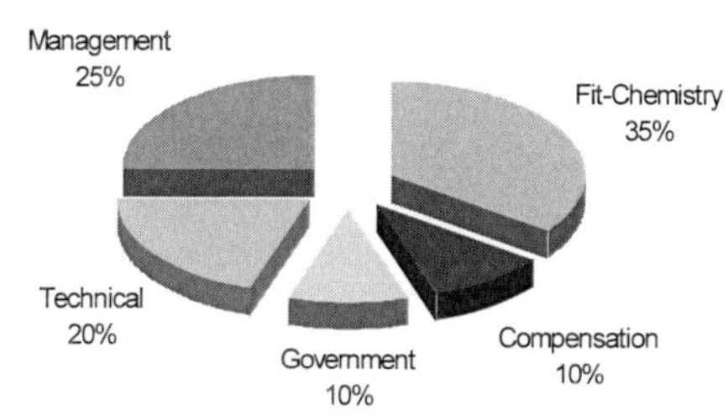

During the interview process you may find yourself talking to: the HR Director; a group of people all asking different questions; the hiring manager; or various other managers that you may have a working relationship with, in the event you are hired. Each situation is unique. One question that often creeps into an interview is "How does your DoD background relate to our civilian business?" Don't despair, by the time you finish this book you will be prepared and will relish answering this question.

What Are They Looking for In a New Hire?

There are three primary factors that are sought after when considering a new hire. They are:

1. **CAN DO** . . . the job – does the person have the strengths and the experience required to perform successfully in the position or, can the person be taught to do the job? ***Demonstrate "Can Do" by conveying personal knowledge, experience and accomplishments which are RELEVANT to the requirements of the job.***

2. **WILL DO (*and wants to do*)** . . . the job – will this person be willing to do the job? To put in the effort required and be willing to get into the details and solve problems? Are you serious? And, willing to work for a reasonable salary. ***Demonstrate "Will Do" by conveying personal initiatives, planning and execution RELEVANT to the requirements of the objective (job/position).***

Aspects of "Fit"

Appearance ... how you look – your attire
Posture ... energy, confidence
Handshake ... are you alive?
Opening remarks ... first things out of mouth
Your referral ... their relationship to interviewer
Service/industry reputation
Demonstrated interest ... in industry/company
Obvious interest ... in industry/company
Knowledge of industry and company
"**M/B Preference** match"
Knowledge of Pentagon (in defense)

3. **FIT** . . . will the person fit in with the company's culture? Your attitude! Of the three factors, in the vast majority of cases, fit is the most critical. Managers will overlook a multitude of sins but no one will hire a person that they don't like or think that they won't work well as a team player, especially someone with a bad attitude.

> **Note: The Strategic Hire.**
> Often a company will hire a person because of their strategic value and practically disregard all other factors. For example, if the company is trying to "break into" a new industry they might hire someone who can provide the necessary entree/s to the appropriate people in that industry. What is your strategic value?

Interview Techniques

How you will be interviewed will differ with the person conducting the interview. Trained interviewers will probably be somewhat more formal in their approach. If the interview is conducted by someone you know fairly well, the interview will be more casual . . . in terms of setting and structure. In either case however, the interviewer will be looking to see if you pass the *Fit, Can Do and Will Do* filters.

Knee-to-knee; one-on-one; tire kickers; courts martial; round table.

Knee-to-Knee interviewing . . . you are seated directly across from the interviewer with no table or structure in between you and the interviewer. Many professional interviewers use this format.

Tire Kickers . . . these are people with whom you will probably be interfacing with if you land the job. They could be the people you will be working with, or for, or the people who will be working for you. They can't ensure that you get hired but they can put a major dent in your efforts to get the job if they don't like or respect you.

One-on-One. . . similar to the Knee-to-Knee structure except you are more comfortably seated, probably on a sofa or easy chair. Senior managers interview this way – they find it more comfortable.

Court Martial . . . the Court Martial structure is how many government organizations interview. The interviewing group (usually four to six people) sit at a long table and you are seated in front of them. Another good description of this kind of interview would be inquisition interviewing. Just keep your cool and do not be intimidated by the numbers. HINT: When you are being interviewed by a group made up of men and women, ensure that you have eye contact with everyone. If you pass over/avoid eye contact with any of them, your action could be interpreted as having a bias. If convenient, give each member a business card.

The Court Martial Interview

Keep eye contact with each member!

Round Table . . . just like the Court Martial except you are seated around a round or rectangular table. . . same considerations apply.

The Stress Interview

Occasionally, you will encounter a *stress interview.* Most people do not subscribe to this technique, but in the event that you encounter one, maintain control and keep your answers objective. If the question really seems out of line, inappropriate or illegal, simply ask for clarification . . . ask how that information relates to the position that you are interviewing for. All interviews are critical . . . never let your guard down. It could be a test or, the interviewer could just be a jerk! ***I have only heard of one stress interview from people who have attended our seminars in the past ten years.***

The Four Stages of the Job Interview

The stages of the job interview are similar to those of the information networking meeting.

1. **Introductions** . . . this is the initial impression stage where the interviewer is looking you over for overall impact. This is your opportunity to establish rapport. This first impression is critical, since most people form an initial impression, positive or otherwise, in the first two minutes or less of the interview. Even at this initial meeting the interviewer is already thinking, "How would I like to work with this person every day for the next five years?" As the saying goes, "You never get a second chance to make a first impression."

And, why do you want to work here?

2. **Questions and answers by the interviewer** . . . once the niceties are over, the interviewer will quickly move into your qualifications for the job. Note: if the interviewer is well trained, they will give you a short description of the job in terms of skill requirements, experience and any special needs or circumstances. At some point, the interviewer will probably ask about your government service, the kinds of jobs you held, and may even ask why you left the service. Remember that many private sector managers think that government personnel stay in the service for 30 some years or more and then retire and live off of their luxurious, tax free pensions. Your goal is to assure them that you enjoy working, are interested in a totally new second career, have the strengths necessary to make that goal a reality, and that *you really want to work.* So, when you describe your service jobs, try your best to give accomplishments and responsibilities and use applicable **key words** that are relevant to the job. Sometime during this stage the interviewer might ask, "What do you think you bring to the table?" meaning, "How will you contribute to the financial profitability, or growth, or benevolent purpose of the organization?" . . . what you can do to fulfill their needs? Don't be long-winded with your answer . . . a minute or two should be all that is necessary. Use business terminology! Give short story examples using the PAR format. Lastly, you should determine the 30 most likely questions that the interviewer will ask and think through the appropriate answers. Use the questions in this book for ideas.

3. **Questions by you** . . . after the interviewer is finished with the direct questions you may be asked if you have any questions about the company. You should . . . NO, **MUST** - have prepared, in advance, at least ten or more questions that will indicate you are more than a superficial candidate. By asking well-founded questions the interviewer will know that you have done your homework and have a genuine understanding of the company and the industry. ***Your questions should contain strengths – key words/skills that are required for the position and short story examples of accomplishments.*** Now is the time to refer to your notebook. You have already asked permission to take notes. Typical questions are listed at the end of this chapter.

4. **Closing** . . . the last five minutes or so of the interview may start with the interviewer asking if there is anything else that you would like to add, or a simple, thank you for coming in for the interview. In any event you should thank the interviewer and prepare to leave. Keep in mind that it is their nickel and, therefore, their call on when the interview should end. You should at least summarize your strengths, the fit, why you are well suited for the position and why you would like to be selected for the job . . . why the "fit" is good.

Note: Don't forget the importance of good eye contact . . . but don't let them cross!

What constitutes an offer?
An offer can come in different forms, such as; "We would like to offer you the position of ____" or, "We will send you an offer letter tomorrow outlining specific responsibilities" or, "What would it take to bring you on board?" or, "We would like to make you an offer contingent on us being awarded _______."

*Note: A verbal offer is good enough to begin salary discussions, but it is **not a done deal until it is in writing**.*

How might the offer come?
The offer may come at the end of the interview or, at a networking meeting or, by letter or email after the interview or, at lunch or dinner or from the HR director or, from the functional manager or, from the CEO or, President or Chairman.

The Offer or No Offer – *and, a thank you note in either case!*
At the end of the interview you might or might not be offered a job. Most smart interviewers won't do this, however, because they will want to talk to their HR/Personnel department or their boss to get the final blessing – it's just protocol. The interviewer will not/should not tell you that you won't get the job – unless he/she is a fool. The HR department will notify you of the bad news by mail or a brief telephone call, or sometimes not at all. Smart companies have a "Don't tell the person that they *will* not be offered the job or any reason *why* they were not offered the job" policy. It has to do with fun stuff like legal matters and law suits.

No offer? Thank them anyway!

In any event, when you are notified either way, you should send the company a thank you note thanking them for the interview and offer, or, if you didn't get the offer, just thanking them for the interview and offering future assistance. Why send a thank you note to someone that did not offer you a job? Three reasons . . . it is a civilized thing to do, it keeps the network open, and, most importantly, the person that was selected instead of you might turn the offer down and you will be more memorable than the other contenders if you were courteous enough to send a letter of thanks. Why might the other person turn the offer down? The other candidates are just like you. They have several irons in the fire, and in the course of events, they get a better offer from another company. It happens all the time! I know it is counterintuitive and you would much rather send a note telling them to *stuff it*, but don't; just do as I suggest!

Preparing for the Job Interview
Just as in the case of networking, your preparation for the interview begins long before you arrive at the office. Some things to consider are:

• **Appearance** . . . follow the attire rules . . . lay your clothes out the night before so you won't have to determine if colors match the next morning when it's too dark to see . . . especially your socks.

- **Research**
  - ✓ know the company and the industry
  - ✓ determine the exact location of the meeting, where the best place is to park, and check it out the day before if at all possible (you may have to call the company and ask for directions – that's okay)
  - ✓ have your questions prepared . . . at least ten
  - ✓ write out twenty answers to questions that you think might be asked (check out Glassdoor)
  - ✓ talk to friends who may have interviewed in the same industry
  - ✓ understand how your strengths meet the company's needs

Needs: Contributions
Make a list of the organization's "needs" . . . their job requirements. Next to each need explain how you fulfill that need. Be prepared to give an example or two.

- **Practice . . . practice . . . practice**
  - ✓ practice with friends
  - ✓ practice in front of a video camera
  - ✓ record yourself and play it back

- **Arrive early**
  - ✓ ten to 15 minutes early will save you sweaty palms. **Not** an hour early.
  - ✓ it will allow you to review your notes and resume before the meeting

The answers you give to the interviewer's questions should contain or imply strengths and experience applicable to the position.

- **Information**
  - ✓ bring a resume with you
  - ✓ bring a small notebook to take notes and write your questions down
  - ✓ you don't need to take a briefcase or portfolio but it is OK if you do

- **Demeanor** . . . smile
  - ✓ be positive and friendly . . . consider body language
  - ✓ don't convey any negative thoughts
  - ✓ maintain good eye contact . . . 80 percent of the time
  - ✓ careful with your quips
  - ✓ language should be squeaky clean - prim and proper

Regardless of how it may appear, the interviewer is only interested in your past as it relates to your future with their company!

- **Show appreciation**
  - ✓ say thank you when you leave . . . leave your business card

- **Write a thank-you letter** . . . **write it that day** . . . **mail it the next day after proofing it twice**

Interview Questions . . . ***they might ask***
One of the best ways to practice for an interview is to write down 25 questions that you think the interviewer will ask you . . . and your answers! Practice answering them with someone you know or on a audio recorder and then listen to how you sound. Good interviewers will not ask very many questions that can be answered with a simple yes or no. Types of interview questions boil down to basically four types:

Behavioral – example: *"Describe a situation where you had to lay a person off from their job."*

Situational – example: *"How would you go about laying off a person who had been a good employee but for 'whatever' reason was no longer needed?"*

Conventional – example: *"How do you manage change?"*

Stress – example: *"What makes you think you are good enough to handle this position?"*

Below are some of the more typical questions you may be asked:

1. Tell me about yourself
2. What are your short term goals?
3. What are your long term goals?
4. How do you work under pressure? Give me an example.
5. What salary did you have in mind for this position? (sensitive)
6. Why do you want to work for us?
7. What are your greatest strengths? . . . Your greatest weakness?
8. Give me an example of:
    - your administrative strengths
    - your analytical skills
    - your leadership strengths
    - your creativity
    - your ability to maintain your self control
9. How do you get along with subordinates?
10. How do you motivate people?
11. How did you get along with your last boss?
12. How did you find out about this position?
13. How would you reduce the G and A of our company?
14. Have you ever developed a budget? How did you go about it?
15. Why are you leaving service in the government? (sensitive)
16. What did you enjoy most about your government career?
17. What would you do if given the chance to do anything that you wanted to do?
18. How would you describe the perfect/ideal boss? (sensitive) How would your boss describe you?
19. How do you think that you could make the biggest contribution to our company?
20. Are you willing to move/relocate?
21. What do you do in your spare time?
22. What were your responsibilities in your last job?
23. How would you go about making improvements to our firm? (sensitive)
24. What could you have done differently at your last job to improve things?
25. How do you define success?

Practice Makes Perfect!

"I hear and I forget,
I see and I remember,
I do and I understand."

Confucius

26. What would you do if you won the lotto? (trick question)
27. What do you bring to the table?
28. What is the most difficult thing you have had to do?
29. Have you ever fired anyone? How did it feel? How did you go about it?
30. How soon do you think that you would be productive if we offer you the job?
31. Do you prefer working with others or alone? Why?
32. What did you enjoy least about your last assignment? Why?
33. How did you prepare for this interview?
34. Are there any questions that you would like to ask about the company?
35. Why should I hire you? . . . the mother of all questions!

The ***Mother*** of All Interview Questions

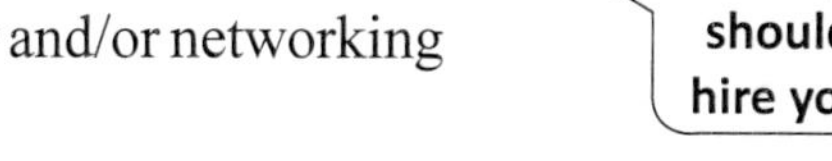

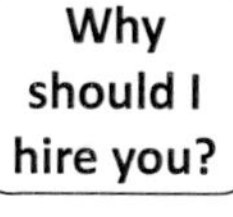

Information You Should Know . . . before the interview and/or networking meeting

- Major competitors
- Product line/s
- Your experience relevant to company operations
- Recent product introductions
- Latest innovations in the industry
- Latest products in the industry
- Stock price and history
- Where you think you would best fit
- Current news in the industry
- Recent changes in company management and/or ownership
- Examples of accomplishments relevant to the industry
- Who owns the company
- Recent articles in business magazines and on-line articles about the company/industry

Questions to Ask the Interviewer

1. What are the priorities in this position?
2. What are the major challenges in this industry?
3. How will my performance be evaluated?
4. Who are the key players in the organization?
5. What makes the company so successful?
6. What will be the criterion for success in the job?
7. What are your concerns about the functional area I would be working in?
8. What are the features that you are looking for in the selected candidate?
9. Who does my department interface with?
10. What happened to the last person who held this job?
11. What are the biggest changes in the company over the past five years?
12. What do *you* like most about working here?
13. What is the company's management philosophy?
14. Are there any specific skill requirements that did not appear in the ad?
15. May I see where this position appears on the company organization chart?
16. How do you like working here and what do you like most about the company?
17. Where would this job lead to?
18. How would you describe the kinds of people that thrive in the company and those that don't fit in?
19. What would success look like in the position?
20. ***Tell me a little about how you came to work here. What have you enjoyed the most about working for this company?*** The "halo" question.
21. What kind of people best "fit in" at this company?

Ask a question(s) about the company which will demonstrate you have done your homework – ensure you do not come across as insulting, too personal, or a smart aleck. By all means, steer away from any hint of compensation . . . salary, benefits or perks UNTIL AFTER AN OFFER HAS BEEN MADE!

Note: Since most senior managers are not particularly good interviewers . . . you may have to keep the interviewer focused on the subject . . . another reason to have good questions.

A good way to frame your questions is around topics such as: the product line, the problems that may exist, the plans that the company has for the future, more information about the job itself, and questions about the people in the organization.

Try Not to Sound like a Drill Sergeant

A good interviewer will expect some questions from you and will think less of you if you don't have any. Or worse than that, if you ask about mundane things that you really ought to know. Relax, if you prepare properly the interview sessions will be enjoyable. In any interview situation you should know at least 10 to 15 facts about the organization and be able to verbalize them. You should also be prepared to link your accomplishments with the questions that you expect to be asked. ***Remember to keep your responses to a max of two minutes***.

How to Destroy an Interview:

- Take a vacation . . . *don't leave a number where you can be located*
- Talk salary too soon and be anxious about it . . . *it will appear that you are only interested in money.*
- Use a flashy resume . . . *bright red or stripes running through it*
- Argue with the interviewer
- Try to wing it . . . go in unprepared. *Remember the story about the young lady who had just arrived in New Your City. She stopped and asked a police officer how you get to Carnegie Hall . . . the officer politely replied, "Practice, practice, practice!"*
- Badmouth a former boss
- Ignore punctuality . . . *call ahead if you are going to be late.*
- Be unfamiliar with the company
- Display poor personal habits . . . *don't scratch where you ought not to!*

How to Succeed in an Interview:

- **DO YOUR HOMEWORK**
- Show that you meet or exceed the requirements
- Explain your relevant previous successes
- Show that you fit the company image
- Explain how you would boost profits
- Display confidence and composure
- Show that you are a sound decision maker . . . give examples
- Express your career goals and interests
- Display your leadership qualities
- Create a rapport with the interviewer
- Follow the process described in the book!
- Have short stories ready that demonstrate your applicable strengths - 2 minute max

Interview Factors – *Behavioral*

The following list of questions was taken from an actual interview prepared by a HR specialist and the functional manager.

Behavioral interviewing takes many forms

Relationships with Others

1. Have you ever been described as hard headed? . . . By whom? . . . Give an example.

2. Tell me about a time when you became involved in a problem faced by a peer or subordinate . . . how did it work out?

3. In what kinds of social situations do you "freeze up"? Provide an example.

4. Have you ever been in a situation where the other person, for some reason, had a negative opinion of you . . . before you said a word? How did you overcome the negative "vibes?"

5. Have you ever ridden in an automobile with someone who talked too much or too little? How did you ensure that you were communicating effectively with him or her?

6. How skillful do you think you are in sizing up people? Give an example.

7. What has been the most difficult situation that you have experienced in establishing rapport with a fellow employee? How did you handle it?

Leadership

1. Briefly review the leadership experience you have had, giving examples that would show what your leadership style is like.

2. Give a brief summary of the leadership positions which you have held. What was your major success and major failure as a leader in each?

3. What do you think are the most important components of a practical leadership philosophy? Describe how you developed your philosophy.

4. Who have you most respected for their leadership qualities? What were these specific qualities? Has there been a time when you tried to use this style?

5. Have you ever had to take over a leadership role unexpectedly? (Perhaps a sudden illness of your boss) How did it work out?

Technical Evaluation

1. Various questions about the technical aspects of the post.

Policy and Procedures

1. Describe a situation in which you had to support the directives of higher management, even when you personally disagreed with them.

2. What work policies or procedures have you found to be personally distasteful? Did you conform? Why or why not?

3. Have you been tempted to break policy for a special situation? If so, explain.

4. Can you describe a situation in which a company's policy and procedures have been unfair to you? How did you cope with the problem?

5. Have you ever worked in a situation where there were continual changes in company operating policies and procedures? How did you react to these changes? What was it like?

Decision Making/problem Solving Strengths

1. Tell me about the biggest work decision you have had to make. How did you come to your decision?

2. Describe a major work problem which you have faced and describe your method of dealing with it.

3. Tell me about a work situation in which you feel you have been part of the problem. What did you do?

4. Would you describe yourself as being more logical or intuitive in solving problems? Give me an example of each.

Commitment to this Industry

1. How you became interested in this career field. What steps have you taken to achieve this goal? What specifically interests you in a career in this industry . . . in this company?

2. What specifically interests you in this company?

3. What do you know about this company?

4. What do you know about this company's competitors? How did you find out?

5. How does your service career relate to this business? Give me an example.

6. Why do you feel you would be a valuable asset to this company? Please explain.

7. In what area of this company do you feel you could contribute the most? Please explain.

The Most Popular Behavior-Based Interview Questions

Modern studies have replaced the "old-fashioned" way of interviewing, which often combined mind-scrambling/brain teaser questions (which don't predict anything) with behavioral assessment questions. Questions which ask the job candidate to describe how they handled a specific situation. The theory being, and frequently validated, that how a person performed in the past solving a given problem is a good predictor of how they will actually perform in the future.

Tell me about a time when you:

- Turned down a great job
- Were required to fire a close acquaintance
- Interviewed and hired the wrong person for the job
- Used creativity to solve a difficult problem
- Didn't finish a project or assignment on time
- Were persuasive in a meeting
- Were required to deal with an emotional situation
- Had to make an unpopular decision
- Submitted a report that drew accolades from your superiors
- Overcame a major obstacle
- Were disappointed in your own personal behavior
- Were unhappy with how a project you were responsible for turned out
- Persuaded a working group to do things your way
- Completely missed the point
- Set your goals too high
- Set your goals too low
- Handled a difficult problem with a subordinate
- Counseled a subordinate in regard to substandard performance
- Mentored an employee
- Had to correct a superior
- Proved a superior wrong
- Made a decision that you knew would not be popular with your employees
- Reviewed your life goals

Illegal Questions and How to Manage Them

Basically, any question that is not relevant to fulfilling the requirements of the position is improper to ask, and many are flat out illegal . . . in terms of the job interview. Please note, however, that once you have been hired, many of the previously illegal questions are now perfectly legal to ask and must be answered.

The list at the right pretty much sums up the basic questions considered illegal. Most of them are obvious. There are borderline questions that can be asked . . . for example, it is legal to ask if there is anything physically that would prevent you from fulfilling the requirements of the job. You must answer truthfully. So, think about the responses to questions like this before you get to the meeting. Most human resource managers know what is legal and what is not, but many of the more senior managers may not know that they are asking an illegal question . . . *they were too busy to attend the training.*

Illegal Interview Questions

- Race
- Color
- Religion
- National Origin
- Ancestry
- Physical handicaps
- Marital status – *sexual preference*
- Age
- Sexual preference
- Medical condition

Things not relevant to performance!

Illegal Interview Questions
possible responses

1. **Answer the question straight out** ***... don't offend***
2. **Address the underlying concern** ***... talk around the question***
3. **Repel the question** ***... not recommended***

Above all-be tactful!

Often, an illegal question seems appropriate. For example, if you are finishing up the interview and the interviewer casually asks what you do for hobbies, or if you are married or things that are common in everyday discussions, the questions could be perfectly honest and asked out of pure interest in you. At this point it will be up to you to decide how you want to handle it. I see three options (on the left). **1**. You can just answer the question and forget it, assuming that it is innocent and is probably just small talk. **2**. Or, if the question refers to your age, you could answer it by saying, "If you are asking me if there is anything about the job that I would have trouble handling or if I have the energy to carry-off the routine that the position calls for, the answer is no." You have just talked around the question. Now it is up to the interviewer to get more to the point, if he or she wants to. **3**. The third option is to confront the interviewer with a comment like, "What does that have to do with the job," or, "Don't you know that is an illegal question?" That response might make you feel good but will probably take you out of the running for the job! It's up to you. For my money, in 99 percent of the cases, I would respond with option 1. Your Call!

Sensitive Questions . . . what are they?

There are many sensitive questions an interviewer might ask. They nearly always ask, "Why did you leave your last job?" They might ask a government person (military or civil service) what you think about women in fighter aircraft, serving onboard ships or submarines, or what you think about the Congressional action allowing gays to serve openly in the Armed Forces, or sexual harassment . . . whatever. Most interviewers would ask those questions out of pure curiosity. Smarter interviewers would ask questions like that to see if you harbor any bias or prejudice against females, gays, minorities or any other situation that could ***result in a law suit based on discrimination***. With all of the TV and newspaper press and cartoons about the armed forces, a *tuned-in* interviewer might just ask questions like those just mentioned in a casual, but deliberate way. I WOULD! To military or civil service! To ANYONE! Not because I might personally care, but because I do not want to get sued because you discriminated against someone . . . in a hire, promotion or personnel action! It can get expensive! Besides, ***when you are the hiring official you want to hire the most capable and "best fit" candidate . . . the one willing to do the job and can do the job!***

Interviewing ...

The three areas that we consider to be the most critical in any job search are: having a career focus, networking and being prepared for networking/informational meetings and the job interview. The hardest part of any job search campaign is the interview . . . and you will almost never get a job without an interview. Many job hunters go down the tubes because of their failure to prepare themselves properly for the interview. I think the need for preparation is obvious. You should:

Interview Preparation

It's the best prepared ...

- **Research the company** . . . by this time you will know a lot about the industry . . . it's time to focus on the company you are meeting with. Check out their corporate website.

- **Anticipate questions** that they are bound to ask. See the questions in this chapter and in Yate's, Knock Em' Dead book.

- **Think through your answers** . . . to all sorts of questions. You don't want to memorize them because you will come off too structured. Know the key words. On the other hand, you don't want to sit there and squirm or you will look like "the lights are on but there is nobody home." And, if you have a slam-dunk answer, pause for a moment, so you don't appear too rehearsed.

- **Have good questions** to ask the interviewer and/or the interviewer's accomplices. Sometime during the meeting, someone will ask if you have any questions you would like to ask about the company or the position. I promise you! Besides, it's a two-way street; you want to determine whether the position and company are right for you.

- **Look the part**. Determine what they are wearing. Always look the best you can. This is no time to be casual. They will be looking to see if you "fit" in and dress is one way that helps them determine it.

- **Be prepared to answer the question, "Why should we hire you**?" Or, you might put it this way: "Why should they hire me?" Your summary statement and bullets from your resume will go a long way toward answering that question if you get stuck.

- **Read a book**, or at least browse through one, on the subject of How to Interview. At every seminar I conduct, I ask the question, "How many here have had a course on how to interview someone for a job?" In the hundreds of seminars I have conducted, no one has ever answered in the positive. So, why not read up on interviewing from the interviewer's perspective. The library is full of good books.

What Do People Do Here? . . . story

I have a good friend who was the Human Resources Director for a fairly large company. He did most of the senior interviewing for the company and all of the final hiring interviews. He told me that once, while he was interviewing a young man, he asked the man if there were any questions that he would like to ask – a reasonable question. The young man responded with, "Yes, what do you do here?" My friend responded with, "Nothing that you will ever be responsible for!"

What the Employer Wants to Know

- **Why you want to work for their company**?
- **Are you willing to haul the wood**?
- **Provide me with some examples of relevant work**
- **What you bring to the table** . . . what are your special talents that would make you valuable to the organization?
- **Will you fit in**? Will they enjoy working with you day after day for the next five years? Will you enjoy working with them for the next five years?
- **Why hire you**? Why bring you aboard instead of the other five people they are interviewing?
- **Could you be overqualified?** Too much experience for the job.
- **Can they afford you**? Are you worth the price you are negotiating?
- **Are you serious about working?**

Why did you hire me?

"I thought it would be easier to teach you the numbers than to teach an accountant how to talk, and you fit in nicely."

While some of these questions seem a bit rough and to the point, they will be easy to answer if you have taken time for your research and have prepared yourself as you know you should. I have had countless people write and tell me that they were *almost sorry* that the interview meeting had been so easy. Trust me, in every case these people were prepared to go into battle!

Body Language

Many people give little credence to body language, but it is alive and well in interview and networking situations. If you are interested in the subject, there are numerous books in the library on the subject, and seminars that teach it. There are a few things that you should be especially tuned in to during an interview.

Body language is critical!

- Crossed arms is a posture that signals that you are on the defensive, or perhaps are not interested in the person you are talking to. It is a contentious posture when communicating!
- Eye contact is critical. Looking at someone in the eyes demonstrates confidence and character. Looking away or down could show a lack of confidence or even trying to avoid telling the truth. The "rule" is that you should have direct eye contact about 80 percent of the time. Careful not to 'stare em down!
- **Don't** . . . put your hands in your pockets.
- **Don't** . . . sit on the edge of your chair . . . like you are about to launch.
- **Don't slouch** . . . like you would rather be asleep.
- **Don't** . . . anticipate what I am going to say and finish my sentence for me!
- **Don't** . . . cross your legs away from the person you are talking to . . . shows disinterest – And, **don't** clutch your ankle like you were holding on for dear life!

- **Don't** . . . nod your head in a hurried fashion or rub your neck or nose or click your pen . . . bad habits that are distracting!
- **Don't** . . . talk too much.

Some Frequently Asked Questions and Answers About Interviews

Why are you getting out of the service? Why did you leave your last job?
Several years ago we were conducting a seminar and during a go-around question and answer session I asked one of the attendees why he was leaving service. He responded with a question . . . "Do you want the real answer or the cushy answer?" I was a little taken back at his response so I said, "Why don't you start with the real answer and we can go from there." So he said, "I am leaving the service because of the leadership!" "Leadership" I said, "Your boss is a great leader . . . what do you mean?"

The Employer Wants To Know

- *Are you willing to "haul the wood?"*
- *Why do you want to work here?*
- *What do you bring to the table?*
- *Will you fit in?*
- *Why hire you?*
- *Are you affordable?*
- *Are you hungry?*
- *Are you serious?*

How will you contribute to our mission?

He said, "I don't mean my boss, I mean so-in-so! I mean that womanizing, pot smoking, gay bashing, thieving, draft dodging so-in-so." With that I said words to the effect: "Once having said that you never have to say it again. Everyone does not have your same beliefs and even if they did, it would be inappropriate for you to take off on that tangent. In fact you may offend someone who had been a supporter of the person in question."

Negative statements about anyone do little to raise your image in the eyes of the person you are meeting with! Remember what you mother taught you, "If you can't say something nice about a person, don't say anything at all." Note that HR interviewers almost **always** ask the "Why did you leave your last job" question as a matter of form; they are not singling you out. They just want what you did and someone probably told them that this is a question they should ask. They do get some really funny responses!

Forthrightness only goes so far!

So, why am I leaving service?
". . . I had a great career in the _______, but it is time to move on . . . and I am looking forward to a second career in the _______ industry."

Note: There is no need to carry "old baggage" into an interview session let alone a new job!

How candid should you be?
We would never suggest that you bear false witness when being interviewed or in any other situation. However, there are some things better left unsaid. The fact that you once played hooky from school or got a speeding ticket ten years ago are of no consequence to the interview or the interviewer. You may have some regrets, but unrelated information just throws a curve ball into the interview meeting. *And naturally, you would not want to tell them that you have been "on the wagon" for several months now and are starting to feel normal again and that your liver is recovering nicely.*

Is it okay to ask when you can expect to hear if you have been selected for the job?
Certainly and you should. You are entitled to know where the hiring process stands and how long before they will make a decision. Some people ask if it is all right to call the interviewer if there is no word within a week or two. That's okay, but I prefer to call them without asking in a week or two. Just assume it is okay to do so.

Is it okay to tell them that you want the job, or, in some cases, to outright ask for the job?
Most certainly. That is not to say that you get down on bended knee and beg, but telling the interviewer that you believe you are a good fit and are very interested in the position is a positive thing to do. You would think that the interviewer would know that you wanted the job – otherwise why are you here taking the interview? But everyone likes to hear positive comments and that you *really* want to work for their company!

How much time can I reasonably ask for when considering an offer?
You first need to determine how long the offer is open. You should understand that once the hiring manager/company makes up its mind to offer you the job, most of the time they want you yesterday. They will probably ask you, "When can you start?" You could reply with, "I am really anxious to get into the job but I would like to take a little time to examine/consider all of the aspects of the offer . . . when do you need to know or when do you need an answer?" Frequently, the time will be stipulated in the offer letter and that will probably be a week or two, but some will want to know in a few days. By the way, as the deadline approaches, you can always call and ask for an extension – like everything else, this is a negotiable item! I have a friend who waited four months to answer – the company wasn't concerned because they didn't need him before that time. However, it is unfair to the company to keep *stringing* them along just to keep all of your options open. They need to get on with life just as you do.

How do I tell a company that I am taking a job with another company and am turning down their job offer?
Do it as nicely and tactfully as possible. Call the person who made the offer to you and/or the senior manager that interviewed you, thank them for their offer and explain that you have decided to accept an offer from another company. You don't have to give a lot of reasons, but again, thank them for the opportunity and wish them well. You should follow this up with a short letter, thanking them for the opportunity to interview and offering to be of assistance to them in any way you can. Never burn a bridge and always keep the lines of communication positive. You want to be remembered in a positive way.

Apart from functional or technical strengths, what strengths are most in demand these days?
Hiring officials are always looking for people who can solve problems, are team players and good communicators. Several years ago the word *leadership* was not in vogue. These days, however, leadership is sought after – even though in most companies there is little time for those at the management level to demonstrate their leadership qualities. How does it go? "When the alligators are nipping at your ankles, you do not have time to worry about who left the flood gates open!" Nevertheless, leadership is a wonderful talent so by all means mention that you have had leadership roles . . . probably in the summary section of the resume. (See the appendix for John Kotter's take on leadership and Warren Bennis comments regarding what makes a good leader.)

Recently, articles in Fortune and Forbes magazines have publicized that according to surveys, companies are looking for people with strong customer relations talent and those with a desire to improve product quality. About time!

Should I mention that my spouse and I run a small business from our home?
No, keep that information to yourself. You don't want the interviewer thinking that you will be worrying about your own business when you should be concentrating on his company's business. Some companies will have a clause in their offer letter stipulating what you may and may not do in regard to extracurricular work.

What should I say if the interviewer asks me if I have other offers or what other companies am I talking to?
That is pretty much a situational call. Most companies will pretty much assume that you are touching base with their competitors so they will not be surprised to hear that you are exploring all of your options. This is especially true in the defense industry. There is certainly no harm in telling them that you are meeting with other companies. If you are asked if you have any offers and you do, then there is no harm in saying "yes." Whether or not you tell them who the offers are from is up to you – all else being equal, I would respond with, "I would rather not say." If you don't have any other offers you could just respond with, "Let me just say that I have several irons in the fire."

"You say I'm overqualified! Give me the job and I will act as stupid as the rest of you!"

What if they say I am overqualified?
This remark can be sincere or can just be a nice way of giving you a wave-off. Companies are concerned, and rightly so, that you may have too much experience for the job and as a result will get bored in a short while and leave. Then they will have to go through this whole process again. You should give serious thought to the matter as well. The last thing you want to do is accept the job and then discover that you are bored and/or unhappy with the mental requirements of the job. If, however, you think their comment represents a wave-off, then you could say something like, "I realize that I would bring a lot of experience to the position and understand your concerns, but let me reassure you that I have given this a lot of thought, and I want to start at this level so that I can understand the business from the ground up." . . . or words to that effect.

What if I receive a contingent offer? ... *Please see Compensation chapter.*

What if they tell me I will or will not be offered the job?

"Dear Mr. Smith, Thank you for not offering me the job."

In either case you send a thank you note for being afforded the opportunity to be interviewed. Chances are that they will not tell you on the spot that you will ***not*** be selected but will say that someone from HR will call you and let you know the results. So why bother to send a thank you note to some *idiot* who failed to comprehend what a great talent you are? Because the person who *was* selected might choose to take a different job and the company may well call you and make you the offer . . . since you were as good as the other non-selectees and had the courtesy of sending a thank you note.

What if they want me to pay my own way to the interview?
Every once in a while we run into a company who has a policy that says, "Prospective employees wanting to interview for a position with our company must bear the expense of traveling from their location to our location." This does not occur very often. So, what to do? If you believe that you are on the "short list" and that they definitely are considering you and you would really like to have the job, then it is probably worth the expense. Some companies will ask you to absorb the air ticket and they will pick up hotel and

food . . . all kinds of combinations. It is a situational call and only you can make it.

How Do I prepare for an interview over a Video/Webcam system? *Please see Marketing chapter.*

When will the offer come? . . . *in many forms and from different people.*

- at the end of the interview
- from the functional manager
- by letter or email after the last interview
- from the CEO, President or Chairman
- at a networking meeting
- by telephone
- from the HR director
- at lunch or dinner

How will the offer sound? . . . *in many different ways.*

- "We would like to offer you the position of _______."
- "We will send you an offer letter tomorrow."
- "What would it take to bring you on board?"
- "We would like to make you an offer as ____ contingent on being awarded _____."

A verbal offer is good enough to begin salary negotiations, but it's not a done deal until the offer is in writing . . . ***an offer letter*** or in very high salary ranges, ***a contract***.

The Meeting/Interview/Telephone Report

The following report should be filled out completely after each telephone call, info meeting or interview . . . before you leave your desk or the area of the meeting.

Name of person(s): ____________________

Title: ____________________

Telephone: ____________________

Company: ____________________

Address: ____________________

Secretary's name: ____________________

Referred by: ____________________

Date and location of meeting: ____________________

Purpose of meeting: ____________________

____

Information gained: ____________________

____

____

Referrals: ____________________

____

Industry problems: ____________________

____

My next step(s): ____________________

____

____

Meeting evaluation: ____________________

____

Job Interview Preparation Check-off Sheet

______ I have researched the company and know why and how I would fit in. Where:

____

____

______ I know the name(s) of the interviewer(s). Name(s):

____________________ ____________________

____________________ ____________________

______ I am prepared to give my 2-minute response . . . ***say it!***

______ I have ten good questions to ask the interviewer about the ***company***:

1. ______________________________
2. ______________________________
3. ______________________________
4. ______________________________
5. ______________________________
6. ______________________________
7. ______________________________
8. ______________________________
9. ______________________________
10. ______________________________

______ I know what the company's stock is worth: ____________________

______ I have ten good questions to ask the interviewer about the ***industry***:

1. ______________________________
2. ______________________________
3. ______________________________
4. ______________________________
5. ______________________________
6. ______________________________
7. ______________________________
8. ______________________________
9. ______________________________
10. ______________________________

______ I know the company's competitors and what they are doing. They are:

____

____

____

______ I know the products of the company and can describe them. They are:

____

____

____

____

______ I know the salary range for the job I am applying for. It is $____________to $____________

______ I have good examples (short stories) which describe my value to the company. They are:

____

____

____

____

____

____

______ I have practiced responding to the book's questions out loud . . . ***do it!***

______ I can give an accomplishment for each of the skills required. They are:

1. ____
2. ____
3. ____
4. ____
5. ____
6. ____

______ The key words that are relevant to the job are:

1. ____________________ 2. ____________________

3. ____________________ 4. ____________________

5. ____________________ 6. ____________________

______ I can answer the question, "Why do you want to work for this company?" Your answer:

____

____

____

______ I have five short stories (2 minutes max) that will help the interviewer better understand how I will fit in: (use PAR format for structure)

1. ____

____

____

2. ____

____

____

3. ____

____

____

4. ____

____

____

5. ____

____

____

______ I have reviewed all of the questions in the ***What's Next?*** book and penciled in my answers.

______ I have read the "Interview" and"Compensation" chapters twice!

______ I know how to find the interviewer's office.

______ I know the secretary's name: ____________________________________

______ I have business cards and an extra resume with me.

______ I have a small notebook to take notes.

______ I know where to park.

______ I have my cell phone with me. (Make sure it is turned off)

______ If traveling, I have an extra set of clothes.

Note: This is also a good preparation check off list for a networking meeting, as well!

CHAPTER 14

REFERENCES

"Be bold . . . and mighty forces will come to your aid."
— Basil King

You probably won't need them, but you *gotta* and *wanna* have them. Most people think of references in terms of someone who will vouch for them and say nice things about their work, their personality, and their character. But of equal or more importance, is understanding ***that references become an important part of your network and could provide invaluable job leads . . . i.e., they could be a referral.*** For that reason they are a significant part of your job hunting network. When you are asked for references, you may want to consider a group of people that include five professional references. If possible, include one person who has worked for you, one who has worked with you, and at least two for whom you have worked. Both professional and social references should be persons who will add to your credibility. **Note**: Ensure you ask your references if they could suggest people that you could talk to regarding your objective area of interest . . . will build your network.

Choose carefully . . . Ideally:

- ✓ Previous boss/bosses (with positive relationship.)
- ✓ Colleague in "like" functional area.
- ✓ Recognized leader in an associated field.
- ✓ Recognized leader in any field.
- ✓ Local professional . . . banker, attorney, etc.

Different references for different jobs

Some Basic Guidelines:

1. Approach your references the same as you would approach a networking contact, regardless of your relationship. Ask the person permission to be a reference. It is thc courteous and proper thing to do. Do it by letter, by email or by phone. The absolute worst thing that a person can do is to give a name as a reference without advising the reference you have done so. Otherwise the reference will be blind sided when an unexpected call comes in and will not appreciate it.

2. Make certain your references know what you want to do . . . your objective. If you don't tell them, rest assured they will ask. Use relevant key words when you describe to them what you want to do and why.

3. Send a resume. Send another when you update the previous one.

4. Send a ***one page*** talking paper so they will have something to remind themselves about you. Just because you worked for

References

- Give them a heads up . . . *ask . . . call or write.*
- Advise objective . . . *send update when objective changes.*
- Send resume . . . *send update when objective changes.*
- Send talking paper . . . *send update when objective changes.*
- Ensure they know the skills and experience required . . . *include them in your correspondence.*
- Write their letters . . .*send update when objective changes.*
- Send thank you notes.

They are important referrals

someone ten years ago doesn't mean that they will remember everything you want them to remember about you. And, make sure that the talking paper is relevant to the position you are after. Tell the reference some facts about the position, what you told the company, and what your goals are.

5. Offer to write a sample (strawman) letter for them to use in the event they are asked for a written response. You might also offer to e-mail them an attachment. That way they won't have to retype the entire letter if asked for one. Don't start it with a "*To whom it may concern*." Reference letters should be addressed to the person who asked for it.

6. Finally, keep them abreast of your progress and make sure that you write them a thank you note when you land your job. Your references will become part of your contact network. More than a few people have written to me that someone they asked to be a reference sponsored them into a job within their organization. Don't forget to ask your references to let you know if they are contacted concerning you.

References are Important Referrals
and
Networking Resources

They will ask:
- **What are you plans?**
- **How can I help?**
- **What do you plan to do?**
- **What are you career objectives?**

. . . and you will say?

NOTE: Since the references will have a focused resume and talking paper, you will have to update them in the event you change your course and strive for a different objective. Also, make sure that you write a slightly different talking paper and reference letter for each reference, or they will all say the same thing about you.

CAUTION: **Fake references** . . . don't play this game. Companies DO check references. If you are caught using fake or weak references, it will have a serious impact on candidacy, and it could also negatively impact your future job search prospects . . . the word gets around.

The Reference and the Offer

An acquaintance of mine was ready to begin her job search. She had her list of references and began to call them to ask permission to use their names. The first person she called had been her boss ten years ago and she had maintained a social contact throughout the years. When she called her old boss the first thing the boss said was "I would be delighted to be your reference, what are you going to do?"

Our job hunter gave her 30-second commercial and after a second or two the reference said, "My company is looking for a person just like you and I think the fit would be perfect." So she went to the company for an interview and was hired.

Your references are part of your networking cheering team, which could have ideas and contacts that lead to job opportunities . . . again, choose them carefully. Be prepared to discuss your objective when asked, and never, never, never take them for granted.

CHAPTER 15

COMPENSATION

Compensation

Is a function of:

- **Where you live** – *supply and demand*
- **What you do**
- **The value of the job**
- **Your experience**
- **Special talents**
- **Your track record**
- **Your negotiation ability**
- **The economy***
- **Your gender***

Compensation or salary negotiation, as it is most often referred to, should result in a win-win proposition. Each party should walk away feeling that a fair deal was struck and everyone is happy. Negotiating for salary, benefits and perquisites (perks) is foreign to most career military and civil service personnel . . . Congress took care of that for you. In the private sector however, negotiating compensation can be a major part of the job interview process and it is usually expected by the hiring party. Salary negotiation is not difficult, and like buying a used car, most companies will usually expect some negotiating to take place. We will spend considerable time discussing salary negotiation and perks in this book . . . largely because you are so unfamiliar with it. Rest assured, most employers are decent people and are not out to take bread from your mouth. However, happiness for them may well be to hire an outstanding candidate at a price somewhat less than they had budgeted. Nearly every job has a salary range, and a maximum. While a new employee at McDonald's burger place may not be able to negotiate a higher hourly wage, nearly everyone else can . . . from secretaries to CEOs. Your up-front goal is to determine what that salary range is and negotiate to the top of it . . . then, go after the perks! **Remember, compensation is based on the value of the job's fair market value, *not* what you may or may not be actually worth.**

The Big Ten + 2 Basic Rules

1. Do not discuss salary until after the offer is made
2. Try to discuss/negotiate salary in person
3. Do not mention salary first
4. Know the job salary range before you negotiate
5. Study the perk list before you negotiate
6. Do not ask if the offer is negotiable, assume it is!
7. Always, always negotiate for more - *salary and perks*
8. If pressed for salary – give a range
9. If stymied . . . move on to the comp package
10. If stymied . . . talk to the 'manager' who made the offer
11. Get the offer in writing
12. Never accept the offer on the day it's made!

Why Negotiate Compensation? . . . *some very tangible reasons:*

- Your beginning salary is the basis for all future increases, therefore, you want it to be as high as possible.
- You will feel better about yourself if you accept the job knowing that your compensation is commensurate with your strengths and responsibilities.
- It will give you a chance to improve your "non-salary" benefits. There are more benefits and perks for those in the higher salary range.
- Your employer will think more highly of you if you can present sound rationale for the salary you believe you are worth.

- Nearly everyone does it, and the more senior and higher paying the position, the more there is to negotiate. Administrative personnel to CEOs negotiate.

Note: When negotiating for the first time you will probably feel a little skittish, nearly everyone does. Just remember, it is part of the game . . . and the negotiation includes the perks, as well as base pay.

An offer will not be withdrawn just because you try to negotiate . . . as long as you negotiate in a professional manner. In every case we have seen, the worst thing that can happen is for the employer to say no. The employer's goal will be to find out what salary or salary range you have in mind. That information will be of great value to them when you begin the salary negotiation ceremony.

Note: You have no leverage until you get an offer*. Once the job offer has been made to you, your position changes; you now have some leverage. The company has now decided that you are their selection (companies do not make an offer for the same job to multiple candidates at the same time) and in most cases will "give" a little to land you and make you satisfied with the compensation package. They do not want you to walk away from the offer! They do not want to have to tell their boss that they were unable to "land" you for the position that is so necessary! They do not want to take their second choice and they do not want to go through this interview process for the same job again. It is just as painful for them as it is for you!*

Basic Strategy *. . . for your consideration:*

- **Salary ranges.** Nearly every job, with perhaps the exception of entry level, has a salary range.
- **Know the salary range** for the job you are being interviewed for before you begin the interview.
- Have **three** numbers in mind:
  A. What you think would be **nice-to-make**
  B. Your "stretch" number – the ***Wow*** number
  C. Bottom line – the **least** amount you can accept

Salary Disclosure!

There is an unwritten law and/or agreement that says: ***"You will not ask your associates or friends about salary."***

Besides, it's tacky to do so ...

- **Your minimum**. To be successful at negotiating, you must have in mind your minimum salary figure and any other requirements.
- **Practice**. If you want to negotiate effectively, you must practice, practice, practice. Just like the job interview, practice with an audio or video recorder.
- **Preparation**. You must be able to recall the research and preparation that went into your resume, networking, and preparation for the job interview. That will be the information you will use to make the employer understand just how valuable you are to the company. Without sounding boorish, be prepared to enumerate the reasons why you are a good fit for the position.
- **Discuss the position** thoroughly and get the offer before getting into salary negotiation.
- **Negotiating . . . must take place *only after* the offer is made and *before* you are hired**. Forget it once you are hired. You only have negotiating leverage/power when they decide that ***you are the person for the job and have made you an oral or written offer.***

Avoid being the first to mention salary . . . two reasons:

1. You will sound as though salary is the most important thing to you . . . *even though it might be!*
2. Mentioning salary first signals the employer what you have in mind and diminishes your bargaining leverage. If your number is too high, the employer might think that you are unaffordable. If your figure is too low, the employer knows you will hire on for a bargain, or worse, that you are a *lightweight* and may not be of the "quality" the company is looking for.

- **If the employer insists** on a figure, and you have used all of the tricks in your bag to avoid giving one, respond with a range, (you have done your research and already know what the job's salary range is) or respond with the salary of your last government job, which includes base pay, perks and tax benefits.
- **When in doubt, ask for more**. (Remember, you already have the offer) If you don't at least ask, you will always wonder what could have been. A few thousand dollars may be a lot to you but to a major corporation it is a drop in the bucket. On the other hand if you are looking at a $XXX,000 job and are within a few thousand, the job is exactly what you want, it's exactly where you want to live, you like the people, and there is good potential, etc., then ask, but don't quibble over the difference . . . *especially if the job is where your spouse wants to live.*
- **Never, never, never accept a salary offer the day that it is made** . . . or a job offer for that matter. Explain that you need some time to think the offer over. *That's code for going home to discuss it with your spouse*. No one will object if you ask for a few days or even a week to think over the offer. In fact, they will expect you to ask for time to consider the offer. They will be anxious to put the "ordeal" to bed but will appreciate your request. ***The best questions will come to you on the way driving home!***

More Basic Training for Salary Negotiations

"Except in very unusual cases, never accept an offer on the day it is made."

Think about it overnight ...

Win-Win Negotiating:

- Don't act as though you are desperate.
- Don't have a deadline . . . keep an open agenda.
- Understand that there are four elements in the process . . . the salary that you are looking for, the person that you are negotiating with, the nature of the company, and yourself.
- When you are all finished and the salary and perks are still not quite enough, you can ask the company if they could "gross up" the overall value. This simply says that after all is said and done, you feel the overall package is a little on the short side. They are going to ask, "by how much" and you are going to have to respond with whatever you think is fair.
- The goal should be a win for each side. You want them to be happy with their offer and you want to be happy with what you are getting!

You will know that you should have bargained for more when you are driving a low-end Kia and all the other cars in the lot are Mercedes Benz convertibles!

The Salary Is Offered ...

Don't go bananas!

Let's assume for a moment that a salary offer has been made. Now is the time to contain yourself . . . regardless if the offer is lower <u>or</u> higher than expected. If the offer is higher than expected and you jump out of your chair and shout, "SOLD!", the employer will realize that he just gave away the farm. If the offer is on the low side, you should realize that the interviewer may be testing you or perhaps the position just doesn't pay what you thought it would. In either case, one tactic is to go into a "quiet contemplation" mode for about thirty seconds. And, while doing so, take out your note pad and do some calculations or doodle. In many instances the employer will offer to raise the original figure quoted with no further encouragement from you.

"The 30 Second Pause" . . . it really works

Situation*: A job offer was made on a Monday and salary discussions were to be conducted with the company's president on Thursday. My friend had not taken our career transition course and was inexperienced in the ways of salary negotiations. Interestingly enough, since the position being discussed was new, the president was unsure about how much to offer – he could/should have asked his HR manager to find out. The HR director would have gone to a salary website (like you will do) and determined the salary range for their size company and informed the president.*

Silent Negotiations
the 30 second pause

- The offer is made
- The salary is quoted
- A thoughtful pose
- Quiet contemplation
- A possible increase

Discuss position, responsibilities, your contributions, future plans ...

Negotiations were held over a quiet lunch and when the meal was finished the president said, "Well, we should get down to business and discuss compensation. What kind of base compensation do you have in mind?" Without the benefit of research, my friend didn't know what to say; he thought the company would make an initial offer and the conversation would go from there. He responded with something like: "Your company has a great reputation for fair play, and I think that whatever you have in mind would probably be okay with me." (A great response, by the way) Now the company president was caught off guard . . . he was as lost as my friend. Then the president had a flash of genius and said, "What were you making in the service?" Fortunately, my friend was familiar with the ***civilian equivalent*** *of his military pay, and he told the president, not believing for a minute that the company would match it. The president thought for a moment and said, "I think we can do better than that! How does $ _____ sound?"*

My friend was speechless and just stared at his plate. He was also trying to contain himself so the president wouldn't think the offer was too much. This silence went on for about thirty seconds. The president interpreted the silence as a sign that his prospective employee wasn't happy with the offer. The president then said, "If that is not enough, I have the authority to offer more." At this point my friend was about to bust out of his suit, but he regained his composure and said, "If you think that's fair compensation for the job, then it's fine with me." They both sighed in relief, shook hands, and departed. The president drove away in his limo and my friend ran home to tell his spouse the wonderful news! They discussed the rest of the package – the perks – at the office a few days later.

A 30 second pause could be profitable.

Analysis: Preparation is key. My friend got lucky! Both parties should know the salary range for the position in question. You should know how little you will accept, and the company should know the max they will offer. Additionally, know what perks are available, and how they can be traded for more or less salary. You have also just seen the power of silence . . . it can be a powerful negotiating tool. Once an offer is made, the last thing a company wants is for you to walk away from the proposal . . . especially if you would have accepted the offer for a small increase in base salary or some additional perks. Pausing for ten or twenty seconds never hurts; I have never heard of a company withdrawing an offer because someone took a few seconds to think about it. On the other hand, I have received countless letters that tell how a 30-second pause resulted in larger salaries and greater benefits . . . all without uttering a word.

An Impasse Occurs – over base salary
If an impasse occurs over base salary, suggest the salary issue be put aside and move onto the rest of the package – the perks. Make a comment such as, "While salary is important to me, the job is foremost on my priority list. Once we can agree on the position, I am sure the salary will fall in place." Or, "I know that salary is but one part of the total compensation, why don't we look at the benefit package and come back to the salary question later?" When you return to salary, review the job out loud with the interviewer, discuss the responsibilities, your contribution and value that you bring to the company.

The "At will" clause . . . unless you are looking at a million dollar or more job, most offer letters will state that this will be an ***"at will"*** position, meaning that you can be let go on short notice and that you can walk away at your will with no legal repercussions. Companies do not like to provide large sum severance packages/contracts that go on for years, unless that is what it takes to get the right person – like the President of GM. The offer might also include a ***"non-compete"*** clause that basically says that you will not compete with the hiring company for some period of time after leaving the company unless you are let go through no fault of your own. These are very common, however in many states the non-compete clause does not hold up except for special nature items . . . such as, a secret formula or expensive research information.

"Work at Will"
No Contract, No Security . . .

Could mean NO JOB!
Work at will . . . means no employment contract!

Good News . . . Bad News – For Women!

The good news is that there are more and more careers available for women and women are now making major strides in the senior management of corporate America.

The bad news is that, in most areas throughout the country, women are paid somewhat less than their male counterparts for doing the same job.

Not fair, especially when military and civil service women have become accustomed to getting the same pay as their male counterparts. According to surveys (USA Today and WSJ) the difference runs between 10 percent and 20 percent. The discrepancies exist in all careers . . . clerks, medical doctors, lawyers, retail sales and so on. I don't have a solution for this gross discrimination other than for you to bargain for the best deal you can get, and write to your congressional representative!

Responses To: *"What Are Your Salary Expectations?"*

- "I'd like to discuss the position more completely before getting into salary."
- "I'd like to come back to that after I have a better understanding of what you have to offer."
- "I think that salary shouldn't be an issue . . . your company has a good reputation for fair play."
- "From what I have been able to determine, the salary range for the position would be from _ to_."
- "I see a lot of possibilities for my contribution here . . . but I would prefer to go according to your scale."
- "From what I have been able to determine, the range of the position would be from _____ to _____."
- "What would the salary range be for a person with my experience, skills and accomplishments?"
- **Classic response**: "While compensation is an important aspect of any job, I am sure that if the fit is right, compensation will not be an issue . . . I would expect to be compensated based on the position's responsibility. What would you have in mind?"

Responses to a Lower than Expected Salary Offer

- "The offer seems a bit on the conservative side, could you do a little better."
- "Perhaps we could review the position requirements again . . . based on the responsibilities as I understand them, I expected the salary to be somewhat higher."
- "Can you do a little better?"
- "Perhaps we could put the base salary aside for the moment and discuss the rest of the compensation package." . . . the perks . . . see the following pages.

Heads Up!

- **People want to know what your offer is!**
- **They will ask:**
  "What did it take to get you to take this job?"
- **Don't reveal your salary ... if you do it will be all over the company.**

Many companies forbid salary discussions between employees

Accepting an offer lower than you are worth (or think you are worth)

It is okay to accept an offer that pays less than you are worth if it allows you to "get in the door" and there is a possibility of bigger and better things. I know of many who have taken jobs for less salary and responsibility than desired and have worked themselves up to senior positions in their company. There is also the case that, while the compensation might be less than desired, the other conditions of the job, such as location, working environment, commute distance, a happy spouse, etc., make takes the lesser salary a smart move.

Some Landing Report Feedback

A. "I was able to negotiate salary and some perks. I remember that you stressed that we military retires often undervalue what we are worth. Other folks I spoke to who were in the seminar with me, but did not negotiate, ended up with much less compensation. You should stress salary negotiation even more during the seminar. I think that was some of the best advice I got."

B. "We met twice. The second time to discuss the job at which time he put an offer on the table. When I told him it was well below my bottom figure he offered another five percent, just as you said. When I again hesitated, he groused a bit about having a budget to live within. I said I was very interested in the job, that

I hoped we could get together on compensation and departed. It was clear that he was going to see his boss about getting additional funds. About two weeks later he asked me back at which time he put the minimum I had asked for on the table and I accepted. It was another 25 percent over his initial offer."

Offer Letter and Agreements - GET IT IN WRITING

I received the following letter from a student who did not heed the warning about getting it in writing. Don't let this happen to you!

Get It In Writing

"As a valuable lesson learned, which you may want to pass on to future seminar members. I committed the exceptionally naive act of trusting a company's stated intentions to hire me without insisting on a signed agreement (Letter Offer). The first week of July, during my second month of networking, I interviewed with a company in Denver – one week later, the company advised me that I was the right person for the job, and generalities of salary and perks were discussed. Salary was higher than expected, perks were great and the area was my number two choice. Shortly after that, I received a letter from the company VPs advising me that my position would be available the second week of October. Several subsequent phone calls confirmed the company's intentions. I ceased my job hunt process and retired from the service on 1 October, the same day the company confirmed my schedule to return to Denver to formalize their offer. The very next day I was called by a mid-level manager who advised me that the company would not, in fact, require my services, as a recent influx of technical managerial personnel talent to a subcontractor had negated my position. In retrospect, I am amazed at how foolish I had been."

More Basic Rules

- **How long is the offer good for?**
- **Need some time to think it over.**
- **In writing, please!**

They won't take the offer back for asking

When the negotiations are <u>verbally</u> all wrapped up, **ask if the agreement could be written in a confirming memorandum . . . an offer letter**. Most companies will be more than willing to do this for you. If you get a negative response to your request, offer to write what you understand about the agreement and send it to them. If they are not willing to buy into your suggestion, you may want to reconsider the position. **Ask when do they need a decision**. In most cases they will want to know within a week or two but often they may be willing to wait several weeks or even months, especially if you bring needed strengths and/or knowledge to the table.

Note: Please don't say, "I want this in writing." Just say, "Could you please formalize the offer in a memo or an offer letter." Chances are that they will be way ahead of you and have the offer letter already in the computer, ready to go once the compensation issue is settled.

Contingent offer

A word to the wise. Some offer letters contain a "contingency clause," which states the offer is contingent upon the company winning a contract they have responded to. This, of course, means you will not be hired unless the company is awarded the contract they are bidding on. It is okay to accept the offer, but it is also okay (and wise!) to continue networking and/or interviewing until the bird is in hand – when the company's offer is final.

The Contingent Offer

Caveat emptor – buyer beware

- No guarantee of a job
- OK to sign - *but keep networking*
- You can always walk away if:
  - *a firm offer develops elsewhere*
- Give contingent offer notice/option

An offer without a contingent clause is always better, but if the company is solid, the offer will probably work out.

Sample Contingent Offer Letter

XYZ INCORPORATED
ADDRESS

DATE

Mr. Tom Hammons
1398 Elm Avenue
Fairfax, VA 12345

Dear Tom:

On behalf of XYZ Corporation, I am pleased to offer you a position as Project Manager with our Atlantic Region. As we have discussed in detail during our recruiting of you, your initial assignment will be as manager of the ABC project. As such you will be responsible for the successful completion of all project tasks on time and within budget.

Your initial salary and base compensation will be at the rate of $ _______ per month ($ ____ annually). In addition, you will participate in the incentive and fringe benefit programs which are standard throughout the company. As we discussed, your first salary review will be at the end of six months and then go on the normal annual cycle. Also, your vacation base will start at two weeks with normal annual increases.

As we agreed, in addition to the normal fringe benefit package, the company will be providing you with a laptop computer and will be leasing you an automobile (American made mid-sized of your choice). You will also be given country club golf privileges.

This offer is contingent upon the company winning the contract you will be managing. If the company is not the successful bidder, this offer will be considered null and void.

We are most pleased to welcome you as an at will, salaried employee with the understanding that you will be available to start work approximately ______ (DATE). Your location will be at our Arlington, Virginia offices. We are pleased to have you join our dynamic team and look forward to your future growth with the company. Please indicate your acceptance of our offer by signing and returning the attached copy provided for this purpose.

Sincerely,

Nelson Hendricks *(Company authorized individual)*

AGREED AND ACCEPTED

_______________________________ YOU

____________ DATE

Benefits and Perks . . . Check-off Sheet . . . *for now and the next time around*

	Company			
	①	②	③	④
Annual physical				
Base salary				
Bonus, signing on				
Bonus, annual				
Commissions				
Company car or allowance				
Cost of living increases . . . *average 4 percent*				
Corporate property, use of				
Country club				
Company telephone card				
Company credit card				
Child care (tax impact)				
Deferred compensation . . . **beware!**				
Dental plan				
Early salary review . . . *average 6 months*				
Education (finance and time off)				
Expense account				
Executive dining room				
Employment contracts				
Employee discounts				
Flex hour options (e.g., 4-day/10 hr per day)				
Free parking				
401 K (qualified plan)				
Home selling expenses				
House hunting expenses				
Incentive pay				
Interim living expenses				
Insurance . . . **first $50,000 free**				
Low interest loan				
Long-term disability pay				
Medical plan				
Moving expenses				
Outplacement counseling				
Out-of-state college tuition				
Professional associations				
Profit sharing				
Pension plan				
Relocation Allowance				
Sick leave and pay				
Severance pay				
Stock options				
Spouse outplacement				
Tele-commute options				
Title				
Travel insurance				
Tax, legal and financial counsel				
Tuition funds				
Vacation . . . with and without pay				

Benefit Descriptions **... Job Satisfaction: Remember that while the perks and base salary may**

be the greatest in the world, if you don't like the job, no amount of money will make you a happy camper!

Base Salary: Base salary should be negotiated before the benefits/perks are discussed if at all possible. Not only because it puts that issue to bed but because the value of some perks are based on the value of the base pay. Sometimes this is not possible but usually it is. (And, never discuss salary or perks until after the offer has been made!)

Commissions: Commissions are normally paid in any endeavor involving sales or selling. Often, commissions are a significant part of the total compensation package. Sometimes when there is a commission involved, employees receive a "draw" – a small amount of money each month to augment their commissions. Therefore, it is important to determine if there is a commission involved and how much, in terms of the percent of sales or some other metric.

Profit Sharing: In good times . . . when the company is profitable . . . many companies offer profit sharing at the end of their financial year when the final returns are in. The amount of the profit that is shared is determined in many different ways. Frequently, the amount is based on your position/level in the company and/or as a percent of your base pay. So, when a company tells you that they have a profit-sharing plan, you want to ask how is it paid out . . . what determines who gets what.

Pension plans: A company will either have a pension plan (sometimes called a cash balance plan) or not have one. Many companies are eliminating pension plans in favor of making contributions to 401K plans. If the company does have a pension fund, most likely there will be a period of time before you will become *vested* (company policy) and able to leave the company with some amount of pension.

Vesting: In plain language, ***vesting*** in a company occurs when you have been employed long enough by that company to be eligible for their pension fund benefits and/or to exercise (cash in) your stock options. Let's face it however, even if you are ***vested***, you won't receive much of a pension unless you have been with the company for a good many years. The amount of time it takes to become ***vested*** will depend upon the individual company policy. Why is knowing the time frame to vest important? Because you might want to stay with a company for a few more months or years so that you will be ***vested***, than leave sooner and lose whatever benefits you would have otherwise received.

401K (a qualified retirement plan): Many companies no longer offer any kind of pension plan. 401K plans have become very popular in recent years because a person can invest pretax dollars in the stock market and often receive a partial or sometimes 100 percent match from their employer. The money then grows, *hopefully*, tax free until it is withdrawn. At that point, the money is taxed at whatever your tax bracket is. Frequently the company will match your contribution with company stock. The company stock match can run from zero to 100 percent, but on the average runs about 20 percent to 30 percent of your contribution. For plans with a fixed dollar match, the most common match is 50 cents per $1 up to 6 percent of pay. So, if you earned $100K and contributed $6K to your 401K, the company, in this case, would contribute $3K. As a friend of mine always says, "Better than a sharp stick in the eye." The max amount of salary that can be invested usually changes each year, and if you are 50 or older, the max increases. Most financial planners will recommend that you maximize your contribution to your 401K plan. A *company stock* match is only a good deal if the company stays alive/solvent . . . think about it!

As a general rule, *but not ironclad,* whenever you can compound money/earnings tax-free, you should take advantage of the opportunity. Don't forget to investigate the 401K– a great deal for those who can qualify!

Heads up! Conventional wisdom says that it is **unwise/dumb** to invest all of your savings in the company you are working for . . . because, if the company goes under you not only lose your job and source of income but most or all of your stock invested. Think about it!

Caution

If the value of the stock goes down the tubes, so goes the value of your stock options and their cash worth. Message: don't put all of your savings in company stock.

Show me the money ... as in cash!

Title: While title may seem of little importance in the civilian world, it can be very significant when it comes to interfacing/dealing with people from other companies or even within your own company. Title can also impact certain benefits that a company offers such as the quality of company car or the year-end bonus. The more senior the title, the *more better*.

Incentive pay: Incentive pay is often given to people involved in a critical or time sensitive program that must be completed on or before a certain date. The pay encourages the program participants to bring in the finished product before or on time. It is also sometimes used to encourage employees to produce more sales.

Expense accounts: These are simply accounts that employee expenses are logged against after entertaining a client or traveling somewhere on company business. If you need one you will be authorized to have one . . . that is, authorized to spend company's money for company business without some kind of purchase document. Normally expense accounts are used by the sales force or business development people and by senior company officials. Most expense accounts have limits set on them and/or are limited for use in certain ways. Like the government, you have to submit a claim to get reimbursed. The company will expect you to be a good steward of their funds.

Vacation time: Most companies authorize time off for national holidays and that is sometimes stipulated in the offer letter. Other time off . . . vacation time . . . is often a negotiated item. There are some companies that don't give any vacation time until you have earned it. The majority offer somewhere between five and ten days for the first year on the job. In general, if you are moving into any kind of management position you should strive for two weeks vacation and try to negotiate for three weeks. Remember that the private sector does not count weekends as vacation time. So, when they say ten days, what are they saying? Make sure you understand the number of days . . . is two weeks 14 days or ten days? . . . it usually means ten days. How do you find out what they mean? You ask. Note that some managers are very sensitive about vacation time. Approach the subject with tact . . . you don't want to sound like vacation time is the biggest thing in your life or that the job is secondary to a lot of time off. They are hiring you to make money for them!

If you have reached an impasse on vacation days, you might want to ask about trading time off for salary . . . time off without pay. Some companies will go for it, most will not, except at the senior levels. It is worth a try and won't hurt anything. This conversation should take place at the very end of the negotiations . . . you don't want to give them the idea that you want a nice salary but a lot of time off!

Sick days: Nearly all companies offer sick days off with pay. The number of days given per year will depend on the individual company. Saved vacation pay can usually be *banked* and when you leave the company you receive compensation for it. Saved sick leave, however, most often cannot be saved and when you leave the company you leave the value of the sick leave behind.

Paid Time Off (PTO): There has been a tendency in the last few years by corporations to lump sick days and vacation days together. They are doing this because some employees use their sick days for vacation. Remember, once you have gone through all of your vacation and sick days, the days off after that will be without pay.

Medical plans: Most organizations of any consequence have some kind of medical plan for their employees. Most plans offer some kind of "cafeteria menu" arrangement that allows you to pick and choose what part of the plan you want to use.

Free parking: Most of us take free parking while in government service for granted. That is because parking is usually free. Try to arrange for free parking or to be compensated for paid parking. Parking expenses can run $100 to $700 a month or <u>more</u> in some cities.

Country clubs: Some companies offer country club memberships to very senior officers and/or to people who are involved in sales. You can always ask but unless you fit into one of the aforementioned groups, you probably won't see such a membership.

Professional associations: Nearly every company will allow and pay the dues for mid-level management employees and above to subscribe to publications or join professional associations that are relevant to the company business.

Company cell phone: If offered, take it. Let the company pay for your business calls rather than be reimbursed for the calls at some later date.

Annual physical exam: Most companies have some kind of medical exam program. Make sure you ask for it and make sure you get an annual physical even if you have to pay for it yourself.

Out-of-state tuition: If you are moving from one state to another and you or your children are going to have to pay out of state tuition, some companies will be willing to pay for the first year of the higher fees. You will have to ask.

Low interest loan: Some companies/organizations will provide a low interest home loan for people who are moving in from an out-of-town area. This is especially true when the economy/job market is hot. In tough times when profits are low, there is a tendency not to give these low interest loans. Asking won't hurt! Banks and other major financial institutions are most prone to offer low interest loans to employees . . . at all levels.

Severance pay: Severance pay is what you get if you are terminated from a company through no fault of your own . . . downsizing, re-organization, merger or what have you. It *typically* amounts to 1.44 week's pay for 'workers', 1.78 week's pay for middle managers, and 3 week's pay for senior

Typical Severance Clause

In the event that this employment arrangement is terminated through no fault of the employee, monetary severance will be provided to the employee in the amount of $ ________ (X months base salary) plus unused vacation time. Employee agrees to the company's stated rules and regulations regarding the disclosure of company information and rules regarding non-compete activity.

Note:
Severance terms are negotiated at the time of negotiating compensation, not when you are notified that you are about to be severed.

managers . . . for ***each year of service***. This can be a negotiable item. The higher your level in the company the higher will be the severance pay. *See outplacement below.*

Outplacement services: While it may sound strange to discuss severance plans and outplacement (career transition) services while negotiating compensation for a new job, it is something that is done every day in the private sector. In fact, in a hot economy, severance plans often play a major role in salary negotiations. This is because of the uncertainty of the job market . . . mergers, acquisitions, reorganizations and the like, that you have no personal control over and oftentimes the company you are working for has no control over. All you have to say is, "In the event that my job ceases to exist through no fault of my own, what provisions do you offer in terms of severance pay and outplacement services." They will understand.

Employee discounts: Employee discounts are often given to employees for items manufactured or sold by the company. This can be a good deal if you need the merchandise. If the item is purchased at or above cost there is usually no tax implication. It the item is purchased below cost, then there is a high likelihood that some of the savings will be a taxable event.

Sign-on-bonus: A sign-on bonus is simply a bonus that a company may give as an extra inducement to accept the job with the company. They are very common and are given to many people in management and sometimes non-management positions. The signing-on bonus can amount to a few thousand dollars to a hundred thousand dollars or more. These bonuses are especially prevalent during times when the economy is booming and there is a high demand for skilled talent. I know of many officers as well as senior enlisted personnel who have received signing-on bonuses. Most military and civil service personnel are reluctant to inquire about a signing-on bonus and as a result leave money on the table. It will never hurt to ask. ***Note: Don't ask if there is one***. Simply say, "What is the signing-on bonus that comes with this offer?" The worst thing they can say to this or any other request is . . . "No." I have never heard of a company withdrawing an offer from a person asking for a signing-on bonus. You may think asking for this and other things mentioned in this section amount to being greedy, but this is the way it is done. **IN MANY CASES, IF YOU DON'T ASK, YOU DON'T GET!**

Bonus: Very often, when there is a job offer, the offering official will tell you that there are bonuses that usually go along with the job. A financial bonus is usually tied to performance . . . you win a big contract or complete an assignment ahead of schedule which makes more money for the company or anything else that has a favorable financial impact on the bottom line. Bonuses are not often given out because you are a nice person or show up on time. And, in poor economic times and/or when the company is not performing well, the bonuses are often few and far between. Just because the person who had the job ahead of you got a big one doesn't necessarily mean that you will get the same amount, if any. Further, a bonus is not counted as part of the base salary when it comes to a negotiating a raise.

Stock options: A stock option is simply a piece of paper given to you by the company that gives you the option to buy a certain number of shares of the company stock at some future date at the price indicated on the paper. For example, you receive an option to buy one share of stock for ten dollars. In two years from now the stock is selling for 20 dollars a share and you decide to *exercise* your option. You go to your stock broker and tell him you wish to exercise your option and he will buy the stock for ten dollars, sell it for 20 dollars and give you a check for ten dollars, less his commission. You net the difference and become a happy camper! Don't forget the IRS gets a cut. Note: I personally prefer cash! How about both?

While in the past stock options were pretty much reserved for the high rollers, today they are being given to employees at all levels . . . from CEO to floor sweepers. There are many ramifications to stock options and before you start selling yours, talk with someone in the financial or human resource area and get some experienced advice. Stock options could be a negotiable item and it wouldn't hurt to inquire about them, especially if you are going in at a relatively high level.

Early salary review: This is a "no-brainer." Let's say that you are somewhat less than satisfied with the offer but it is close to what you are looking for. You could ask the person you are negotiating with if you could have an early salary review, say in six months, to review the job and how well you are doing with the idea that salary could be enhanced. This is a give-away perk because it costs the company nothing. And, in six months you will both probably forget to meet and discuss it, or if you do meet your boss can always say that they think the original arrangement is okay. Keep in mind that if you aren't doing as well as you thought you might, an early salary review could be counter productive. OOPS!

Cost of living increases: In good times, most companies offer cost of living increases. These can range from a few percent to as much as 3 percent of your base salary (the average is three to four percent) and therefore, have the potential to be significant. The amount will depend on the economy, the company, your performance and the discretion of the senior. If your performance is outstanding you may get a higher amount, if your performance is marginal you may come in at the low end of the totem pole. In any event something is better than nothing.

Deferred income: This is basically a perk for those at the upper income levels. Many companies offer a plan that permits senior employees to defer receiving some of their income until a later date, and therefore avoid paying income tax on the amount deferred each year (like an IRA or 401K). The mechanics of such a plan are simple . . . the company withholds the money and puts it in an investment account where it grows in value (hopefully) unencumbered by federal or state income taxes. The account is usually managed by a professional pension fund manager and invested very conservatively. The good news about deferred income is that it avoids taxes until it is withdrawn, when you might be at a lower tax rate. The bad news is that if the company goes under, your money stays with the company and you become another creditor. Normally you will have sufficient warning that your company is about to fold and you will be able to retrieve your funds . . . but the risk is always there. And, remember that the entire amount will be taxed when you withdraw the funds from the account . . . again, hopefully when you retire and are in a lower income tax bracket.

Caution: *if you had a crystal ball and could determine that you would be at the top of the tax bracket forever, then you might be better off not choosing the deferred route (because you will be paying the same tax then as now) and instead invest the after-tax money in items that are taxed at a lower capital gains rate and pay less in taxes in the future. Gets complicated . . . see your tax person for guidance.*

Company car or allowance: Company cars are often given to senior people in the company and to others who may require a car to conduct their work . . . like sales people and those who must travel to conduct business. Usually, a company will give you a choice between a company car or receiving compensation for expenses in lieu of the car. The choice is yours. My advice is that if you need a car, a company car is a good deal but if you don't need a new or another car, take the cash. The cash will be a taxable item and reported to the IRS. And, some portion of the company car will probably be taxed. See your finance department or human resources department for details.

Life Insurance: Presently, the first $50,000 of insurance provided by a company is **tax free**. Some companies provide senior officers with more insurance but if the amount exceeds $50K it will be a taxable event. The point here is simply this . . . if you need the extra insurance taking the company's offer for more will probably be the most economical way of getting it. If you do not need it, then you are wasting money. Always accept the $50,000 or whatever the standard amount is at the time of the offer . . . there is no tax consequence making it a freebie! Remember, the $50,000 insurance is only good while you work for the company.

Dental plan: First, get all of your dental needs cared for before you leave government service. Dental work is very expensive and dental insurance, such as TRICARE Dental doesn't help very much. A few companies offer extensive dental coverage for the more senior officers but that perk like others is not what it used to be.

Executive dining room: If the position is high enough and there is an executive dining room then this is good deal. Unfortunately executive dining rooms are rapidly going away and this as a perk may soon be a moot point.

Corporate credit card: Like the US government, some companies offer a company credit card for those with a need. If you are offered one take it.

Travel insurance: Most companies offer travel insurance while traveling on company business.

Health clubs: Sometimes offered in-house and sometimes at a gym nearby. More frequently, not at all.

Corporate Property: Use of corporate property would include things like notebook computers and smart phones . . . devices that might be necessary in conducting your day-to-day work. For senior personnel, corporate property might also include use of a company condo at the shore or some other nice to have benefit. Ask about them.

Tuition assistance: There are very few companies that do not offer some kind of tuition assistance if you are taking courses that will make you a better employee. The company may pay for all or a portion of the tuition, and reimbursement may be based on how well you do in terms of grades. There might be some payback time associated with helping with tuition assistance.

Long term disability Insurance: Most large companies offer long term disability insurance if you are injured or unable to work for some legitimate reason. The amount differs from company to company but in general amounts to around 75 percent of your base pay for five to seven years. This will be company policy and probably not negotiable unless at a very senior position.

Moving expenses: In good times, when the economy is hopping, most companies are willing to pay for moving expenses. They might also be willing to pay for house hunting trips and expenses while you are getting settled in. I know of several companies that will reimburse your spouse to come and "have a look" at the area. Some companies will offer this perk up front but most will wait until you ask. Defense industry companies will know that the military will move you free when you retire so they may not be inclined to pay themselves. Ask anyhow. Many, many people have been able to negotiate a good deal by having the company pay them what it would have cost the company for the move, and then move themselves using the government's last move benefit. There is nothing wrong or illegal about doing this and it is probably one of the most often good deals received. This can also be a way for a company to give you a signing-on bonus (and call it a moving expense) without having eyebrows raised elsewhere in the company. Many people get both . . . signing-on bonus and the cost of the move.

Contracts: Whereas a offer letter usually includes a statement that you will be an *at will* employee, an employment contract will stipulate a time frame . . . normally about three years. What a contract usually means is that if you are let go before your contract expires, you will be paid for the balance of the contract or whatever has been negotiated. Contracts are written in many different ways with many different considerations. Employment contracts are not normally used unless the salary is very high . . . $800,000 or more. They are very popular with senior management but not popular with shareholders. If you are getting paid a salary high enough to warrant a contract you should hire a contract lawyer in the state where the job is located to help you read and understand the fine print. And there will be fine print!

Tax, legal and financial counsel: At high management levels, companies often provide free financial counseling. This can be a great perk. Understand that ***the perk could be a taxable event***, especially if it is done by an outside firm. The company will be billed by the outside firm and the company will then show it as a tangible benefit and you will incur a tax burden. It can be a good deal if you need outside financial assistance but not if you don't need it. Do the math.

Child care: For those with young children, some companies will pay for child care and then deduct the amount of costs attributed to you from your pay check. This really amounts to paying for the child care with your pre-tax dollars instead of your after tax dollars. This is a good deal if you require the service. This is still a new concept and you will have to inquire about this benefit. Some companies offer child care at or near your work location.

"Perks"

- 19% of total compensation
- Can almost always get some
- More senior = more perks
- Higher salary = more perks
- Asking won't hurt
- It all adds up
- Don't get greedy

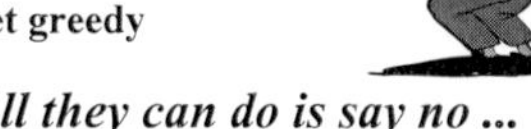

All they can do is say no ...

Summary and Salary Range

Salary Range

- Ask Associates
- Associations
- Websites . . . Yahoo
- Newspaper ads and articles
- Business magazines
- People in like positions
- Retired business people
- Salary Surveys

You will find that negotiating compensation is a little stressful but very rewarding. You will be better prepared to negotiate if you do some homework. The first thing is to determine the salary range for the position in question. Unlike the government where everyone knows what everyone else is paid, in the private sector those facts are well guarded. You can ask friends, however, who are in the same or similar line of business. They won't tell you what they make, and you shouldn't ask, but they will usually give you a range. If you are working through a recruiter, the salary range will probably be available and even offered. You can also look in the newspapers for similar jobs and get an indication of the range. Many associations publish average salaries paid to various levels in their business. **Try www.salary.com for a salary information or Glassdoor.com**, ***but beware: a WSJ study found that salary Websites can overstate salary figures by 10 percent +.*** Remember that compensation differs throughout the country for the same jobs and responsibilities. A job in LA pays three or four times what the same job would pay in other parts of the country . . . but the cost of living is much higher . . . compare apples to apples. Another salary site to check out is Indeed.com ... there are many.

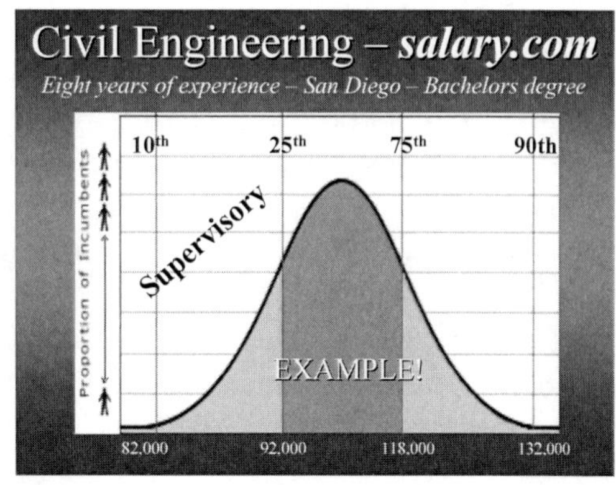

Before you even begin to negotiate, you must know what you bring to the table . . . how you will help make the company profitable. List the requirements of the job and match them with your experience and accomplishments. Your goal is to make the employer understand your value to the company's or organization's bottom line.

Leverage
By the time you do get to compensation, the employer's negotiator has obviously decided that you are the right person for the position. When you get to this point, you have some leverage . . . they want you and you know it! Remember however, the goal is win-win:

- Be positive
- Don't try to get the last drop of blood . . . don't over-negotiate
- Try to get the company to commit to a salary or range before you begin
- If they ask what your salary in the government was, try to avoid an answer by saying that the responsibilities are different as well as the benefits.
- Remember that silence is a powerful negation tool
- Do your homework
- Always remember that you are negotiating and that some compromise is bound to take place
- Go for your goal but be prepared to back off . . . know what you need

Letter from a seminar attendee . . .
"Retirement pay was not considered in the compensation package. I attribute my successful interview to the preparatory strengths you laid out for me during the class. It really worked!

Of special note was the tip about what to do after the initial offer was given. I followed the book's suggestion and drifted off like I was calculating in my mind. After an apparently uncomfortable period of time the HR supervisor offered up more money and reminded me that "since I was new at this" I could come back with a counter offer. I said that I would like to take the weekend to think about it. On Monday afternoon I called her up and asked for another two thousand above her second offer. She groaned, but conceded . . . I would have gladly taken the first offer."

The moral to the story is this: Following the rules in the *Ruehlin Associates*' book really works. The resume was right, the cover letter was right, the interviewing technique was right (practice really helps too), and above all else, don't be afraid to be yourself and ask for what you think is fair. Note: She probably groaned with happiness because she got him so cheap!

A word to the wise: Compensation is important and we all want to be paid according to the value we bring. However, there are many other aspects to job satisfaction, such as those discussed in Chapter One . . . Profile of The Ideal Job . . . and doing what you want to do!

Example Compensation Negotiation Scenarios (Dialogue)

Scenario 1 . . Job being offered

HR: What kind of salary do you have in mind?
You: Do I understand that you are offering me a job?
HR: Yes . . . what salary do you have in mind?
You: While salary is certainly an important component of a job, I have always thought that, if the fit was right, the appropriate compensation would follow. What would be the range for this position?

What Are You Worth?

You will get paid based on the *value of the job*, not your intrinsic value!

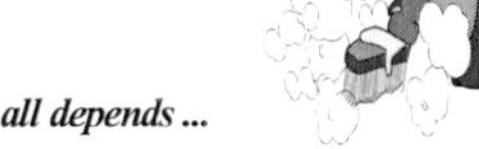

It all depends ...

Scenario 2 . . . Job not yet offered

HR: What kind of salary do you have in mind?
You: Do I understand that you are offering me a job?
HR: Well no, I was just trying to determine what salary you would expect to receive.
You: While salary is certainly an important component of a job, I have always thought that, if the fit was right, the appropriate compensation would follow. I would prefer to know the status of the offer before getting into the salary question.

Scenario 3 . . . If Pressed

First, ask "Is there a salary range for the job?" If pressed further, say "Based on my salary research and talking with people in similar situations, the range would seem to be between _____ and _____." *Be careful here because you can believe the HR person will not offer you the high side of the quoted range. Do your homework and try to get close to what you really think the job is worth. Consider quoting a low number equal to what you would "expect" to make, and a high number equal to your "WOW" number.*

Typical Salary Dialogue

"We would like to make you an offer of $_________. How does that sound?"

"The base salary of the position would run between $____ and $_____. Is that figure within your range?"

"What kind of salary are you looking for?

"What would it take to get you on board here?

Playing One Salary Offer Against Another – *Strategy*

I am often asked if it is okay to play one offer against another. For example, company A offers you X amount and company B, which is okay but you prefer company A, offers you X plus more.

Question: It is fair to go back to company A and explain that you have two offers, and, that for the same position, another company has offered more, but that you prefer to work at company A, and could company A match company B's offer?

Answer: Yes – as long as you do it in an honest and polite manner, *AND* are **positive** that you **have both offers in writing**. The last thing you want to happen is for company A to say, "Sorry, we can't go any higher and good luck with company B" . . . and company B's offer goes away!

Personal note: Unless the difference in salary and perks is really significant, if company A represents true happiness, I don't think it is worth squeezing the turnip. It won't hurt but think it through before you act. There are no two situations exactly alike in this salary negotiating business.

"And, What Salary Are You Looking For?"

The story goes like this . . . At the end of job the interview the HR person asked the recently retired Colonel, *"And, what starting salary were you looking for?" The Colonel responded confidently, "In the neighborhood of $250,000 a year depending on the benefits package. The HR person said, "Well, what would you say to a benefits package of 6-weeks vacation, 14 paid holidays, full medical and dental, a company car leased every two years – say a red Corvette, and a company matching retirement fund to 50 percent of salary, and the salary that you mentioned?" The Colonel sat up, mouth agape and said, "Wow! Are you kidding?" And the HR person said, "Of course . . . but you started it!"*

Websites . . . For Salary Information

There are numerous ways to obtain salary information and many are discussed in this book. The websites are presenting more and more opportunities to find out salaries for any given position. Sometimes the information is provided on a national basis, and other times it is shown by state. Websites that I have found to have good tables/info which will at least provide an idea of what different occupations pay – even though they are usually overstated – are (* popular favorites):

Economic Research Institute at: www.erieri.com
US Bureau of Labor Statistics at: www.bls.gov
WSJ career journal at: http://careers.wsj.com*
www.Salary.com*
www.pay-scale.com*
www.glassdoor.com *

Also: try Google . . . just ask,*"What is the salary of a program manager in the aerospace industry,"* for example. It might give you some idea or at least a starting point.

Employers determine pay:
... by the seat of their pants or,
... professional salary surveys:
(not available to individuals)
Hay Group
Mercer Corp

Employees determine pay:
... asking around
... library research
... web sites:
Pay-Scale.com
Salary.com
Payscroll.com
Glassdoor.com
www.indeed.com.salary

The problem with most salary websites is that they often show a spread so large that the information is nearly worthless. Better than nothing at all, but not very valuable. Another problem is that normally, no two management job descriptions/responsibilities are exactly the same. And, zip code can play a major role. So, the best way of determining what a given job should pay is to ask a knowledgeable friend, who is familiar with the industry, what they think a ball park number might be. And then compare it to what you have *found* in one or two of the above mentioned websites.

Those who brag about how much they earn are either: very insecure; or very full of it; or both!

Attendee Feedback Regarding Salary Negotiation

"Unquestionably, the most frightening aspect of transition for me was salary negotiation. Despite all the research, you still have little idea of your current and future worth to a given company. I simply started with my total service compensation and worked down from there. Their initial offer was well below my absolute bottom line where salary plus retirement pay - even though it's not part of the negotiation - would have matched current income. I took their offer home for the weekend and came back with a counter, and after a few quick phone calls they met it. It wasn't hard negotiating an additional 20 percent in salary over their initial offer. In retrospect I probably may have gotten even more."

In the Final Analysis

Career Decision Factors ... which job?

- Location
- Best fit
- Commute
- Base salary
- Perks
- Size of company
- Future opportunities
- Growth potential
- Demands
- Personal time
- Prestige
- Stability

Culture and ethics!

"Better to have a job that you enjoy and is located where you want to live but pays a conservative salary, than a job that you dislike but pays on the high side. And, better to have a job that pays "a little less" than you might be worth, than to have no job at all!"

— Confucius

Salary Take-away

- Have **three** numbers in mind:
  1. What you think would be **nice-to-make** ... fair market value
  2. Your "stretch" number – the ***WOW*** number . . . *the very high end of the range*
  3. Bottom line – the **least** amount you can accept
- You will be paid based on the value of the job, what you are worth to the organization in this particular position, not your intrinsic value.
- If asked about salary expectations: Respond with "What is the salary for someone with my qualifications?" or "Can you suggest a range for the position?"
- If pushed: Offer a range with "nice-to-make" number at the bottom and the "Wow" number at the top.
- You can't bargain until there is an offer on the table. Until the employer thinks that you are worth bringing aboard, don't discuss money.
- If you don't ask, you don't get. Don't undervalue yourself. Do your homework and know approximately what the salary/perks should be for the position in question.
- Talk to the hiring manager. Whenever possible you should be negotiating with the person who will be hiring you.
- By the numbers. You should always try to negotiate your base salary first. There might be times when you "set it aside" and go to perks, but your goal should be to put the base salary to bed.
- Don't be afraid to speak up. If the offer is lower that expected, let them know . . . in a nice way.
- Be prepared to offer alternatives . . . if the company won't give on one item perhaps they will give on another.
- If stymied, try to talk to the person/manager who made you the offer or who you will be working for.
- Promises are great, but the promise of a big bonus at the end of the year won't put food on the table. Make sure the tangible compensation will take you where you want to go.
- Win-win negotiations. Try to make the situation a win-win for both sides. Squeezing the last drop of blood from the employer might make you feel good, but it might also create some bad feelings.
- I've said it before . . . get the offer in writing. It's okay to negotiate compensation based on a verbal offer, but before you say "Sweet dreams," you want the offer in writing.
- It is okay to take a job that pays lower than you are worth (or you think you're worth) if it allows you to **"get in the door"** and there is a probability of bigger and better things.

Do not be afraid to negotiate . . . keep the door open!

CHAPTER 16

RESEARCH *and* PREPARATION

Serendipity is wonderful, but
"Luck Favors The Prepared Mind"
— Peter Drucker

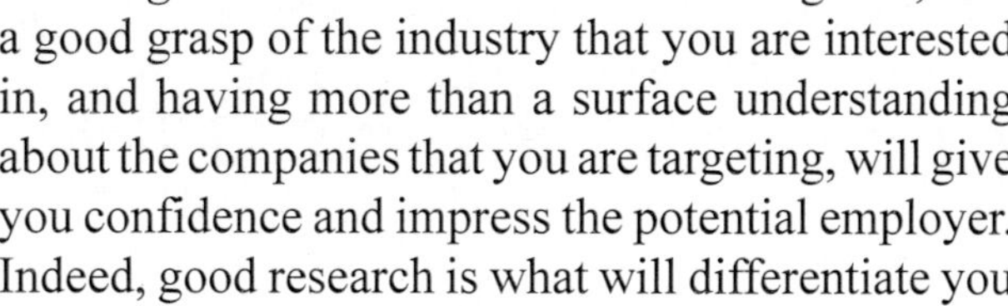

Research is a critical element of a successful career transition.

Together with having a career focus and networking, research is a critical aspect of any job hunting campaign. It is the very foundation of job hunting and those who invest the time and energy researching industries and companies will reap the benefits accordingly. There are many kinds of research . . . scanning the newspapers for information, talking to friends and acquaintances, digging out information at the local university or business library and *scouring* websites. It is a time-consuming task, but one that ***must*** be undertaken. Having a good grasp of the industry that you are interested in, and having more than a surface understanding about the companies that you are targeting, will give you confidence and impress the potential employer. Indeed, good research is what will differentiate you from the competition! As Peter Drucker, the renown management guru said, *"Luck favors the prepared mind."*

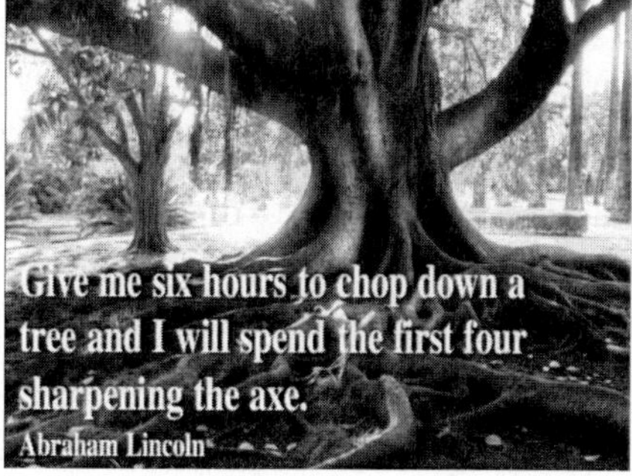

Targeting Companies

Many people begin their career transition by going around shaking hands with whomever is willing to shake their hand. And, when asked what industry or companies they are interested in, often as not, they give you a blank stare. Knowing that you have decided upon an objective, and by the way, it is impossible to research without an objective (either written or just in your mind), the first action is to develop a list of target companies that interest you. Come up with a list of as many names as possible. Consider ...

- ✓ Personal contacts
- ✓ The Yellow Pages
- ✓ Newspapers
- ✓ Trade magazines
- ✓ Directories of Corporations
- ✓ Chamber of Commerce
- ✓ Service clubs
- ✓ Professional clubs
- ✓ Websites
- ✓ Friends

> "The job I have was advertised and had 330 applicants. I found out about the job, and got an interview through networking. The search committee interviewed 12 candidates. The final three made presentations to all 19 board members. I would have never been interviewed were it not for networking! I was well prepared by your course. I had interviews with six organizations, and three offered positions: one reject; two were in final interview phase when I decided to accept this position. Preparation is truly the key. ***I out-worked my competition."***

The next step is to review your contact/networking lists and see if there are any matches. If you find a match, and you will, you have an initial starting point: for entry into the company, for finding more information about the company, to find out salary structure within that company or industry and who are the decision makers in the company.

Why Bother to Research? . . . The Value Line Story

The night before George was to meet with a senior member of a large bank, he thought that he had better go to the library and find out what banks do . . . other than the obvious. He went to the local library and after finding out where the business research section was, proceeded to research. Note that this was a new adventure for him because up to this time he had never bothered to learn much about any company he was talking to . . . dumb, he knew, but that is how it was. He found a research company named Value Line and started to look up the bank. Now you would think that any company with assets of 20 billion dollars would be "covered" by a stock analyst. But try as he might, the bank was not to be found . . . there were some larger ones and some smaller ones but not the one he was looking for. He finally gave up and went home. Hey, he tried . . . didn't he ?

If you meet with a company without fully understanding its business and having good questions to ask, you are not very smart!

Who Gets Hired?

It's Not The Best Qualified who gets the job ... it's the best prepared and a positive attitude!

Lest we forget !

The next day he was seated before the head of the bank talking about his career, how nice the weather was, and other important things like that. He had experienced similar conversations like this many times before . . . not talking about the industry but just general thoughts . . . which is probably why his hosts always looked at him wondering why he was there. At the end of the meeting . . . his time was up . . . the head of this 20 billion company asked if he had any questions he would like to ask him about his bank. True to his previous encounters, he had nothing substantial to ask . . . after all, Value Line didn't have anything so why should he ? As he was about to say that he had no questions, he blurted out, "I was wondering why Value Line does not analyze/maintain coverage on your bank." Turns out that the Chairman didn't know that, nor did the Chief Financial Officer. Also turns out that they had been talking for some time about creating a position that would interface with companies like Value Line so that they would be analyzed/followed (reported on) by all of the major stock analysts. Note that publically owned companies want to be analyzed and reported on by companies like Value Line so that stock brokers and potential investors have information readily available. If no one knows about you then no one will buy your stock and the stock won't go up and the shareholders won't be happy and nor will the Chairman.

Knowing something about the company could open doors.

To make a long story short, the banker turned to him and asked what he was going to do in his second career. George gave a lame reply and the banker said, "Why don't you come and work for me and help us do a better job of communicating with Wall Street? So he did, and became the Director of Shareholder-Investor Relations. How about that? Heck, if Value Line had included an analysis of the company, George could have found some really pertinent data about the company, and they might have made him the President . . . doubt it!

Lesson learned: **Information is power.** In this case one piece of information opened a door of opportunity. Knowing something about the company will take you a long way. Knowing a lot about the company, one key significant comment, will take you even further! **Knowing nothing will get you nothing**!

Researching Companies

When you research these companies you should plan to spend four to eight hours in the library or at a Website, in addition to the time spent talking with personal contacts and other means . . . and that is for each company. ***Just Google the company and you will most likely find useful information***. Information that you should obtain:

- The culture of the company.
- Key managers and some personal information about each.
- The products or services that they market.
- Current problems/situations in the industry and the company.
- What their present needs are . . . problems that you can solve.
- What new products are appearing in the industry.
- Who are their competitors and what are they doing?
- What is their long-term business strategy?
- Their current stock price and trend . . . if traded on the exchange?
- Is the industry/company in a growth stage or are they a potential dinosaur?

Company Profiles

- Dun and Bradstreet's Million Dollar Directory
- Secretary of State's office – for private corporations
- Dun's Business Locator – small companies
- The American Business Disc – small companies
- IBISWorld – global industry market research and trade journal articles

There are many ways to get this information. Personal contacts are usually the best, but sources like the library, web research, calling the company and asking for their annual report or 10K/10Q or stopping by the lobby and picking up information all pay dividends. If you do call the company just tell them that you are interested in their company and would like some information. Ask for the Investor Relations Officer, or the Chief Financial Officer or the Director of Marketing . . . one of these offices will have company information and be happy to provide it to you. Annual reports are easy reading . . . the front section will tell you about the products and where the Chairperson of the Board thinks the company is heading. The second section is composed of easy-to-read numbers that describe the financial condition of the company. The 10K and 10Q are the nitty-gritty numbers and are *not fun* to read. If you have trouble sleeping at night, a 10Q is a good cure. ***Another great source is the Internet***. Just Google the company name and the words *Annual Report* and there it is, endless amounts of information as well as other companies like the one you are examining.

Using data at networking meetings and job interviews.

Most people find that taking and keeping research notes on 3x5 index cards makes sense. You can sort the cards alphabetically and carry them with you to an information meeting or job interview . . . not to be shown, however. The index cards should contain all pertinent information about the company. Of course you can always use the memo pad in your cell phone. Or consider using Post-It notes in a small, Day-Timer like notebook filled with all of the data and questions you want to ask. We cannot overemphasize the importance of research. The knowledge that you gain will give you a definite edge over the competition. The computer will be worth its' weight in keeping track of information.

I was more prepared!

"I found that I was more prepared for the job interview than the person conducting the interview! I asked questions they had to think about. They were not expecting to be asked any in-depth questions."

Card/Fact Sheet Format

Company Name:

____

____

____

Background/Overview:

____

____

____

Products/Services:

____

____

____

Clientele:

____

____

____

Facts:

____

____

____

Industry Comments:

____

____

____

Using Reference Books

1. Go to the reference section of the library. Ask the librarian if you don't know where it is.

2. Look up the industry and find the appropriate NAICS code . . . Standard Industrial Classification . . . an eight-digit code.

3. Use the North American Industry Classification System (NAICS) to target companies.

4. Research the companies, their management and other data.

5. Review their Annual Reports, 10K and 10Q ... use the internet.

6. Select other materials . . . magazine articles, newspaper clips, industry surveys.

A great source of research information is your librarian. The librarian will be ecstatic to assist and will save you time and effort in your research efforts.

The ***NAICS codes*** (North American Industry Classification System) classify establishments by the type of activity in which they are involved. There are 20 classifications and cover a vast range of economic activities, such as ...

- Agriculture
- Mining
- Construction
- Manufacturing
- Transportation, communication, electric, gas, and sanitary services
- Wholesale trade
- Retail trade
- Finance, insurance and real estate
- Personnel services, business services, repair services, and other services
- Public administration

For example: One NAICS code relates to the Printing and Publishing industry; another relates to the Sheet Metal Work industry; still another relates to the Manufacture of Space Vehicles and Satellites. The code lists the companies, addresses, telephone numbers, number of employees, CEO, Human Resources Director, etc.

Sources for Information and Research . . . ASK GOOGLE ANYTHING!

There are innumerable sources of information available. There is more information to research than you can possibly read, let alone digest. Most cities of any size will have the following publications or something similar:

- Chamber of Commerce Referral Directory
- Websites . . . Google will find most anything, including you.
- Source Book
- Economic Development Corporation Manufacture's Directory
- Business Journal
- Manufacturer's Directory
- Business Journal Book of Lists
- Contacts Influential
- Local newspapers and magazines - The Wall Street Journal
- 10K and 10Q . . . available free in the Internet at www.sec.gov (Securities and Exchange Commission's EDGAR database)
- Annual Reports
- Library of Congress Business Research Site.

In addition, there are a host of national publications and websites that offer information of every kind imaginable and in every format possible. Here is a list of research resources that will assist with your job hunt:

Library Research on Companies

Dun & Bradstreet Million-Dollar Directory
Dun & Bradstreet Consultants Directory
Mergent - America's Corporate Families
Mergent - Handbook of Common Stocks
Mergent - Moody's Investor Manuals
Standard and Poor's Register of Corporations, Director and Executives
Standard & Poor's Stock Reports
National Trade and Professional Associations of the United States and Canada
National Directory of Non Profit Organizations
Gale – Encyclopedia of Associations
Value Line Investment Survey

Web Research on Companies

Businesscredit.dnb.com
Barrons.com
Spglobal.com
Gale.com
Valueline.com

Hoovers.com
Inc.com
Fortune.com
Money.cnn.com
Dowjones.com
Wsj.com
Bloomberg.com
Bizjournals.com

Job/Career Opportunities via the Internet

Indeed.com
Careerbuilders.com
Monster.com
Usajobs.gov
Vault.com
Chronicle.com/jobs
Glassdoor.com
LinkedIn.com
Google.com

Also, be sure the check out our list of Useful Websites in **Appendix D**. We have tried to give you the latest and greatest sites for effective job hunting but websites are continuously changing and morphing. By the time we publish this edition of our book, there are probably newer, shiner and glossier sites. Good Luck surfing the web, but don't get sidetracked; the most effective way to find a job is through Networking!

OTHER

Bloomberg Industry Categories – The S & P 500 – *Examples*

1. **Aerospace and Defense** - *Lockheed Martin, General Dynamics*
2. **Automotive** - *Ford, Goodyear Tire and Rubber*
3. **Banks** - *Chase Manhattan, Wells Fargo*
4. **Chemicals** - *Dupont, Monsanto*
5. **Conglomerates** - *Allied Signal, General Electric, TRW*
6. **Consumer Products** - *Maytag, Coca-Cola*
7. **Containers and Packaging** - *Owens Illinois, Avery Dennison*
8. **Discount and Fashion Retailing** - *Home Depot, Wal Mart Stores*
9. **Electrical and Electronics** - *Intel, Tektronix*
10. **Food** - *Safeway, Campbell Soup*
11. **Fuel** - *Exxon, Mobil*
12. **Health Care** - *Schering Plough, Johnson and Johnson*
13. **Housing and Real Estate** - *Masco, Sherwin-Williams*
14. **Leisure Time Industries** - *Walt Disney, Marriott International*
15. **Manufacturing** - *Johnson Controls, Applied Materials*
16. **Metals and Mining** - *Bethlehem Steel, Alcoa*
17. **Nonbank Financial** - *Charles Schwab*
18. **Office Equipment and Computers** - *Microsoft, Oracle, Dell, Novell*
19. **Paper and Forest Products** - *Kimberly-Clark, Boise Cascade*
20. **Publishing and Broadcasting** - *Gannett, New York Times, Dow Jones*
21. **Service Industries** - *IMS Health, Waste Management*
22. **Telecommunications** - *AT&T, Verizon, Bell Atlantic*
23. **Transportation** - *Delta Airlines, Ryder System*
24. **Utilities** - *PECO Energy, Edison International*

S & P 500 Industry Sectors (Weightings (%)

Technology -20.70
Telecom - 2.79
Materials - 2.91
Utilities - 3.45
Energy - 6.73
Industrials - 9.90
Cons/staples - 10.14
Cons/Discrete - 12.41
Health care - 15.25
Financials - 15.72

"Research is formalized curiosity. It is poking and prying with a purpose." — Z. N. Hurston

Homework: Research Exercise (use Google or another search engine)

______ Select an industry that appeals to you (e.g. aerospace, shipbuilding, education, banking, medical):

____

______ Select a company within that industry (e.g. Lockheed Martin, Northrop-Grumman, Boeing):

____

______ List three things the company (whichever one you have selected) produces:

1. ______________________________
2. ______________________________
3. ______________________________

______ List five pieces of information about the company (e.g. recent merger, stock price, new product(s)):

1. ______________________________
2. ______________________________
3. ______________________________
4. ______________________________
5. ______________________________

______ List a functional area where you would be of service to the company (e.g. sales, finance, training):

____

______ List the six skills/strengths required by that functional area:

1. ______________ 2. ______________
3. ______________ 4. ______________
5. ______________ 6. ______________

______ List three major of the company's major competitors:

1. ______________________________
2. ______________________________
3. ______________________________

______ List the names of the company Chairman, President, CEO and CFO:

Chairman ______________________________

President ______________________________

CEO ______________________________

CFO ______________________________

______ What Standard and Poor business category is the company in?

____

______ List three people you know that work in the company or knows someone who works in the company:

1. ____

2. ____

3. ____

______ Why would you be of value to this company? . . . *no more than three short sentences*

____

____

____

____

____

____

____

____

____

____

____

____

____

____

______ List ten key words associated with the company and their industry:

1. ____________________ 2. ____________________

3. ____________________ 4. ____________________

5. ____________________ 6. ____________________

7. ____________________ 8. ____________________

9. ____________________ 10. ____________________

Staying Current

by hard copy or electronically

- Wall Street Journal
- Local newspaper ... *in area of interest*
- Industry focused magazines
- Business Week
- Fortune or Forbes
- New York Times - Sunday
- Local business newspaper

Keep abreast of business news!

CHAPTER 17

ORGANIZATION

My Life Is A Disorganized Mess! - *Letters from the "front lines"*

"I can see how easy it is to put the transition stuff off in the pile marked "when you get time." It is even more difficult for those of us who are in no big hurry because we haven't established a retirement date. I've decided however, that if I don't get an organization together this week, I will lose the energy created by your process. I see now that transition does not have to be an act of desperation, rather the product of an organized plan."

"I see that ***my life is a disorganized mess****. Not my military stuff. Not my family. But anything that has to do with anything other than those two are totally disorganized. Over the last two days, I have found business cards in 14 different spots . . . files, briefcases, pockets, drawers and dressers. With very little focus I have found a two-inch stack of people with whom I have worked or met, but not followed from the initial meeting. I'm currently putting together the three ring binders to get organized. My spouse and I have a lot of work to do. Thanks so much for your insight and wit. I hope to prove to be a good student. As previously discussed, staying organized can be a monumental task all by itself. After years of having a staff, some large and some small, you suddenly find yourself doing it all, all by yourself. That makes you the writer, director, player, producer, marketeer, distributor, etc. A true entrepreneur. When you first begin to job hunt, this record-keeping and organization task seems like an easy thing to do. After several weeks or months, however, you will soon find that it takes a lot of effort just to stay on top of your schedule."*

Get Organized

- **Management system that includes:**
  - **Calendar**
  - **Tasks**
  - **Email**
  - **Contacts**
- **Three ring binders, 2 Alphabetic indexes** – *for critical backup*
- **Global Voice Messaging**
- **Scanner/Printer/Fax machine** *Archaic?*
  ... many companies still use fax machines
- **File cabinet and folders**
- **Computer with Auto and Cloud backup**
- **Separate telephone number for transition**
- **Cell phone/smart phone**
- **Home office space**

You'll kill for a secretary!

Computer knowledge. You won't have your own secretary in the next office to help you and it is expensive to hire someone to do the work, let alone impractical. If you are not computer savvy, ask any 18-year-old E-3, or the 6-year old who lives next door to show you!

Computer Technology

- Word processing
- Basic graphics
- Spreadsheets
- E-mail
- Texting
- The Web
  ... for research

You ***must*** *be computer literate!*

You can use your Outlook or Smart Phone for scheduling. This will allow you to keep information backed up on your computer and/or on hard copy. Keeping track of appointments and a record of your meetings is mandatory. And don't forget that ***good grammar and word choice counts in email or texting as well as in a formal letter.*** Don't allow yourself to get sloppy. It will not impress the recruiters.

You could research the company you are about to visit on your smart-phone using Google, while sitting in the company lobby waiting for the appointment. I have a love-hate relationship with my Samsung Galaxy S-20. Enough said on this subject – it is changing faster than we can get the words on the paper. ***PS . . . I still use a pocket Calendar notebook as backup for important notes and scheduling . . . doesn't breakdown and the batteries don't ever rundown.***

Personal Information Management Systems

Documentation such as your personal marketing plan, a weekly campaign plan, a weekly schedule, key people contact cards, a record of all interactions, an event calendar and meeting/interview report records are basic to the process. Using a personal management system such as ***Outlook*** helps to keep things in order. ACT is high powered, costly and probably not worth the investment unless you are going to be a salesperson.

Day-to-day Management

Everyone develops their own system for the day-to-day management of their search. A system that many of our successful candidates use consists of the following:

- ✓ A calendar.
- ✓ Two three-ring binders with alphabetical tabs . . . one for people and one for companies. Record **all** correspondence and telephone calls. Cross reference!
- ✓ 3 x 5 alphabetic index cards . . . to keep notes on if you don't use your smart phone
- ✓ A cell or smart phone with an emergency battery booster.
- ✓ An answering machine and/or voice mail service . . . your message, not your three-year-old grandson's . . . whose message would probably be something like: "High dilly-dilly, Dad's in Philly and Mom's out mowing the lawn." Not very professional!
- ✓ File folders and a large 2 to 4 drawer file cabinet . . . information will grow
- ✓ A second telephone line . . . especially if you have teenagers at home
- ✓ A fax machine . . . perhaps combined with the home answering machine

Maintaining Control . . . *Some hints for staying in control of your job search*:

- ✓ Write out a weekly plan, in great detail, Thursday or Friday, for the following week.
- ✓ Have your records organized and readily accessible.
- ✓ Keep a record of <u>all</u> phone calls, meetings and interviews and letters that you write.

As mentioned earlier and worth repeating, maintain a special 3 x 5 card file of "hot" or selected contacts. On the front of the card you should write: the name, title, company, address and telephone number, secretary's name, and the person's name that referred you. On the back of the card write miscellaneous information such as: spouse's name, children, interests, schools attended, associations,

Document Your Efforts

- **Personal Marketing Plan**
- **Weekly Campaign Report**
- **Weekly Schedule**
- **Key Contact Cards**
- **Interaction Record**
- **Events Calendar**
- **Meeting/Interview Report**

Stay In Control!

home phone and any other information that might help to connect you with the contact. Or, put all of that stuff on some electronic gadget. ***Carry them with you*** – always.

> If you have not already done so, establish a file in Outlook or whatever management system you use, and label it "Career Transition." Then establish sub-files for: people, companies, research and any other categories that will help you manage paperwork and information. Do it now!

Interaction Records and Forms

We find that forms are great to help you maintain a record of your conversations and meetings. We also have found that there is a direct and positive correlation between the completeness of the records maintained, and the time it takes a person to land a job. Another purpose of the forms is to give some structure to your career pursuit and your life. You should design your own forms to meet your requirements, but we recommend, as a minimum, you use the forms in this book . . . either in hard copy or on your computer or smart phone. *Tailor them to fit your needs.*

Reality Check

Getting and staying organized will not only give you the confidence that you know what is going on, but will also give you a sense of control. This latter feeling is an important one to have since your transition records are perhaps the only thing that you now control. As you get further and further into the process, stop and ask yourself these questions to ensure that you are keeping things in perspective:

> **Employing three ring binders in these days of high technology probably seems somewhat archaic, but we have found that keeping critical letters, research and information where they can be located quickl its advantages. Not to forget that three ring binders don't have power outages or hard drive crashes. Your call.**

- Are my goals realistic?
- Are my deadlines too ambitious?
- What should I be doing differently?
- What seems to be working?
- What does not seem to be working?
- What roadblocks am I running into and what action can I take?
- How do I feel about how things are progressing?
- If not working, am I spending at least 8 hours daily on my job hunt?
- What efforts are yielding the most potential?
- Who or where should I go to get additional support?
- Am I following up on all leads?
- Am I maintaining up-to-date records?
- Am I writing out my plan of action sufficiently in advance . . . at least weekly?
- Am I researching enough?

The infamous "hard drive crash!"

NOTE: *You may wonder why we recommend that you maintain manual records in these days of sophisticated "electronics," and especially since we just told you to become computer literate. The reason is that you must be able to retrieve information quickly when you receive a telephone call and that is often difficult when your* *computer is not running, or when you are using your cell phone and can't get to your notes/memo's file. It is also easy and reliable to carry around a few 3x5 cards in your pocket. Trust us . . . it is very effective, and corporate executives earning $500,000 and more use the same system. One last thought . . .* ***manual records don't "crash!"*** *(Note: Investing in a computer backup system, is a smart investment and, in my opinion, mandatory! . . . or backup on a thumb drive.)*

You Are Going to Be Busy!

There will be lots going on in your life during the transition process and there will be a tendency to let some things go . . . "Just too busy to do everything." All I can tell you is that when you least expect it, an opportunity will present itself. So keep track of everything and don't allow anything to drop through the cracks. You can't catch a fish if you don't go to the pond and put your baited hook in the water!

Have a Plan - Stay Productive

You will accomplish more if you have and work a plan. Set up your "To-Do" list in priority sequence and try to accomplish something or *some things* that relate to your job search every day. People that are the most successful during career transition establish a routine – that's what you did in service – and follow it. If you have a good To-Do list and it is prioritized properly, you will get past the tendency to procrastinate . . . a common failing for many undergoing transition.

By setting reasonable goals and tracking your progress you will be more productive, and you will start your next career sooner. Playing golf with the "guys" is fun, but unless one of them is Bill Gates or Jeff Bezos, you are probably just procrastinating. If you are playing golf because you feel you need a break from the routine, that's fine – it's a stress reliever. If you are playing golf (or another non-productive activity) because you don't want to tackle a difficult task, it is procrastination.

Planning for Career Transition (Milestones) – *Example*

The question of when to begin career transition planning is easy to answer . . . you should always be planning for change. Trouble is, we all know that things will change, but few of us do much about it until the moment of truth . . . job loss. The chart below is meant to be an example of a milestone chart that could be used for career transition planning purposes.

Some people say that you should begin the planning to leave the service five years before retirement. I believe that 18 months is desirable and one year in advance is really a necessity. Once again, *you should always be planning for change!*

Milestone Chart for Career Transition . . . example

Days to Retirement

	360	300	240	180	120	60	0
Objective							
Resume 1							
Contacts							
Corps							
Network 1							
Resume 2					(Continue to refine)		
Research							
Network 2							
					(At 180 days you		
Office					should be in a		
Organize					full-court press)		
Computer							
Attire							
Validate							

Chart for overall transition to the private sector

You can make a strong case for developing a similar milestone chart for home/family planning. It would include such things as moving dates, house selling, new wills and trusts, VA disability screening, selecting the Survivor Benefit/insurance options and so forth. That way everyone in the family could look ahead and see what must be done, before, and shortly after the retirement date.

Manage your information

Create a 'Master' file:

<u>CAREER TRANSITION</u>

in your Outlook or computer management program. Create sub-files for people, industries, information, etc.

Do it now!

Marketing Action Plan Form

Date ________________

Activity	**Action Planned**	**Priority**	**%**	**Results**
Answering Ads	____________________	_______	____	____________
Writing Letters	____________________	_______	____	____________
Talking with Search Firms	____________________	_______	____	____________
Networking One-on-One	____________________	_______	____	____________
Networking Associations	____________________	_______	____	____________
Other	____________________	_______	____	____________

Marketing . . . Planning Form

Date ____________

Career Objective: ____

Companies/Industries to Consider	**Possible Contacts**

A. ____

B. ____

C. ____

D. ____

E. ____

F. ____

G. ____

H. ____

I. ____

J. ____

New contacts to meet:

____

____

____

Other:

____

____

____

Weekly Review Form

Date ____________

OBJECTIVE: ____

1. Information meetings held:

Date	Person	Company	Comments	Action

2. Job Interviews:

Date	Person	Company	Position	Action

3. Meetings/Interviews Scheduled for next week:

Date	Person	Company	Position	Purpose

4. Advertisements Answered: ____

____

____

5. Pending Actions: ____

____

The Meeting/Interview/Telephone Report

The following report should be filled out completely after each telephone call, information meeting or interview . . . before you leave your desk or the area of the meeting.

Name of person(s): ______________________________

Title: ______________________________

Telephone: ______________________________

Company: ______________________________

Address: ______________________________

Secretary's name: ______________________________

Referred by: ______________________________

Date and location of meeting: ______________________________

Purpose of meeting: ______________________________

____

Information gained: ______________________________

____

____

Referrals: ______________________________

____

Industry problems: ______________________________

____

My next step(s): ______________________________

____

____

Meeting evaluation: ______________________________

____

____

CHAPTER 18

RETIREMENT PLANNING

"Every morning I get up and look through the Forbes list of the richest people in America. If I'm not in there, I go to work."

— Robert Orben

"When Should I Retire From Service, and, When The Time Comes, From Work?"

Life is good!

Other than the question, "Where do I go from here," the question I am asked more than any other is, "When *should* I retire?" . . . ***NEVER!*** The question comes from people in their early years of work, from people who were just promoted, and from people who have been working for more years than anyone can count. There are no easy answers to the question, and in the long haul, only you can make the decision. One answer could be, work or do what you are doing as long as you are enjoying it . . . as long as there are challenges and opportunities to accomplish meaningful goals. The problem with that logic is that perhaps there is a requirement to move away from your present job location, or perhaps there is a money issue because you have nine children all starting college next year. Everyone has their own set of special circumstances. There are many people 55 years old and over (and some younger) who retired with plenty of money only to find that when the stock market crashed, a major part of the nest egg that was earmarked to keep them financially in good health, vanished. As a result, many of those people are in their later years and are struggling financially, and are afraid to attempt a re-entry to the job market. Worse than that, they find themselves in a situation where no one wants to hire them. Consider this: An American Medical Association study reported in Bottom Line Magazine said, **"People who work between the ages of 50-70 are half as likely to die in any given year than those who do not."** So, maybe working at *something* until you drop over isn't such a bad idea after all. Depends how soon you want to drop! You just never know!

"Sorry, you have come too soon, I am still working."

Considerations

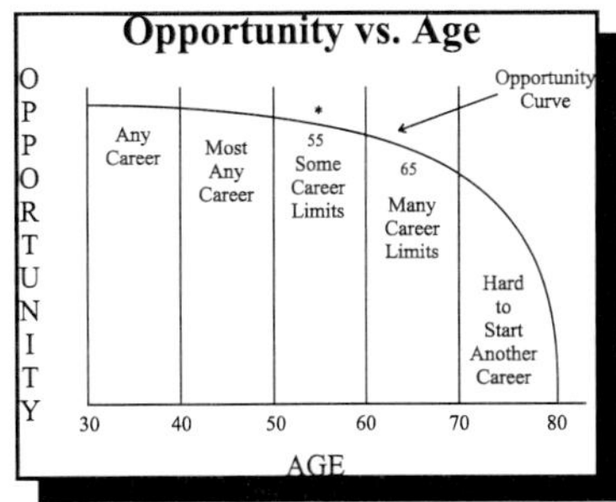

The older you get, the fewer opportunities!

There are several personal factors that you should consider. First of all, if you want a full-blown second career after whatever you are doing now, then you can't wait too long to begin or you will run out of time. When you are 40 years old, there is time to do most anything you want to do. At 50, you are still young, at least in a 60-year-old person's eyes, but at 65 and beyond, there begin to be limitations. Not overwhelming, but some limitations.

Energy

Another item to consider is how much energy (I call it thrust) you will have as the years roll by. Some people lose their "thrust" at a very early age. Others go on to high positions and are able to maintain a high energy level regardless of what is going on. And, others somehow are able to continue to take on more and more responsibilities, or work, and never seem to tire. Much depends upon how much you enjoy what you are doing. You should decide where you are on an energy scale and/or if you want to continue like a comet. It's another personal choice. There are no value judgements in making this decision. Some would prefer to retire and teach school part-time or manage a nonprofit organization for little pay or on a volunteer basis, and others prefer to make President of AT&T their primary focus. An aviator friend described this situation as deciding if you want to continue burning your afterburners, or would you prefer a more "normal," and at a not so dramatic pace. I have a good friend who works for me as a consultant 1/3rd of his time; donates time to his church 1/3rd of the time; and plays golf the other 1/3rd of his time. *He believes that he has found Shangri-la and so does his wife, since he is out of the house 2/3rds of the time!*

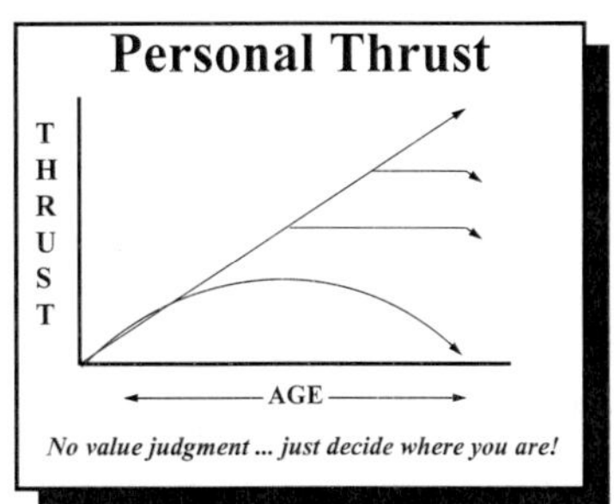

Planning Ahead

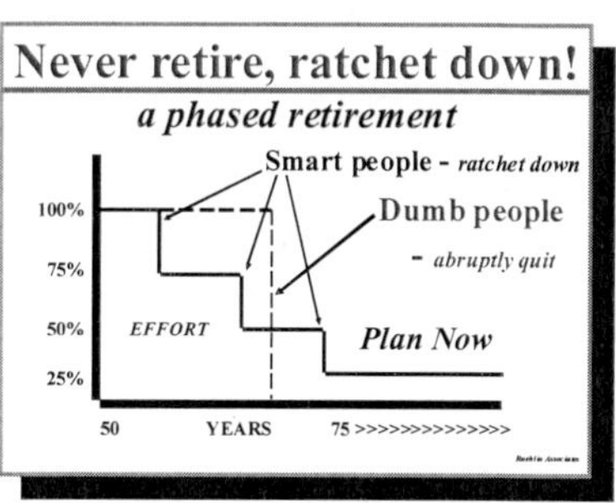

For those who want to continue with another career, you should give some thought to the out-years and work. For many, the ideal situation in their later years is to work at a great job on a part-time basis. For people who own their own business and have someone whom they can turn the business over to, this is fairly easy to accomplish. And, for those who have a technical specialty, it is fairly easy to become a consultant in the technical field and work your own hours. For others, it may be working for the same company on a consulting basis . . . as a retired annuitant. In any event, you should begin now to determine how to accomplish what I have termed ***ratcheting down***. For those who want to work *forever* and for whatever other reason, *ratcheting down* is the best of all worlds. It provides an income stream and the feeling of accomplishment that work provides, and it keeps you out of the house and out of your spouse's way. Remember, "For better or for worse, but not for lunch." Many people, especially males according to studies, more closely identify their self-worth and self esteem with their jobs, and they feel less than complete if they don't have something to identify with.

"For better or for worse."

Speaking of for better or for worse, a few years ago my spouse of many years suggested that I stop working and retire. She said that we are growing older and she wanted more time to do more things together. So I said, "That's okay with me, and I will be home with you all day long!" Then she gave a second thought about what she had said and the conversation went something like the following:

She: "I want you to retire!"
He: "Great! I'll get to spend all day with you!"
She: "But I don't want you here *all* day!"
He: "So what should I do?"
She: "I dunno, just go some place, anyplace!"
He: Replying sarcastically, "Fine, I'll just go stand outside in the backyard for eight hours each day!"
She: "Sounds like a good plan to me!"

"For better or for worse, but not for lunch" . . . every day?"

While it may sound like a good idea, the total togetherness idea is probably not for everyone, at least not immediately following a career that has been consuming you for the past many years. Much has been written on this subject and for the most part the experts agree that it may not be such a red-hot idea. Too much togetherness may be too much! So, think about it before you take the total togetherness plunge. A little *"absence makes the heart grow fonder!"* . . . and, allows sanity to prevail!

"It's a new reality show. Week by week, a newly retired man slowly drives his wife insane."

The Vase On The Piano Story

There once was a job hunter who, like the rest of us, suddenly found himself at home a lot. Now this job hunter liked to play the piano in his spare time . . . for pleasure and to help relieve the stress of the job hunt. One day when he was playing he noticed that there was an expensive vase sitting very close to the edge of the piano. So the job hunter moved the vase to the center of the piano where it would not be apt to get knocked off.

"Play it, but don't move it!"

The next day he returned to play and found that the vase had somehow moved back to the edge of the piano. Strange he thought as he moved the vase back to where he had placed it the day before. The next day he returned and found the same situation along with a small yellow sticker that read, **"Leave it alone."**

Lesson learned: Don't mess around with stuff in the house unless you are asked to do so. And, then get permission in writing!

Keep Your Options Open

<u>You can always retire</u>! You can always make the decision that "I am out of here and want to do what everyone says is the good life." (It really ain't that good). What is hard to do, and for some nearly impossible, is to retire from work for several years and then try to get back into the job market. If you do think you want to retire, my recommendation is that you go through the career search process, find a job that you can enjoy, take it and see how it goes. If, after a year or so you decide that this is not for you, then retire with no regrets. Never look back. On a personal note, when the first private sector corporation I was with went under, I contemplated retiring from work. Just as I was about to make a decision, I picked up a book that described a couple who retired early and one that continued to work at something they enjoyed. The difference they described astounded me and I concluded that I would work "forever." Or at least until I could comfortably rachet down. As an aside, the consultants who deliver my transition seminars all have a military or government background, have all transitioned successfully into the private sector at senior level positions and at this point in their lives, have all *ratcheted* down and conduct our seminars on a part-time basis.

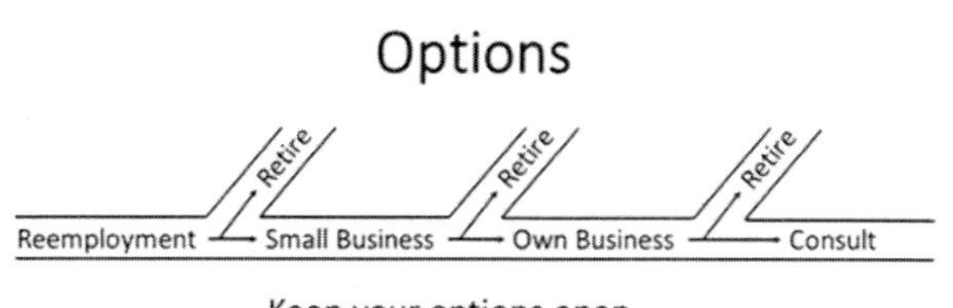

Keep your options open . . .
You can always
RETIRE!

But, once your out, it's hard to get back in the mainstream!

Why Not Work? Why Do People Continue To Work?

After talking to countless people on the subject of retirement, it seems to boil down to this: people continue working, for however long, for one of five primary reasons: (1) to preclude boredom, (2) for purposes of self esteem, (3) for income and (4) for the pure joy of doing what they do, (5) so they might live longer or some combination of each. People usually quit work when they are no longer happy with what they are doing. Ditch diggers quit because they are just tired of digging holes in the ground. Many great artists, writers, actors and other creative people work until they are physically no longer able. A good friend once told me that the basic goal in life was to be happy. So, if you are happy working and move onto the next life while working, then that's about all you can expect out of life. **Note**: All of the *Ruehlin Associates* team falls in the *rachet* down category. All have had successful service careers, all have had successful private sector careers, all are financially secure and all want to continue to make a contribution to something worthwhile . . . but not full time and no 50 hour weeks. Net-net, while we all receive some remuneration, it is the enjoyment of what we do that keeps us going. Think about it!

Increased Longevity

"People who work between the ages of 70-90 are 1/3 less as likely to die in any given year as those who don't."

The French Medical Institute study.

Yep, that's what I said!

In 473 BC, Confucius said,
"Choose a job you love, and you'll never have to work a day in your life."

Same Old Grind? . . . some philosophy!

It's not that we tire of working . . . it's that we tire of the work that we are doing! People who enjoy their work tend to work forever, or so it seems. Just think about all those people in the arts that just keep working forever. They like their work!

Too long, too hard? Try something you enjoy!

How much does it cost to retire?

It really doesn't cost much to retire if you don't worry about having to impress your friends, but if you like to indulge in a lot of life's little pleasures like travel and eating well, and not worry about finances, then work will provide the wherewithal to do that. There are numerous retirement calculators available. Just Google "Retirement calculators" and pick one.

Desperate Souls

As a child I can remember going shopping with my mother. It was always boring and I usually got tired after twenty minutes or so. I can also remember looking for a place to sit or lay down. She didn't like me to lie down for fear that someone would step on me. The problem was that in the available chairs there were old men, or so it seemed, already sitting in the chairs making strange guttural noises . . . sometimes I would touch them to see if they were breathing. They were sitting there waiting for their spouses to return after a day (or more) of shopping in the mall.

I will never forget the totally blank look on their faces . . . just sort of staring into space like they were waiting for the Starship Enterprise to return or "ET" to call home. Sometimes there would be two or three on a couch in the lady's lingerie area.

On the mall!

One would be asleep and the other two watching silently and waiting for their wives to return and take them home, shopping having been completed. "What a pity," I used to think. These men are the forgotten heros of the shopping mall. They are probably still there.

Lesson learned: You figure it out.

Food For Thought – In a recent book, The Number by Lee Eisenberg, he discusses "A completely different way to think about the rest of your life." He poses three big questions: (1) What would you do with your money if you had all you could ever need, (2) How would you live your life if you knew you were going to die feeling perfectly healthy in five or ten years, and (3) What would you feel you'd missed if you found out you had but 24 hours to live? ***Note: "I should have bought and drank that $1,000 bottle of single malt scotch," is not the answer we are looking for.***

It's problematic

Summary

The good news is that we are living longer and longer. The bad news is that we are living longer and longer – but may not be able to afford it. So, plan ahead! The first of the baby-boomers turned 60 years old in 2016 and many are in a panic state over the uncertain stock market and financial solvency and what to do with the rest of their lives. Don't let that happen to you! Keep on work'n and truck'n, albeit not necessarily full time and not too hard. And remember, the longer you work and earn, the less you will need in full retirement and the longer you will probably live. How about them apples?

A good friend once told me that:
"Happiness is when you have a full or part time job you love
and are good at, and get paid for doing it,
but don't need the money."

So, when *should* a person retire? Well, it's like playing the old game of marbles when you were a kid. You kept on playing as long as you were winning the other guy's marbles. But, when you lost all of your marbles, you had to go home. So like the game of marbles, ***when you lose all of your marbles, or forget where you put them, it's time to retire!***

So . . . It's time to retire when you lose all your marbles!

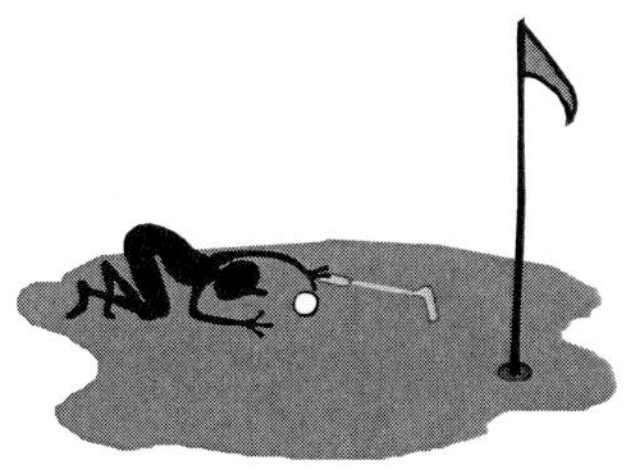

Still want to retire, retire?

Write a two page combination resume

Objective: To retire from work

Follow our protocol …

- write a summary of your retirement plans
- list skills required to successfully retire
- list skills you will use
- write accomplishments supporting skills
- list retirement courses you have taken

What will you do each hour of each day while awake?

CHAPTER 19

FINANCIAL PLANNING

Get Your Financial House in Order

This book is not intended to provide authoritative advice on financial planning. However, there are some prudent actions everyone should take to get their "personal finances house" in order.

"I planned to retire so I could spend more time with my wife and family, but my wife and family talked me out of it!"

Everyone should have a will, if for no other reason than to save their heirs from a needless struggle . . . *unless you think that they deserve it!* I recommend that while you are getting the will, you get the other documents, relevant to personal planning, taken care of also . . . such as a marital trust which might reduce the tax bite for your heirs. Do it now, before you retire!

Survivor's Benefit Plan (SBP)

Military personnel will have to make a decision about the Survivor Benefit Program . . . should you take it or not? Your career counselor and/or the service Transition Assistance Program Office can fill you in on the details. After talking to the presidents of the service's Mutual Aid Insurance Associations and a major private sector insurance company, the SBP appears to be the most cost effective way of providing insurance for your family and, all else being equal, it beats commercial insurance. It beats commercial insurance because SBP is paid for with <u>pretax dollars</u> and is cost-of-living adjusted. Since everyone is a unique case, take some time to run the numbers and determine which is best for you. Another tangible benefit is that no one can ever take the retirement benefit away from your spouse!

The saved leave question.

Saved Leave

Lump sum leave payment of base pay <u>or</u> two months, *for example,* drawing base and allowances?

There are two schools of thought on this subject. One says that you should draw full base pay and allowances for whatever leave time is coming to you; the other says that you should take the leave time you have accumulated in a one lump base payment and begin drawing retirement pay immediately. ***For <u>most</u> of us, conventional wisdom says to take the lump sum and begin drawing retirement pay immediately***. It is all in the numbers. Sit down with a calculator and determine what is in ***your*** best interests. ***Remember to take allowances, special pay and any health care requirements in your calculations.***

Financial Planners

I recommend that people use financial planners unless they are extremely astute at managing their own financial matters. I personally prefer the financial planner arrangement where you pay up-front for advice and then execute the plan yourself. That way you don't have to worry about the planner making financial decisions that benefit them but maybe not so good for you. They are not costly and a good one will make you see shortfalls in your financial planning and enable you to make better decisions with your money. In any event, buy a copy of a good basic financial planning book, such as <u>Personal Finance For Dummies</u>, and study it. Start saving now! Another great book to read is The Millionaire Next Door, by Stanley and Danko. Another great book is Rich Dad, Poor Dad. You too can be a millionaire!

How Much Will it Cost to Retire?

As we discussed previously, that all depends on what your future spending plans are. Many financial planners tell us that it takes between 75-85 percent of your current working income to retire on a satisfactory financial basis. Their assumption is, of course, that you will need fewer clothes and won't be buying a new car every year. However, there are some financial planners who believe you will need 100 percent *or more* of your present net income to be happy in retirement. I side with this group. They say that because retired people like to do things and stay active . . . like traveling and buying things for their kids and their grandchildren, and that all takes money . . . *and I can vouch for the latter case.* Therefore, you will have to supplement your retirement income.

It depends on whom you ask!

An issue of great importance is . . . how long do you intend to live? If you think you are going to see your maker at 75 years old that's one thing. If you think you might make it to 90, it is another thing. Financial planning for retirement is easy if you know when you and/or your spouse will expire, but unfortunately it doesn't work that way. Which is why so many seniors are still working and continue to work – at least part time. Personally, I don't know when I'm going to leave this planet so my plan is to work, part time at least, until I drop so I can maintain the life style I have become accustomed. But more importantly, because I thoroughly enjoy what I do, and so do all of my associates.

Can You Afford to Retire?

In the past several years nearly every major weekly business magazine, Fortune, Business Week, Kiplinger's, Forbes, etc., has published a report on retirement and the *afford-ability* of retirement. They were all very good and all made just about the same points.

- You may not be able to depend on Social Security.
- Medical costs will continue to climb . . . the government will increase the medical insurance fee.
- Most people are not saving enough.
- People are living longer and therefore will require more money to live out their lives in the manner they desire. Read New Passages, by Gail Sheehy.
- The longer people work, the lesser the burden on their retirement income needs and possibly on their families.
- If you are on a government pension, there is nothing that says that the government won't control/reduce/cap the annual COLAs.
- Inflation is an uncertainty, but will always be here at some level.

Bennitt's Curve . . . *for military personnel*

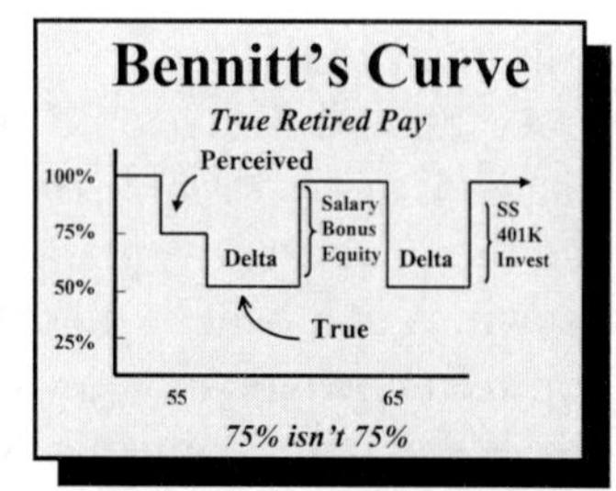

Everything gets taxed!

Many people believe/perceive that when they retire after 30 years of active duty they will receive 75 percent of their perceived present pay, which in fact they will not – for several reasons.

The chart on the right tells us that, when we retire after 30 years, for example, we won't receive 75 percent of our pay (*perceived*). It will be closer to 50 percent of what you were really earning when you left active duty (*true*). By the time you eliminate the items like BAS and BAH, the tax advantage and so forth, you end up with about 50 percent of what you were making on active duty. Therefore, if you want to continue your present life style, you will have to earn enough to make up the difference ***and*** accommodate the tax impact. Remember, the tax man will gobble up a big chunk of all the money you are going to make in your next career so *you will have to earn more than the delta between what you were making and your retirement pay* . . . just to break even! You can do that fairly easily from your next career income. However, there will come a time when you will want to stop working altogether . . . *I don't recommend it* . . . so you will have to earn *more* than the "50 percent" delta while you are working, if you want to have the same quality of life you had before you retired. Needless to say, if you want to *enhance* your quality of life, you will have to earn much, much more. Pick up a Turbo-Tax program and plug in your own numbers and see what your requirement will be.

Making it Last . . . *more on the subject*

Since we are all living longer, you will have to calculate just how long you will work after leaving government service and how much you will have to earn while working to accommodate your desired life style. If, for example, you intended to leave your government career after a thirty-year career at 50 years old, and stop working at 65, you have but 15 years to earn enough money to maintain your current life style and save enough for the probable 20 or more years to follow. It's fairly easy to maintain your life style while working. It will take some doing to make enough to continue it during the non-working years. I think it was easier in the old days when we knew we would retire around the age of 65 and pass on at 69 . . . that made financial planning much easier. Now we are living longer, messing up all of the social security calculations, and making ourselves financially miserable! And, what do we do with our free time if we don't work - for profit or not for profit?

Making it Last!

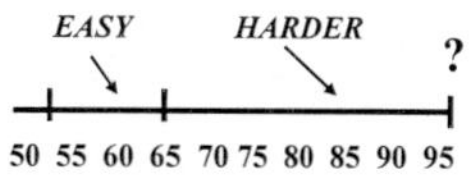

EASY *HARDER* ?

50 55 60 65 70 75 80 85 90 95

Providing for the out-years

Rule of Thumb

For every $1,000 you will need each month (in addition to social security) you should have at least $230,000 moderately/aggressively and conservatively invested when you stop working. So, if you want to receive $10,000 each month, you will need to have $2,300,000 in savings. That's right, $2,300,000 in savings*! (So I will never stop working!)* The good news here is, that <u>if</u> you have made the service a career and have 20-30 years of service, you will receive a substantial sum of money from your retirement pension. So, you are partly there, at least. Naturally, much depends upon where you end up living and the lifestyle you choose.

A Word to the Wise

Since you will be busy with your career transition effort when you retire, try to take care of as many personal matters as possible before you do retire. So give serious consideration to updating, starting or considering personal programs such as:

- Your will
- A marital or A-B trust . . . *see your tax advisor*
- Life insurance
- Saving plans
- Long term care insurance – if you think you will need it.
- A Roth IRA

How Much Income Do You Really Need?

Many of us worry about not having enough money to be happy and press ourselves to earn as much as we can. Every book and article I have read in the past ten years stresses the point that you can be happy without an enormous amount of money . . . not to live in a state of poverty of course, but that you don't have to have it all. In the chart on the right, one person makes 3X dollars and the other makes 2X dollars, but neither need those amounts to truly enjoy life. Everything above the dotted line is in excess to their needs. Many people I know have more than they need and spend countless hours worrying about what to do with it. Also, there is a price to be paid for *having it all!* Before you make the *money god* your guiding light, make sure you have considered the repercussions . . . what you will get as a result and what you might lose in terms of family, friends and health.

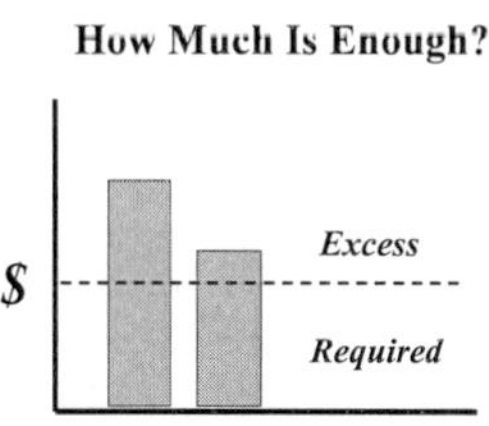

How Long Will Your Money Last When Not Working?

Conventional wisdom used to say that a 4 percent annual withdrawal rate from your retirement funds would allow your money to grow and have a 75 percent chance of lasting through retirement. Current thinking says that a lower withdrawal rate of 3 ½ percent is a more accurate rate. A nine percent annual withdrawal rate on the other hand will most likely deplete your retirement funds in less than ten years . . . which of course is okay if you are certain you will pass on in ten years.

All of the studies that I have read say that there are so many variables that it is impossible to predict exactly how much you can withdraw, so the above numbers are only guesstimates. Some articles indicate that you can probably withdraw 4 percent of your retirement funds each year and still be on the safe side of not running out of money before you exit out. Obviously, these numbers are contingent on the quality and performance of your investments. If you are in an extended down market, things will look more bleak than if the economy and your investments are booming. ***Note: better have some cash on hand so that you don't have to withdraw invested money during a down market.***

The chart shows the impact of different withdrawal rates during the period 2011 to 2044 on an investment of $500,000.00 – taking in to account inflation. As you can see, all else being equal, a 4 percent withdrawal rate allows the investment to grow and a 9 percent withdrawal rate depletes it in short order (4 percent providing about $20,000 a year and 9 percent providing about $45,000 a year).

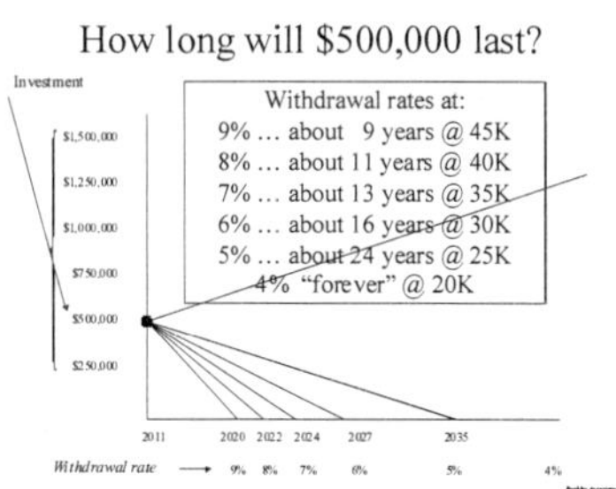

Last comment: *The longer you work, part time at least, the less you will worry about running out of funds and the more apt you will be able to spend, travel and enjoy your later years. Think about it!*

Useful retirement calculators:

- Go to the **Vanguard** or **Fidelity or AARP** Websites. They both have excellent retirement calculators.

CHAPTER 20

READY TO GO

You have now completed reading the basics of military/civil service to private sector career transition. You realize that career transition is not a part-time job. You understand that the elements of looking for a job link together and that you must consider job hunting as a process. You are Ready to Go! You have:

> ***"Many of life's failures are people who did not realize how close they were to success when they gave up."***
>
> — Thomas Edison

- ✓ ***A plan*** . . . an objective . . . a focus.
- ✓ ***A resume*** . . . you have re-rewritten it 50 times and are now satisfied that it represents your strengths as they relate to what you want to do.
- ✓ **LinkedIn** . . . you have built your profile on LinkedIn.
- ✓ ***You know how to . . . Network,*** and you understand the difference between purposeful networking and just knocking on doors. You know the significance of key words.
- ✓ ***You know how to interview*** . . . and understand that you must practice and be able to relate your accomplishments to the position. You know the significance of key words.
- ✓ ***You know how to negotiate*** for compensation and have an idea of the salary range before you enter negotiations.
- ✓ ***An organizer*** . . . and it is filled with your prospective contacts and target companies.
- ✓ ***An office*** . . . you have carved out a space that you can use as a work center.
- ✓ ***A global messaging service.*** A dedicated business phone.
- ✓ ***A computer*** . . . and attendant equipment . . . and you know how to use them.
- ✓ ***A uniform*** . . . a sincere blue suit.
- ✓ ***An opening statement*** that describes your background, accomplishments and goals in two minutes . . . you can do nearly the same thing in thirty seconds.
- ✓ ***You have researched the possibilities*** . . . companies and industries.
- ✓ ***You are organized*** . . . have a system to keep track of your telephone calls and meetings . . . you can retrieve data almost instantly.
- ✓ ***You have business calling cards*** . . . name, telephone number., email, LinkedIn
- ✓ ***A computer back-up system*** . . . and know how to use it!

Pitfalls ... *most common mistakes made during career transition*

From years of experience we have observed that senior job hunters are prone to make judgement errors during the transition process. The following, in no particular order, is a list of the most common:

Many pitfalls!

- ***Depending on recruiters*** . . . it is fine to deal with recruiters as long as you don't wait around or go fishing while you wait for their results. This is especially true for senior military/civil service personnel the first time around. Even when you have established private sector credentials, don't depend upon anyone coming through for you. They work for the company, not you!
- ***Depending only on computer job listings/classified ads*** . . . there is a tendency to respond to an ad when you feel you are the perfect candidate and then sit around doing nothing because you are so certain that you will be selected. The "How can I miss?" syndrome.
- ***Putting you resume/profile on LinkedIn*** and waiting for the offers to pour in!
- ***Assuming that people will follow through*** . . . while your job search is the most important thing in your life right now, other people have other things on their minds. Be persistent – follow up, follow up, follow up! Many people are lousy at following through.
- ***Taking rejection <u>personally</u>*** . . . this will cripple your efforts . . . *"It's just business."*
- ***Having no clear focus*** . . . enough said on this one!
- ***Presuming that people will know what you want to do*** . . . even your close friends will have trouble with this one . . . you must let people know . . . the 30-second commercial.
- ***Waiting for hot leads to work out*** . . . as with the ads and the recruiters, don't stop the process until you have the job offer in hand and are working.
- ***Winging it /being unprepared*** . . . you will get caught if you do.
- ***Talking compensation too soon*** . . . let them bring the money subject up!
- ***Lack of consistency in effort*** . . . if you take a vacation in the middle of your search you must start all over . . . you will lose momentum.
- ***Not following the process*** . . . career search is a process. If you try to go from A to Z without understanding what is between, you will not be prepared.

Weekly Career Planning . . . Prior to Retirement

If you are still working and actively involved in your job, it will be not be possible to spend eight hours a day in search of a new career. In fact, many say that they are so busy that there is *not a moment* available to think about and take some action about their future . . . and their family's future. We have all felt that way, but why not take 10 minutes in the morning and 10 minutes in the afternoon to do some quick research on a Website? And, you should be eating something for lunch so why not have lunch once or twice a week with a contact in your network? Believe me, *if you do not look out for yourself, no one else will*! Give it a try and, on a weekly basis, make it a goal to:

1. Research one industry of interest – gather ten facts – use the Internet. Google can answer most any question.

2. Research two companies within that industry – learn major products and any problems.
3. Make three calls to industry connections – discuss your interest, set up an info meeting.
4. Conduct one info meeting related to the industry.
5. Write out six major strengths and your related experiences – analyze your interest and fit.
6. Consider getting additional education in the area of interest.
7. Talk to a good friend who has been successful in a new career after service.
8. Review the milestone chart in the "Organization" chapter – determine where you are.

Hiring Hurdles
Everyone faces hiring hurdles when looking for a job but there are some special hurdles that senior personnel must overcome. The most common ones, in addition to age bias, are:

- ***"You are overqualified"*** . . . this may in fact be the case. Or it may be a way of getting you on your way and out of the office. A serious reason for an employer to be concerned with your possible over-qualification is the fear that you will keep on looking for a position that is more suitable to you and then depart. No employer wants to go through the agony of hiring again, let alone the cost of training. You should know the nature of the job in terms of responsibility before you begin the interview process. If you are told that you are overqualified, ask them to explain in what ways are you over qualified. Don't let them off the hook. Lastly, if you find you really are overqualified for the position, and would not be willing to begin at a level lower than you could "tolerate," then bow out gracefully and accept it as a lesson learned.

- ***The reluctance to network*** . . . as discussed earlier, many senior personnel just don't like to network . . . to "use" their friends and acquaintances. My only answer to this dilemma is to tell you that this is how it is done in the marketplace. The market expects it and once you begin to network, you will understand it's value. Just do it!

- ***Interviewers are not convinced that you really want to work*** . . . some private sector civilians believe that if you are retired from the government/military service, your pension is so sufficient that you really don't have to work – that you are just looking for something to do when not playing golf. You must make them understand that you are interested in a full second career. You will be more convincing if you demonstrate knowledge and interest about the subject, company and the industry.

- ***The employer can't believe that you would be willing to work*** at this level. When you start telling them about all of the major responsibilities you had during your government career and the millions and billions of dollars you have managed, they begin to think that you would be unhappy working at anything less than the President's job . . . and while that may be true, it probably isn't going to happen.

- ***"I should be working for you"*** . . . for the same reason as above.

- ***Resentment*** . . . not by the functional manager who hired you, but perhaps by others who believe that you haven't earned your place in the company. You may also be seen as a threat . . . "why is so and so bringing in an outsider?" . . . especially a government outsider.

- ***Ego impairment*** . . . being unable to cope with the reality of having to go out and market yourself. We kid about this, but for some people it is the major hurdle . . . "It's below my level, below my status to do that." And, there are people who are not willing to begin working at a lower level even though there is a good future with the company and the pay is more than they were getting in the service. Duh!

Where to Go and Where *NOT* to Go for Help

Although you have read this book, (and probably read everything else that you have seen in the book stores), after working the process for several months you may begin to wonder if there might not be a better way. The bad news is that there isn't . . . the good news is that there are some good places to go for help and some places that you should revisit. The really good news is that everything I have told you to do in this book, works!

Where to Go for Help

Help yourself by helping yourself!

- If you have not already read What Color Is Your Parachute pick up a copy at the library give it a **brief** read. It will reinforce everything that you have read here, but sometimes with a different twist. Remember that ***most career transition books are written for private sector employees*** . . . so, if they differ from what we have said here previously . . . *"they are wrong!"*
- Knock 'Em Dead - the current edition, by Martin Yate - great interview questions
- Visit your local library or the largest college business library around and talk to the librarian. Discuss your objective. That can be your best resource.
- Call some friends who have been successful in their career transition . . . it will remind you that if they can do it, so can you.
- Go to the gym for a good workout . . . often . . . it will change your perspective, make you feel good and get you out of the house for a few hours!
- "What's Next?" Reread this book again . . . more carefully the next time!
- Browse/Google the websites . . . determine skills required for various careers

Where *NOT* to Go for Help

- The refrigerator . . . don't start eating. How does it go? . . . a moment on the lips and forever on the hips and then your new clothes won't fit!
- The local watering hole . . . don't start drinking!
- The SOAPS in the afternoon . . . or to bed.
- An expensive resume writing service . . . it's your resume . . . you must write it yourself.
- An expensive career "packaging" company . . . you know more than they do . . . and it will cost you thousands of dollars!

Some Special Things to Do

Before you transition from government service, or if you are going to a new city to conduct your career transition, there are some things that you can do that will assist your transition and enhance your networking opportunities.

- Attend and/or speak at as many conferences or meetings as possible and especially those that relate to your *new* career objective.

- Make appointments with companies that you want to network with or are interested in, before you leave government service. Your platform (the organization that you are presently assigned to) goes away when you leave service.

- Volunteer for charity work . . . the Red Cross, Cancer Society, major charitable fund raisers.

- Join the local Chamber of Commerce . . . offer to serve on the fund-raising, marketing or membership committees of the Chamber.

- Get involved with the local community . . . the theater, the symphony . . . museums.

- Look up your college alumni associations. Call old high school buddies.

- Find out if there are alumni chapters of your fraternity or sorority in the area.

- Subscribe to the local newspaper and Business Journal.

- Find out who the high rollers are in the community and how you might go about talking to them . . . via your network.

- The idea is to get actively involved in civilian business affairs as soon as possible once you decide to leave the government service.

Occupations - Where are they working?

Ruehlin seminar grads are working everywhere and doing everything imaginable. One Navy Commander built motor homes in Florida. A Marine Major is an administrative officer for a Law office in California. A senior civil service person is the senior contracting officer for a major non-defense corporation. A Vice Admiral manages support services for a major aerospace company in the East. A Master Chief Petty officer works in a IT business in Los Angeles. A Marine MSGT runs his own business. A retired General turned around the Seattle school system . . . another is a senior officer at Sears. A Navy Captain heads a major automobile spare parts distribution operation. A Marine Colonel works for a major bank in San Francisco. A Coast Guard officer manages quality control for a company in the marine industry. An Army officer heads a Volunteers of America region. A retired Navy Captain is the HR director for the LA unified school system. And so on.

Where The Jobs Are

they are e v e r y w h e r e

- **Reorganizations**
- **Mergers**
- **Retirements**
- **Quitters**
- **Promotions**
- **Acquisitions**
- **Created positions**

Some parts of the country are better than others

Do they only hire from within?

Even when companies say they are not hiring, they are. And when they say they only hire senior people from within, it ain't necessarily so. One person I know conducted networking meetings with a company who told him flat out that they only promoted from within. Three months later he was hired as a senior Program Manager for expansion into South America. The bottom line is, there are jobs everywhere, and if you bring something to the table, demonstrate knowledge of the business and fit their corporate image, you will be considered and have a great chance of working there.

You meet a high roller – a prominent business person

From time to time, we all have the opportunity to meet and speak with what I refer to as a "high roller." A highroller would be someone of stature in the business community or the federal government and who is known by a multitude of people . . . in today's business world the name that comes first to mind is billionaire Bill Gates. If you have an opportunity to conduct a networking meeting with someone like him, don't spare the dollars . . . they can open up any door in the country. They will ask, "What do you want to do?" (Do you know what to say?) ***Hint: 30 second response***.

Networking/Interviewing on the Road - Who Pays?

Travel Tips

interviewing on the road

- **Carry on luggage**
- **Is spouse included?**
- **Determine who pays***
- **How to get reimbursed**

**If you ask, you pay*

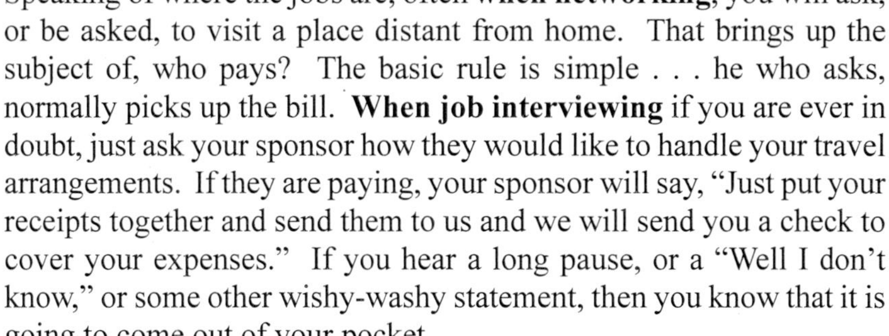

Speaking of where the jobs are, often **when networking**, you will ask, or be asked, to visit a place distant from home. That brings up the subject of, who pays? The basic rule is simple . . . he who asks, normally picks up the bill. **When job interviewing** if you are ever in doubt, just ask your sponsor how they would like to handle your travel arrangements. If they are paying, your sponsor will say, "Just put your receipts together and send them to us and we will send you a check to cover your expenses." If you hear a long pause, or a "Well I don't know," or some other wishy-washy statement, then you know that it is going to come out of your pocket.

What if they ask you to pay for traveling to a job interview?

It doesn't happen often but it does happen. Some companies, but very few, have a policy requiring interview candidates to pay for all or some portion of travel to the company for an interview. If that is their policy and you are on their short list and you believe they are really serious about hiring you then give it some thoughtful consideration. If nothing else was on the horizon and I liked the company and thought I met or exceeded their qualification requirements then I would probably make the journey . . . but this is a situational decision and one that no one can make for you.

Large or Small Company?

Another question that we are frequently asked is, "Where is it easier to find a job, in a small or a large company?" Sometimes it is easier for a large company to hire a newcomer because they have the resources to cover the costs if the deal doesn't work out . . . as opposed to a smaller company who can ill afford to take many financial chances. In regard to the hiring process, a large company might have layers of approval managers to go through before hiring someone, whereas a small company manager can probably hire you without consulting with anyone. For what it is worth, the Wall Street Journal published a survey that indicates that the majority of people are happier in smaller companies. My advice is that you decide what you want to do, and go for it, large or small . . . just like the government, you don't work with everybody.

Work for the Federal Government?

There are many senior officers and enlisted personnel who would be a great benefit to the federal government . . . taking years of tried and true experience and using it for the benefit of our country. So, if that is your bag, go for it. The same career transition rules apply when looking for a federal job as in the private sector . . . know your objective, preparation and networking. And, believe it or not, you can negotiate with the federal government. Check out Kathryn Troutman's Website for assistance in writing a government resume.

Typical Second Careers

One of the most frightening things about career transition is that you, as an individual, think that you are all alone in your pursuit of a new career. Many think that there is probably not a suitable job out there and wonder where all of the retired government personnel land jobs. The answer to that concern is . . . they land jobs everywhere. There is no one kind of occupation that is especially attractive to retired government personnel, except that the majority of them land jobs in the defense industry . . . mainly because that is where the majority of their contacts are found.

Typical Occupations

It would be just as easy to list all the occupations in the country than to attempt to list the ones where former military/civil service personnel are working. Here are a few:

- Defense contractors
- Home construction . . . The trades
- Banking
- IT
- Retailing
- Project/program management
- Financial management
- Human Resources management
- Own business
- Life insurance
- Education
- Law, and law firm administration
- Computer education
- Shipyard management
- Chancellor
- Purchasing/contracting
- Data Processing
- Health care
- Airport management
- Energy
- Teaching
- University administration
- Various corporate positions
- Information technology
- Federal Government
- Nonprofit charities
- Associations
- Home Land Security

Everything and anything . . .

CHAPTER 21

REALITY

What Is Really Gonna Happen? . . . The Joys of Job Hunting!

She: "How is the job hunt going?"
He: "Well I think it is time to switch to plan B."
She: "What is plan B?"
He: "Depending upon the kindness of strangers!"

"What's plan B?"

It really won't be that bad, but many people begin thinking in those terms when things don't jell or work out as fast as they would like. In reality, people end up getting jobs in one of six different ways:

1. You have a lifelong friend or relative who has been coaxing you to come with them in their company for the past 15 years and now the time has come. Bingo!

2. You walk into someone's office for a networking meeting and after your *2-minute, letter perfect*, "Tell me about yourself" response, the person says that the company is looking for someone just like you, and the meeting becomes a successful interview leading to a job. Bingo again!

3. You see an opportunity posted on a job website or see an ad in the newspaper. And in spite of knowing the success rate is low when answering ads and postings, you do it anyhow. And whoa-and-behold the company calls you, interviews you and offers you the perfect job!

4. A head hunter hears about your incredible talents, meets with you and offers you up as a candidate for a great position . . . and you get the job.

5. You join LinkedIn and Facebook and an old school buddy reads your profile, remembers that you were voted the person most likely to succeed in your class and hires you.

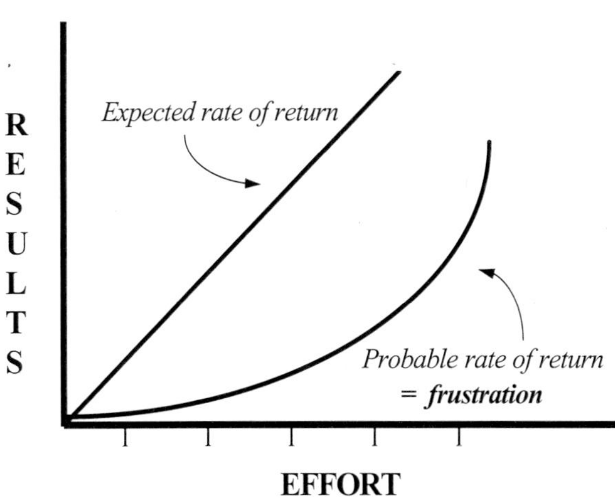

6. None of the above happens and your brother does not own a mega-million dollar company and no one seems to be offering you a job while standing on a street corner, so you begin the chore of networking. The vast majority of job hunters end up taking this networking route. The trouble with this route is that it all takes time. Historically, the average time to land a job in the USA, starting from scratch, has been about four months . . . longer for some and shorter for others (by the way, it is common for it to take a year or more, to find the right position). The reason for this is the time it takes for preparation and to build an awareness in the marketplace. This is frustrating for most of us because we have come to believe that if we contribute an ounce of effort, we will get an ounce of return . . . a one for

one ratio. Unfortunately, when looking for a job, you must build up what we call a ***critical mass*** before things begin to ignite . . . in terms of interviews and offers. What must occur is having many people in the same functional area/industry impressed with you and thinking about how you might fit into their company. This is the fundamental reason why networking, used properly, is such a powerful career transition tool. It is exactly how many of the most productive salespeople sell their wares . . . by referrals. However, if they don't know what you are selling, there won't be many referrals. There could come a time however, when you realize that whatever career field you are after is not going to work for you and you will have to change course direction and pursue a new/different objective.

The Old Sandwich Board Trick

A great idea, but it didn't work!

A few years ago, a San Francisco newspaper carried a photo of a man carrying a 3'x5' sandwich board with his resume printed on it, walking down the streets of the San Francisco Financial District. The article described the man as desperate and willing to do anything to get a job. The article went on to say, nice try, but that he had no takers.

Another desperate attempt was made by a man who printed his resume on a bed sheet and hung it out of an office building window to get the attention of an executive in the building across the street. That didn't work either. These are good tries, but a little outlandish, and usually don't get results.

Expected Compensation

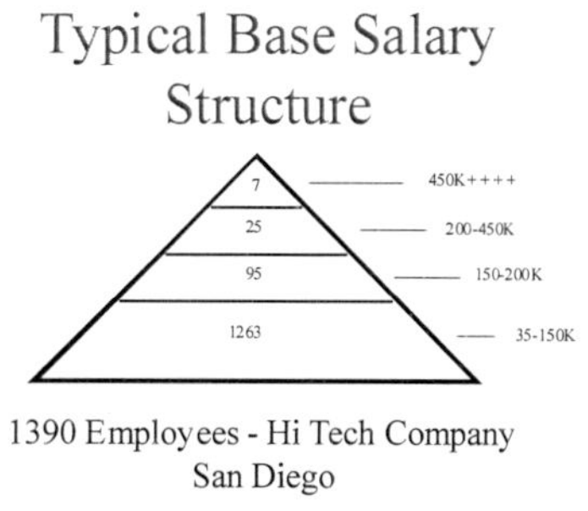

The good news about private sector employment is that it is possible to make more money . . . in terms of base pay and perks . . . than you did in the government. It is not a given, however. The bad news is that you probably won't start at the top of the pile. A few do. Most don't. The chart at the right shows a nearly 1400 person IT company's breakdown of base pay. Assuming that you have something to offer this company, it would not be hard to start at a salary around the $85K mark, but to get much more, you would probably have to bring in business. A good friend of mine, who is president of a very successful IT company, advises senior job hunters to just get in the door of a company they like as long as the compensation is reasonable. And, that if the fit is good, the newcomer will move up quickly. In my friend's case, he started as a project manager, moved to a program manager's position and because of excellent performance, was ultimately promoted to president of a spin-off company. I think his advice is right on!

The Truth of the Matter

Caveat Emptor!

Some people are never quite able to move on. They never seem to get their life in gear. There might be some hurdle that they are unable to get over, or they can't make up their mind as to what their objective should be, or whatever. Others convince themselves that they never want to work again and that their goal, their passion, is to retire . . . the *bad* word. Retirement is fine if that is what you really want to do, but for some, it is an excuse not to try and therefore they forego a second career. See more on this subject in the "Retirement" chapter.

Another case of reality is the job situation where you are asked to contribute money to the company or sign a document that obligates you to the company's debt. In either case, I can only say buyers beware. There have been several cases that I know of where government personnel, and I'm not talking about O-1s, E-3s, or GS-3s, have been cajoled into investing in a company in order to get a job, only to lose their shirts. And remember, the higher the return on your investment, the greater the risk! It is up to you to decide. All I can advise you to do is get a lawyer before signing anything. ***There is no such thing as a free lunch***! Tell that to yourself over and over again!

Is It Beneath Me?

Several months after I had been hired by a major financial institution I found myself in downtown New York City riding in a limo with three other corporate officers en route to visit some Wall Street high rollers. Halfway to our destination one of the corporate officers queried me about being a senior officer in the military service and having had several large commands. When I replied that his information was correct he replied, "Why do you do work like this?" (Meaning, "Isn't this work beneath you?") As I was thinking of a clever reply, the President, who was one of the other passengers, replied for me with, "He does it for the same reason that we all do it . . . he likes it!" And, he meant it!

Many people that you will encounter will wonder why you would take a job that *seems* to be less important than what you were doing while in government service. It doesn't make much difference if you were a four star Admiral or Master Sergeant or senior civil servant, some people will wonder why you would be willing to take the job you are applying for, or have just landed. The belief is that most people should strive to always go higher in their career structure and when someone accepts a job that is "lower" than the previous one, their motives become suspect. In fact, you may very likely have to convince the hiring official that you are willing to work at "this" level.

Another facet of this situation has to do with what your friends will say if you take "that" job. There is the story of a senior flag officer who wanted to manage his own business. He ended up running a porta-potty company (no pun intended) and you could hear the gossipers talking all over Washington saying . . . "How could a person with his rank and position do something like that?" Well let's face it, he isn't cleaning them out, he is managing a business and most likely working out of a nice office on the umteenth floor of a high rise office building somewhere, and making 'pots' of money ... *sorry.*

If you have been in charge of a division, or command of a battalion or whatever, you have had an enormous amount of responsibility. Most likely you will never have that much responsibility again . . . but the chances are that you will earn more money and be just as happy or happier.

The last part of this story of course is about self and how do you feel about "working below your status?" My answer to that problem is simple . . . if you like what you are doing and the compensation, in whatever form it takes is reasonable, go ahead and take it. Let's face it, the Head of the Joint Chiefs will never have a job as responsible as the one he has today.

The "beneath me" feeling is more prevalent than most people think and more prevalent in men than in women. Most of us deny that there are things beneath our dignity to do, but in truth, most of us do them on a daily basis . . . like cleaning the bathrooms and taking the garbage out. ***Next time your spouse asks you to carry out the garbage, try telling your spouse that carrying the garbage out is beneath your dignity . . . then run for cover!***

In the best-selling book Angela's Ashes, written by Frank McCourt, the Irish father would not take a job that was beneath him even though his wife and children had to pick up bits of coal off of the street from passing coal trucks in order to have enough fuel to heat their shabby shelter. The father lived off the government dole and spent most of it in a nearby pub buying drinks for himself and others, because "That is what Irish *gentlemen* do!" I have talked with senior military and civil service personnel who were struggling to find work but were unwilling to take a job that they thought was beneath them. So, they didn't work. And it's not just government people . . . private sector managers are no different. I had a client once who had been the CEO of a fairly large hi-tech firm. He lost his job but was soon offered a job with another company as the CFO . . . making nearly as much money. He refused the offer because it was less stature than what he had previously and ended up taking his children out of college, selling his home and moving away. This is your call. As I have mentioned before, most of us will never again have a job with as much responsibility and stature as we had in government service . . . more money perhaps, but not the same status!

Advice: Get this "it's beneath me" hurdle out of the way before you begin your new career search. An uncontrolled ego can strangle an otherwise good career transition effort!

Perceptions

There are many wrong perceptions in the private sector about senior military and civil service personnel. As with many perceptions, most of these are unfounded but all have some basis. Nevertheless, sometime in the past someone, or *someones* did or said something that created a bad impression and/or bad perception, that got applied to all those who came after. The perceptions differ somewhat for military and civil service. There are many and you have probably heard of most of them. My theory is that if you know what the perceptions are, you can cope with them and use them to your advantage.

We military and civil service also have perceptions about the private sector. We think that the only thing people in the private sector think about is making money . . . period. We think that lawyers are basically dishonest and that most, if not all politicians are on the take. I could go on and on but I think you get the idea. The reasons we have these perceptions are obvious.

One CEO of a IT company told me that he needed senior government personnel but not those who want to pass a problem to the subordinates and have them find a solution. He wants the senior military/civil service manager to use their brainpower to reach a solution. He went on to say that half of those military/civil service personnel who have worked for him fail to do this and move on within six months of joining the company. Another CEO said that only half of the seniors that he has hired are able to adapt to the company culture for whatever reason.

Another CEO of a defense company once asked me to send any good senior officers and/ senior enlisted personnel to him . . . that he was always looking for good project and program managers. I agreed to do that and told him that I knew some Flag Officers who would be good Program Managers also. He replied, "Don't send me any Generals or Admirals . . . they don't want to work!" Wow! Wow, because he is one . . . he was a senior officer in the service for thirty years. So some of the perceptions prevail among retired military personnel who are now managing private sector companies. Note – they don't fail because of brainpower, it's because they can't or don't want to adapt!

Knowing these perceptions exist should help you prepare to counter them. By studying the company and giving examples of how you accomplished tasks yourself, you can eliminate some, if not all of the concerns that drive the perceptions. You can also do some soul searching and determine if you really do want to work and if you really are willing to get into the details. Remember, most private sector companies have small staffs . . . people cost money and the fewer you have on the payroll the more the profit! The most prevalent perceptions that I have heard senior business people say about senior military are:

- They are not profit motivated
- They are easily buffaloed
- They don't like to get into details
- They need big staffs
- They have trouble adapting
- They are overqualified
- They are not street smart
- They really don't want to work
- They think business owes them
- They don't document/benchmark/quantify progress

There are many incorrect perceptions about military and civil service personnel! Don't be threatened – turn lemons into lemonade!

Note that the more senior you go in the military, the greater the perception.

And what about the civil service?

- They are not profit motivated
- They will not move out of their hometown for any reason
- They are rigid in their thinking . . . like the military
- They are not street smart
- They can only do it the "government way"

Your objective is to think of ways to convince the private sector why their perceptions/concerns do not apply to you. You do that with giving relevant examples and discussing relevant strengths. Turn lemons into lemonade, as the old saying goes.

On the other hand, there are many positive perceptions about the military and civil service. For example:

- Team-oriented
- Ability to conform to roles and structure
- Ability to work under pressure and to make deadlines
- Leadership
- Team builders
- Drug free
- Mature
- Integrity

- Healthy – physically fit
- Ability to work in diverse groups . . . and so on

Long-term Career Planning

The second and third careers after your initial career transition will be easier to obtain/land if you stay in the same line of work – industry and functional area. In that regard, working in the defense industry will initially enable you to move more easily into other defense companies. This is a major factor to consider because the same advantage does not present itself in the non-defense industry. The defense industry needs retired military personnel and really doesn't care how old you are . . . within reason. They know that you have government medical coverage and that you have a government pension. The private sector however is wary of older managers because of potential health problems and because they will probably want and/or *demand* higher compensation. They can hire younger people who are healthy and willing to work for less. Lastly, a career in defense will facilitate consulting after your full time job-life is over.

CHAPTER 22

ON THE JOB

Having survived step one of the career transition, you are now ready for step two . . . making the most of the position that you have landed. When you begin your new career it is important that you get accustomed to your surroundings ***before*** you suggest that they move the corporate headquarters from Boston to San Diego. You want to show that you have a lot to offer, but we suggest that you tread lightly until you feel secure about your position. When that will be . . . only you can tell!

> **Please Take Note**
>
> ***No one achieves success without hard work, a little luck and the help of many others ... mentors. Take a moment to call and/or drop a note and thank ten people or more, who helped you succeed in your service career . Don't wait! Make yourself memorable.***
>
> ***They may also be the ones who can help you most in your next career.***

Considerations:

- **LEARNING CURVE** . . . no one is going to expect you to make dramatic changes the first day on the job. In fact, you may not be around very long if you try to do so.

- **CULTURE SHOCK** . . . different companies operate in different ways . . . even those within the same industry. Many will want you to find out who's who, and to understand their policies before you begin making waves . . . good advice!

- **TURF ISSUES** . . . this situation exists everywhere, even though everyone says we are all one happy family. That's right, all one happy family as long as you realize that I am the "Godfather." Figure out who's who, in the company.

- **RANGE OF AUTHORITY** . . . establish this with your boss, before you flex your muscles. You will find that it may be much more limited than what you have been accustomed to. All organizations have a formal and informal power structure.

- **BUILD ALLIES. WIN RESPECT** . . . makes sense in any situation. If you want to change the product lines, get the support of your fellow line operators, before you make your suggestion.

- **SOME HELP** . . . you will find that many will welcome you with open arms, as long as you are a "good guy/gal."

- **SOME RESENT** . . . some of them will hate your insides because you may have taken part of their turf or landed the job they wanted, deserving or not. You, an *outsider*, got the job!

- **WATCH THE EGO** . . . you may or may not have a position equal to what you had in your last job. You may or may not be making more money.

The Power Structure

All organizations have a formal and informal power structure. During your first few weeks or months on the job, try to determine where the power lies. Some people have authority by virtue of their title . . . others, more junior, may have equal or more power by virtue of their relationship with the President and higher-ups. While most organizations have an organizational chart which represents the management system, just like the government there is also an informal organization system that really gets the job done. You need to understand that *informal* system as well as the formal system. Below is a typical organization chart for a manufacturing company. In some companies the top three positions are held by one person and in others there are three separate people. You should know:

- Who makes the personnel decisions?
- Whose advice is sought after?
- Who does the president/functional manager turn to for guidance the most?
- Who is the company spokesperson?
- Who reports to whom?
- Who travels with the boss?

Corporate Organization Chart

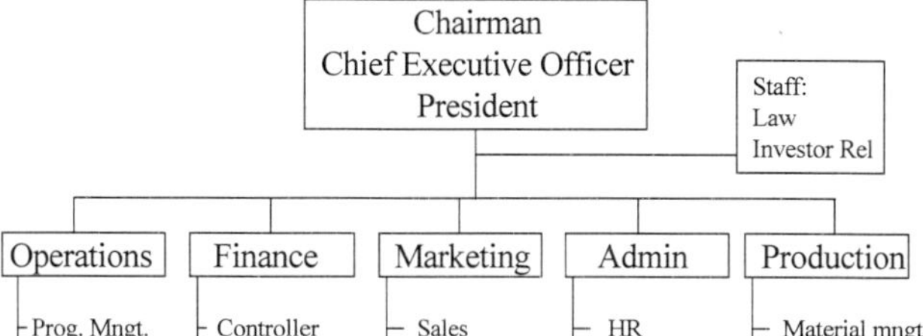

Every corporation will be different!

- Whose suggestions are treated like orders?
- Who is the final authority when it comes to funds obligation?
- Who has the authority to hire? . . . to fire?
- Who is the acknowledged expert in each area of the company?
- Who does the president/functional manager confide in?

Who Has The Power . . . *sizing up your fellow employees*

Don't assume, for example, that the assistant controller is just another accountant. That person may be the key player in developing financial presentations and have the President's ear more than anyone else. Most companies try to hire from the inside. When you arrive, you are an outsider and will be perceived by some as a *threat* . . . especially in a non-defense company. They will ask themselves, "Why did the boss bring this outsider, who doesn't know anything about our business, into the company?" Others may resent the fact that you have not paid your dues . . . this feeling could last until the next newcomer shows up . . . then, *you* will have the same concerns, and wonder if the new guy is going to get *your* job. However, most employees will be happy to help you get settled into your new job. Bottom line . . . take it easy . . . get the lay of the land!

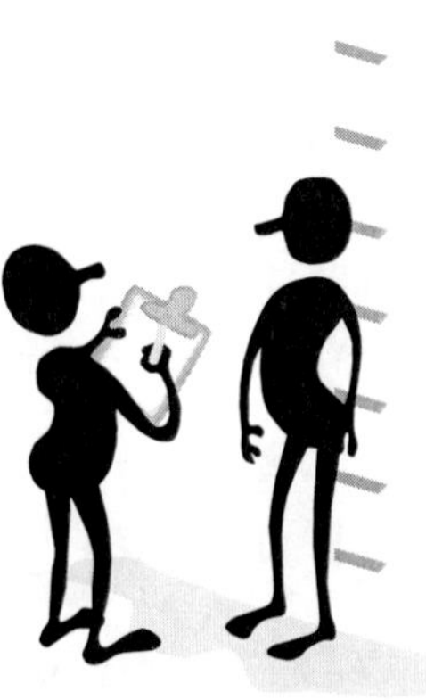

Take care when sizing people up!

"Jobs That Last for Never"

Several years ago I picked up a newspaper and blinked when I read the headline . . . ***"Jobs That Last for Never."*** At first I thought there was some kind of error, that it should read, "Jobs That Last Forever." A year later the company I was working for went under. I watched people who thought they had it "made"until retirement, suddenly go into a state of panic. Jobs do not last forever. There are countless reasons why . . . just a few:

- **Corporate failure** . . . *company fails*
- **A recession** and attendant layoffs
- **Merger** . . . *the small guy gets gobbled up*
- **Acquisition** . . . *one company acquires another*
- **Reorganization** . . . *and out you go*
- **Downsizing** . . . *not enough action/business to keep everyone*
- **Re-location** . . . *company moves to another location and you choose not to go*
- **Bad fit** . . . *after taking the job you find yourself the proverbial square peg in a round hole*
- **Change of management** . . . *and the new guy brings in his own team*
- **Company fails to get a contract or contract renewal** = *no contract, no work to do, no job*

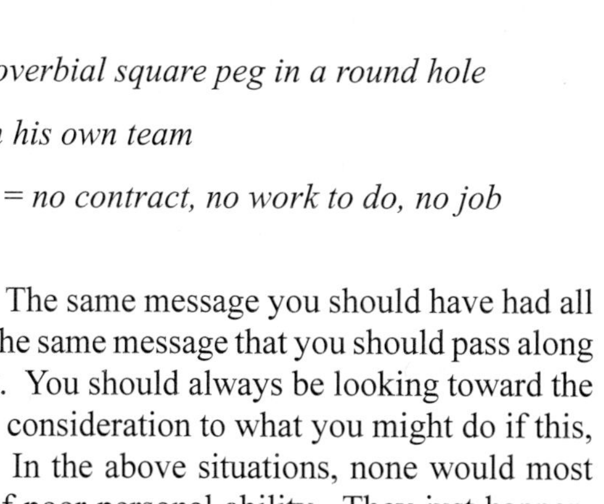

So, what's the message? The same message you should have had all of your working life and the same message that you should pass along to anyone you care about. You should always be looking toward the future and giving serious consideration to what you might do if this, "sure-thing" goes away. In the above situations, none would most likely occur as a result of poor personal ability. They just happen. When I was the general manager of a human resources consulting firm, I observed people being laid off for all of the above reasons . . . over and over and over. No fault of their own . . . just happened to be there. Typically, most jobs only last between three and five years in the private sector.

Caution

Regardless of the circumstances surrounding your layoff, and no matter how good it might feel at the moment, ***never, never, never burn a bridge***. You never know when you might need help or a reference from your previous company. That goes for leaving the military/government service as well!

Legal Considerations

WARNING! For those of you who have been involved in government contracting, or are in a position to influence a contract, or who may know people or have friends who are in positions to influence a contract . . . **BEWARE**. Know the rules regarding *contracting/procurement integrity* before you start calling around and asking a lot of questions about a contract that your company is bidding on. Your company's legal counsel will be happy to fill you in . . . could avoid a huge lawsuit and/or elimination from the qualified bidder's list. Enough said.

Know the DOD restrictions!

"How Long must I Stay, Once I Begin?"

Sounds like a strange question coming from someone who just landed a great job after struggling for the past four months. However, it is a question that we get asked frequently. What seems to happen is this . . . you are in the new job for six months and a company you interviewed with months ago, and liked very much, calls and asks if you would like to come with them. More money - doing the same thing. A dilemma. Give it careful thought. Moving, in less than a year on the job, may not be the best thing to do. If it were a great opportunity and/or a promotion, I would *probably* wish you well. If it were for a few thousand dollars, I would not have nice thoughts about you. The impact of job hopping can be serious. Most managers are wary of job hoppers. They will ask you why have you moved so many times. And, the word gets around – especially in the defense industry! To illustrate: I once received a telephone call from a friend telling me that he had just received an offer from another company to manage a fairly large program and offering more money than he was currently making. There were several drawbacks . . . first, the company making the offer had not yet won the contract he was to manage, but they wanted to hire him and put his name on the solicitation. Secondly, my friend had only been with his present company for ten months. This is real life and it happens frequently. I told him that this was a risky situation - a slippery slope! First, if he agreed to go with the "new" company and they did not get the contract, he could be without a job. Next, even if he just allowed his name to be used on the proposal and his immediate company found out he would be dead meat! Third, unless the increase in salary was really significant, it probably would not be worth the change; meaning that he would have to go through the learning process again, figuring out who is who is the company and how they operate. Net-net . . . proceed with caution. *Note: it would take a heck of a lot of money and significant increase in responsibility for me to leave a company that I was happy with and where I could see future growth.*

Changing jobs - Considerations

1. Try not to leave a present job until you have another firm offer.
2. It is somewhat unethical to look for another job on the present job's time.
3. Read adjacent paragraph - *slippery slope.*

Boorish Bosses

An interesting article appeared in a local newspaper concerning bosses who display other than civilized characteristics in the workplace. This is not an infrequent occurrence and you should be sensitive to the fact that it does take place. (Note that you may have a boorish boss while in the service but you always knew that one of you would be transferred in a year or so.) The best way to avoid a boorish boss is not to work for one in the first place. Hopefully, during an interview session you will get some indication of the type of personality that you will be working for. It is not always easy to detect a boor but you should be on the lookout. The article said that the situation was so prevalent in the workplace that there is a Website where people can go to for assistance . . . *How about them apples?*

Private Sector Layoffs . . . *just thought you would want to know!*
Layoffs in every industry are commonplace. Even in good times companies lay off employees. The layoff can be a result of a merger, an acquisition or a reorganization or a downsizing because of a poor economy or poor performance on the behalf of the employee. Unless there is obvious discrimination, and since you will probably be working "at will," there is not much that an employee can do other than take a severance check and look for work elsewhere.

How the layoff is conducted is another story. Companies have a great fear that, once an employee/s is notified that their employment is being terminated, the employee may do physical damage to the company. Most susceptible of course is the company's computer system. As a result, it is not unusual for a company to terminate an employee and then escort the employee to the front door without ever returning to the employee's office. (Someone goes to the employee's office and boxes up the personal belongings.) What's worse is that the employee is often paraded through the office in front of the other employees . . . even if the employee is being terminated through no fault of his/her own. While this procedure is not practiced by every company, there are enough of them doing it to generate many vitriolic articles in human resource magazines on the subject.

The infamous "pink slip"

Terminating an employee, a good or bad one, is probably the most difficult personnel action that a manager has to take. It is so distasteful that many senior managers delegate it to the HR manager (a rotten and cowardly thing to do) so they can avoid the emotional tirade that often comes with the message. Emotions range everywhere from the employee going into a stupor, to shouting, to getting a gun and shooting people like what happened at a U. S. Post Office years ago. There is just no easy way. While there are probably some employees that deserve to be paraded before their peers and lead out the door, it is considered very bad manners for a company to do so.

The worst case is when a good and responsible employee is terminated through no fault of their own and treated in the manner described above. Military members will have a hard time appreciating this kind of situation because the government doesn't weed out their employees in the same manner. And, most military leadership tends to take more responsibility when notifying subordinates of bad news . . . non-selection, crummy orders and things like that. It is very bad form to delegate giving bad news . . . have the courtesy/guts to do it yourself! At any rate this is the real private sector world . . . *just thought you would want to know.*

You "Work At Will"
The vast number of offer letters will contain the phrase, "your employment will be on a ***"work at will"*** basis. This simply means that you can be let go (terminated) at any time and conversely, you can walk out the door (bag it) at any time. (Note: If you are serving on active duty in the military you do not work at will . . . you have a contract and cannot be fired. However, since you do have a contract you cannot walk away from your responsibilities, unless you want to go to the brig for a spell!) Some companies abuse the *letter offer* agreement but most do not let good employees leave unless there is a situation beyond their control . . . like a downsizing because of poor business or a merger or acquisition. This is a good reason to understand what the company's severance policy is . . . in the event you are let go through no fault of your own. By the way, if you leave your job on your own volition, your severance will most likely be ZIP!

How to Protect Yourself Financially If Laid Off

The key to re-employment is NETWORKING!

So, how do you protect yourself from the financial implications of being severed from your job through no fault of your own? One of the last perks you negotiate after you get the job offer, is severance pay . . . refer to the Compensation Chapter and the perks section. In the nicest way possible, you say something like this . . . "If I were to be let go for a reason such as reorganization or a merger or acquisition, that is to say, for no fault of my own, what would the severance package be." Don't ask if there is one, assume it is so. Nearly all large companies have a severance policy and it can be a negotiable item during compensation discussions. You will be reluctant to bring this subject up but you will wish you had! The worst that can happen is for the company to advise you that they don't offer severance. Also see Outplacement services – a related issue – in the perk section. Typically, severance pay is about one week's pay for every year you worked for the company. ***(Better than a sharp stick in your eye!)***

Severance Pay and Job Loss Rationale

If you are laid off through no fault of your own you should always ask for a severance package . . . compensation, medical, outplacement assistance, et al. Review the paragraphs on severance pay and outplacement services in the perk section of the "Compensation" chapter. You should also have an agreement with the company, in writing, as to why you were let go. Note that if possible, severance provisions should be addressed at the beginning, before you sign your offer letter.

CHAPTER 23

SUMMARY

Some perspective from a 30-year Navy Captain at his retirement ceremony. . .

> ***"On Looking Ahead . . .***
>
> ***Government service has been rewarding, fun and a challenge, but it has been secure too. I do not regret my decision to leave the service. Many approach me and express condolences. I view this change much like completing a book. I have turned the last page. It is time to put the book on the shelf with the other classics and select my next piece of reading material. I have no desire to reread the book. I have no desire to read the last page very slowly to "make it last." I will recommend the book to someone who has not yet read it, but I will make another selection."***

What I Know for Certain!

There are many actions that must be accomplished when leaving one career and starting another. I have tried to explain the most important ones in this book in a way that makes sense to everyone. Some of the readers will disagree with me and that is to be expected – all I can tell you is that the information contained herein is based on professional career transition consulting training, more than 20 years of teaching and writing on the subject, and reading letters and feedback reports from thousands of people who went through the process. Having said that, the following is what I know for certain, and I mean for certain!

Jack of all trades!

1. **You must be Pro-active -** You can pray every hour of every day for assistance from above but the Lord helps those who help themselves. Success will not happen by itself. No one can network for you, and no one can take the job interview for you. You must make the calls and conduct the research. When looking for a new career you become a jack-of-all-trades . . . from Marketing Director to Chief Financial Officer, to CEO, to coffee maker, to the head of janitorial services. Try it, you might like it . . . or at least some of it!

2. **You must have an objective - some kind of focus.** Launching on any new adventure without having some kind of focus will lead to frustration. You will always be looking over your shoulder and second guessing yourself. I can't think of any successful person I know who didn't start with a fairly specific objective in mind. That is why we have strategic planning sessions in business and government organizations. You can always change your objective but at least have one to give yourself direction, if nothing else. Don't forget to determine the ***key words*** associated with your objective!

3. **Preparation and research and are the keys to success -** The single most common comment I receive from people who have followed the process described in this book, and have gone on to begin new and successful careers, is the value of preparation . . . for networking meetings and for interviewing. I cannot overstress the value of having good background data about the company you are networking or interviewing with . . . it will truly separate the pros from the amateurs. With websites like Google available for research there is no reason not to be ready to go! **Remember. Two thirds of the effort involved in successful career transition is preparation.**

4. **Networking is how the vast majority of people land jobs -** The feedback data, both verbal and written, validate all the surveys I have read about the value of networking. This is especially true for former government employees be they military or civil service. Nationwide, 75 percent of all jobs are found by word-of-mouth and the statistics from feedback forms provided me by previous seminar attendees are even higher . . . like more than 95 percent. Websites like LinkedIn and Facebook can help you find acquaintances and provide referrals and leads, but for senior managers, at least, face-to-face networking is what will ultimately get you the job.

5. **A positive attitude is imperative -** Just as with any other effort you might undertake, a positive attitude is imperative. It is important during an interview as well as with those you meet with on a day-to-day basis. You know that your job search will be successful if you give it a chance. A short time for some, and longer for others, but in the end you will reach your goal.

Emotions will go from one extreme to another!

6. **If I am persistent and determined, I will get there -** Philosophers have said it, Presidents have said it, and you have heard it over and over throughout your life. Follow the process and just hang in there with a persistent attitude, and the power of the momentum you create will help you obtain your goal.

7. **The first two minutes are critical to the first impression -** We all know first impressions are critical and at an interview or networking meeting even more so. Your dress, your demeanor, and what you say will set the tone in the first few minutes . . . so be prepared!

8. **I will encounter some rejection -** There is absolutely no doubt that you will encounter some rejection. It happens to everyone and it is simply the way things are. Seniority is not protected from the feeling of rejection. The secret is to acknowledge that it will happen and get on with the process.

9. **Feeling depressed at times is perfectly normal -** Just as rejection is a normal happening when looking for a job, so is a little depression. That is not to say it is normal for it to last for days or weeks, but when someone fails to return your call or you don't get the job when you thought you would, feeling a little *down* is perfectly normal - you wouldn't be human if being rejected didn't hurt a little.

10. **Emotions will go from one extreme to another -** I can tell you from personal experience and the feedback from thousands of others that your emotions will go from an all-time high to the pits . . . and back. Just remember that this, too, is part of the process and everyone experiences it. And, remember how good it is going to feel . . . *the high* . . . when you receive the offer you worked so hard to get!

11. **It is okay to negotiate for an increase in compensation -** It will seem strange for you to negotiate for a better compensation package. You must understand that it is an expected reaction to an offer. I'm not saying you should be greedy, just ensure you are not leaving salary or perks on

the table. And, as strange as it may seem, even people who have been in the private sector for years are hesitant to negotiate for more . . . they do, but most are uncomfortable when doing so. You will be too, but just do it!

12. **Most people are willing to assist -** People are basically kind, and are willing to assist you as long as you go about it in a polite fashion. Certainly, you will meet some *"back-ends*," but for the most part, you will be surprised at the number of people whom you have never met before and are willing to help. Always remember: those people got their jobs through networking with friends and people whom they had never met before.

The Successful Job Hunter

There are no strict rules for what makes or breaks a successful military/civil service to private sector career transition campaign. In this book we have covered a multitude of Things-To-Do that we know, through practical experience, work. A survey was taken of professional career consultants and they were asked, "What are the traits of the successful job hunter?" The response was as follows:

1. ***The successful job hunter begins immediately*** . . . it's okay to take some time off after retirement but the longer you wait the cooler you get. The standard guidance is, it is always easier to get a job, if you have a job.
2. ***Takes personal responsibility for the job search*** . . . does not rely on others.
3. ***Has a career focus*** . . . has taken the effort to translate his or her strengths in the civilian marketplace needs.
4. Is aware of ***how his/her activities relate to fulfilling the objective*** . . . are you achieving or relieving?
5. ***Has a plan*** . . . works on it daily.
6. ***Maintains a positive attitude*** at all times.
7. ***Is constantly networking***.
8. Has a minimum of ***three informal networking meetings a week*** . . . *best is two per day.*
9. ***Never underestimate who can be of help*** . . . realizes that everyone is a potential contact.
10. ***Understands the difference between networking and a job interview***.
11. ***Follows up*** on all leads and referrals.
12. ***Is always prepared***.
13. ***Researches*** all leads and companies thoroughly.
14. Keeps ***balance*** in his/her life!
15. **Joins LinkedIn and Facebook**.

The Seven Habits (now eight) of Highly Effective People and *Career Transition*

Steven Covey writes that highly effective people have seven common habits. The same habits apply to career transition and starting a new career. Think about it. Following are the original seven habits:

Pro-active – While there are all kinds of people who will help you look for a job, no one can do it for you. You must be pro-active. Sit around and wait for it to come to you and you will either be sitting for either a long time or end up with a job you really don't want.

Begin with the end in mind – you must have an objective or you will wander around aimlessly. Have an idea of the kind of industry you want to work in and hopefully what you want to do in that industry.

Put first things first – this just means that when you are looking for a job, finding that a job is the most important thing you have to do, so keep your focus on the goal.

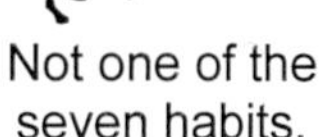

Not one of the seven habits.

Think win-win – you want to get hired and want the organization to like you but you want to be happy in the organization as well. It should be a win-win proposition . . . and that goes for compensation too!

Seek first to understand – Pay attention to what is being said during a networking meeting or a job interview. Gather as much information as possible. They will want to get your views on various subjects but be careful not to hog the conversation . . . let alone pontificate!

Synergize – use everything at your disposal. Your friends, and their friends, and all of your past acquaintances. Don't worry that you have not spoken to an old school chum for twenty years – pick up the phone and call them.

Sharpen the saw – the career is but one part of the life equation. Covey focuses on the importance of bringing balance to your life – your physical well-being, your mental health, your emotional and spiritual health. There are many aspects to having a happy and satisfying life – the career, albeit important, is but one of them. See "Life Planning" in the following section.

Some Thoughts to Leave You With

Happiness

I once asked a successful businessman what his definition of success was, and he replied, "Happiness!" In the working world, happiness is having a job that you are interested in, where you have the strengths to carry it off, and one where you can make a reasonable income and/or be compensated through the personal satisfaction of doing good for others. That should be everyone's goal. The other part of that equation of course is living where you want to live. There is almost always a compromise!

Happiness Is ...

You only go around once ...

LIFE PLANNING

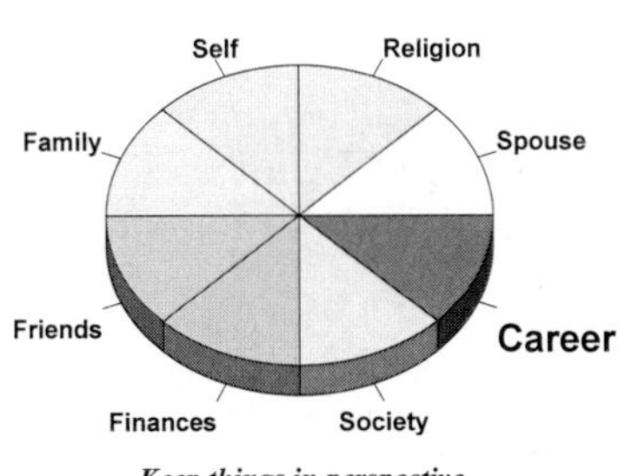

Keep things in perspective

There Is More in Life than a Working Career

However, as we have said earlier, the job . . . the career, is only one part of the equation. The other parts are where you are going to live and the income that will be derived from the job. If you have a significant other, it is a two-person decision. Planning for a follow-on career involves more than just you, it must fit in with your life planning scheme.

That means your family, ethics, religion, social aspects, spouse, society, self, friends and finances. A lot to take into consideration. And, speaking of finances, there was a recent article in the Sunday paper that talked about millionaires and how they spend their money. It went on to say that the majority of millionaires do not spend lavishly. They don't drive brand-new cars, they live in the community where real people live and for all intents and purposes live a modest life. Under that criteria, we are all already millionaires. If you think about it, it takes mega-bucks to make a significant difference in your life!

Have a Bucket List

Whatever you do, don't put off doing those things you have always wanted to do! The 2008 movie "The Bucket List" describes the life of two old geezers (Jack Nicholson and Morgan Freeman) who are about to pass on, desperately trying to accomplish everything that is on their list of things to do before they "kick the bucket!" Nearly panic driven, they realize that they should have managed their personal lives more carefully . . . years before. Have no regrets, do both . . . work and play . . . think ahead!

What to Expect during your job hunt

How Long?

Plan on 5-7 months or longer if the economy is suffering . . . *It took me nine months.* If you were to survey a group of 100 senior military members (officer or enlisted) or civil service personnel within six months of retirement, you would find that about half of them have jobs or are well into the process of getting one. Many of these opportunities come from family and close friends. There is another small percentage who just seem to fit in perfectly with the needs of a company. Perhaps they are nuclear engineers, or procurement specialists, or construction engineers or specialists in some field where there is an immediate need. Or, perhaps they just fall into a good deal. The majority however, are required to use their contacts and get involved in networking. If you are among the majority then stand by to be in the job hunting market for *three to five months* or more . . . depending on the level of the position, salary requirements and current economic conditions. There is also a very small group that try job hunting for a while and then, for whatever reason, decide not to pursue a second career. If you are in the first two groups, lucky you. If you are in the group that decides to *"retire-retire,"* make sure that you really don't want to work. Try working first. You can always quit.

JOB SEARCH

Is a step by step *process*

There are no shortcuts!

How Much?

On the average, for the past three years it has taken four to seven months for a *private sector* job hunter, expecting a salary of $125,000 to $175,000, to land a job. It is not unusual for the process to take a year or more, depending on the area and type of job that you want. The average salary differs widely between locations. There are many websites that compare the cost of living between areas.

How Come?
The people that appear to be the most successful in landing a job are those that start immediately and follow the process. Dennis Waitley, the well known motivational speaker, says that when you want to pursue something important, do so with gusto . . . and make certain that everything that you do somehow benefits that pursuit. In his words, "achieve, don't relieve." Achieving means eight hours a day, five days a week, or more. Relieving is occupying yourself with tasks that, however important they might seem to be, have nothing to do with finding a job. Treat the job search as you would a full time job and you will be successful sooner!

CAVEAT EMPTOR! There is no such thing as a free lunch! If you receive an offer that is two or three times more than you expected, or believe the job is worth, beware. If you are asked to sign papers on the company's behalf, don't . . . see your lawyer first in both cases. Make sure that you do your due diligence before jumping in with both feet. Meeting with a good contract lawyer could save you lots of grief later. As I said before, if the deal is too good to be true, it is too good to be true!

***Note: Full and Open Disclosure**. If you begin this process while still in government service and you are subject to the rules of employment, check with your organization's legal department and let them know what you are doing. To be certain that everything that you do is in the clear, write the legal officer a memo regarding your intentions to visit a private corporation or business before you go. It's called full and open disclosure.*

14 Steps to Success - check them off!

- ❏ Determine your objective
- ❏ Determine the skills required
- ❏ Research
- ❏ Develop the accomplishments to support the strengths
- ❏ Write resume #1
- ❏ Conduct level one networking - gather information and validate objective
- ❏ Write resume #2
- ❏ Develop a target list of people who can help . . . ***focus on referrals***
- ❏ Develop a target list of companies
- ❏ Research
- ❏ Conduct level two networking
- ❏ Conduct interviews that will result from the above
- ❏ Negotiate salary and perks
- ❏ Start preparing for next job

Personal Letter - from a seminar attendee

"Dear John,

It has been about one year and nine months since I took your class and I am happy to report that I have just begun my job with the company that I targeted. I had a signed job offer one month before leaving service and started working while on terminal leave.

Some observations that you may find useful and might want to pass along to others:

No matter how difficult it may seem in the beginning, networking is absolutely necessary. I had exactly 100 networking contacts that I had talked to or met with by the time I accepted this job. These were all people working in the industry (high technology manufacturing) that I wanted to work in. And it was growing exponentially.

I managed my network on Touch base Pro. (Apple computer software) It keeps basic information regarding people as well as records of meetings and phone calls. And it allows you to attach documents to the person's file. (Note: the ACT PC software does the same thing) This way, I always had a copy of the tailored resume that I had sent that person handy if he or she called.

I read the classified in the San Jose Mercury Newspaper each Sunday and applied for two positions each week. I received ten standard reply cards and no interviews out of the 36 positions I applied for. Interesting exercise, but you were right. This is not a good way to go.

I spent a year and four months preparing for the hunt. I joined the USO of Northern California and was elected to the board of directors. I joined a professional society in the manufacturing area and was elected to the board of directors. I researched the key words. I also completed both of the organization's certifications. Several people I interviewed with told me that the certifications were important because it demonstrated that I was interested in the industry that I wanted to work in and that I was willing to work to get into a new area.

Before I began the search, I had completed my final resume and had it on the computer in a way that was easy to modify and change to fit several different types of positions. I had also memorized my two-minute opener and my 30-second commercial. And my wife had grilled me with questions from the Knock 'Em Dead book every night after dinner for two months. After she worked on me, I was almost disappointed at how easy the interviews seemed. In short, I was prepared before I began my search.

I began with the idea that I wanted to work in the high technology manufacturing industry with a company not associated with government contracting. The locale was the San Francisco bay area. From there I developed a list of fifteen companies and ordered all of their annual reports.

It is important to note that I spent one year and four months preparing and only five months actually looking for a job. The longer preparation resulted in the shorter search. I believe I spent 10 hours a week during the preparation and search phases on the transition to the new career. This may seen like a lot of time to some, but I started this job for a compensation package worth $51,000 per year more than what I thought I was going to get. Assuming that differential remains constant for the next 15 years that I plan to work, that equates to $877 per hour for that preparation. Not bad after one takes into account the time value of money.

I found the whole experience trying but fun. In the end I not only got a job, but I also learned a significant amount about the industry I wanted to work in and I met many very nice people.

When I would get rebuffed or ignored, I would not take it personally but would look at it as a salesman would. I was selling a product, me! To sell one unit a salesman must make many contacts. Some work and some don't, but the salesman still keeps on selling and so did I.

In short, I really got a lot from your course and my results seem to prove that the process works. Thank you for everything. Call anytime I can help."

Conclusion

Throughout this book and our seminar, you have read and/or heard about the importance of having a focus . . . the importance of research and preparation and the importance of the networking process. You will receive advice of all kinds as you go through your career transition . . . some of it good and some of it off the wall . . . "Don't buy used clothes from a person that scratches a lot." There are countless books on the market for sale on the subject of career transition . . . most of them say about the same thing and nearly *all are written for a private sector manager* who is job hunting within the same field. Most of you are a different animal! Remember the warning about who is correct!

My goal with this book is to make *you* sensitive about *you* in terms of what you really want to do and to expose you to the various facets of job hunting. You have also been made aware that civil service and military personnel, as compared to their private sector counterparts, have a different set of problems. The good news is that you bring strong management qualifications to the table. The best news of all is that having read this book you understand the process and are prepared to get on with your search.

The bad news is that you may be *perceived* by many as having strengths that are not applicable to the private sector. We know that nothing could be further from the truth, but convincing others is another story. More bad news is that you are probably transitioning into a new vocation. That is difficult for private sector civilians as well as senior military and civil service. So your work is cut out for you. It may seem like an impossible task, but the process described throughout this book works. If you follow the process that I have laid out for you, you will have a major advantage over those that are wandering from door to door trying to sell their wares without knowing what they want to sell or knowing what they really have to sell. I have received thousands of letters attesting to the fact that the process we describe in this book really does work!

More bad news, or perhaps not so bad, is that the first job you land out of service will probably not be the last one you will have. So don't worry about the first job being the perfect new career. Worry instead about the second or third job being the perfect new career.

Choose carefully

There are millions of job openings in this country and millions of jobs turnover each year. Many of those turnovers are simply economic fatalities but many are the result of a round peg in a square hole. According to a study by Korn/Ferry International, the world's largest recruiting firm, 51 percent of the people interviewed said that if given the opportunity to do over again, *they would have chosen a completely different career field*. The study also found that 25 percent of those interviewed said they would have stayed the course and 24 percent were not sure. The secret to career happiness is knowing what you want to do, assuring yourself that you have the strengths or can get the strengths to do it, and having the persistence to make it happen. Major outplacement companies process tens of thousands of people through group and individual career transition programs yearly. Those that follow the process land jobs, and according to their surveys, most people are happier in their new jobs and make equal to or more compensation than they did in their previous jobs.

One final note. Keep in mind that there are thousands of senior military and civil service personnel that have gone before you and are now working in careers that not only compensate well but also bring a great deal of personal satisfaction. There is life after a career in the government service . . . enjoy it!

. . . Have a great new career! Good Luck

What it means to have succeeded in life:

> ***"To laugh often and much; to win the respect of intelligent people and the affection of children; to earn the appreciation of honest critics and endure the betrayal of false friends; to appreciate beauty; to find the best in others; to leave the world a bit better; whether by a healthy child, a garden patch or a redeemed social condition; to know even one life has breathed easier because you have lived.***
>
> ***This is to have succeeded."***
>
> **— Emerson**

PERSONAL ASSESSMENT

Understanding yourself is one of the first things you should do before diving into the process of career transition. In the following pages you will find a series of questions that will help you to better understand the course you should be following. Many of the questions are straight forward but others will require some serious thought. Remember the goal in your next career is to be happy in your work and satisfied with how you are being compensated . . . financially or by some altruistic feeling.

CAREER PLANNING

1. What do you like to do *outside* of your present government duties?

2. What do you like to do best in your job-related activities?

3. During your present government career, in what kind of jobs/duties did you find the greatest satisfaction? . . . in what kind the least?

4. What are your favorite hobbies?

5. Given no restrictions, what kind of a *civilian*/private sector job would you like to have? Why?

6. What do you consider to be your greatest:

   Strength:
   Why?

   Weakness:
   Why?

7. Where do I want to live when I leave government service?

8. Where does my spouse want to live when I leave government service?

9. List your three favorite vacations and what you did.

10. List the three qualities for which you are most complimented.

11. List the three times in your life when you felt most exhilarated.

12. List three activities you used to enjoy but think you have outgrown.

13. Ask yourself . . . what's missing in my life?

14. Ask yourself . . . what's right with my life?

15. Ask yourself . . . is there any kind of common thread running through my answers in this personal assessment?

APPENDIX A

PERSONAL CONSIDERATIONS

1. What are your income objectives?

2. What factors do you consider most important in your next career?

3. What family considerations must you keep in mind?

4. What is more important to you . . . salary, the position, location? Why

5. What special concerns do you have? (Income, aging parents, children, location, health)

6. What would I like to learn/gain from this seminar?

7. What concerns me most about career transition is?

8. I will consider this seminar a success if afterwards, I can:

9. What I really want to do in the time I have remaining in the government service.

10. What are my options?

11. What do I really want to do when I leave government service?

12. What do my friends think I should do when I leave government service?

13. What will you do if you retire and don't work?

YOUR NEXT CAREER

1. Describe your ideal work position. What functional area? What industry?

2. List the kinds of things that you enjoy doing the most . . . work or home life.

3. List the things that you enjoy doing the least . . . you may do them well but given the option would rather NOT engage in the activity . . . work related.

4. Going back to number one, your ideal position, what would prevent you from achieving that position?

5. Write down five possible things that you would like to do.

6. List 40 people that you believe could be of significant assistance to you in locating your next career and briefly describe how they might help you.

7. Industries and companies that are of interest to me.

YOUR ACCOMPLISHMENTS

One of the most difficult things that a career government person must do in career transition is decide what he or she wants to do in the private sector after leaving the service. The more senior the person is, the more difficult that decision becomes. The other tough decision is when to leave the service. Answering the questions in this personal assessment and giving serious thought about your accomplishments will help to clarify the direction you are headed.

You have done things that you are proud of . . . things that you have received recognition for and things that are meaningful to you. These accomplishments or achievements are the result of your leadership, your personal ideas, or your energy. You may have accomplished them alone or while working with your fellow service members . . . junior or senior . . . civil service or military.

It is important to identify these accomplishments/achievements since many will most likely be used in your career transition preparation.

- Write down 12 accomplishments or achievements that you consider your best . . . work or non-work related . . . but mostly work related. Your personal evaluation reports and evaluations on others are a good place to begin. After you have written the 12, expand on the six that are the most significant from a work-related viewpoint.

- Briefly describe 12 achievements or accomplishments from your government career.

  Examples:
  A. Instituted a procedure for streamlining the budget preparation.
  B. Implemented a record management system that reduced the cost of operation.

SPECIFIC ACCOMPLISHMENTS

The next step is to expand upon the accomplishment. Using the format in the example below, describe six achievements /accomplishments in the following terms:

A. Describe the situation . . . or the problem

B. What you did about it . . . describe the action taken

C. The results . . . what was accomplished

Example:
Situation: The error rate in file maintenance had increased by 20 percent in the past eight months.

My Action: I assembled all of the players involved and conducted an in-depth analysis of the contributing conditions and designed a new procedure for error control. Results: Within two months the error rate returned to normal and within another six months the rate was reduced by 10 percent . . . with no increase in man-hours expended. Overtime was reduced by 14 percent for a quarterly savings of $25,000.

APPENDIX A

CAREER CHRONOLOGY . . . *list in reverse chronological order.*

1. Title:

    Organization:

    Major Responsibilities:

2. Title:

    Organization:

    Major Responsibilities:

. . . *etc. If the position/role or responsibilities changed significantly within the* <u>*same*</u> *organization, consider that a new organization. Feel free to include additional early positions.*

EDUCATION

Educational History

1. School:

    Major Subjects:

    Subjects Enjoyed Most:

2. School:

    Major Subjects:

    Subjects Enjoyed Most:

. . . *etc.*

ORGANIZATIONS AND AFFILIATIONS

List present and past memberships in professional organizations. Describe your responsibilities and any leadership positions that you held.

SPOUSE PERSONAL ASSESSMENT

These questions should be answered independently of your spouse's (the "job seeker's") Personal Assessment. When you have both completed your assessments, compare and discuss.

1. What do you think your spouse's three greatest strengths are?

2. What are his/her major weaknesses?

3. What kind of job do you think your spouse would be best at doing?

4. What do *you* want to do when your spouse leaves his/her present job?

5. Where are three places/locations that you would like to live? (in order of preference)

6. How much money do you and your spouse need to earn each month to supplement your retirement income and be happy?

7. Do you intend to work outside the home if you are not already doing so? Doing what?

8. What is your greatest concern about retirement from government service?

9. What are three hobbies that you have and/or plan to continue to pursue?

10. Do you think that your spouse is prepared to retire? Why? Why not?

11. What would make you the most happy?

12. I fully understand our personal financial situation? Yes! No?

APP

HOMEWORK

Objective Exercise & Research Homework
Day 1

Objective:

1. What is your Career Transition Objective (pick one)?

   Level ____________________

   Functional Area ____________________

   Industry ____________________

2. Using Indeed.com, CareerBuilder, or USAjobs.gov, find a job that matches your objective.

   Job/Company ____________________

3. Go to that company's website. What are the six key skill/keyword sets required for that job/occupation?

   1. ____________ 4. ____________
   2. ____________ 5. ____________
   3. ____________ 6. ____________

PAR

4. Describe one accomplishment in your career that proves you have one of these skills; be sure to include data/metrics.

   Problem ____________________

   Action ____________________

   Results ____________________

   ____

5. Does the company have an opening located where you (and your spouse) desire to live? Yes / No

6. Complete the "Objective Exercise" in Chapter 5 ("Objectives") and be prepared to present your work to the class.

Objective Exercise & Research Homework
Day 2

Compensation:

1. Using Salary.com – or PayScale - or Occupational Outlook Handbook (bls.gov/ooh/): what is fair market value (Median Salary) for this occupation in the location that you wish to live?

____

Does this company offer a 401K/403B/457? Yes/No

2. With your spouse, calculate your personal salary requirements:

Survival (The least amount that you could live with) $ ______________

Fair Market Value (What you believe to be realistic) $ ______________

The 'Wow' Number (The very highest number you could imagine) $ ______________

Research:

3. Using Glassdoor.com:

Does the company receive good reviews from it's employees?

____

Who is the CEO and what is his/her rating? ______________________________

What are two typical interview questions?

1. ____

____

2. ____

____

4. Using Wall Street Journal wsj.com:

How are their stocks trading? Up? Down? Price? ___________________________

5. Using Hoovers.com:

What are their total sales? ______________________________

Who are their top competitors? ______________________________

6. Using Bloomberg.com – or Forbes.com - or BusinessInsider.com:

Have there been any recent articles written about the company? Negative or Positive? ____________

7. Google the SEC 10K report for the company:

What are the company's main products/services? ______________________________

Networking:

8. Using LinkedIn.com:

Do you know anyone that works at that company? List them.

______________________________ ______________________________

______________________________ ______________________________

______________________________ ______________________________

9. Using NAVNET Resources.com or any other professional networking group you are affiliated with:

Do you know anyone that works at that company? List them

______________________________ ______________________________

______________________________ ______________________________

______________________________ ______________________________

10. Complete the "30 Second Commercial Exercise" at the end of Chapter 12 ("Sound Bites"). Be prepared to practice your commercial with the class.

Suggested Reading . . . in addition to this book

- ★ What Color Is Your Parachute . . . Richard Bolles
- ★ The Three Boxes of Life . . . Richard Bolles
- ★ Job Hunting for Dummies . . . Max Messner
- ★ **Knock 'Em Dead . . . Martin Yate**
- ★ The Seven Habits (now eight) of Highly Effective People . . . Stephen R. Covey
- ★ The 12-Hour MBA . . . Milo Sobel
- ★ Starting and Operating a Business . . . Michael Jenkins
- ★ **Please Understand Me . . . Keirsey, Bates**
- ★ The Millionaire Next Door . . . Stanley and Danko
- ★ Rich Dad, Poor Dad . . . Robert Kiyosaki
- ★ **Game Plan . . . Bob Buford**
- ★ **LinkedIn for Dummies**
- ★ **Social Media Networking for Dummies**
- ★ Angela's Ashes . . . Frank McCourt
- ★ The Consulting Bible . . . Alan Weiss
- ★ Getting Started In Consulting . . . Alan Weiss

Note: Buy the books in **bold text** . . . the others are available in the library.

Useful Job Hunting Websites

General Support

Job Hunt - An amazing collection of articles written about careers and job searches:

https:www.job-hunt.org

VETS - Department of Labor site for Veterans:

https://www.dol.gov/veterans/findajob/

Career One Stop - Comprehensive workforce information and tools for job seekers:

https://www.careeronestop.org

Change

Career Shifters - Helps with dealing with change and making a career shift:

http://www.careershifters.org/start-here

Personal Preference

Assessment.com - Provides a free career test to help you decide what job suites your personality type:

http://www.assessment.com

Objectives

MyNext Move - Helps you find careers by industry and key words/skills:

http://www.mynextmove.org/vets/

Occupational Outlook Handbook - helps find career information regarding the duties, education, pay and outlook for hundreds of occupations:

https://www.bls.gov/ooh/

Resumes

O*NET OnLine - Helps identify the skills and education needed for a career in a particular industry:

https://www.onetonline.org/skills/

Jobscan - Compares your resume to a job listing and gives suggestions on how to maximize your chances of being called in for an interview:

https://www.jobscan.com

APPENDIX D

Job Market

Flexjobs - Helps find part-time, telecommute, freelance and contract jobs:

https://www.flexjobs.com

Frannet - Helps people find a good franchise match:

http://www.frannet.com

Networking

Association Directory - Great site to connect and network with the Association that governs whatever industry you plan to work in:

http://www.directoryofassociations.com

American Corporate Partners - Non-profit that connects you with mentors that help guide you through the military to civilian transition:

http://www.acp-usa.org

Interviews

Livecareer - Excellent interview prep site:

https://www.livecareer.com

Research

Vault - Known for it's ranking's and reviews of thousands of top employers:

http://www.vault.com

Other excellent websites for Researching Company information:

Businesscredit.dnb.com
Barrons.com
Spglobal.com
Gale.com
Valueline.com
Hoovers.com
Inc.com
Fortune.com
Money.cnn.com
Dowjones.com
Wsj.com
Bloomberg.com
Bizjournals.com

Organization

Jibberjobber - Helps with organizing your job search:

http://www.jibberjobber.com/features.php

Ruehlin Associates

917 B Ave
Coronado, CA 92118
619-435-2220

Landing Report Feedback

Name: ______________________ Service Background: ______________________

Level: ______________________

Home Address: ____

Home Phone: ______________________ Office Phone: ______________________

Date Landed Job: ______________ Company: ______________________

Position/Title: ____

Address: ____

Phone: ______________________ Email: ______________________

Job Description: ____

____

Found job through: Networking ____ Ad in Paper ____ Recruiter ____ Internet ____

Other ____

How long did it take? ________ months (from retirement)

Number of interviews (within company): ________

Most difficult interview question: ____

____

Your Answer: ____

____

Salary Range: 0-50K __ 50-75K __ 75-100K __ 100-125K __ 125-150K __ 150-200K __ 200K+ __

Perks? ____

____

Other ____

____

Others may call me for advice and networking. ___ Yes ___ Rather not

______________________ ______________
Signature Date

ALL INFORMATION WILL BE TREATED AS CONFIDENTIAL!

Where Do Leaders Come From

"They are mostly self made" . . . Dr. Warren Bennis

WRITE AN EXAMPLE OF EACH AS IT PERTAINS TO YOU AND YOUR OBJECTIVE

Business literacy . . . knowledge and feel for the business

People strengths . . . the capacity to motivate

Track record . . . done it before and well

Conceptual strengths . . . thinks systematically, creatively, and inventively

---

Taste . . . picks the right people

Judgment . . . can make quick and reasonably good decisions with imperfect data

---

Character . . . the core competency of leadership

A guiding vision . . . a strongly defined sense of purpose

Management and Leadership

John B. Kotter, Harvard Business School Press

MANAGEMENT: A set of processes that can keep a complicated system of people and technology running smoothly. The most important aspects of management include:

- Planning
- Budgeting
- Organizing
- Staffing
- Controlling
- Problem solving

LEADERSHIP: A set of processes that creates organizations in the first place or adapts them to significantly changing circumstances. Leadership defines:

- What the future will look like
- Aligns people with that vision
- Inspires people to make the vision happen despite the obstacles.

Note: Some of the above aspects of management and leadership might be used in a resume, in a two minute opener and/or during a networking meeting or job interview.

APPENDIX H

Career Transition Quiz

(Answers at the bottom of Appendix I *(Employment Application - Example)*)

T F 1. About 50 percent of all jobs are filled through recruiters, personnel agencies newspaper ads, Job Fairs, and Websites.

T F 2. Schedule your first networking meetings with companies in which you are most interested.

T F 3. There is no such thing as job security.

T F 4. Do not contact prospective employers with phone calls after you have written to them. They will call you if they are interested.

T F 5. The first five minutes of a meeting (networking/job interview) are by far the most important.

T F 6. It is nearly impossible to determine the salary range of a job before the interview.

T F 7. If the base salary offered is really not what you want, there is no point in wasting time trying to get the job offer.

T F 8. When asked to describe your background in an employment interview, ideally you should spend no more than two minutes.

T F 9. It is important to contact as many people as possible *immediately* upon making the decision to leave your present job.

T F 10. If you are a smoker, when being interviewed you should *always* ask permission to smoke.

T F 11. The addition of Website capabilities in the job search process (like LinkedIn) has significantly reduced the importance of personal contacts and networking.

T F 12. There is no point in answering a newspaper ad or Website job posting, even though you seem to be a perfect fit for the position.

T F 13. It is bad interview form to ask questions about the company.

T F 14. The best qualified candidate gets the job.

T F 15. In planning a second career, it is best not to become too specific with what you want to do.

T F 16. You should argue with the job interviewer because it shows that you have your own opinions and are not afraid to espouse them.

T F 17. My really good friends will know exactly what I want to do in my second career.

T F 18. A good recruiter will be able to find you a job if you have a clear objective.

T F 19. With the advent of LinkedIn, the resume has become passe.

Employment Application – Example

ABC Industries, Inc.

Date: ________

Name: ______________________________ Telephone Number: _______________

Social Security Number: _________________

Address: ____________________________ ________________ ____ _______

(Street) (City) (State) (Zip)

Years of occupancy: _____

Position applying for: ________________________ Salary requirement: $_________

How did you learn about this position? ____

____

Have you ever applied for a job with or worked for ABC Industries? Yes__ No__

Explain: ____

____

In the event of an emergency, contact: ____

Have you ever served in the U.S. Armed Forces? Yes__ No__ If yes, Branch of service _____

Date of discharge: ___________

Keep the "duties" description relevant to the position you are seeking.

Employment Record

Name and address of employer: ____

Supervisor's name: ____

Job Title and duties: ____

Career change.

____

Reason for leaving employment: ____

(Note: A typical employment application will ask the same questions for your past three to five jobs.)

Have you ever been discharged from a job? ____________________________________

Have you ever been convicted of a crime? _____________________________________

Have you ever received unemployment compensation? ____________________________

Have you ever filed a claim for Workman's Compensation? _________________________

Driver's license (State and Number): ____

Printed Name: ______________________ Signature: _________________________

Answers to *Career Transition Quiz*: 1-F, 2-F, 3-T, 4-F, 5-T, 6-F, 7-F, 8-T, 9-F, 10-F, 11-F, 12-F, 13-F, 14-F, 15-F, 16-F,17-F, 18-F, 19-F.

Sample Disqualification Memorandum

(Date)

MEMORANDUM FOR (Your Supervisor)

FROM: (Your Name/Office Symbol)

SUBJECT: Request for Disqualification – Employment Discussions

My (approved)(contemplated) date of (retirement)(separation) is_____. I expect to begin terminal leave on_____. I anticipate entering into employment discussions with certain defense contractors prior to my (retirement)(separation). Pursuant to 18 U.S.C. 208(a) and 5 CFR 1635.604, I submit the following notice of disqualification, subject to your approval.

Both the Joint Ethics Regulation (DoD 5500.7-R) and the Standards of Ethical Conduct for the Executive Branch (5 CFR 2635) require me to conduct my personal affairs in a manner which upholds the public trust. I am aware that I must disqualify myself from participating in any particular matter that will have a direct and predictable effect on the financial interest of a person or organization with whom I am seeking employment. Therefore, I am giving formal notice that I plan to seek employment with the following, persons/companies:

(List persons/companies here)

I request to be disqualified from any official action that might have an impact on these persons/companies and I will avoid my involvement in matters affecting these companies. In the event that any matter brought to me for action may have a direct or predictable impact upon these companies, I will immediately inform you and make arrangements to insure that I am not involved.

(Your Signature Block)

Ruehlin Associates

John Ruehlin *transitioned* from active Naval service as a Rear Admiral. His most recent active duty assignments prior to leaving active duty were Commanding Officer of the Naval Supply Center Oakland, Commanding Officer of the Aviation Supply Office Philadelphia, and Commander, Defense Personnel Support Center, Philadelphia. He served as the Supply Officer aboard USS ENTERPRISE deployed in the Tonkin Gulf during the Vietnam conflict.

Upon leaving the Navy, John served as Senior Vice President of Great American Bank, a $15 Billion financial institution in San Diego, CA. As the Director of Institutional Investor Relations he was the Bank's principal interface with Wall Street and other major financial centers and leaders around the world. As the Bank's Director of Internal Consulting he was involved in every facet of the Bank's internal operations, with a focus on efficiency and cost reduction.

In 1990, John was recruited by an international career transition management and human resources consulting company as a Managing Principal. In that capacity, he worked with Fortune 500 corporations providing management consulting services and career transition assistance for senior private sector executives. In 1992, John was asked to develop government career transition programs and has since designed and delivered career transition programs for civilian and government organizations throughout the world. As a Senior Vice President and the Director of Government Relations, he played a major role in developing programs that address the special needs and requirements of military and civil service personnel undergoing career transition. John also provided management consulting for Fortune 500 companies and government organizations involved in base closure, realignment, relocation and downsizing.

In 1993, John launched his own business, *Ruehlin Associates*, providing Career Planning and Management assistance (career transition) for senior officers, including Flag and General Officers, and senior enlisted personnel of all services. He and his Associates, all with successful military backgrounds, advanced degrees and successful private sector corporate experience, also design and conduct career transition programs for senior civil service personnel, including SES. In addition to his Career Transition Management focus, John serves as an expert witness in private sector legal cases involving wrongful termination. He also serves as a conference keynote speaker on the subject of career management and planning, and has conducted junior and senior officer and enlisted Career Decision counseling workshops at military commands throughout the country and abroad. More than 67,000 people, including over 3,000 Flag and General Officers and their spouses have attended his career seminars. He is the author of *What's Next?,* a comprehensive book on the process of career transition.

John has served as Vice President of the World Affairs Council of San Diego, the Chamber of Commerce, the Board of Directors of the USO and the Family Literacy Foundation. He received his undergraduate education from **The** Ohio State University and earned an MBA, with honors, from Michigan State University.

He and his wife Peggy reside in Coronado, California and have three children: Dave, a Captain in the Navy Supply Corps (ret); Rick, a Navy SEAL Captain (ret); and Kim Pittner, a professional educator . . . married to a Navy fighter pilot (ret).

Visit *Ruehlin Associates* online at: www.RuehlinAssociates.com

Ordering Additional Books

Additional books can be obtained via any of the following:

Write to (please enclose check with your order):

Ruehlin Associates
ATTN: MJ
917 B Avenue
Coronado, CA 92118

By phone (using credit card):

619 435 2220

or visit
www.RuehlinAssociates.com (secure order using credit card or PayPal)

or email
careers@ruehlinassociates.com (payment made by check)

The price of the book is $30 plus $6 (postage and handling)

Index

Index

N

O

P

R

Index

Index